T0352094

From Africa to Brazil

From Africa to Brazil traces flows of enslaved Africans from identifiable
points in the large African region of Upper Guinea to Amazonia, Brazil.
These two areas, though separated by an ocean, were made one by a
slave route. Walter Hawthorne considers why planters in Amazonia
wanted African slaves, why and how those sent to Amazonia were
enslaved, and what their Middle Passage experience was like. The book
is also concerned with how Africans in diaspora shaped labor regimes,
determined the nature of their family lives, and crafted religious beliefs
that were similar to those they had known before enslavement. This
study makes several broad contributions. It presents the only book-
length examination of African slavery in Amazonia and identifies
with precision the locations in Africa from where members of a large
diaspora in the Americas hailed. *From Africa to Brazil* also proposes
new directions for scholarship focused on how immigrant groups created new or re-created old cultures.

Walter Hawthorne is a professor of African history at Michigan
State University. He is the author of *Planting Rice and Harvesting
Slaves: Transformations along the Guinea-Bissau Coast, 1400–1900*
(2003) and has published in scholarly journals such as *Journal of
African History, Luso-Brazilian Review, Slavery and Abolition, Africa,
Journal of Global History*, and *American Historical Review*. Before
joining the History Department at Michigan State University, he was a
visiting assistant professor at the University of Vermont and assistant
and associate professor at Ohio University.

AFRICAN STUDIES

The African Studies Series, founded in 1968, is a prestigious series of monographs, general surveys, and textbooks on Africa covering history, political science, anthropology, economics, and ecological and environmental issues. The series seeks to publish work by senior scholars as well as the best new research.

EDITORIAL BOARD

David Anderson, *University of Oxford*
Catherine Boone, *University of Texas at Austin*
Carolyn Brown, *Rutgers University*
Christopher Clapham, *University of Cambridge*
Michael Gomez, *New York University*
Nancy J. Jacobs, *Brown University*
Richard Roberts, *Stanford University*
David Robinson, *Michigan State University*
Leonardo A. Villalón, *University of Florida*

A list of books in this series is found at the end of this volume.

From Africa to Brazil

Culture, Identity, and an Atlantic Slave Trade, 1600–1830

WALTER HAWTHORNE

Michigan State University

CAMBRIDGE
UNIVERSITY PRESS

CAMBRIDGE UNIVERSITY PRESS
Cambridge, New York, Melbourne, Madrid, Cape Town,
Singapore, São Paulo, Delhi, Tokyo, Mexico City

Cambridge University Press
32 Avenue of the Americas, New York, NY 10013-2473, USA

www.cambridge.org
Information on this title: www.cambridge.org/9780521152389

© Walter Hawthorne 2010

This publication is in copyright. Subject to statutory exception
and to the provisions of relevant collective licensing agreements,
no reproduction of any part may take place without the written
permission of Cambridge University Press.

First published 2010
Reprinted 2011

A catalog record for this publication is available from the British Library.

Library of Congress Cataloging in Publication Data

Hawthorne, Walter.
From Africa to Brazil : culture, identity, and an Atlantic slave trade,
1600–1830 / Walter Hawthorne.
  p. cm. – (African studies ; 113)
Includes bibliographical references and index.
ISBN 978-0-521-76409-4 (hardback) – ISBN 978-0-521-15238-9 (pbk.)
 1. Slaves – Amazon River Region – History   2. Slave trade – Africa – History
 3. African diaspora – History.   I. Title.   II. Series.
HT1129.A426H39   2010
306.3′6209811–dc22   2010025329

ISBN 978-0-521-76409-4 Hardback
ISBN 978-0-521-15238-9 Paperback

Cambridge University Press has no responsibility for the persistence or accuracy of URLS
for external or third-party Internet Web sites referred to in this publication and does not
guarantee that any content on such Web sites is, or will remain, accurate or appropriate.

Contents

Figures

Maps

Tables

Abbreviations Used in Notes

AAM   Arquivo da Arquidiocese do Maranhão (São Luís)
AHMF   Arquivo Histórico do Ministério das Finanças
AHU   Arquivo Histórico Ultramarino (Lisbon)
AJ   Arquivo Judiciário
ANRJ   Arquivo Nacional do Rio de Janeiro
ANTT   Arquivo Nacional da Torre do Tombo (Lisbon)
APEM   Arquivo Publico do Estado do Maranhão (São Luís)
BNA   British National Archive (Kew)
BNP   Biblioteca Nacional de Portugal (Lisbon)
CGPM   Companhia Geral do Grão-Pará e Maranhão
CO   Colonial Office
MISD   Maranhão Inventories Slave Database
TJEM   Tribunal de Justiça do Estado do Maranhão (São Luís)
TSTD   *The Trans-Atlantic Slave Trade: A Database on CD-ROM*
TSTD2   Voyages: The Trans-Atlantic Slave Trade Database

Acknowledgments

It is a great pleasure to thank the funding agencies, colleagues, friends, and family members who have played a part in the making of this book. In 2004 and 2005, a Fulbright-Hays Fellowship funded my research in Guinea-Bissau, Portugal, and Brazil. In 2008 and 2009, a National Endowment for the Humanities Fellowship funded the writing phase of my project. Without those generous fellowships, this project would not have been possible. I am also grateful for financial support from the Michigan State University (MSU) History Department Sesquicentennial Fund and the MSU Intramural Research Grant Proposal Award.

Linda Heywood, James Sweet, Peter Mark, Toby Green, David Bailey, David Robinson, Paul Lovejoy, and Benjamin Lawrance read a near-final draft of the entire manuscript. Each gave me particularly detailed and insightful comments and criticisms that helped me hone my arguments. I am forever in their debt. Readers who remain anonymous provided valuable feedback. Further, the following people helped me personally and professionally through their support, criticisms, challenges, responses to inquiries, assistance in archives, or helpful suggestions: John Waller, Erica Windler, Peter Beattie, David Wheat, Tom Summerhill, Peter Alegi, Nwando Achebe, Laura Fair, Ben Smith, Peter Limb, Joe Lauer, Peter Berg, Mary Jo Zeter, Christine Root, David Wiley, James Pritchett, Assan Sarr, Bala Saho, Lumumba Shabaka, Josh Grace, José Silva da Horta, Ramon Sarró, Marina Padrão Temudo, Maria João Soares, Maria Manuel Torrão, Philip Havik, Mariana Candido, Clara Carvalho, Jorge Fernandes Nascimento, Maria Luisa Abrantes, Mário Pires Miguel, Domingos Nagague, Mamadú Jao, Carlos Intigue, Agostinho Clodé Suba Nania, Emily Osborn, Lynn Schler, Richard Roberts, Thom McClendon, Marty

Klein, John Thornton, Gwen Hall, Edda Fields-Black, Pier Larson, Jose Lingna Nafafe, Jelmer Vos, Bruce Mouser, Josh Forrest, Allen Howard, George Brooks, David Eltis, Daniel Domingues da Silva, Luiz Felipe de Alencastro, Phil Misevich, Clifton Crais, Pamela Scully, Kristin Mann, Judy Carney, Ralph Austen, Michael Gomez, Paul Richards, Patrick Griffin, Joe Miller, Don Wright, Eric Crahan, Jay Harward, Soniya Ashok, Jason Przybylski, Kevin Conru, Mariza de Carvalho Soares, Antônio Wilson de Souza, Cleber da Silva Reis, Diogo Gualhardo Neves, Roque Ferreira, Matthias Röhrig Assunção, João José Reis, Flavio Gomes, Antonia da Silva Mota, Mundicarmo Ferretti, Sergio Ferretti, and Regina Helena Martins de Faria. At MSU, I am fortunate to have a dean, Marietta Baba, who is supportive of faculty research endeavors. In the History Department, my chairs, Mark Kornbluh and Keely Stauter-Halsted, facilitated my research and writing.

I was aided in countless ways by the staffs at a number of libraries and archives: the Arquivo Judiciário of the Tribunal de Justiça do Estado do Maranhão in Brazil, Arquivo Publico do Estado do Maranhão in Brazil, Arquivo Nacional do Rio de Janeiro in Brazil, Arquivo Histórico do Instituto Nacional de Estudos e Pesquisa in Guinea-Bissau, Biblioteca Nacional in Portugal, Arquivo Histórico Ultramarino in Portugal, Arquivo Nacional da Torre do Tombo in Portugal, and Michigan State University Library. My many requests were met by those working in interlibrary loan, in special collections, and with the African and Latin American collections at MSU. Further, my research was shaped greatly by the faculty and students at the Universidade Federal do Maranhão and Universidade Estadual do Maranhão, who guided me in archives and invited me to present my findings. Obrigado.

Warm thanks also to my extended family for their encouragement: Walter and Judy Hawthorne; Sarah, Steve, Benjamin, Paul, and Liam Covert; Carolin Belden; David Belden; and Paul Belden.

My greatest debt is owed to those I hold dearest. My wife, Jackie, and our daughter, Katherine, who was then less than a year old, moved with me to Portugal when I started research for this book. They later sent me off to Guinea-Bissau and moved with me to Rio de Janeiro and later São Luís, Brazil. What great adventures we had along the way to seeing *From Africa to Brazil* published! Best of all, we welcomed my son Jonathan, or J. D. as we affectionately call him, into the world while I was writing up in East Lansing, Michigan. For their love, companionship, patience, and unending support, this book is for Jackie, Katherine, and J. D. I could not have done it without you.

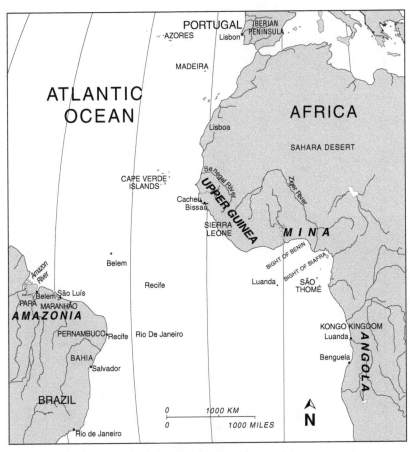

MAP 0.1. The Atlantic, Upper Guinea, and Amazonia.
Courtesy of Jackie Hawthorne.

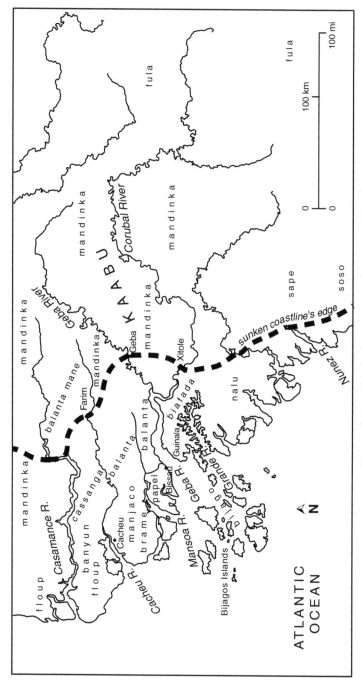

MAP 0.2. Upper Guinea Ethnic Groups around Bissau and Cacheu.

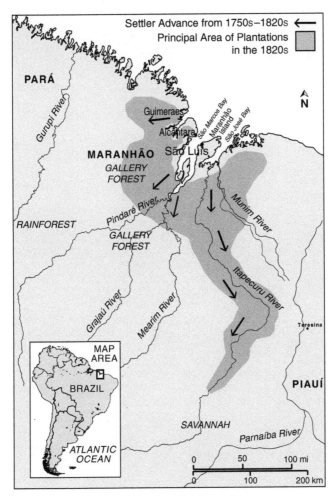

MAP 0.3. Amazonia, 1750s–1820s.
Courtesy of Jackie Hawthorne.

Introduction

In 1492, the Early Modern Atlantic was born. After that date, sailing ships connected distant parts of the Atlantic in new and dynamic ways. As people, trade goods, and ideas flowed across the ocean, African, American, and European cultures and economies were radically reshaped. For several hundred years, American Indians would die in tremendous numbers from diseases that white explorers and settlers introduced and wars they waged; Europeans would colonize much of the Americas and establish plantations that produced exports for Old World metropoles; and blacks would labor on those plantations as Europe shipped what ultimately was about 12.5 million enslaved Africans from coastal ports in the largest forced migration in human history. To illustrate the magnitude of this migration, before 1820 about three-quarters of all people arriving in the Americas hailed from Africa.[1]

It is only over the past several decades that studies using the Early Modern Atlantic as a unit of analysis have become popular. Many scholars who examine Atlantic history see Europeans as dominating Atlantic interactions and shaping transformations. They equate the Atlantic basin with European civilization. These scholars marginalize Africa and reduce Africans' contributions to the construction of an Atlantic World to merely labor alone.[2] However, historians who reject Eurocentric approaches to

---

[1] David Eltis and David Richardson, "A New Assessment of the Transatlantic Slave Trade," in *Extending the Frontiers: Essays on the New Transatlantic Slave Trade Database*, eds. David Eltis and David Richardson (New Haven: Yale University Press, 2008), 1–2, 37.

[2] See, especially, Jorge Cañizares-Esguerra, "Entangled Histories: Borderland Historiographies in New Clothes?" *American Historical Review* 112 (2007), 794; Alison Games, "Atlantic History: Definitions, Challenges, and Opportunities," *American Historical Review* 111 (2006), 741–57.

the past see considerable African and Afro-American agency. That is, they view Africans and their descendants in the Americas as controlling some of the processes that led to the creation and metamorphosis of an Atlantic economic and cultural system. Following John Thornton, "Africans were active participants in the Atlantic world, both in African trade with Europe ... and as slaves in the New World."[3]

This book focuses squarely on people from Africa. In simplest terms, it traces the flow of enslaved Africans from identifiable points in Upper Guinea (what the Portuguese came to call *Guiné*) to plantations in Amazonia, Brazil. It is concerned with the period from about Portugal's establishment of a colony in Amazonia in 1621 to the legal abolition of the oceanic slave trade into the region in 1830. I am particularly interested in how Upper Guineans effected change in the Atlantic economic and cultural network that connected the Upper Guinea ports of Bissau and Cacheu – cities in the present-day country of Guinea-Bissau – to the ports of São Luís and Belém in the captaincies of Maranhão and Pará, which together comprised Amazonia. In the period covered by this book, captains of sailing ships embarked slaves at Bissau and Cacheu and disembarked iron, cloth, beads, guns, gunpowder, rum, tobacco, and other trade items. The vessels were mostly Portuguese-owned. The enslaved were shipped, for the most part, to Amazonia.

The slave trade from Upper Guinea to Amazonia reached its zenith in the second half of the eighteenth century. Before then, Amazonia was an underdeveloped backwater of the Portuguese empire. Few whites were settled there, and over a period of about 150 years, fewer than 3,500 African slaves (mostly Upper Guineans) had been shipped there. In 1755, Portugal sought to stimulate Amazonia's economy by encouraging increased levels of African slave imports. For this, the crown granted a monopoly on shipments from Bissau and Cacheu and into São Luís and Belém to a joint stock company called the Company of Grão Pará and Maranhão (*Companhia Geral do Grão Pará e Maranhão*, or CGPM). High volumes of trade from Bissau and Cacheu to São Luís resulted in an Upper Guinean majority emerging in colonial-controlled rural areas of Maranhão. Parts of Pará, too, saw the emergence of an Upper Guinean majority. However, fewer slaves went to Pará than went to Maranhão (and many who went to Pará were traded elsewhere), so the bulk of my analysis focuses on Maranhão. Trade from Bissau and Cacheu declined

---

[3] John Thornton, *Africa and Africans in the Making of the Atlantic World, 1400–1680* (New York: Cambridge University Press, 1992), 6–7.

sharply after 1815 when Portugal, under pressure from Britain, forbade its nationals from engaging in the transoceanic shipment of slaves north of the equator. From 1755 to 1815, about 70,000 Upper Guineans entered Amazonia, and most of those entered before 1800.

With those 70,000 and the hundreds of thousands more in the communities from which they were taken as its subject, this study makes several historiographical contributions. First, this is one of a handful of accounts of Upper Guineans in diaspora and is the only book-length examination of African slavery in Maranhão before the early nineteenth century. Second, this is one of few studies to identify with precision from where members of a large diaspora in the Americas hailed in Africa. Finally, this book proposes new directions for scholarship focused on how immigrant groups who crossed the Atlantic in the Early Modern period created new or re-created old cultures in the Americas. I will expand on each of those points.

AN UNDERSTUDIED DIASPORA IN AN UNDERSTUDIED PART OF BRAZIL

This book fills large voids in scholarship about slavery and the Atlantic slave trade. It is one of few works to examine the cultural linkages between Upper Guinea and its diaspora in the Americas. Considerable research has traced flows of captives from West Central Africa (especially the Kongo and Angola areas) and the Bights of Benin and Biafra (what the Portuguese called Mina). Scholars have been especially concerned with the degree to which slaves from West Central Africa and Mina re-created in the Americas aspects of the cultures from which they came.[4] However,

---

[4] On West Central Africans: Linda M. Heywood, ed., *Central Africans and Cultural Transformations in the American Diaspora* (New York: Cambridge University Press, 2002); Linda M. Heywood and John K. Thornton, *Central Africans, Atlantic Creoles, and the Foundations of the Americas, 1585–1660* (New York: Cambridge University Press, 2007); James H. Sweet, *Recreating Africa: Culture, Kinship, and Religion in the African-Portuguese World, 1441–1770* (Chapel Hill: The University of North Carolina Press, 2003); Roquinaldo Ferrira, "Atlantic Microhistories: Slaving, Mobility, and Personal Ties in the Black Atlantic World (Angola and Brazil)," in *Cultures of the Lusophone Black Atlantic*, eds. Nancy Naro, Roger Sansi and David Treece (New York: Palgrave Macmillan, 2007), 99–128; On Minas: Toyin Falola and Matt D. Childs, *The Yoruba Diaspora in the Atlantic World* (Bloomington: Indiana University Press, 2004); João José Reis, *Slave Rebellion in Brazil: The Muslim Uprising of 1835 in Bahia* (Baltimore: The Johns Hopkins University Press, 1993); Douglas B. Chambers, *Murder at Montpelier: Igbo Africans in Virginia* (Jackson: University of Mississippi Press, 2005); York/UNESCO Nigerian Hinterland Project, http://www.yorku.ca/nhp/areas/nhp.htm.

only a handful of studies focused on the transfer of rice-growing techniques and one looking at the transfer of an architectural aesthetic have considered Upper Guinean cultural contributions anywhere in the New World.[5] Several notable studies explore the economic links between Upper Guinea and Amazonia in the era of the CGPM. But beyond speculating about the ethnic groups to which slaves arriving in Amazonia belonged, no single work pays attention to the cultural implications of the trade.[6]

[5] Peter Mark, *"Portuguese" Style and Luso-African Identity: Precolonial Senegambia, Sixteenth-Nineteenth Centuries* (Bloomington: Indiana University Press, 2002), 59–80; Judith A. Carney, *Black Rice: The African Origins of Rice Cultivation in the Americas* (Cambridge, MA: Harvard University Press, 2001); Judith A. Carney, "'With Grains in Her Hair': Rice in Colonial Brazil," *Slavery and Abolition* 25, 1 (2004), 1–27; Judith A. Carney and Richard Nicholas Rosomoff, *In the Shadow of Slavery: Africa's Botanical Legacy in the Atlantic World* (Berkeley, CA: The University of California Press, 2010); Edda L. Fields-Black, *Deep Roots: Rice Farmers in West Africa and the African Diaspora*, (Bloomington: Indiana University Press, 2008); David Eltis, Philip Morgan, and David Richardson, "Agency and the Diaspora in Atlantic History: Reassessing the African Contribution to Rice Cultivation in the Americas," *American Historical Review* 12, 5 (2007), 1329–58; Reinaldo dos Santos Barroso Júnior, "Nas rotas do atlântico equatorial: tráfico de escravos rizicultores da Alta-Guiné para o Maranhão (1770–1800)," (Ph.D. thesis: Universidade Federal da Bahia, 2009); S. Max Edelson, "Beyond 'Black Rice': Reconstructing Material and Cultural Contexts for Early Plantation Agriculture," *American Historical Review* 115, 1 (2010), 125–35; Gwendolyn Midlo Hall, "Africa and Africans in the African Diaspora: The Uses of Relational Databases," *American Historical Review*, 115, 1 (2010), 136–50; Walter Hawthorne, "From 'Black Rice' to 'Brown': Rethinking the History of Risiculture in the Seventeenth and Eighteenth Century Atlantic," *American Historical Review*, 115, 1 (2010), 151–64; David Eltis, Phip Morgan, and David Richardson, "Black, Brown, or White? Color-Coding American Commercial Rice Cultivation with Slave Labor," *American Historical Review* 115, 1 (2010), 164–71. Also, Sylviane A. Diouf, *Servants of Allah: African Muslims Enslaved in the Americas* (New York: New York University Press, 1998); Michael A. Gomez, *Exchanging Our Country Marks: The Transformations of African Identities in the Colonial Antebellum South* (Chapel Hill: The University of North Carolina Press, 1998).

[6] António Carreira, *As companhias pombalinas de navegação, comércio e tráfico de escravos entre a costa africana e o nordeste brasileiro* (Bissau: Centro de Estudos da Guiné Portuguesa, 1969); Manuel Nunes Dias, *Fomento e merchantilismo: A Companhia Geral do Grão Pará e Maranhão (1755–1778)* (São Paulo: Universidade de São Paulo, 1971); Ilídio Baleno, "Reconversão do comércio externo em tempo de crise e o impacto da Companhia do Grão-Pará e Maranhão," in *Historia geral de Cabo Verde*, ed. Maria Emília Madeira Santos (Lisbon: Centro de Estudos de História e Cartografia Antiga, Instituto de Investigação Científica Tropical, 2002), III: 157–233; Daniel B. Domingues da Silva, "The Slave Trade to Maranhão, 1680–1846: Volumes, Routes and Organization," *Slavery and Abolition* 29, 4 (2008), 477–501; Rafael Chambouleyron, "Escravos do Atlântico equatorial: Tráfico negreiro para o estado do Maranhão e Pará," *Revista brasilleira de história* 26, 52 (2006), 79–114; Jeronimo de Viveiros, *História do comércio do Maranhão (1755–1778)* (Belém: Universidade Federal do Pará, 1963); Benedito Carlos Costa Barbosa, "Em outras margens do Atlântico: Tráfico negreiro para o Estado do Maranhão e Grão-Pará (1707–1750) (Ph.D. thesis, Universidade Federal do Pará, 2009).

As well as being one of few studies about Upper Guineans in diaspora, this is the only book-length examination of African slavery in Maranhão before the early nineteenth century. Despite the fact that the slave trade to the region is relatively well documented and that archival sources about African slave life are plentiful in Maranhão's well-organized state archive, Anglophone scholars have paid little attention to black slavery in the region.[7] Beyond articles mostly published by a handful of dedicated scholars living in Amazonia, little, too, has been published in Portuguese.[8] This might be because the region's historical trajectory was very different from the rest of Brazil. Maranhão and Pará were largely cut off from regions to the south by contrary currents and winds. Indeed, it was faster to sail from São Luís to Lisbon than from São Luís to Rio de Janeiro.[9] Further, whereas much of the rest of Brazil had vibrant export economies in the seventeenth century, Amazonia's economy, as noted above, floundered until after the mid-eighteenth century. Added to this is the fact that ocean currents and winds linked Amazonia to a very different part of

---

[7] Colin M. MacLachlan, "African Slave Trade and Economic Development in Amazonia, 1700–1800," in *Slavery and Race Relations in Latin America*, ed. Robert Brent Toplin (Westport, CT: Greenwood Press, 1974), 112–45; Sue A. Gross, "Labor in Amazonia in the First Half of the Eighteenth Century," *The Americas* 32, 2 (1975), 211–21.

[8] Regina Helena Martins de Faria, "Escravos, livres pobres, índios e imigrantes estrangeiros nas representações das elites do Maranhão oitocentista," in *História do Maranhão: Novos estudos*, ed. Wagner Cabral da Costa (São Luís: EDUFMA, 2004), 81–112. Information about slavery in this period can also be gleaned from Mário M. Meireles, *História do Maranhão*, 2nd ed. (São Luís: Fundação Cultural do Maranhão, 1980); Antonia da Silva Mota and José Dervil Mantovani, *São Luís do Maranhão no século XVIII: A construção do espaço urbano sob a lei das sesmarias* (São Luís: Edições FUNC, 1998); Antônia da Silva Mota, "Família e fortuna no Maranhão setecentista," in *História do Maranhão: Novos estudos*, ed. Wagner Cabral da Costa (São Luís: EDUFMA, 2004), 51–80; Regina Helena Martins de Faria, "Trabalho escravo e trabalho livre na crise da agroexportação escravista no Maranhão" (Ph.D. thesis, UFMA, 1998). On slavery in Pará, Vicente Salles, *O negro no Pará sob o regime da escravidão* (Rio de Janeiro: Fundação Getúlio Vargas, 1971); José Maia Bezerra Neto, *Escravidão negra no Grão Pará: (séculos XVII–XIX)* (Belém: Paka-Tatu, 2001); Anaiza Vergolino-Henry and Arthur Napoleão Figueiredo, *A presença Africana na Amazônia colonial: Uma notícia histórica* (Belém: Secretaria de Estado de Cultura, 1990); Barroso Júnior, "Nas rotas"; Rafael Chambouleyron, "O 'senhor absoluto dos sertões': O 'Capitão Preto' José Lopes, a Amazônia e o Cabo Verde," *Boletín Americanista* LVIII, 58 (2008), 33–49; Patricia Melo Sampaio, "Escravidão e liberdade na Amazônia: Notas de pesquisa sobre o mundo do trabalho indígena e africano," unpublished paper, 2007. For a notable publication in German that explores slavery in Maranhão in the first half of the nineteenth century, Matthias Röhrig Assunção, *Pfanzer, sklaven und kleinbauern in der brasilianischen provinz Maranhão, 1800–1850* (Frankfurt: Vervuert, 1993).

[9] Luiz Joaquim de Oliveira e Castro, *Historia do Brazil* (Rio de Janeiro: Garnier, 1862), 383.

the Atlantic World. The region looked to *Guiné* for slaves. This can be contrasted with the southern reaches of Brazil, which drew slaves mostly from Angola, and with Bahia and Pernambuco, which drew slaves mostly from the Bight of Benin.

What this book does is explore two understudied areas on the Atlantic's periphery that were united by a slave trade. I argue that through much of the Early Modern period the Amazonia and Upper Guinea areas were two sides of the same coin. They comprised one unit – one region that stretched across an ocean. Processes of historical change in one part of that region reverberated throughout the rest, effecting change thousands of miles away. Neither area should be seen in isolation. Both are best understood through a study that takes a broader, Atlantic perspective.

ORIGINS AND IDENTITIES

Within *Guiné*, I trace the origins of slaves exported to Amazonia after 1755 to specific and relatively small areas.[10] Recent scholarship about African diasporas in the Americas has made use of data generated from records of slave ship voyages to detail flows of slaves across the Atlantic. Particularly important has been data generated from two sources. The first is David Eltis, Stephen Behrendt, David Richardson, and Herbert Klein's 1999 *The Trans-Atlantic Slave Trade: A Database on CD-ROM* (TSTD) – a dataset with information from the Atlantic crossings of 27,233 slave ships. The second is the same team's Voyages: The Trans-Atlantic Slave Trade Database (TSTD2), an Internet-based dataset that documents about 35,000 slave ship voyages.[11] Users of the datasets

---

[10] Gwendolyn Midlo Hall calls for studies like this in *Slavery and African Ethnicities in the Americas: Restoring the Links* (Chapel Hill: The University of North Carolina Press, 2005). Gomez traces African slaves to large regions within the continent in *Exchanging Our Country Marks*. Similar is Chambers, *Murder at Montpelier*; Heywood and Thornton, *Central Africans, Atlantic Creoles*; Reis, *Slave Rebellion*. Notable works use ethnonyms in notarial records to trace the origins of Upper Guinean slaves in Peru: Stephan Bühnen, "Ethnic Origins of Peruvian Slaves (1548–1650): Figures for Upper Guinea," *Paideuma* 39 (1993), 57–110; Frederick P. Bowser, *The African Slave in Colonial Peru, 1524–1650* (Palo Alto, CA: Stanford University Press, 1974); Jean-Pierre Tardieu, "Origins of the Slaves in the Lima Region in Peru (Sixteenth and Seventeenth Centuries)," in *From Chains to Bonds: The Slave Trade Revisited*, ed. Doudou Diène (Paris: UNESCO, 2001), 43–54.

[11] David Eltis, Stephen D. Behrendt, David Richardson, and Herbert S. Klein, eds., *The Trans-Atlantic Slave Trade: A Database on CD-ROM* (Cambridge: Cambridge University Press, 1999); *Voyages: The Trans-Atlantic Slave Trade Database*, http://slavevoyages.org/tast/assessment/estimates.faces.

can trace particular flows of slaves from ports in Africa to ports in the Americas and can generate information about, among other things, the volume of those flows over time. Together, the datasets show better than any other scholarship the nature of the linkages between broad regions of Africa and wide areas of the Americas. Africans in the Americas, the datasets make clear, were not any more randomly distributed than were Europeans.[12]

But what the datasets do not show is from where within Africa slaves embarking on Atlantic vessels hailed and to where in the Americas slaves disembarking from those vessels went.[13] That is, the datasets contain information about how many slaves embarked at particular African ports and disembarked at particular American ports, but they contain no information about the birthplaces of the Africans aboard any ship or the final destinations of African slaves who reached the Americas. It should go without saying that Africa has always been a vast and varied place. Supply routes stretching from deep in the interior brought slaves to ports as did shorter routes connecting to communities tens of miles from the coast. Moreover, there was a substantial coastal trade in slaves, which involved merchants moving captives from place to place in the open ocean and through intercoastal waterways before boarding them on ships bound for the New World. It is also clear that America, too, was a vast and varied place, with supply routes stretching from coastal ports to the deep interior of many colonies in addition to the not-so-distant hinterland. Further, it was not uncommon for slaves to disembark at one American port and then embark on a new ship for another distant place – a different colony hundreds of miles away. The TSTD and TSTD2 contain no information about intra-African or intra-American supply routes.

Hence, studies making use of TSTD and TSTD2 generally discuss Africa using generalities. That is, they focus on the likelihood that slaves in particular plantation zones were "Angolans" and "Minas," without pinpointing from where, exactly, those Angolans and Minas came. In the case of Upper Guinea, those arguing for and against a thesis that Upper Guineans brought with them the technologies necessary for plantation

---

[12] For conclusions drawn from the datasets, Eltis and Richardson, "New Assessment"; David Eltis, "The Volume and Structure of the Transatlantic Slave Trade: A Reassessment," *William and Mary Quarterly* 58, 1 (2001), 17–46.

[13] Philip D. Morgan, "The Cultural Implications of the Atlantic Slave Trade: African Regional Origins, American Destinations and New World Developments," *Slavery and Abolition* 18, 1 (1997), 122–45; Paul E. Lovejoy, "Extending the Frontiers of Transatlantic Slavery, Partially," *Journal of Interdisciplinary History* 40, 1 (2009), 57–70.

rice production in the Americas (the "black rice thesis") have failed to determine the exact origins of the people they study.[14] Were they from rice-producing parts of Upper Guinea or weren't they? Can we know?

To the latter question, I say yes. We can know. In this study, I pinpoint the locations in Africa of Upper Guineans who were enslaved and shipped into the Atlantic by making use of postmortem inventories recorded in Maranhão between 1767 and 1832.[15] When a property owner died in the captaincy, a representative of the state tallied his or her possessions – including slaves. Inventory takers usually made extensive notes about slaves. Typically, they recorded slaves' ages, marriage partners, children, professions, values, and "defects" (injuries and illnesses). In addition, they asked slaves from what "nation" they hailed. To the question "What is your nation?" Upper Guineans in Maranhão most often responded with the name of an ethnic group – Balanta, Bijago, Papel, Banyun, Brame, Mandinka, Floup, and Fula, for example. Sometimes, too, slaves responded with a place such as Cacheu, Geba, and Bissau. Such responses, Gwendolyn Midlo Hall argues, can tell us who slaves thought they were – what identities they chose to emphasize. It is clear from sources she has collected in Louisiana and I have collected in Maranhão that African ethnic or national identities often survived the Middle Passage and continued to have meaning for African slaves in the Americas.[16]

Ethnic identities were, indeed, significant for Upper Guineans. From some of their first visits to the Upper Guinea coast, Europeans recorded the ethnonyms of the peoples with whom they came into contact.[17] And they would continue to gather this information for hundreds of years.

---

[14] Carney, *Black Rice*; Eltis, Morgan, and Richardson, "Agency"; Barroso Júnior, "Nas rotas"; Hawthorne, "From 'Black Rice' to 'Brown'"; Fields-Black, *Deep Roots*.

[15] I assembled those into a database – the Maranhão Inventories Slave Database (MISD). The documents are at the Arquivo Judiciário of the Tribunal de Justiça do Estado do Maranhão (TJEM).

[16] Hall, *Slavery and African Ethnicities*, xv, 49, 55–79; Michael Gomez, "African Identity and Slavery in America," *Radical History Review* 75 (1999), 111–20; Gomez, *Exchanging*, 11, 38, 150; Reis, *Slave Rebellion*, 154; Paul E. Lovejoy, ed., *Identity in the Shadow of Slavery* (New York: Continuum, 2000); Paul E. Lovejoy and David V. Trotman, eds., *Trans-Atlantic Dimensions of Ethnicity in the African Diaspora* (New York: Continuum, 2003); José C. Curto and Paul E. Lovejoy, eds., *Enslaving Connections: Changing Cultures of Africa and Brazil during the Era of Slavery* (Amherst, NY: Humanity Books, 2004); José C. Curto and Renée Soulodre-La Crance, eds., *Africa and the Americas: Interconnections during the Slave Trade* (Trenton, NJ: Africa World Press, 2005).

[17] Duarte Pacheco Pereira, *Esmeraldo de situ orbis*, ed. Damião Peres (Lisbon: Academia Portuguesa da História, 1988).

Further, Portuguese, French, English, and Dutch observers, acting independently, drew maps noting territories in which people from particular ethnic groups lived. In their conceptualization, European observers believed ethnicity was determined by language, although they often noted differences in political structures and customs – dress, scarifications, foods, and so forth. Within ethnic groups, there is often a notion of shared descent. In Upper Guinea, oral traditions also speak of ethnolinguistic territories, which people in Guinea-Bissau refer to as *chão* (*tchon* in the singular) in a widely spoken creole language called *Kriolo*. In an exhaustive study of written sources from the years 1440 to 1700, P. E. H. Hair shows how these *chão* have been stable over time. That is, ethnic groups remained established in more or less the same locations for many centuries.[18]

Although European colonial policies did, in the twentieth century, bring ethnic identities to the fore, hardening them and raising their importance by linking economic and political opportunities to group inclusion, there is no evidence that Europeans "invented" ethnic identities from whole cloth in Upper Guinea – in the nineteenth or twentieth centuries and certainly not before. Simply put, in Upper Guinea before the nineteenth century, Europe's representatives were rent-paying guests of local African landlords. For the most part, they exercised little direct political influence beyond the boundaries of small coastal areas. And in the enclaves of Bissau and Cacheu, Portugal's political and military position was tenuous indeed.[19] Africans responded to both internal and external forces by defining and redefining identities; to describe their identities as "European inventions" would be to misunderstand the nature of power in Upper Guinea. Here and elsewhere – although perhaps not everywhere – in Africa, ethnic identities were salient from the fifteenth through the nineteenth centuries.[20]

---

[18] P. E. H. Hair, "Ethnolinguistic Continuity on the Guinea Coast," *Journal of African History* 8, 2 (1967), 247–68.

[19] Joshua B. Forest, *Lineages of State Fragility: Rural Civil Society in Guinea-Bissau* (Athens: Ohio University Press, 2003), 27–63.

[20] My purpose here is not to compare and contrast the salience of ethnic identities in places across Africa. That said, I think people on the Upper Guinea coast may have emphasized ethnic identities more than people in many other parts of Africa. In Maranhão, slaves from West Central Africa in the eighteenth century were most often identified as Angolan in plantation inventories. Those from Upper Guinea most often identified themselves and were identified by others with more narrow ethnonyms – Balanta, Bijago, Biafada, Papel, etc.

This is not to say that ethnic identities, as misguided European colonial administrators and intellectuals thought through much of the twentieth century, were innate and unchanging. Many people in Upper Guinea were multilingual.[21] People from different groups sometimes married. Some changed locations, moving from one *tchon* to another. Others settled down with people from other ethnic groups, eventually becoming members of that group. As Boubacar Barry writes, "There were Toures, originally Manding, who became Tukulor or Wolof; Jallos, originally Peul, became Khaasonke; Moors turned into Naari Kajor; Mane and Sane, originally Joola, surnames were taken by the Manding royalty of Kabu."[22] In the northeast of Guinea-Bissau, Balanta who interacted and intermarried with Mandinka over time adopted new political structures, cultural styles, and social customs. Their language changed to integrate Mandinka words, and eventually they adopted an identity for themselves that was neither Balanta nor Mandinka. They became Bejaa.[23]

But no Bejaa was only a Bejaa. That is, no Bejaa held one and only one identity – an ethnic identity. Indeed, members of all ethnic groups held multiple and overlapping identities – some more important at times than an ethnic identity. A Papel could identify himself as a member of a rural, village-based community and as a *grumete* (canoe-hand) employed by a white merchant in Bissau. He could work as a *grumete* alongside Balanta, Bijago, Mandinka, and people from other Upper Guinea ethnic groups, joining with them at times in common cause to protest treatment by an employer or to defend an employer's interests against threats from an African landlord. A Papel could wear, like all people in Upper Guinea, protective amulets acquired from Muslim priests. Further, he could attend a multiethnic mass when Catholic priests were in Bissau, and he could visit shrines to Papel ancestral spirits. He could have many identities – identities linked to a very local religion and to Catholicism *and* Islam; identities linked to his profession, village, and ethnicity. Ethnic identities were not the only identities that Upper Guineans possessed, and

---

[21] Almada noted in the late sixteenth century that Biafada had a word (*ganagoga*) for "a man who speaks all languages." Andre Alvares de Almada, *Brief Treatise on the Rivers of Guinea*, trans. P. E. H. Hair (Liverpool: University of Liverpool, 1984), 1: 23.

[22] Boubacar Barry, *Senegambia and the Atlantic Slave Trade* (New York: Cambridge University Press, 1998), 35.

[23] Avelino Teixeira da Mota, *Guiné portuguesa* (Lisbon: Agência Geral do Ultramar, 1954), 141; Cornélia Geising, "Agricultura e resistência na história dos Balanta-Bejaa," *Soranda* 16 (July 1993), 125–76; Diane Lima Handem, *Nature et founcionnement du pouvoir chez les Balanta Brassa* (Bissau: Arquivo Histórico do Instituto Nacional de Estudos e Pesquisa, 1986), 10–19.

they were not frozen in time. But ethnicity was one way Upper Guineans defined themselves – in West Africa and Brazil.

Given this, I argue that in Maranhão, African slaves' responses (as recorded in postmortem inventories) to the question "What is your nation?" can allow us to determine who slaves thought they were and where slaves hailed from within Africa. In making these arguments, I recognize that plantation inventories might, in some ways, distort the complexities of African identities.[24] What did Upper Guineans make of the question "What is your nation?" Why did a small percentage respond with the name of a place – Cacheu, Geba, and Bissau? Why did most respond with an ethnonym? Did some fail to provide an answer? If so, were they assigned an ethnic identity? Were others around them consulted? Did slaves on plantations for a period of time become Balanta, Mandinka, or something else? That is, did they change their ethnic identities in the Americas? Did record keepers use only generic or common ethnic labels, redefining more complex ethnicities as belonging to what they saw as major ones?

Unfortunately, my sources do not allow me to provide satisfactory answers to all of these questions. Nonetheless, I am convinced that on the whole, plantation inventories can be used to identify elements of Africans' identities and, for Upper Guineans, to trace from where they came. Simply put, inventory takers had nothing to gain from recording one ethnic label rather than another. They had no reason to write down anything other than what they heard from slaves. Further, the range of ethnic labels they recorded was large, indicating that they were more interested in writing what they heard than in simplifying and redefining ethnic labels when confronted with complexities. It is also clear that inventory takers often made corrections, returning to documents to make sure a Papel was not labeled a Balanta or Bijago or Floup. This is not to say that all record keepers were diligent. Indeed, a small number of Maranhense inventories list slaves only by the broad regions from which they came – *Guiné*, *Mina*, *Angola*, and *Moçambique*. Hence, Balanta, Bijago, Mandinka, and others shipped through Bissau and Cacheu became *Guiné* in some records. But in most inventories, very localized ethnic labels were logged, evidence that Upper Guineans sometimes chose to emphasize ethnic identities.

---

[24] Paul Lovejoy, "Methodology through the Ethnic Lens: The Study of Atlantic Africa," in *African Historical Research: Sources and Methods*, eds. Toyin Falola and Christian Jennings (Rochester, NY: University of Rochester Press, 2002), 103–17.

Given this, it follows that one can use Upper Guinean ethnonyms recorded in Maranhão (or elsewhere) to determine where slaves came from within Africa. There are myriad sources from the eighteenth and nineteenth centuries describing the locations of the ethnic *chão* of Balanta, Papel, Floup, and other groups near Bissau and Cacheu. These *chão* could often be measured in tens of square miles. Hence, when slaves responded to the question "What is your nation?" with "I am Balanta," "I am Papel," or "I am Floup," they revealed much about where they were captured.

When many responses to the question "What is your nation?" are compiled into a database, patterns of slave production can be discerned. As one of the evidentiary bases of this study, I have assembled data from about 8,500 inventories into the Maranhão Inventories Slave Database (MISD). With it, I show that most slaves exported from the Upper Guinea coast after 1750 hailed from an area stretching tens of miles from the ports of Bissau and Cacheu. My data challenges long-held notions that most of the slaves who passed through Bissau and Cacheu and into the Atlantic were made captive in the more distant interior and were the products of wars waged by states, especially the Mandinka state of Kaabu and a Fula state on the Futa Jallon plateau.[25] Using the MISD, I argue that most slaves exported from Bissau and Cacheu were the victims of conflicts among and within relatively small-scale and politically decentralized coastal societies. The MISD also reveals much about the gender ratios of slaves exported from parts of Africa, marriage practices of African slaves in Maranhão, the value planters placed on the skills that slaves brought with them from particular parts of Africa, and the impact of plantation labor on slave health and reproduction.

AFRICAN CULTURES IN AMAZONIA

Finally, this study draws on information about precisely from where African slaves in Amazonia hailed so as to test old and advance new theories about the extent to which Africans in the Americas re-created cultures of their homelands.[26] Decades ago, scholars such as E. Franklin

---

[25] Walter Rodney, *A History of the Upper Guinea Coast, 1545 to 1800* (New York: Monthly Review Press, 1970); Barry, *Senegambia*.

[26] Lovejoy argues that one of the tasks of Atlanticists is to find ways to understand "to what extent enslaved Africans were able to determine their cultural survival; to what extent they were the agents in the continuation of traditions." For me, doing so requires developing an understanding of from where within Africa those enslaved in the Americas came. Paul E. Lovejoy, "The African Diaspora: Revisionist Interpretations of Ethnicity,

Frazier and Stanley M. Elkins argued that the horrors of the slave trade and plantation life traumatized African slaves so much that they were rendered culturally void; they became receptacles that were filled with their masters' cultural assumptions.[27]

Frazier's and Elkins's ideas gave rise to waves of scholarship taking a variety of approaches. One group of scholars argued that particular and scattered African cultural and spiritual forms "survived" the Middle Passage and could be documented over time and space in the Americas.[28] A second group of scholars built on the work of Sidney W. Mintz and Richard Price, who famously argued in an essay focused on the Caribbean that the slave trade served to randomize Africans shipped to that region. That is, African slaves on Caribbean plantations were not, they said, from one cultural group but were thrown together into multicultural "crowds" in which no one culture dominated. Randomization combined with the harshness of the Middle Passage and of life under slave regimes separated African slaves from the cultures from which they had come, creating what Mintz and Price saw as discontinuities in cultural transmission. However, rather than seeing Africans from widely scattered places as recipients of a European-based culture, the pair argued that Africans became cultural creators who drew on many African and non-African cultural forms to create something unique in the New World. Later, this process of African cultural creativity under oppression was labeled "creolization," a term that has been widely applied to situations that Mintz and Price insist do not resemble the historical circumstances that they describe in their scholarship.[29] Indeed, creolization has come to mean "cultural mixing"

Culture and Religion under Slavery," *Studies in the World History of Slavery, Abolition and Emancipation* II (1997), 4.

[27] E. Franklin Frazier, *The Negro Family in the United States* (Chicago: The University of Chicago Press, 1966); Stanley M. Elkins, *Slavery: A Problem in American Institutional and Intellectual Life* (New York: The Universal Library, 1963).

[28] Writing before Frazier, Melville J. Herskovits pioneered this line of thought. See *The Myth of the Negro Past* (New York: Harper Brothers, 1941). Others built on it to counter Frazier and Elkins. For example, Roger Bastide, *African Civilizations in the New World*, trans. Peter Green (New York: Harper Torchbooks, 1972); John W. Blassingame, *The Slave Community: Plantation Life in the Antebellum South* (New York: Oxford University Press, 1979); Joseph E. Holloway, *Africanisms in American Culture* (Bloomington: Indiana University Press, 2005).

[29] Sidney W. Mintz and Richard Price, *An Anthropological Approach to the Afro-American Past: A Caribbean Perspective* (Philadelphia: Institute of the Study of Human Issues, 1976); Sidney W. Mintz and Richard Price, *The Birth of African-American Culture: An Anthropological Perspective* (Boston: Beacon Press, 1992); Sidney W. Mintz, "Enduring Substances, Trying Theories: The Caribbean Region as Oikoumene," *Journal of the Royal Anthropological Institute* 2, 2 (1996), 302. Similar is Sylvia Frey and Betty Wood, *Come*

(and not necessarily under oppressive systems) and has been applied to a host of situations and locations.

Although many today accept versions of a creolization model, James H. Sweet argues that neither the creolization nor survival approaches fully explain the complexity of African cultural and spiritual experiences under enslavement in the Americas. He, like others, recognizes that Africans were not always randomized in the New World. "Rather," he writes, "many were arriving in coherent cultural groupings that shared much in common – language, kinship, religion, and so on." Further, Sweet asserts that within these cultural groupings "an essential character or worldview, based on the cultural values of a specific African region," was re-created in the Americas, where it continued largely intact. Most of Sweet's watershed *Recreating Africa: Culture, Kinship, and Religion in the African-Portuguese World, 1441–1770* is concerned with how West Central Africans in diaspora clung to what he calls "core" spiritual beliefs, which he sees as relatively fixed and unchanging over time.[30]

Although a considerable amount of historical research over the past few decades has proven Frazier and Elkins wrong, scholars actively debate whether African cultures survived in small and scattered fragments, became something wholly new through processes of creolization, or were re-created in the Americas. These debates are not without their problems. I will highlight two. One has been a tendency for scholars to draw conclusions based on evidence from one African diaspora and to apply them broadly to other diasporas. That is, some have failed to acknowledge the particularities of slave-trading patterns across the Atlantic over space and time. Some parts of the New World drew from one African port or from a set of closely neighboring ports. But during periods of their history, parts of the New World drew from a great variety of widely dispersed ports. In the former case, Africans in diaspora may have shared a common culture, aspects of which might have been re-created under oppressive conditions in a foreign land. In the latter, they may not have shared a common culture and, therefore, might have engaged in processes of

Shouting to Zion: African-American Protestantism in the American South and British Caribbean to 1830 (Chapel Hill: The University of North Carolina Press, 1998); Laura de Mello e Souza, *O diabo e a terra de Santa Cruz: Feitiçaria e religiosidade popular no Brasil colonial* (São Paulo: Companhia das Letras, 1994).

[30] Sweet, *Recreating*, 116, 227. Supporters of the "black rice thesis" can be placed in the "re-creations" school. Especially Carney, *Black Rice*; Fields-Black, *Deep Roots*. Also on randomization, Thornton, *Africa and Africans*, 184–205.

cultural creativity – creolization.[31] This is to say that time and place matter in historical analyses.

A second problem with scholarship on African cultural survivals, re-creations, and creolizations has been the failure on the part of many scholars to identify the multiple and overlapping "boundaries" of African cultures and cultural identities. Decades ago, Melville J. Herskovits saw similarities in all cultures from which African slaves were taken. In the Americas, he argued, broadly African cultural forms survived and could be identified, particularly in Brazil. However, researchers today often see great differences in African societies, even within relatively small regions. To argue for a general African culture is, some claim, to depict as homogeneous what was a heterogeneous continent. Summarizing, Mintz and Price write that "knowledge of West African cultural complexity suggests that ... allegedly widespread or universal West African cultural 'elements,' 'traits,' or 'complexes' are not at all so widespread as Herskovits supposed."[32]

So to what extent did African cultures differ over space? With regard to Upper Guinea, it is clear that there were cultural differences from ethnic group to ethnic group – even among groups occupying a relatively small area (a zone within tens of miles of the ports of Cacheu and Bissau, for example). People who were part of particular ethnic groups used dress, jewelry, bodily markings, and language to identify who they were. From group to group there were differences in political structures. Ethnic groups also embraced certain forms of labor organization for large-scale rice projects, and there were variations from group to group with regard to how rice was planted, processed, and prepared for meals.

But across ethnic groups in Upper Guinea there were also cultural similarities. Indeed, there was a cultural unity.[33] Barry notes this about

---

[31] In a study of Cuba from 1789 to 1865, Oscar Grandío Moráguez finds that Africans' backgrounds were diverse and that they "did not share a 'unique' culture." If Sweet is right about Angolans elsewhere at particular times, Moráguez is not necessarily wrong. Oscar Grandío Moráguez, "The African Origins of Slaves Arriving in Cuba, 1789–1865," in *Extending the Frontiers: Essays on the New Transatlantic Slave Trade Database*, eds. David Eltis and David Richardson (New Haven: Yale University Press, 2008), 181. Also on the Caribbean, David Eltis, "Volume and Structure," 17–46.

[32] Herskovits, *The Myth*, 81–5; Mintz and Price, *The Birth*, 9.

[33] Forrest, *Lineages*; Eve Lakshmi Crowley, "Contracts with the Spirits: Religion, Asylum, and Ethnic Identity in the Cacheu Region of Guinea-Bissau" (Ph.D. thesis, Yale University, 1990); Carlos Lopes, *Kaabunké: Espaço, território, e poder na Guiné-Bissau, Gâmbia, e Casamance pré-coloniais* (Lisbon: Comissão Nacional Para as Comemorações dos Descrobrimentos Portugueses, 1999). On cultural zones elsewhere, Thornton, *Africa and Africans*, 184–92; Paul E. Lovejoy, "Ethnic Designations of the Slave Trade and the

the region to the north of Guinea-Bissau: "Nowhere ... where population settlement patterns assumed stable outlines ... did any Wolof, Manding, Peul, Tukulor, Sereer, Joola, or other ethnic group feel they were strangers."[34] And in the area around the ports of Bissau and Cacheu – the area from which most of the slaves exported to Amazonia hailed – the same could be said of Balanta, Biafada, Papel, Floup, Bijago, Brame, Mandinka, and Fula. They were not strangers; they shared a common regional culture. In the Guinea-Bissau area, Joshua Forrest emphasizes, ethnic identities were salient and conflicts sometimes flared across ethnic divides. Nonetheless, in the precolonial period there was "a recurrent capacity for constructive interethnic ties, which reflected the social malleability and incorporative capacity of most groups, as well as their economic and trading interests."[35]

As noted above, many people in Amazonia were multilingual, something emphasized by the Jesuit missionary Alonso de Sandoval in the early seventeenth century. Observing slave arrivals in Cartagena, he wrote that the "Wolofs, Berbers, Mandingas, and Fulos" could "usually ... understand each other because they have [in Africa] frequent communication." Mandingas (Mandinka), particularly, "are spread out among many kingdoms and know many different languages." Continuing, he said that "Bootes call themselves Banhun, and ... they understand the Fulupos." As for Banhuns (Banyun), they "can understand the Cazangas ... [and] also speak Bran and Mandinga." Brans, he said, "understand many languages, including Banhun, Fulopo, Balanta, Mandinga, and Biafara."[36]

None of this is surprising given that Upper Guinea's languages all belonged to two large families – West Atlantic and Mande. Within those families, linguistic differences existed, but there were also many similarities. Moreover, all groups in Upper Guinea were involved in regional trade, communicating regularly at great markets, in port towns, and in interior entrepôts. Upper Guineans did not live in isolated, inward-looking communities. They engaged with one another and, as oceangoing vessels began arriving with great regularity, with the broader Atlantic.

Reconstruction of the History of Trans-Atlantic Slavery," in *Trans-Atlantic Dimensions of Ethnicity in the African Diaspora*, eds. Paul E. Lovejoy and David V. Trotman (New York: Continuum, 2003), 34–7.

[34] Barry, *Senegambia*, 35.

[35] Forrest, *Lineages*, 43.

[36] Nicole von Germeten, ed. and trans., *Sandoval, Treatise on Slavery: Selections from De Instauranda Aethiopum Salute* (Indianapolis: Hackett Publishing, 2008), 44–5. Sandoval makes clear, too, that not all Upper Guineans could understand one another.

And connect with the Atlantic they did. I argue that as West Africans made themselves part of the dynamic commercial and cultural network that linked Bissau, Cacheu, and the surrounding area with Maranhão and Pará, they made *Guiné*. That is, they fashioned a dynamic regional culture that was shared by members of myriad ethnic groups. Trade with Atlantic merchants had a profound effect on how people in Upper Guinea saw themselves, on what they did, and on how they interacted with one another. Engagement with the Atlantic brought goods and ideas that circulated widely. This connection with the Atlantic, too, brought Upper Guinea communities into increased interactions with one another as people in many localities fostered alliances, entered into competition (which was often violent), and traded goods. This give and take with the Atlantic was a catalyst for people to make and remake cultural identities. One of those identities was regional; it was found throughout *Guiné*.

As a geographic unit, *Guiné* (or Guinea in English) was named by Europeans. That is, people with whom Europeans came into contact as they made their earliest voyages down the coast of Africa in the fifteenth century did not identify themselves as living in an area they called *Guiné* nor did they say they were *Guineense* (Guinean). The word *Guiné* was first used by Portuguese and is of unknown origin. One theory holds that it is from Djenne, an important city of the powerful West African empire of Mali. Another claims that it is from the Berber *guinwi*, which means "blacks" or in this case "land of the blacks." And, indeed, in the early years of Atlantic exploration Portuguese meant "black Africa" when they wrote of *Guiné*.[37] However, by the early seventeenth century, *Guiné* had come to mean areas between about the Senegal River and Cape Palmas, as distinguished from *Mina* (Cape Palmas through the Bight of Biafra, which was called "Lower Guinea" in English), and *Angola* (south from the Bight of Biafra).[38]

In Brazil from the early seventeenth century, Portuguese sometimes identified slaves embarked at ports on the Upper Guinea coast as *Guiné* – as part of what they saw as a Guinean *nação* or "nation." But Portuguese colonists did not invent that nation in Brazil any more than they invented ethnic groups across the ocean. Portuguese named a region, but what

---

[37] Chouki El Hamel, "Constructing a Diasporic Identity: Tracing the Origins of the Gnawa Spiritual Group in Morocco," *Journal of African History* 49 (2008), 241–60; Luigi Scantamburlo, *Dicionário do Guineense* (Lisbon: Edições Colibri, 1999), I: 19.

[38] Mariza de Carvalho Soares, *Devotos da cor: Identidade étnica, religiosidade e escravidão no Rio de Janeiro, século XVIII* (Rio de Janeiro: Civilização Brasileira, 2000), 47–51; Thornton, *Africa and Africans*, 184–92.

made Guineans Guineans resulted from processes occurring in black communities in Africa and Brazil. That is, by engaging with one another and with Atlantic merchants, Africans fashioned a broad regional identity that overlay smaller ethnic identities.

In Amazonia, slaves shipped through Cacheu and Bissau continued to identify themselves as being from ethnic groups – Balanta, Papel, Bijago, Mandinka, Biafada, and others. However, when thrown together on plantations and in colonial towns with slave populations consisting of people from various Upper Guinea ethnic groups, Upper Guineans did not see themselves as comprising heterogeneous crowds; they did not see their identities or cultures as ethnically bound. Rather, they saw themselves as part of a homogeneous community. They looked back to *Guiné* as a culturally unified region, and it was a regional identity that they sought to re-create under oppressive conditions in Amazonia. Indeed, I see no evidence that in Maranhão, people from Upper Guinea fostered ethnic languages, celebrations, cuisines, approaches to agriculture, dress, or spiritual ceremonies (although I do not doubt that some ethnically based traditions may have "survived" for some time in scattered places). Rather, Upper Guineans sought to re-create institutions they had known across the ocean as crosscutting and incorporative – institutions that served to unify and not to divide.

It should go without saying that in Amazonia, as elsewhere, Africans could not re-create all aspects of the cultures they had known before their enslavement. Indeed, it is my argument that they could re-create precious few. On Amazonian plantations, slave owners called many of the shots. They used violence – which was often swift and severe – to force slaves to submit to their will, shaping much about black life. Moreover, the physical environment of Amazonia was different in many ways from that of Upper Guinea, meaning that African slaves often had to improvise, invent, and innovate – developing, as they did, new cultural forms.[39] Nonetheless, where narrow spaces in the plantation regime allowed, captives sold through Bissau and Cacheu drew on their common cultural traditions to remake Guinea in Brazil.

So what did Upper Guineans in Amazonia forge that was new and re-create that was old? Through a rich analysis of African agency in the Americas, Thornton argues that much of African culture disappeared rapidly under oppressive plantation regimes. Quick to vanish, he argues, were African languages because in most American towns and on most

---

[39] Eltis, Morgan, and Richardson, "Agency and the Diaspora."

American plantations, slaves embraced a lingua franca, which was most often a creole version of the dominant European language. This is not to say that Africans speaking the same homeland language did not use it when they were together. It is to say that creole versions of European languages emerged over time as the language of daily interaction.[40] And, indeed, in Maranhão, I see no evidence that Upper Guinean ethnic languages survived for long. Extant documentation for Amazonia makes no reference to Upper Guineans speaking Bijago, Mandinka, Fula, Balanta, or any other homeland language. Rather, they communicated with their masters and each other through a creole that utilized much Portuguese vocabulary.[41]

Other aspects of African culture also disappeared in the passage across the ocean. Most obviously, political structures vanished (except, perhaps, in scattered communities of runaways) as African slaves were subordinated to white masters and plantation hierarchies. In parts of the New World, African "kings" and "queens" held sway during festivals, but their duties and powers were quite different from those back home.[42] In the case of coastal Upper Guineans, ruling institutions that took the form of councils of elders in the Old World were not re-created in the New. In Amazonia, planters controlled high politics.

But in other realms of their Amazonian lives, African slaves exercised some agency. In this book, I focus particularly on three realms of slave life in Amazonia – work, family, and religion. I find that in each of these realms, planter power manifested itself in different ways. The rice regime that emerged in Maranhão was, I argue, "creolized." That is, it resulted from inputs of people from multiple corners of the Atlantic World and was not transplanted intact from West Africa. Planters and Upper Guinean slaves contributed varying degrees of knowledge to different stages of the annual rice cycle. Planters cared a great deal about how rice was planted, harvested, and processed and, therefore, sought to

---

[40] Thornton, *Africa and Africans*, 206–18.
[41] In early periods of Amazonia's colonial history, Brasílica, a standardized version of Indian Tupi-Guarani languages in Brazil, was spoken widely, including by black slaves who learned it. As for creole, a version that utilized much Portuguese vocabulary (called *Kriolo*) was spoken in parts of the Upper Guinea coast. It was a language of trade used among people from different ethnic groups and with Portuguese. Available sources do not allow me to compare creoles spoken on both sides of the ocean. However, *Kriolo* has been seen as an African or Africanized language. Further study may show it was reproduced in Maranhão.
[42] John Thornton, *Africa and Africans in the Making of the Atlantic World, 1400–1800*, 2nd ed. (New York: Cambridge University Press, 1998), 325–6.

control agricultural processes. However, they did not care how Africans prepared rice for consumption in slave quarters. For this, Upper Guinean women in Amazonia, almost all of whom were from rice-producing societies, re-created cuisines known widely throughout their native region. Planters, too, did not care about their slaves' family lives and spiritual beliefs and practices. Slaves exercised considerable control in these realms of their lives and, I show, re-created familial and spiritual institutions that were common throughout the whole of *Guiné*.

In sum, I argue that a close look at slave life in Amazonia reveals that Africans were able to exercise different degrees of agency in particular realms of their lives. The nature of plantation regimes and of physical environments meant that much African cultural knowledge was ill-suited for conditions in the New World and was lost. Through violence, masters dictated how things would play out in many areas of plantation life. Masters and slaves contributed varying levels of knowledge to other realms, creating creolized spaces in plantation regimes. But in Amazonia, Upper Guineans found a few narrow openings where they could "make Guinea" – or some aspects of the Guinea they had known. When brought together on plantations, Balanta, Papel, Floup, Mandinka, Fula, Biafada, Brame, Banyun, and Bijago re-created some cultural institutions found throughout *Guiné*. Where they could, they re-created traditions that they remembered as unifying the members of different ethnic groups and not as dividing them.

THE CHAPTERS

I have divided this book into two parts. Part I examines why and how Upper Guineans from an area only tens of miles from the ports of Bissau and Cacheu were enslaved and shipped to Amazonia after 1755. Chapter 1 focuses on the demand side – Amazonia. In this chapter, I explore the long history of Portuguese colonialism in Maranhão and Pará. From the time the Portuguese made a forceful claim to Maranhão Island in 1621 to the establishment of the CGPM in 1755, Indians were the backbone of the colonial labor force in Amazonia. The chapter is concerned with why white settlers in Amazonia saw Indian slaves as inferior to African slaves and why, ultimately, Upper Guineans replaced Indians on plantations. Chapter 1 also charts a history of the African slave trade to Amazonia and shows where the Africans exported to Amazonia hailed from in Upper Guinea.

Chapter 2 explains how those who were shipped to Amazonia were made captive in Upper Guinea. Why after 1755 did Upper Guineans in an area stretching only tens of miles from the ports of Bissau and Cacheu take actions to meet a Portuguese demand for labor in Amazonia by supplying captives in dramatically higher numbers than they had in previous decades? The answer lies in the convergence of factors – an Upper Guinean need for iron to expand paddy rice farming, a Portuguese willingness to supply increasing quantities of iron in exchange for slaves, and the fractured nature of Upper Guinean coastal societies and politics. Ultimately, most communities found ways to control and manage the slave trade – keeping losses to a minimum while at the same time garnering the goods they needed from Atlantic ports.

Chapter 3 focuses on the movement of captives from myriad and scattered villages to interior entrepôts, to the ports of Bissau and Cacheu, and then onto slave ships. From there, the chapter traces the flow of captives across the ocean to Amazonian plantations. I argue that when captives from a variety of ethnic groups were forced together on slaving routes, they looked to one another for support and community, emphasizing unity in the face of great adversity. For Balanta, Papel, Bijago, Floup, Mandinka, and people from other ethnic groups who were enslaved and sent through Bissau and Cacheu, their time together in transit was central to their later emphasis of a Guinean identity.

Part II begins an examination of how people from numerous Upper Guinean ethnic groups fostered cultural links with one another in Africa and Brazil. Chapter 4 examines what Upper Guinea slaves did most of the time – work. In Amazonia in the second half of the eighteenth century, most slaves worked over two crops – rice and cotton. However, the physical environment in Maranhão was different from that of Upper Guinea, meaning that not all Upper Guinean knowledge of rice was appropriate to this new setting. Further, planters wielded considerable power and dictated much about how fields would be cleared and rice planted, harvested, and processed. This is not to say that Upper Guineans contributed nothing beyond labor to the rice complex that emerged in Amazonia. Upper Guineans drew on shared knowledge of rice to shape their working lives when and where they could. If it was anything, the rice regime that emerged in Maranhão was a creolized one. It resulted from Portuguese settlers and Upper Guinean slaves drawing on their respective traditions and improvising new agricultural methods in a land that was very different from anything either group had known before.

Chapter 5 explores slaves' sex and family lives. After puberty, more than 30 percent of African slaves married in Maranhão. Evidence from the MISD shows that an impressive percentage chose to marry others from the same region of Africa. Upper Guineans most often married other Upper Guineans, re-creating endogamous marriage patterns they had known across the ocean. They made choices about whom to marry and their selections were informed by the cultures from which they had come. However, the nature of the group in which Upper Guineans married endogamously was different in Amazonia from what it had been in their native land. In Upper Guinea, Africans married most often within ethnic groups. In Amazonia, they married most often within a regionally defined group.

In Chapter 6, I argue that spiritual beliefs were the most stable aspect of Upper Guinean culture over time and across space. Although many aspects of spiritual belief and practice differed from ethnic group to ethnic group, all Upper Guineans held a set of overlapping beliefs that changed little over time. All believed that there was one creator god who rarely interacted in daily life; that spirits inhabited the earth, interacting with humans and affecting them for better and worse; that certain material objects and natural substances contained supernatural powers; and that some people were "gifted," knowing better than most how to receive messages from spirits, to please them with gifts in the form of sacrifices, and to manipulate the supernatural powers of natural substances and material objects. Using Church books of denunciation and some Inquisition cases, I examine how Upper Guineans re-created *some* of those commonly held beliefs in Amazonia. The chapter also examines what disappeared rapidly in Amazonia – mainly ethnically based spiritual practices that were not widely known in Upper Guinea.

PART I

THE WHY AND HOW OF ENSLAVEMENT AND TRANSPORTATION

I

From Indian to African Slaves

In 1767, Judge Antonio Jozé Araújo of the captaincy of Maranhão in Brazil's Amazonia region visited the home of Ventura de Almeida in Vila de Viana to conduct an inventory of the deceased's possessions. Along with a variety of personal items, some land, cattle, and fields of cotton and rice, he owned eleven slaves. All of Almeida's slaves had been given Christian names, only one maintaining an African surname. Diogo was a Mandinka male who was about thirty years old and married to Rita, a twenty-five-year-old *cafuza*, or racially mixed woman of black and Indian descent. The thirty-five-year-old Manoel Beyam was listed as a *Guiné*, or a person from the Upper Guinea region of Africa. His last name, which is not Portuguese, indicates that he, like Diogo, was of Mandinka origin.[1] Eugenca, Beyam's twenty-three-year-old wife, was also from *Guiné*, of an ethnic group unnamed. Francisco, a Biafada who was forty years old, was in good health like most of his fellow slaves. However, Vicente, a Papel who was thirty, was either sick or injured, as he was valued at only 50,000 réis, which was a little less than half the value of those who labored beside him for Almeida. Francisco and Vicente likely shared some of the same memories of the Upper Guinea coast's Grande and Geba Rivers, on which people from their two ethnic groups lived, farmed, and traded. At eighteen, Anna was the youngest of the Upper Guinea–born slaves. Three slaves, Jozefa (age eighteen), Bendito (thirty-five), and Agostinho (twelve), were all listed as *crioulo*, meaning that they were blacks who had been born in Brazil.

[1] Bayo (or Beyam) is a common Mandinka name in the region around the Gambia River.

Antonio, who was thirty-five, was simply listed as *negro*, or black, giving us no hint as to where he might have been born.[2]

Had Almeida's inventory been generated in 1747 instead of 1767, it would have been an odd document indeed. In the 1740s, both the African and *crioulo* populations of Amazonia were miniscule. At that time, the backbone of the landholders' labor force was made up primarily of Indians. However, to Almeida's contemporaries in Maranhão as well as in Pará, the other Amazonian captaincy, there would have been nothing unusual about any of Almeida's possessions. In the 1760s, most Amazonian colonists grew cotton and rice. Most owned relatively few things, the region being undeveloped compared to the rest of Brazil.[3] And many held African slaves, the majority of whom were from Upper Guinea. Over a short period of time, a revolution had taken place in Maranhão, as Upper Guineans replaced Indians in the fields.

If Almeida's inventory is typical when compared to others in Amazonia, it is startlingly different when compared to others from Brazilian regions to the south during the same period. Indeed, nowhere else in South America did Upper Guinean slaves comprise a majority of the captive population – or a majority of the total immigrant population – as they did in Amazonia in the third quarter of the eighteenth century.[4] Further, in few other parts of Brazil would Almeida, with his meager possessions, have been seen as a person in fairly good economic standing.[5] Understanding why Amazonia was an economic backwater through the mid-eighteenth century and what sparked a revolution that brought tens of thousands of Upper Guineans into Maranhão and Pará requires a deep look into the region's history.

WHITE SETTLERS, INDIANS, AND *MAMELUCOS* BEFORE 1750

In 1621, the Portuguese established the State of Maranhão, which was composed of the captaincies of Maranhão and Pará. That year, Portugal

---

[2] TJEM, AJ, Inventory of Ventura de Almeida, 1767.

[3] Jeronimo de Viveiros, *História do comércio do Maranhão, 1612–1895* (São Luís: Associação Comercial do Maranhão, 1954), 63–7; Ernesto Cruz, *História do Pará* (Belém: Universidade do Pará, 1963), 43; Manuel Nunes Dias, *Fomento e merchantilismo: A Companhia Geral do Grão Pará e Maranhão (1755–1778)* (Belém: Universidade Federal do Pará, 1970), I: 166–7.

[4] To find a population of similar composition, one would have to look to South Carolina after about 1750. David Eltis, Philip Morgan, and David Richardson, "Agency and the Diaspora in Atlantic History: Reassessing the African Contribution to Rice Cultivation in the Americas," *American Historical Review* 12, 5 (2007), 1329–58.

[5] Celso Furtado, *Formação econômico do Brasil* (São Paulo: Companhia Editora Nacional, 2001), 89–90.

ousted French settlers, who had established themselves in 1612, from Maranhão Island and began settling Portuguese in their place. Not long after claiming the island, the Portuguese put effort into setting up farms in the Mearim and Itapecurú River Valleys, which stretched tens of miles south, the rivers feeding into the São Marcos and São José Bays. Abundant rain and tropical heat made the valleys ideal for crop production. Moreover, the rivers facilitated transport to and from the oceanic port that was situated at São Luís, Maranhão Island's principal town.

Throughout the State of Maranhão, annual average rainfall and natural vegetation varied greatly. Maranhão Island and the Upper Mearim and Itapecurú Rivers received between 1,600 and 1,800 millimeters (63 to 71 inches) of annual precipitation. To the west, rainfall was greater – between 2,000 and 2,300 millimeters (79 to 91 inches) annually. It increased farther west toward the Amazon River. The area around the Upper Mearim and Itapecurú was swampy, transitioning into gallery forests that reached dozens of miles south and west. Farther west, gallery forests transitioned into rain forests that continued through the great Amazon River Valley. South of the gallery forests and toward Piauí and Bahia was savannah. In Maranhão's savannah, annual rainfall totals (1,000 to 1,200 millimeters, or 39 to 47 inches) were considerably less than around the Upper Mearim and Itapecurú. As a consequence, the savannah area had low population densities, eventually attracting colonial cattle herders.[6]

Through the nineteenth century, Indians who had not yet suffered colonization occupied much of the forest beyond the immediate coast and south and west of the Mearim Valley. These Indians can be distinguished based on language. In the early sixteenth century, the first Portuguese to arrive in Brazil – in the region that came to be known as Bahia – met Tupi-Guarani speakers. Eventually, missionaries and settlers reduced Tupi-Guarani speakers' multiple, complex identities to the prefix "Tupi," so they became known as Tupis in histories of the New World and in letters written by administrators and Jesuits. In Maranhão the Tupinambá (who occupied Maranhão Island and much of the coast), Tabajara, and Caeté tribes spoke languages that belong to the Tupi-Guarani language family. Early in Brazil's history, Jesuits standardized Tupi-Guarani as a language called Brasílica to which they applied a written form. From the early seventeenth century, Brasílica was spoken in Amazonia as a language of interaction between whites and Tupis. It, too, was taught to

---

[6] See, especially, *Atlas do Maranhão* (Rio de Janeiro: Fundação Instituto Brasileiro de Geografia e Estatística, 1984).

Indians and whites in colonial-controlled areas and became the general language, or *lingual geral*.[7]

The other major Indian group in Amazonia consisted of speakers of languages in the Jê family. Jê languages were quite different from Tupi-Guarani languages and appeared to be "broken," or *travadas*, to Portuguese. In Maranhão, Jê speakers included Guajas, Guajajaras, Gamelas, and Tapuias. They occupied territory south from Maranhão Island along the Mearim and Itapecurú Rivers, some of the forests to the west, and the savannahs.[8]

Over time, Indians from both groups who were integrated into Portuguese-controlled areas as laborers learned to speak Brasílica and developed a generalized "neo-Indian" identity known as *caboclo*. Following Matthias Röhrig Assunção, *caboclo* "can be characterised as detribalised … sharing nearly all of the Indian material culture and remaining attached to elements of Indian beliefs, but living in Catholic-inspired family structures and sharing the Catholic faith."[9] However, throughout the colonial period, Indians that the Portuguese considered "wild" occupied much of Maranhão's forested area and parts of the savannah. The range of social organization of Indian tribes in the area was great. Some were hunter-gatherers and others practiced agriculture, planting especially manioc and maize.

With few settlers and much Indian-controlled territory, Maranhão remained an isolated and underdeveloped outpost of the Portuguese empire until the mid-eighteenth century. It was largely cut off from the rest of Brazil by contrary winds, hidden shoals, and difficult ocean currents. Thus, transport to Bahia and regions south took place in part by land and river routes. Further, because European and African immigrants were few and because Indians who were forced into agricultural labor often died quickly from disease, Maranhão did not experience the economic growth that resulted from increases in sugar production on plantations elsewhere in the seventeenth century.[10] Indeed, although colonial

[7] Robert H. Lowe, "Eastern Brazil: An Introduction," in *Handbook of South American Indians*, ed. Julian H. Steward (Washington: U.S. G.P.O., 1946), 381–400; "The Northwestern and Central Ge," in *Handbook*, 477–517; "The 'Tapuya,'" in *Handbook*, 553–9; M. Kittiya Lee, "Conversing in Colony: The Brasílica and the Vulger in Portuguese America, 1500–1759" (Ph.D. thesis, The Johns Hopkins University, 2005); Carlos de Lima, *História do Maranhão* (São Luís: Senado Federal, Centro Gráfico, 1981), 23–50.

[8] Ibid.

[9] Matthias Röhrig Assunção, "Popular Culture and Regional Society in Nineteenth-Century Maranhão, Brazil," *Bulletin of Latin American Research* 14, 3 (1995), 270–1.

[10] For economic comparisons: Furtado, *Formação*, 89–90; Roberto C. Simonsen, *Historia Economica do Brasil, 1500–1820* (São Paulo: Companhia Editora, 1937), 109–10. On

troops and European diseases had a devastating effect on Indians in the seventeenth and early eighteenth centuries, it was not until the mid-eighteenth century that Portuguese settlers would begin to establish themselves far beyond Maranhão's immediate coastal zone. In the second half of the eighteenth century, Portuguese steadily carved out plantations up the Itapecurú River and its tributaries, along the Munim River to the east, and west of Maranhão Island across the Bay of São Marcos past the town of Alcântara. Through the nineteenth century, colonial settlers had less success south along the Mearim and west, where forests were denser.[11]

Although it was undeveloped, the seventeenth-century Amazonian State of Maranhão, which Portugal claimed as its own, was enormous. It consisted of what are today the states of Maranhão, Pará, Amazonas, Piauí, and Goiás – as well as parts of Ceará, Mato Grosso, and Goiás. Its capital, São Luís, was situated on Maranhão Island. The size of the state made governing it difficult, so at different times it was divided into smaller administrative units and the capital resituated. Most importantly, in 1751 the capital of what was then named Grão Pará and Maranhão was moved northwest to Belém on the Marajó Bay. Nonetheless, Maranhão, with its seat of government still in São Luís, maintained some independence. Its leading officials, *capitães-mores*, wielded great authority but were technically subordinate to the *capitães-generais* in Belém. Finally, in 1772 two independently administered states were created with governors in São Luís and Belém.[12]

In the seventeenth and early eighteenth centuries, Amazonia's non-Indian population was tiny, and mortality rates were significant. Throughout

Indians: John Hemming, "Indians on the Frontier in Colonial Brazil," in *The Cambridge History of Latin America*, ed. Leslie Bethell (Cambridge: Cambridge University Press, 1984), 529. For histories of Amazonia, see J. Lúcio de Azevedo, *Os Jesuítas no Grão-Pará, suas missões e a colonização*, 2nd ed. (Coimbra: Imprensa da Universidade, 1930); J. Lúcio de Azevedo, *Estudos de história paraense* (Pará: Typ. de Tavares Cardoso, 1893); João Francisco Lisboa, *Crônica do Brasil colonial: apontamentos para a história do Maranhão*, 2nd ed. (Petrópolis: Editora Vozes, 1976); *Obras de João Francisco Lisboa* (São Luís: Typ. de B. de Mattos, 1866); C. A. Marques, *Dicionário histórico-geográfico da Província do Maranhão*, 3rd ed. (Rio de Janeiro: Cia. Editora Fon-Fon e Selta, 1970); Ernesto Cruz, *História do Pará* (Belém: Universidade do Pará, 1963); David Graham Sweet, "A Rich Realm of Nature Destroyed: The Middle Amazon Valley, 1640–1750," (Ph.D. thesis, University of Wisconsin, 1974).

[11] Matthias Röhrig Assunção, *Pfanzer, sklaven und kleinbauern in der brasilianischen provinz Maranhão, 1800–1850* (Frankfurt: Vervuert, 1993), 385. Portugal's efforts in Maranhão were also challenged by threatening European outsiders – most especially the Dutch who invaded from Recife and Olinda in 1641 only to be ousted by the Portuguese in 1644. Carlos de Lima, *História do Maranhão* (São Luís: Senado Federal, 1981), 23–50.

[12] Dias, *A Companhia Geral*, I: 153–7.

the region's early history, most white settlers came from Portuguese island possessions. In 1618, for example, 300 Azoreans were sent to Maranhão, another 200 arriving in 1619, and 700 more between 1620 and 1627.[13] Estimates put the colonial populations of Maranhão's commercial and production centers in 1637 at the following: São Luís, 310; Tapuitapera, 300; Belém, 130; Itapecurú, 100; Ceará, 35; and Gurupá, 30.[14]

Over the next century, the settler population fluctuated with little colonial effort being put into transplanting whites from elsewhere. A mid-seventeenth century estimate for the entire State of Maranhão put the Portuguese population at 700.[15] In 1675, 50 Azorean couples were moved to Maranhão, another 234 people of both sexes following in 1676.[16] Where they ended up is unclear, but few seem to have settled in Pará, as a report from 1684 estimated its settler population at "one hundred and fifty households and a little more than two hundred men."[17] In 1698, the crown arranged for the settlement of 200 men from the Azores and Madeira in Maranhão, and in 1705 the monarchy promised to settle another 150. Again in 1707, it turned to the Azores for recruits to populate Amazonia. The crown resisted sending men from the Portuguese mainland, and in 1718 reneged on a promise for 200 Iberia-based soldiers for Maranhão and Pará.[18] With few settlers arriving, the white population of Amazonia showed few gains. In 1720, the total white population of Maranhão's capital and its five villas was reported to be only 1,378 inhabitants. São Luis's population was 854; Alcântara's 332; Vila de Santa Maria do Icatu's 54; the Mearim Rivers's 64; and the Itapecurú River's 74.[19] Historian David Graham Sweet figures that from 1650 to 1750 the Portuguese population of the captaincy of Pará increased from 200 to only about 1,500.[20]

Because few women immigrated into Amazonia and male immigrants looked to the local Indian population for sex (see Chapter 5), Amazonia's white population was destined to stagnate until some change took place.

---

[13] Simonsen, *História*, 110–11; Lima, *História*, 59.

[14] Carlos de Lima, *Vida, Paixão e morte da cidade de Alcântara-Maranhão* (São Luís: Plano Editorial SECMA, 1998), 44.

[15] Ibid.

[16] José Almada Pereira, *Cultura do arroz no Brasil, subsídios para a sua história* (Teresina: Embrapa, 2002), 66.

[17] BNP, códice 585, fl. 326.

[18] Sue A. Gross, "Labor in Amazonia in the First Half of the Eighteenth Century," *The Americas* 32, 2 (1975), 220.

[19] Viveiros, *História*, 63.

[20] Sweet, "Rich Realm," 111.

As will be seen, that change came in 1755 with the recognition of the legitimacy of white–Indian marriages. Until then, the state and the Church discouraged white–Indian sex, and *mamelucos*, who were the products of white–Indian sexual encounters, were not counted in censuses. They were discriminated against, having fewer rights than their white fathers.

Although free and slave Indians lived in white settler areas, they, too, were not counted in early censuses, as they were not Portuguese. Nor, of course, were the Indians who lived outside white settlements. Even in the late eighteenth century, such groups were seen as "barbarous" and threatening to Portuguese interests. Indeed, few whites left their villas because of fear of attack. Those who ventured inland went in raiding parties that struck Indian settlements and seized captives or purchased them from the victors of intertribal wars.[21]

The production of Indian captives reached such a scale that the few Portuguese settled in Maranhão in the early seventeenth century could afford to orchestrate the export of Indian slaves to the Spanish Caribbean. Spanish sources mention Indian slave imports from Maranhão in 1609. In 1616, Portuguese ships from the Amazon landed on the island of Hispaniola with as many as 100 Indians. In 1627, a Portuguese vessel arrived in Santo Domingo with about 200 Indians, who were said to have been acquired from other Indians who held them in bondage. Reports from 1628 and 1630 also note Indians (and a small number of blacks) being imported into the Spanish Caribbean from Maranhão. Precise figures for this trade may never be known, but it seems likely that thousands of Indian captives were exported from Maranhão in the first three decades of the seventeenth century.[22]

Far larger numbers of Indian captives were held as slaves in Maranhão. As they lived in an underdeveloped corner of the Portuguese empire, Maranhão's settlers could not afford African slaves, the backbone of the labor force elsewhere in Brazil. Instead, Indian laborers were the only option for those wanting to produce exports. Indian slaves were put to work growing and processing primarily sugarcane and tobacco, the first export crops experimented with in the region.[23] Under the hot equatorial sun, agricultural work was grueling, and contemporaries described Amazonian masters as exceptionally cruel. A missionary in Pará said that

[21] BNP, códice 585, fl. 326.
[22] John David Wheat, "The Afro-Portuguese Maritime World and the Foundations of Spanish Caribbean Society, 1570–1640" (Ph.D. thesis, Vanderbilt University, 2009), 50–1.
[23] BNP, códice 585, fl. 326.

Indians were "forced to do very heavy labor such as making tobacco, in which they work for seven or eight months on end by day and night."[24] Indians, too, gathered *drogas*, or natural products of the jungles, which included cacao, vanilla, cloves, other spices, indigo, and trees for lumber.[25] But no matter how hard Indians were forced to work, exports from Maranhão through the mid-eighteenth century were insignificant compared to the rest of Brazil.[26]

Hard work and Portuguese attacks led to the deaths of an untold number of Indians, but even more died from European diseases, particularly measles and smallpox. In 1621, smallpox decimated Tupinambá Indian populations on Maranhão Island, facilitating the Portuguese conquest. Observers wrote of "an epidemic ... of such virulence that any who caught it – most of whom were Indians – did not survive for more than three days."[27] In 1663, another epidemic killed many people "principally of the Indian class."[28] Two years later in 1665, a plea went out from Maranhão to King Afonso VI for "slaves for the agriculture of the plantations," which lacked laborers because of a "plague of smallpox in the whole of the state."[29] Epidemics struck again in 1695 and 1700, when 200 people died in São Luís and many more unrecorded in interior Indian villages. That year, the king acknowledged "new heights of misery in which the residents of the state [of Maranhão] find themselves with the great barrenness that continues and the deaths of [Indian] slaves."[30]

Despite the fact that settlers often replenished their slave holdings with Indians taken from the interior, shortages from death were a constant problem. Hence, in 1714 officials in Maranhão wrote that "there has been a great lack of Indians the result of which has been an inability to continue farming."[31] A 1725 report from Belém noted a "terrible contagion of smallpox that spread through the entire state in September last year.... It took from the city many whites, and more than 1000 slaves, most of whom were Indians, who are the instruments of all of the commerce and sustenance of the people and without whom most cannot

---

[24] Hemming, "Indians," 530.
[25] BNP, códice 585, fl. 326.
[26] Simonsen, *Historia*, 115–16.
[27] Bernardo Pereira de Berredo, *Annaes historicos do estado do Maranhão* (Lisbon: Typographia Maranhense, 1749), 6:211.
[28] Lima, *Vida*, 63–4; 70; Hemming, "Indians," 520–1.
[29] AHU, Maranhão, cx. 4, doc. 506.
[30] "Livro grosso do Maranhão," v. 1, in *Anais da Biblioteca Nacional* 60 (Rio de Janeiro: Imprensa Nacional, 1948), 155, 171.
[31] AHU, Maranhão, códice 269, fl. 21.

sustain themselves."[32] In 1726, the governor of Maranhão emphasized the need for more slaves because "many have died from an epidemic of smallpox."[33] In 1727, there was another report of massive Indian slave deaths from the disease in Pará and in Maranhão.[34]

Disease spread quickly in Indian populations in part because many Indian groups were encouraged to, and others forced to, change their settlement patterns. Before the establishment of Maranhão, Portuguese law in Brazil required that Indians who were not slaves live in Jesuit mission villages, or *aldeias*. Under arrangements known as *descimentos*, Jesuits in the mid-seventeenth century ventured up the main tributaries of the lower Amazon and Negro Rivers, returning with some 200,000 Indians whom they located near the coast in fifty-four villages. Indians were lured by the promise of salvation and material prosperity. However, in fixed and densely populated *aldeias*, Indians had prolonged contact with Europeans carrying contagions that had been unknown in the Americas before 1492. *Aldeias* were, then, perfect breeding grounds for disease.[35]

Aldeias were also sites of struggles between Jesuits and planters over control of Indian bodies and souls, because colonists sought to force mission-administered Indians to labor on farms and serve in the military. As best they could, Jesuits –motivated by humanitarian concerns, a desire to control Indian labor, and their fear that Indians who worked for colonists would not become good Christians – opposed colonists' demands that resettled Indians be made available to them. Hence, settler–Jesuit tensions ran high. "It was," a planter wrote in the mid-seventeenth century, "deplorable to compare the situation of this captaincy to that of the State of Brazil, where every month large numbers of Negro slaves enter. Here [in Maranhão] the only help is the Indian; and the new settlements [*aldeias*], placed on islands and on the shores of rivers, at great distances, will not dispense with the service of this people [Indians]."[36]

In the mid-seventeenth century, Father António Vieira, a Brazilian-born priest who was close to King João IV, articulated Indian "rights" in the face of growing planter frustration with colonial labor shortages.[37]

---

[32] AHU, Maranhão, cx. 9, doc. 768.

[33] AHU, Maranhão, cx. 9, doc. 855.

[34] AHU, Pará, cx. 10, doc. 941; AHU, Maranhão, códice 270, fl. 27.

[35] Simonsen, *História*, 122; Hemming, "Indians," 533, 512–13; Gross, "Labor," 211; Mathias C. Kiemen, "Indian Policy of Portugal in America, with Special Reference to the Old State of Maranhão, 1500–1755," *The Americas* 5, 2 (1948), 141–2.

[36] AHU, Maranhão, códice 270, fl. 27.

[37] Dauril Alden, "Some Reflections on Antonio Vieira: Seventeenth-Century Troubleshooter and Troublemaker," *Luso-Brazilian Review* 40, 1 (2003), 7–16.

When Vieira arrived in Amazonia in 1653, he was shocked by the treatment of Indians. He preached against planter expeditions to capture and purchase (or, as the Portuguese euphemistically called it, "ransom," or *resgate*) Indians, telling colonists, "All of you are in mortal sin; all of you live in a state of condemnation; and all of you are going directly to Hell!"[38] After returning to Portugal, Vieira convinced King João to pass legislation in 1655 against Indian enslavement.[39]

Disease, wars, and forced labor took a tremendous toll on Indian populations. As early as 1617, an observer noted that on Maranhão Island "there is not a single Indian village left. Within a hundred leagues of Pará [Belém] there is not a single Indian who is not at peace or has not been domesticated by the Portuguese." Of Indian populations, Father Vieira wrote in 1652 that "the entire region of Maranhão has been worn down, depopulated and reduced to one or two scanty villages, and vast numbers of people have been wiped out."[40] Manuel Teixeira, the vicar-general of Maranhão, wrote in 1662 that in only a few decades, several hundred Portuguese settlers had contributed to an astonishing number of Indians deaths – *about two million* in his estimation.[41] If recent projections of Brazil's Indian population are correct, Teixeira's figure was an exaggeration; nonetheless it does serve to highlight the gravity of the Indian plight during the period. Indian populations were devastated.[42]

And in the decades that followed, things did not get any better. In 1663, settlers rose in revolt against the Jesuits. The priests of the order were expelled and lay overseers were placed in Indian villages to allocate male workers to settler farms. Seventeen years later, Vieira managed to convince a new king, Pedro II, to allow Jesuits to reassume the administration of Indian villages. Dissatisfied with this and other crown decisions, settlers rebelled again in 1684 under the leadership of Manoel Beckman, who expelled the religious order for a short time before his uprising was crushed.[43]

---

[38] Hemming, "Indians," 532–3.
[39] Kiemen, "Indian Policy," 157–9.
[40] Maria Luiza Marcílo, "The Population of Colonial Brazil," in *The Cambridge History of Latin America*, ed. Leslie Bethell (Cambridge: Cambridge University Press, 1984), 42–3.
[41] Hemming, "Indians," 532. Vieira agreed. Marcílo, "Population," 43.
[42] John Hemming estimates 2,431,000 Indians in Brazil in 1500. *Red Gold: The Conquest of the Brazilian Indians* (Cambridge, MA: Harvard University Press, 1978), 487–501. In 1819, the Indian population was 800,000, one-third the population of 1500. Marcílo, "Population," 45.
[43] Hemming, "Indians," 534–5.

Reestablishing themselves quickly after Beckman's revolt, the Jesuits compromised with settlers on two points of contention. First, the fathers agreed that Indians under their administration would work for settlers for six months of every year for a wage to be paid in coarse white cloth (which had little value). Second, the Jesuits agreed to the reinstitution of legalized slave labor for Indians captured in intertribal wars and for those seized by Portuguese expeditions against tribes for which there was "certain and infallible fear" that they threatened crown interests. Settlers dubiously argued that prisoners captured in intertribal wars – who were called *escravos decorda* or "slaves of the cord" – were destined for execution (and were to be eaten), if not "ransomed" by settlers. Enslavement, the argument went, was better than death. Whatever the case, the Portuguese willingness to "ransom" captives encouraged tribal warfare, as powerful groups aligned with Portuguese interests assumed an offensive posture so that they could gain trade goods. As for their own raids, when Portuguese bothered to justify them, they used questionable evidence to brand tribes "threatening" and wars "just."[44] Those unfortunate to be captured in Portuguese expeditions were often branded with a hot iron on the chest to indicate who owned them.[45]

Raids were not without their risks, however. Indians knew the terrain and sometimes claimed the lives of better-armed Portuguese soldiers, as well as of priests who tried to move them to the coast. Such was the case with Father Antonio Pereira who was "killed by the savages of Cabo do Norte" in 1687.[46] Such incidents, of course, only confirmed in the minds of Portuguese the justness of their actions against Indians.

Some Portuguese incursions for Indian slaves were conducted illegally. For example, in 1703 Portugal's king complained of "many people" enslaving Indians in the interior "against my orders."[47] Similar illegal raids followed, some of which caught the attention of officials. In 1724, Portugal's king was again disturbed to learn of more "assaults and the capture of people living in the interior," which were "against the law." Further, the king had learned, that when settlers employed Indians, they

---

[44] AHU, Pará, cx. 10, doc. 935. For proclamations about *escravos decorda* and discussions of "just wars," "Livro grosso do Maranhão," 1: 23, 138–9. Also, Angela Domingos, *Quando os índios eram vassalos: colonização e relações de poder no norte do Brasil na segunda metade do século XVIII* (Lisbon: Commissão Nacional Comemorações dos Descobrimentos, 2000), 27–8.

[45] Azevedo, *Estudos de Historia Paraense*, 39.

[46] BNP, coleção pombalina, no. 4, fl. 3. Others met a similar fate. See fl. 3–4.

[47] AHU, códice 268, fl. 194.

were often not paid.[48] In 1740, a report from Maranhão's governor to Lisbon again raised the ire of the king over the "unjust capture of Indians without prejudice by the whites of the state."[49]

Other Portuguese expeditions occurred with legal licenses granted by the crown.[50] For example, the governor of Maranhão, Bernardo Pereira de Berredo e Castro, wrote to King João V in 1721 about a request by planter Francisco de Potflis, who wanted to "ransom only one hundred Indian slave couples from the Tapuia [Indian] nation to work in his sugar mill ... in the captaincy of Pará." Like most planters, Potflis found that Indian slaves "died or fled making impossible the good use and cultivation of his vast cane fields and of the work required in his sugar mill." Nonetheless, Indians were his only labor option. The governor explained to the king that many thought African labor would be preferable, but "black slaves from Guinea do not come." He asked the king to grant a contract for the purchase of "two hundred slaves from the pagans of the land [Indians] ... who customarily sell them to ransoming parties."[51]

Indians also served the state as troops commanded by Portuguese officers. Recruits were sometimes taken in raids in the interior but more often were obtained from mission villages. Missionaries protested when "their" Indians were ill-treated. Thus in 1702, a father complained that Captain Netto of the Troop of Cabo do Norte "treated very badly fifty Indians of the mission giving to all many beatings and subjecting them to hunger." Other Indians were conscripted into the military – as onto plantations – as punishment for a variety of crimes.[52]

Despite conflicts with settlers and officers over the proper employment of slaves, many Jesuits, too, used Indian laborers. In the early eighteenth century, each of the fathers of the Franciscan order had thirty Indian couples to perform household work.[53] Further, around mid-century, the

---

[48] AHU, Maranhão, códice 269, fl. 250.
[49] AHU, Maranhão, códice 270, fl. 332.
[50] Examples abound. AHU, Maranhão, códice 268, fl. 208 for João de Forres Berera "ransoming" slaves in 1705. For the 1720s, AHU, Maranhão, códice 269, fl. 260–6.
[51] AHU, Pará, cx. 7, doc. 593. In 1722, Manoel da Mota, in Belém, reported "most of the slaves" in his service died from smallpox. AHU, Maranhão, códice, 269, fl. 202. In 1727, a report of smallpox noted sugar mill owners left "destitute." A plea was included for a contract to "ransom" Indian slaves. AHU Pará, cx. 10, doc. 941. In 1705, a planter complained of a shortage of labor and requested "80 ransomed slaves." AHU, Maranhão, códice 268, fl. 210. Colonists who made a living by hunting and fishing or who needed canoehands often preferred Indian to black slaves for their particular skills in the natural environment. Dauril Alden, "Indian Versus Black Slavery in the State of Maranhão during the Seventeenth and Eighteenth Centuries," *Bibliotheca Americana* 1, 3 (1983), 103.
[52] AHU, Maranhão, codíce 268, fl. 179, 181 and 184.
[53] AHU, Pará, códice 270, fl. 101–2.

governor of Maranhão described Jesuit orders holding 12,000 Indians at 63 missions and working enormous ranches, some having upward of 100,000 cattle.[54] A 1760 inventory showed 15,600 cattle and 500 horses in the village of Maracú. The Society of Jesus also controlled plantations upon which they employed Indian slave labor. Some slaves they purchased, and some they were willed. At São Bonifácio, a sugar plantation near Maracú, eight stills were in operation alongside workshops for plank making, weaving, blacksmithing, carpentry, and canoe making. The plantation, too, had large fields of sugarcane, orange trees, manioc, and cacao.[55]

Although they employed Indian slaves, most Jesuits seem not to have subjected them to the brutality that was characteristic of slave plantations employing Africans elsewhere in Brazil. Moreover, although they objected to the harsh treatment of Indian slaves by settlers, they did not express the same level of concern over the Africans employed in Maranhão and Pará. The reasons for this are complex. Settlers and missionaries alike accepted that Brazil's economic prosperity depended on slave labor. In addition, they believed that the trade in slaves from Africa was justified because it ultimately led to slaves' souls being saved. If the price was human suffering, it was a price worth paying. Finally, they thought Africans could better withstand the demands of labor and disease. Many historians argue that Vieira was among the elites shaping Amazonia's labor policy and encouraging the use of African slaves in place of Indians in Maranhão. As early as 1653, he urged the king to "order to this State some ships of slaves from Angola." And Vieira was responsible for legislation in 1680 that mandated that "every year five or six hundred Negroes shall be offered for sale in the State of Maranhão at moderate prices to take the place of Indian slaves."[56]

AFRICAN SLAVE IMPORTS BEFORE 1750

Despite crown, Church, and settler desires, nowhere near "five or six hundred" Africans would be imported annually into Amazonia until the second half of the eighteenth century. There are three reasons for this.

---

[54] Hemming, "Indians," 542; Teodoro Braga, *História do Pará, resumo didactico* (São Paulo: Comp. Melhoramentos de S. Paulo, 1931), 99.

[55] Serafim Leite, *História da Companhia de Jesus no Brasil* (Rio de Janeiro: Instituto Nacional do Livro, 1943), 3: 189–90.

[56] Kiemen, "Indian Policy," 167–8. Also, Vicente Salles, *O negro no Pará sob o regime da escravidão* (Rio de Janeiro: Fundação Getúlio Vargas, 1971), 5; Alden, "Some Reflections," 13–14.

First, the region's economy stagnated until the mid-eighteenth century, meaning that Amazonian planters had little capital with which to purchase African slaves. Yet, in other regions of Brazil – Pernambuco and Bahia, for example – demand for slaves was high *and* sugar planters were comparatively prosperous. For shippers, then, Amazonia was not attractive. Second, Amazonia was farther from Africa's most important slaving ports – those of West Central Africa – than any other region of Brazil. Because longer voyages brought with them greater costs and higher risks of slave mortality, it was economically rational for shippers to stop at ports to the south rather than to travel the additional days to the northern ports of São Luís and Belém.[57] Finally, although the sailing times from Africa's Upper Guinea coast were relatively short, the Portuguese proved unable to flex much economic or political muscle at its forts at Bissau and Cacheu between about 1650 and 1750 and were, therefore, unable to orchestrate the export of large numbers of slaves.[58]

Nonetheless, some Africans trickled into Amazonia. The first Africans to reach the region were brought in small numbers by the English in the late sixteenth and early seventeenth centuries to establish trading posts near the Macapá River.[59] Further, a handful of English settlers grew tobacco in the Amazon during the period, including Johnston and Harcourt, the latter having "many negroes of Angola." North of Pará, English, French, Irish, and Dutch settlers produced considerable amounts of tobacco using Angolan slaves seized from Portuguese ships. A Portuguese expedition noted the production of more than 800,000 pounds of tobacco by Angolan slaves in 1625 and 1626. Troops seized some of those Angolans, returning with them to Brazilian territories.[60]

Hoping to develop Amazonia, the Portuguese crown encouraged monopoly companies to ship slaves from Cacheu beginning in 1664, when the Company of the Coast of Guinea (*Companhia da Costa da Guiné*) was established. Extant documents tell us little about the company's activities.[61] Then in 1676, Portugal attempted anew to develop

[57] Joseph C. Miller, *Way of Death: Merchant Capitalism and the Angolan Slave Trade, 1730–1830* (Madison: University of Wisconsin, 1988), 502–4.
[58] Walter Hawthorne, *Planting Rice and Harvesting Slaves: Transformations along the Guinea-Bissau Coast, 1400–1900* (Portsmouth, NH: Heinemann, 2003), 69–75.
[59] Flávio dos Santos Gomes, "A 'Safe Haven': Runaway Slaves, Mocambos, and Borders in Colonial Amazonia, Brazil," *Hispanic American Historical Review* 82, 3 (2002), 469.
[60] Linda M. Heywood and John K. Thornton, *Central Africans, Atlantic Creoles, and the Foundation of the Americas, 1585–1660* (New York: Cambridge University Press, 2007), 28–9.
[61] Cândido da Silva Teixeira, "Companhia de Cacheu, Rios e Comércio da Guiné," *Boletim do Arquivo Histórico Colonial* 1 (1950); António Carreira, *Cabo Verde, formação e*

the slave trade from Cacheu and into Amazonia by granting a monopoly to the (first) Cacheu Company (*Companhia de Cacheu, Rios e Comércio da Guiné*). It was founded under the direction of the powerful merchant Barros Bezerra, who lived on Santiago of the Cape Verde Islands, and by Manuel Preto Baldez.[62]

Bezerra and Baldez would also become involved in another monopoly company, the Maranhão Company (*Companhia do Estanco do Maranhão*), which replaced the Cacheu Company in 1682. This company was to develop Maranhão by bringing "goods from Lisbon of any quality and blacks from the whole of the coast of Africa."[63] Those slaves were to number 10,000 over a period of 20 years. It was this monopoly, in addition to Jesuit control of Indian laborers, that prompted Beckman's revolt in 1684.[64] That same year, residents of Cacheu, the Upper Guinea coast port from whence company owners hoped the slaves bound for Maranhão would come, also protested the establishment of the Maranhão Company, telling the crown's *capitão-mor* that they could not accept the granting of a twenty-year monopoly. After the protests, the company existed for some time in name only.[65]

Despite efforts to organize monopoly companies, few slaves arrived on Portuguese ships in Maranhão in the seventeenth century (Table 1.1). It may have been the Company of the Coast of Guinea that sent a ship with "some blacks" to Maranhão around 1665. A report describes them arriving with a disease that spread quickly among Indian populations. In 1673, fifty Africans arrived in Maranhão from Angola to work in the production of indigo and an unknown number arrived on a second ship, likely from Upper Guinea.[66] Also in 1673, reports say that 900 Africans from Angola arrived on a Dutch ship at the plantation of João Dias in Maranhão. Although the Dutch and Portuguese were at odds, the ship's

---

extinção de uma sociedade escravocrata (1460–1878) (Lisbon: Instituto Caboverdiano do Livro, 1983), 22.

[62] AHU, Cabo Verde, papéis avulsos, cx. 7, doc. 27.

[63] Bernardo Pereira de Berredo, *Annaes Historicos do Estado do Maranhão* (Lisbon: Officina de Francisco Luiz Ameno, 1749), 583–4.

[64] António Carreira, *As companhias pombalinas de Grão-Pará e Maranhão e Pernambuco e Paraíba* (Lisbon: Editorial Presença, 1982), 23; Marques, *Dicionário*, 265.

[65] Ilídio Baleno, "Reconversão do comércio externo em tempo de crise e o impacto da Companhia do Grão-Pará e Maranhão," in *Historia geral de Cabo Verde*, ed. Maria Emília Madeira Santos (Lisbon: Centro de Estudos de História e Cartografia Antiga, Instituto de Investigação Científica Tropical, 2002), III: 211.

[66] Braga, *História*, 86; Salles, *O negro*, 17; João Felippe Betendorf, *Chronica da missão dos padres da Companha de Jesus no estado do Maranhão* (Rio de Janeiro: Imprensa Nacional, 1910), 291. The indigo project did not amount to much. On second ship, AHU, códice 270, fl. 358.

TABLE 1.1. Slave Imports into Maranhão and Pará before 1750

Source	Year	Known # of slaves contracted for shipment to Amazonia	Known # sent	Known # of slaves arrived in Maranhão	Known # of slaves arrived in Pará	Shipped from	Organizer
1	to 1620			unknown	unknown	Guiné, Cacheu	The British
10	c. 1665			"some"			
1	1673			50		Angola	
1	1673			900		Angola	Dutch ship
11	1676–84			250		Cacheu	Bezerra and Baldez
3, 4	1680				350	Cacheu	Joseph Ardezicus
8	1684			200		Cacheu	
2, 3, 4	1692			145		Cacheu	Gaspar de Andrade
2, 4, 9	1693		159	145		Cacheu	Gaspar de Andrade
9	1695		116	102		Cacheu	
9	1696		179	158		Cape Verde	Companhia de Guiné
4	1698			218		Mina coast?	Antonio Francisco de Ucanha
9	1701		120	115		Cacheu	
2, 4, 5, 6	1702	200		110		Mina coast	Antonio Francisco de Ucanha
9	1703		200	170		Mina (Benin)	
2, 4, 5, 9	1708	200	102	87		Mina (Benin)	João Monteiro de Azevedo
9	1714		406	356		Mina (Calabar)	
9	1715		100	85		Mina (Benin)	
4	1718	150					Manoel de Almeida e Silva

4	1721	150					Diogo Moreno Franco
5	1740			109		Cacheu?	
9, 12	1740		77	69		Cacheu	
7, 9	1741		130	7		Cacheu	
9	1743		101	92		Cacheu	
Total				3368+	350		

Sources:

Braga, *História*, 86–7; Salles, *O Negro*, 17;

ABAPP, 1: 104; ABN, "Livro Grosso do Maranhão," 1: 135–6, 225–8; 2: 38;

Carreira, *Companhías*, 26;

Lopes, *Escravatura*, 136;

Gross, "Labor," 218–9;

AHU, Maranhão, códice 268, fl. 177;

AHU, ACL CU 013, cx. 24, doc. 2263;

Berredo, *Annaes*, 608–9;

TSTD2 (accessed 20 May 2009);

AHU, códice 268, fl. 2. Domingos Santos, Master of the Navio Nossa Senhora do Rozario de Almas;

Extant documents do not show any slave exports by Bezerra and Baldez from Cacheu to Amazonia;

AHU, códice 270, fl. 358.

captain was afraid that his captives would die if he did not discharge them in Maranhão. Therefore he offered them for a low barter price accepting "sugar and tobacco, good trees [for lumber], hides and everything else including nets, cotton, thread, monkeys and birds."[67] Records show the arrival of about 250 slaves in Maranhão and 350 in Pará in 1680, probably shipped by the (first) Cacheu Company.[68] Under the Maranhão Company, 200 slaves arrived in Maranhão in 1684.[69]

A second Cacheu Company was chartered in 1690 under the name *Companhia de Cacheu e Cabo Verde*.[70] The company, which was in existence until 1706, sought to supply slaves to Spanish possessions. However, Portugal's king recommended that it introduce 145 slaves per year to Pará and Maranhão, and he set aside funds to purchase slaves for the company for sale in the underdeveloped captaincies. The subsidy was not enough to encourage directors to steer ships to Amazonia, as few slaves would arrive under the auspices of any entity before the mid-eighteenth century. In 1692, the company sent 145 slaves to Maranhão and in 1693 another 145.[71] Reports went out from Maranhão predicting that these slaves would increase the productivity of the region, but some complained that the Company of Cacheu's prices were too high. More slaves were needed, a report said, for the production of sugarcane, tobacco, and indigo.[72] The king of Portugal was pleased at hearing of the "great utility that the State received with the supply of Blacks," and he wanted to see more arrive.[73]

Data on the distribution of African slaves among Maranhão settlers in the seventeenth century is scarce. However, a document from 1693 indicates that Africans from a single slave vessel were sold to many purchasers, few able to buy large numbers. Of 145 Upper Guineans who arrived in Maranhão on the ship, 101 were sold to farmers – small holders and some who owned sugar-processing facilities. They purchased between one and nine slaves each, paying 160,000 réis per slave. (This price was high compared to much of the rest of Brazil. In Bahia, for example, sugar slaves sold for about 60,000 réis in the 1690s.) Thirty-eight more slaves

---

[67] Betendorf, *Chronica*, 292; Salles, *O negro*, 17–18.
[68] Salles, *O negro*, 18; Carreira, *Companhias*, 26.
[69] Bernardo Pereira de Berredo, *Annaes Historicos do Estado do Maranhão* (Lisbon: Officina de Francisco Luiz Ameno, 1749), 608–9.
[70] Ibid., 212.
[71] *Annais da Bibliotheca e Archivo Público do Pará* (São Paulo: Ed. Brasiliense, 1959), I: 104–106; "Livro grosso do Maranhão," I: 135–6.
[72] AHU, Maranhão, cx. 8, doc. 869.
[73] "Livro grosso do Maranhão," I: 149.

were sold in São Luís to people not involved in farming. Most urban purchasers bought only one slave, although one man bought three and four men each purchased two. Prices ranged from 100,000 to 200,000 réis with the average price paid slightly higher than that paid by farmers. All told, 139 slaves from a shipment of 145 were sold. Apparently, the remaining six died in transit or before sale.[74] No rural planter or urban dweller, then, was able to increase significantly his African slave holdings when a single slave ship arrived. And because so few ships reached Maranhão, whites had very small holdings of African slaves. Most, therefore, relied as they long had on Indian labor.

After 1693, it would be years before more Africans arrived in Maranhão. In 1695, crown officials in the captaincy complained to the king of no recent arrivals and begged him to send more "black slaves" to meet a labor shortage. In another letter of the same year, officials wrote of "sicknesses" that had killed many Indian slaves, saying that more "blacks from Guinea" would help meet planters' needs.[75] Later that year, 102 slaves reached the region from Cacheu and another 158 arrived from Cape Verde in 1696.[76] But these slaves were not enough to quench Maranhão's thirst for African labor. In 1696, planters in Maranhão wrote to the king of the need for more "slaves from Guinea" and asked for a "lowering of the price for it being excessive for each slave." A similar plea for black slaves was made in 1697, with 218 slaves reaching Maranhão in 1698.[77]

It would be three years before another slave shipment reached Amazonia. In 1701, 115 slaves arrived in São Luís from Cacheu. They were followed in 1702 by another 110 from Africa's Mina coast. Thirty of the Mina slaves were sold to settlers in the Villa Nova de Santo Maria on the Icatú, who had petitioned the king for preference in slave sales. The remaining slaves were offered at a price of 160,000 réis each to sugar mill owners on Maranhão Island. This was much more than Maranhense sugarcane planters and mill owners could afford and more than most crown officials earned in Maranhão in an entire year. Hence, complaints went out about the "excessive" sums required to acquire *negros*. Although they needed laborers, no mill owners appeared to buy the Mina slaves. Eventually, they were offered to all of the residents of São Luís at public

---

[74] AHU, Maranhão, cx. 8, doc. 869. On prices in Bahia, Stuart B. Schwartz, *Sugar Plantations in the Formation of Brazilian Society, Bahia, 1550–1835* (New York: Cambridge University Press, 1985), 190.

[75] AHU, Maranhão, cx. 8, doc. 869.

[76] TSTD2, http://www.metascholar.org/TASTD-Voyages/index.html.

[77] "Livro grosso do Maranhão," 1: 167.

auction. All of this prompted residents of the captaincy of Pará to complain to the king that they had received no slaves from the shipment. Because of this, the king ordered that in the future, African slave imports should be divided between the two captaincies.[78]

Despite the crown's instructions, a shipment of 170 slaves from Benin on the Mina coast went to Maranhão in 1703. Sources indicate that no more African slaves arrived for years to come. A colonist in Pará wrote the king in 1705 to complain of a shortage of Africans and to request first claim to eighty Indians who had been "ransomed" in the interior. The "shortage of Indians for work in fields" was a chronic problem in the early eighteenth century. Settlers frequently complained that "there has died the better part of those [Indian slaves]," and colonists proposed more raids and additional African imports.[79] However, extant records indicate that it was not until 1708 that another slave ship reached Maranhão, this one with eighty-seven slaves. Crown officials sold these to planters, mill owners, and others for 160,000 réis each, not sending any up the coast to Pará.[80] Records show an arrival from Calabar on the Mina coast of 356 slaves in Maranhão in 1714 and another 85 from Benin in 1715. Slaving contracts were issued in 1718 and 1721, but there is no indication that any slaves arrived in Maranhão or Pará in these years.[81]

In fact, sources show that only four other slave shipments reached Amazonia before mid-century.[82] In 1740, 109 Africans arrived from a place unknown, and then 69 arrived in a different shipment from Cacheu. The governor knew of no precedent dictating how import duties should be charged, meaning this must have been a very unusual occurrence.[83] Finally in May 1741, the *Madre de Deus, Santo Antonio e Almas* arrived in Maranhão after a disastrous journey from Cacheu during which only 7 of its 130 slave cargo survived.[84] Two years later, 92 slaves arrived from Cacheu.

All told, in the century before 1750, it is doubtful that more than about 3,500 Africans entered the vast and forested regions of Maranhão and Pará. In 1752, merchants João Fernandes de Oliveira and António Ferreira, who asked the king for a license to take slaves from Guinea

---

[78] Ibid., 2: 53–4; AHU, códice 268, fl. 177–80, 185.
[79] AHU, códice 268, fl. 184–5.
[80] Gross, "Labor," 219; Lopes *Escravatura*, 136.
[81] AHU, códice 268, fl. 251.
[82] In 1725, planter Vitoriano Pinheiro requested "slaves from Guine" to work his fields and mill, but nothing indicates his request was met. AHU, Maranhão, códice 270, fl. 27.
[83] Gross, "Labor," 218–19.
[84] AHU, Pará, cx. 24, doc. 2263.

to Maranhão in their two ships, summed up the state of Maranhense labor. "There is," they wrote, "a great scarcity of slave traffic to provide labor for sugar factories and plantations." Many African slaves who had arrived earlier, they said, had died. There were no other merchants who wanted to supply the region.[85]

MARANHÃO AFTER 1750

After the mid-eighteenth century, labor shortages in the northern reaches of Brazil started to abate as Sebastião José de Carvalho e Melo, who is best known as the Marquis de Pombal, put great effort into bolstering Portugal's economy. Part of his plan involved developing Amazonia. From 1750 to 1777, Pombal was the Portuguese interior minister under King José I. Particularly influential, he was considered the de facto head of government, his status being elevated greatly as the result of his decisive leadership in the aftermath of a devastating earthquake that struck Lisbon in 1755.

To lead efforts in Amazonia, Pombal nominated in 1750 his brother, Francisco Xavier de Mendonça Furtado, to be the governor of what was then known as Grão-Pará and Maranhão. What Furtado found was a region in dire straits. Shortly after his arrival, complaints and recommendations from settlers began filling his desk. In December 1753, for example, white planters and merchants in Maranhão begged Furtado to arrange for the importation of African slaves for a "land that was in great poverty." Lacking money to purchase many laborers, settlers proposed state subsidies, tax breaks, and extended finance plans to enable them to get the black hands they desperately sought.[86]

Furtado passed locals' concerns onto his brother. "These states, and principally this Captaincy [Pará and Maranhão]," he wrote, "have been reduced to extreme misery." "All of the inhabitants," he continued, "are in a state of consternation." And he stressed, "There are few who yet cultivate any foodstuffs."[87] Furtado's words echoed those of the previous governor, João de Abreu de Castelo Branco, who complained in 1744 of "great poverty for a lack of slaves." With few African imports at the time, Branco's solution was to organize his troops for slave raids on area Indian populations.[88]

[85] AHU, Maranhão, cx. 33, doc. 3330.
[86] BNP, Collecção Pombalina, PBA 627, fl. 27.
[87] Viveiros, *História*, 68.
[88] AHU, Pará, cx. 27, doc. 2541.

However, Furtado objected to what he saw as settler and Jesuit abuses of Indians, so he called for state intervention to end slave expeditions and redefine the status of Indians. His objections may have arisen from humanitarian concerns. He did report gross injustices to his brother. But Furtado's attempts to end abuses were also aimed at undercutting the power of Jesuits who wielded greater authority and controlled more resources in Amazonia than did the crown. Hence, he proposed measures to deny Jesuits unfettered use of Indian laborers by releasing Indian villages from Church administrative control. This would, he thought, destroy the order's political and economic might and bolster the state's. At his brother's urging, Pombal convinced the king to issue the Law of Liberty in 1755, freeing Indians from Church administration and settler enslavement. Indian villages were to be given Portuguese names, and Indians were to rule over them. Trade with Indians was opened to anyone, and Indians, according to the law, were free to work for whomever they wished with pay rates fixed by governors.[89] If the Law of Liberty undermined Jesuit power, what little was left was obliterated in 1759 when King José expelled all Jesuits from Portugal and their possessions. José's actions followed an assassination attempt in which some Jesuits were said to have been complicit.[90]

Whatever benefits Indians gained from the 1755 proclamation of their liberty, they did not reap them for long; for in 1757, Furtado began to have second thoughts. He told his brother that Indians were reverting to "laziness," focusing their energies on subsistence rather than wage labor. Hence, Furtado issued a new law that placed a white "director" over each native village. In theory, these directors were to be altruistic protectors of Indian interests, teachers of "civilized" ways, and organizers of projects that would produce exports, the wealth from which would enrich Indians themselves. In practice, white directors abused their charges. Indian males between thirteen and sixty years of age were required to labor in public works and to dedicate half of each year to work for settlers. One observer warned that settlers would continue to raid "wild" Indians "without the slightest impediment and [would rule] Indians of the villages, using them all as if they were their slaves, without paying them for their labor."[91]

---

[89] Marcos Carneiro de Mendonça, *A Amazônia na era pombalina, correspondência inédita do governador e capitão-general do estado do Grão Pará e Maranhão Francisco Xavier de Mendonça Furtado, 1751–1759* (Rio de Janeiro: Instituto Histórico e Geográfico Brasileiro, 1963), 493.

[90] Kenneth Maxwell, *Pombal, Paradox of the Enlightenment* (Cambridge: Cambridge University Press, 1995), 82–3.

[91] Hemming, "Indians," 544.

But although some settlers continued to subject Indians to forced labor, they universally disparaged Indian workers, arguing that they were ill-equipped for fieldwork. This impression was summed up by one observer who wrote in 1755, "One Black Slave is much more useful than seven or eight Indians."[92] In 1760, Company of Grão Pará and Maranhão (CGPM) officials noted that after over a hundred years of Indian labor in Pará, "the principal object of the introduction of [African] slaves is the establishment of agriculture."[93] Later, a plantation owner wrote, "The service of Indians is much inferior to that of the African slaves as has been demonstrated from experience." Settlers, the writer continued, "were served by Indians, in the time when they were slaves, but it was only with the introduction of African slavery that agriculture has prospered so much."[94] Francisco de Souza Continho, a governor of Pará, stated a clear preference for "black and *mestiço*" (or mixed race) slaves, who, he said, were "more robust and capable" than Indians.[95]

Settlers criticized Indian labor for several reasons. First, in the mid-eighteenth century Indians continued to succumb to diseases introduced by Europeans and Africans.[96] In 1750, Captain General Francisco Pedro de Mendonça Gorjão described the "deplorable" conditions in Maranhão and Pará resulting from an elevated number of Indian deaths from contagious diseases. To fill a labor void, he requested the importation of black slaves from "Angola, Guinea, the Coast of Mina and the Islands of Cacheu" because of their "robust physiques." Reports from 1748 and 1749 listed the deaths of people in particular districts, one of which lost a total of 3,061 people to disease, most likely smallpox. Of the dead, only 35 were white settlers and an astonishing 3,026 were Indians. One slave owner lost 79 Indians, another 60, one lost 200, and another 82. In one mid-century report, 265 slaveholders reported 3,348 Indian slave deaths.[97] A different report described difficulties in Pará from "a lack of Indians since they are frequently the victims of contagions."[98] And a 1750 expedition on the Negro River in Pará described Indian villages "diminished because of a contagion."[99] Another document from the same year lists more than 18,000 Indian deaths in Church- and state-administered towns

---

[92] AHU, Pará, cx. 38, doc. 3561.
[93] ANTT, AHMF, CGPM, copiadores, cartas para Pará, livro 97, fl. 8.
[94] AHU, Pará, cx. 71, doc. 6033.
[95] ANRJ, diversos códices SDH, códice 807, vol. 11, fl. 9–44.
[96] AHU, Pará, cx. 38, doc. 3561.
[97] AHU, Pará, cx. 31, doc. 2976.
[98] AHU, Pará, cx. 32, doc. 2988.
[99] AHU, Pará, cx. 32, doc. 2993.

and on plantations.[100] Although African slaves also died from outbreaks of smallpox, their deaths were proportionately much lower than those of Indians and no greater than those of Europeans. Further, Africans died in no greater numbers than Indians from tropical diseases, such as malaria. In the eyes of planters, Africans were much hardier and, therefore, were much more reliable workers.

A second complaint was that Indians made poor slaves because they knew the terrain and could flee more easily than Africans, who were foreigners in a strange, new land. To be sure, the destruction wrought by wars and disease left many Indians with no relatives with whom to seek solace. Nonetheless flight was an option that Indians had been pursuing since the early days of Portuguese colonization. In 1637, Jesuit Luis Figueira wrote that because of the oppression of white landowners in Maranhão and Grão Pará, Indians "flee into the forests and depopulate their villages. Others die of despair in this labor without remedy."[101] A 1684 report about Pará noted that "when slaves are ransomed from neighboring [Indian] friends, there is no guard against their fleeing … because it is not difficult to flee to their friends who are those to whom they flee." As for slaves "taken with violence in war," they too "knew where to flee."[102] In 1702, reports noted "some Villages of [Indian] Slaves … who have fled their masters" on the Turiassu River.[103] A 1741 account also described "Indians who had been slaves" forming *mocambos*, or villages of runaways, in the interior. And in 1750, King João V responded to new notices from Grão Pará and Maranhão about Indian slaves who had escaped from their masters to form *mocambos*.[104]

Finally, Indians often rejected settled agricultural work, as it was anathema to their way of living and something for which those born outside settler- and Jesuit-controlled areas had no knowledge. Traditionally, Tupis and Tapuia subsisted, for the most part, by hunting, fishing, and gathering in Amazonia's rich forests. They were never iron producers, knew nothing about the intensive cultivation of the land, and had no skills appropriate for plantation work. Further, as John Hemming writes, "The ideas of working for someone else, either for reward or from coercion, and the production of a surplus beyond the immediate needs of a

[100] AHU, Pará, cx. 32, doc. 3001.
[101] Hemming, "Indians," 530.
[102] BNP, códice 585, fl. 326.
[103] "Livro grosso do Maranhão," 212–13.
[104] AHU, Pará, cx. 31, doc. 2977. For a 1752 account, AHU, Pará, cx. 33, doc. 3151.

man's family, were utterly repugnant to them."[105] Hence, in Maranhão in 1787, an administrator noted that Indians, even those who were "civilized," "detest" fieldwork, preferring to "leave their homes to be vagrants in the jungles." He continued, "All of the labor [in agriculture] they hate, and what they like is guiding canoes along the rivers."[106] On the other hand, all of the Africans who were shipped to Maranhão and Pará came from settled agricultural societies that had long used iron tools to produce surpluses in tropical environments. Amazonia's African slave population knew very well how to grow crops.

With prohibitions on Indian enslavement in place in 1755, it was to Africa that Portuguese policy makers and settlers looked as a likely source for productive labor. Hence, from Pará, Bishop Miguel de Bulhões e Sousa wrote to Secretary of State Sebastião José de Carvalho e Melo in 1755, "With respect to the tillage of this land, it is certain that there is nothing more efficacious for its increase and improvement than the introduction of Blacks into this Country."[107] And, indeed, it was a labor-hungry land. In August 1760, when the slave vessel *São Sabastião* arrived in Pará, its cargo of 208 slaves was sold in less than two hours to landowners.[108]

Who were those landowners? At his brother's urging, Pombal encouraged the expansion of the Portuguese population in Amazonia through immigration and childbearing. His plan for the 1750s was to send settlers to Maranhão and Pará on new, more comfortable ships. As an inducement, each settler was to receive a small subsidy to help with costs upon arrival.[109] In 1751, a contract was agreed upon to ship 1,000 families from the Azores to Maranhão and Pará. Although thorough studies of white immigration into Maranhão have yet to be done, some evidence exists that 430 Azoreans reached Amazonia (probably destined for the Amazon River) in 1752, and 100 more (50 couples) went to Belém in 1766. In the 1750s, unknown numbers of Azoreans also settled in Macapá, on the Amazon River and in locations along the Xingu, an Amazon tributary. During this period, many new towns rose up in the interior of Pará and Maranhão with settlers growing a range of crops for export.[110]

---

[105] Hemming, "Indians," 512.
[106] ANTT, Ministério do Reino, mç. 601, cx. 704.
[107] AHU, Pará, cx. 38, doc. 3561.
[108] AHU, Pará, cx. 72, doc. 6110; ANTT, CGPM, Livro das carregações, 45A, no. 101; ANTT, CGPM, Diário, livro 2, no. 774.
[109] Viveiros, *História*, 80.
[110] Pereira, *Cultura do arroz*, 68.

A sample of wills recorded in Maranhão between 1768 and 1799 reveals much about the origins of the white population. Most men (65 percent) who recorded wills hailed from mainland Portugal or the Azores Islands, with 4 percent originating from Spain and France. The remainder (31 percent) had been born in Brazil, almost exclusively in Maranhão. After Pombal's initiatives, then, the white male portion of Maranhão's population increased steadily, primarily as the result of immigration. The same cannot be said of the "white" female portion of the population. Of women, 90 percent of those who recorded wills between 1768 and 1799 had been born in Maranhão.[111]

Given that there were few white colonists in Maranhão before 1750 and that most white immigrants to the region after 1750 were male, we might ask how it is possible that Maranhão had a concentration of locally born white women in the second half of the eighteenth century. The answer is that they were "white" by convention, being the product of immigrant male relationships with Indian females. Such relationships had long been the norm in Maranhão but had always been viewed as illegitimate by the state and Church. However, in 1755 Pombal legitimized them to encourage population growth. In April of that year, the governor of Pará and Maranhão was informed that there was now "no infamy whatsoever" in unions between Portuguese and Indians. White settlers were free, then, to marry Indian women.[112] In 1787, Maranhão's governor, José Teles da Silva, noted the effect of this declaration on the region's population. *Brancos*, or whites, he said, "almost always have a mixture with other blood."[113]

AFRICAN IMMIGRATION AFTER 1750

Historians have put forward various estimates for the numbers of slaves imported from Africa into Maranhão and Pará during the period of the CGPM's monopoly (1757–1778).[114] The expansive Voyages: The

---

[111] Antônia da Silva Mota, "Família e fortuna o Maranhão setecentista," in *História do Maranhão: novos estudos*, ed. Wagner Cabral da Costa (São Luís: EDUFMA, 2004), 67.

[112] AHU, Pará, cx. 38, doc. 3568; "Ley sobre os casamentos com as Indias, 4 de Abril de 1755," in *Collecção das Leys, Decretos, e Alvaras* (Lisbon: Officina de Antonio Galhardo, 1791).

[113] ANTT, Ministério do Reino, mç. 601, cx. 704.

[114] Colin M. MacLachlan, "African Slave Trade and Economic Development in Amazonia, 1700–1800," in *Slavery and Race Relations in Latin America*, ed. Robert Brent Toplin (Westport, CT: Greenwood Press, 1974), 137–9; J. Mendes da Cunha Saraiva,

Trans-Atlantic Slave Trade Database (TSTD2) provides the most thorough list of ships and cargos arriving in Amazonia. During this period, the database lists 26,731 slave imports into Maranhão and Pará.[115]

After the CGPM's monopoly ended, slave imports increased substantially. The crown managed to jump-start Amazonia's economy by providing cheap African labor through the CGPM. By 1778, plantations were producing significant quantities of cotton and rice, and planters were able to afford large purchases of African slaves, so shippers increasingly visited the region. All told, from mid-century to 1787 (which is when the CGPM was dissolved, having operated since 1778 in a competitive market), an estimated 41,602 slaves entered Amazonia from Africa. Slaves also arrived in Amazonia from other parts of Brazil. From mid-century to 1787, I estimate slave imports into Amazonia from other parts of Brazil to be 3,293 (1,489 went into Pará and 1,804 into Maranhão). Of total slave imports into Amazonia from 1751 to 1787, 22,481 went to Pará and 22,414 went to Maranhão.[116]

So from where did these slaves hail? Who comprised the population of captives that entered Amazonia from mid-century to 1787? Records of slave ship voyages kept by the CGPM and Portuguese authorities reveal that from mid-century to 1787 most (29,565, or 66 percent) black immigrants into Amazonia were from the Upper Guinea region of Africa. Of the slaves imported into Pará from 1751 to 1787, 58 percent (13,133 people) came through the Upper Guinea ports of Cacheu and Bissau or from the neighboring Cape Verde Islands; 35 percent were shipped from other parts of Africa, primarily West Central Africa; and 7 percent from other parts of Brazil. Maranhão showed an even higher proportion of imports from Upper Guinea for the period; 73 percent (16,432 people) of Maranhão's slave imports came through Bissau and Cacheu, most of the rest coming from West Central Africa (19 percent) and other parts of Brazil (8 percent) (Table 1.2).

As the century wore on, average annual slave imports into Amazonia increased. From 1788 to 1800, 23,771 slaves entered the region (6,404 going to Pará and 17,043 to Maranhão) from Africa. Another 8,142 slaves entered Amazonia from other parts of Brazil (1,998 going to Pará and 6,144 to Maranhão). During this period, shipments into Pará showed a substantial reorientation, with only 13 percent of known slave shipments

Companhias gerais de comércio e navegação para o Brasil (Lisbon: Sociedade Nacional de Typografia, 1938), 84.
[115] TSTD2.
[116] Ibid.

TABLE 1.2. *Slave Imports into Amazonia, 1751–1842*

	Mina		Upper Guinea and Cape Verde		West Central Africa and São Thome		Mozambique		Other parts of Brazil		TOTAL
	Estimated #	%	Estimated #	%	Estimated #	%	Estimated #	%	Estimated #	%	Estimated #
PARÁ											
1751–1787			13,133	0.58	7,859	0.35			1,489	0.07	22,481
1788–1800	328	0.04	1,097	0.13	4,979	0.59			1,998	0.24	8,402
1801–1815	424	0.05	2,282	0.26	5,953	0.69			11	0.00	8,670
1816–1841			658	0.15	3,652	0.85				0.00	4,310
Total	752	0.02	17,170	0.39	22,443	0.51			3,498	0.08	43,863
MARANHÃO											
1751–1787			16,432	0.73	4,178	0.19			1,804	0.08	22,414
1788–1800	368	0.02	13,597	0.59	2,707	0.12	371	0.02	6,144	0.26	23,187
1801–1815	599	0.02	21,770	0.66	6,571	0.20	531	0.02	3,664	0.11	33,135

						Total
1816–1842	831	4,874	14,388	668		20,761
	0.04	0.23	0.69	0.03		
Total	1,798	56,673	27,844	1,570	11,612	99,497
	0.02	0.57	0.28	0.02	0.12	
TOTAL	2,550	73,843	50,287	1,570	15,110	143,360
	0.02	0.52	0.35	0.01	0.11	

Sources: TSTD2 (accessed 20 May 2009); ANTT, Ministério do Reino, mç 598, cx. 701; ANTT, CGPM, Memorial, Livro 63; ANTT, CGPM, Livro de demonstrações, livro 77; ANTT, CGPM, Diário, livros 1–3, 7, 9–15; ANTT, CGPM, Copiadores, cartas para Pará, Livro 97; ANTT, CGPM, Livro das carregações, 45A, 46B, 47C, 48D, 49E, 50F, 51G, 52; ANTT, CGPM, Livro dos navios, 65; ANTT, CGPM, Copiadores, Cartas para Pará, Livro 97–8; ANTT, CGPM Borrão do diario, livro 236; ANTT, CGPM, Cartas para o Maranhão, livro 230; ANTT, CGPM Cartas aos Administradores do Maranhão, livro 215; ANTT, CGPM, Copiadores, Maranhão, Administradores, livro 220; ANTT, CGPM, Livro mestre, 27; ANTT, CGPM, Pará – Copiador dos administradores, livro 216; ANTT, Junta do Comércio, mç 62, cx. 202; ANTT, Ministeriio dos negócios estrangeiros, Arquivos dos Legações, cx. 175; ANTT, Negocios estrangeiros, Commissão Mista, cx. 224, 228; AHU, ACL CU 013, cx. 72–80, 82–4, 86, 88, 117, 131; AHU, ACL CU 009, cx. 47–8, 53, 55, 58, 61, 64, 67–8, 70, 73, 75, 77, 79, 81, 84, 86, 89, 93, 97, 107; AHRJ, Vice-Reinado, cx. 371, 747; ANRJ, Junta do Comércio, 7X, cx. 371, 448–9; ANRJ, Série interior, Ministério do Reino. Maranhão. código AA. notação, IJJ9–42, 129, 130, 552; APEM, Secretaria do Governo, Inventários dos avulsos, no. 203.

coming from Upper Guinea. Most slave imports into Pará during this period were from elsewhere in Brazil (24 percent) and the broader West Central Africa region (59 percent). However, slave imports into Maranhão continued to be dominated by Upper Guineans, who were 59 percent of all imports. Only 12 percent were from West Central Africa and 26 percent were from elsewhere in Brazil.

From 1801 to 1815, slave imports into Pará declined, but they increased into Maranhão. An estimated 8,670 slaves entered Pará and 33,135 entered Maranhão. Of Pará's imports, only 26 percent were from Upper Guinea. However, of all slave imports into Maranhão during the period, 66 percent were from Upper Guinea. It was not until after 1815 that West Central Africans would enter Maranhão in proportionately large numbers. In 1815, the Portuguese abolished the slave trade north of the equator. The slave trade from West Central Africa into Amazonia continued unabated, being legal until 1830. But after 1815, the slave trade from Upper Guinea became illegal with ships arriving from Bissau and Cacheu at São Luís and Belém only sporadically. Some ships' captains successfully avoided antislave squadrons, which were established to end the trade. Others used loopholes in antislave trading laws to bring large numbers of "personal" and "crew" slaves across the ocean legally.

If shipping records demonstrate that Maranhão had a large Upper Guinean population well into the eighteenth century, other sources provide different sorts of information about the people who colonized the region. One of those sources is census data. In 1787, Portuguese Governor José Teles da Silva reported findings from a tally of Maranhão's population. His census indicates that the population of government-controlled regions of Maranhão and Piauí (a subcaptaincy controlled by Maranhão and populated by settlers and slaves that entered through São Luís) was 98,743 (Table 1.3). Of the total, 9,804 were Indians and 30,238 were whites. Blacks numbered 57,556 (58 percent of the total population).[117] The Maranhão survey illustrates the dramatic shift in labor patterns that occurred over the course of a forty-year period. In the early 1750s, there

---

[117] ANTT, Ministério do Reino, mç. 601, cx. 704. In the early nineteenth century, there were 66,668 free people and 200,000 slaves in Maranhão. Slaves were 67 percent of the population, meaning Maranhão had the greatest proportion of slave to free in Brazil. Affonso de E. Tauney, "Subsídios para a história do tráfico africano no Brasil," in *Anais do Museu Paulista* X (1941), 256; Antonio Bernardino Pereira do Lago, *Estatistica historica-geografica da provincia do Maranhão* (Lisbon: Academia Real das Sciencias, 1822), 23–40.

TABLE 1.3. *Population of Maranhão and Pará, 1777–1820*

Source	Date	Total pop.	White	Brown	Black	Free	Slave	Indian
Maranhão								
A	1777	[47,803][1]						
B	1778	47,410	[15,366]	[11,757]	[20,291]			
C	1787	61,699	[18,894]		[35,963]			[6,125]
D	1798	78,860						
A	1821	152,893[2]						
Maranhão with Piauí								
A	1777	76,504						
C	1787	98,743	30,238		57,556			9,804
D	1798	130,581						
Pará								
B	1773	55,315				24,779	11,413	19,123
E	1788	80,000						
F	1801	80,000[3]						
G	c. 1820	123,901				90,910	33,000	

Notes:

[1] Brackets indicate estimate. In the late eighteenth century, Piauí was a subcaptaincy of Maranhão, which would later become independent. Estimates in this section do not include Piauí.

[2] Tauney figures a much higher population of 200,000 in c. 1820. Of the total, he says 66 percent were slave. Affonso de E. Tauney, "Subsídios para a história do tráfico africano no Brasil," in *Anais do Museu Paulista X* (1941), 256.

[3] Includes Rio Negro.

Sources:

ANRJ, Diversos códices, códice 798, NP; Lago, *Estatística*, 23;
Alden, "Population";
ANTT, Ministério do Reino, mç 601, cx 704;
Alden, "Demography";
Sweet, "Rich Realm," 111;
MacLachlan, "African," 136;
Tauney, "Subsídios," 256.

were few black slaves in Maranhão. Indians performed the lion's share of labor in fields and in towns. By 1787, Indians constituted less than 10 percent of the population in colonial-controlled areas – blacks having become a clear majority of the population and the linchpin of the colonial labor force.

But the survey also raises a question about that new labor force. If the black population of Maranhão was small at mid-century and if 22,414 Africans (most from Upper Guinea) were imported into Maranhão from mid-century to 1787, why were there 57,556 blacks in the region in 1787? From where did the additional 35,142 blacks come? First, some were the descendants of Africans who had arrived in Maranhão before 1750. Second, because the census did not distinguish categories beyond white, black, and Indian, some may have been *cafuzos, mamelucos,* and *mulatos* (products of white-black sexual encounters) who did not fit neatly into the categories that Teles da Silva chose for this census.[118] Third, after the 1755 decree banning Indian enslavement, an untold number of Indians "became" *negros* in official records. That is, some whites conveniently said that their Indians weren't Indians but were *negros*, allowing them to keep them as slaves.[119] Fourth, it is possible that some black slaves entered Maranhão and were not counted in official import records. Some may have come along river routes from parts of Brazil, remaining uncounted because they did not go through São Luís.[120] Others may have entered from the ocean, brought illegally by ships from Africa or other parts of Brazil.[121]

Finally, and most importantly, the black population in Maranhão in 1787 had grown beyond the number of slaves imported into the region because black women in Maranhão were bearing children. This point is made very clearly by the Maranhão Inventories Slave Database (MISD). It shows that between 1767 and 1800, some 33.8 percent of slaves in Maranhão were *crioulos* – Brazilian-born blacks, the overwhelming majority of whom had to have been the product of relationships between

---

[118] ANTT, Ministério do Reino, mç. 601, cx. 704. In a 1778 estimate of Maranhão's population, "brown" people numbered about 12,000, "black" about 20,000 and "white" about 15,000. There was no designation of Indians. We can assume that there were substantial numbers of "mixed race" people in Maranhão in 1787, as in 1778.

[119] "17 Agosto 1758, Directorio que se deve observar para o governo dos Indios do Maranhão," in *Collecçaõ das leys, decretos, e alvaras, 1750 a 1760* (Lisbon: Miguel Rodrigues, M. DCC, LX), 1: no page numbers.

[120] Projecto Vida de Negro, *Frechal terra do preto* (São Luís: 1996), 35.

[121] Silva suggested in the 1780s that some slaves entered through Piauí's port, though that number was not significant. ANTT, Ministério do Reino, mç. 601, cx. 704.

Upper Guinea–born slaves.[122] It is important to note that the MISD figures are only for slaves. There was, at the time, a substantial population of free *crioulos* as well.

Black family life will be explored in Chapter 5. For now, suffice it to say that the growth of the black population through reproduction in Maranhão is impressive because only 38 percent of slaves loaded in Africa on ships bound for Maranhão between the mid-eighteenth century and 1787 were female.[123] The number is also notable because few other places in Brazil demonstrated a positive black population growth rate at the time. Maranhão was unusual, then, in that it had a high concentration of slaves from Upper Guinea, and its Upper Guinean slaves reproduced their population at a much faster rate than slaves in most other parts of Brazil.[124]

If shipping records and population surveys tell us much about the African population of Amazonia after the mid-eighteenth century, two other sources reveal much about the ethnic makeup of that population. One source is a registry from the slave ship *São José*, which departed Cacheu in 1756. Of hundreds of eighteenth-century ship registries from Upper Guinea departures that I have examined, this is the only one to list the ethnic origins of captives held onboard in the eighteenth century. A total of ninety-seven slaves (including infants and children) were forced onto the vessel. Fifty-seven percent had been taken from the immediate coastal region not far from the ports of Bissau and Cacheu and occupied by politically decentralized groups such as Balanta, Bijago, Papel, Floup, Banyun, and Brame among others. The remaining 43 percent of the captives were from the interior, and most of them were from a large, politically centralized group known as Mandinka.[125]

Another source is the MISD. Data from it confirms other statistics from shipping records, showing that the overwhelming majority of Maranhão's African-born population came from Upper Guinea. In addition, the

---

[122] Walter Hawthorne, Maranhão Inventories Slave Database (MISD).

[123] Calculated with TSTD2.

[124] Although it was not the norm in the colonial period, slaves reproduced their populations in some parts of Brazil. Schwartz, *Sugar Plantations*, 351–2; Clotilde A. Paiva and Douglas Cole Libby, "The Middle Path: Slavery and Natural Increase in Nineteenth-Century Minas Gerais," *Latin American Population History Bulletin* 23 (1993), 13; Linda Wimmer, "Ethnicity and Family Formation among Slaves on Tobacco Farms in the Bahian Recôncavo, 1698–1820," in José C. Curto and Paul E. Lovejoy, *Enslaving Connections: Changing Cultures of Africa and Brazil during the Era of Slavery* (Amherst, NY: Humanity Books, 2004), 149–62.

[125] BNP, Collecção Pombalina, códice 628, fl.179–82.

TABLE I.4. *Known Regions of Origin of Slaves in Maranhão Plantation Inventories, 1767–1800*

Region	#	%
West Central Africa	49	17.3
Africa unknown	4	1.4
Brazil	96	33.8
Mina coast, Africa	8	2.8
U. Guinea, unknown	2	0.7
U. Guinea coast	90	31.7
U. Guinea interior	35	12.3
Total	284	100

Source: Hawthorne, MISD.

TABLE I.5. *Known Regions of Origin of Slaves in Maranhão Plantation Inventories, 1801–1830*

Region	#	%
Angola-Congo	1353	17.9
Africa unknown	116	1.5
Brazil	3009	39.7
Cape Verde	8	0.1
Mina coast, Africa	564	7.4
Mozambique	152	2
Portugal	3	0
São Tomé	9	0.1
U. Guinea, unknown	49	0.6
U. Guinea coast	1406	18.6
U. Guinea interior	904	11.9
Total	7573	100

Source: Hawthorne, MISD.

MISD reveals from where in Upper Guinea captives came. For the period 1767 to 1800, it shows that almost two-thirds of Upper Guinea slaves in Maranhão had been born very close to the coast (and were from the Balanta, Bijago, Papel, Floup, Banyun, and Brame groups). The other third hailed from the interior and were principally Mandinka. For the next period, 1801–1830, coastal populations continued to comprise the bulk of slaves taken from Upper Guinea and shipped to Maranhão (Tables 1.4 and 1.5).

To put this data into perspective, I should make clear that the Upper Guinea coastal zone groups (Balanta, Bijago, Brame, Papel, etc.) – from which a large proportion of Maranhão's slave population was derived from the mid-eighteenth through the early nineteenth centuries – occupied an area that was situated very near the ports of Bissau and Cacheu. This was only about 3,000 square kilometers (1,160 square miles) in size, which is an area smaller than the state of Rhode Island in the United States. Mandinka occupied a larger zone, which stretched hundreds of miles into the interior, but as will be shown in Chapter 2, most Mandinka who found themselves in Maranhão were from a relatively small area only tens of miles from the ports of Bissau and Cacheu. They had regular contacts with coastal people, and their merchants regularly visited coastal villages and the ports of Bissau and Cacheu.

CONCLUSION

In sum, from 1751 to 1842, about 143,360 slaves were imported into Amazonia. To 1815 most of those slaves came from Upper Guinea. After 1815, most came from West Central Africa. Nonetheless, from 1750 to 1842, more of the Africans arriving in Amazonia hailed from Upper Guinea than any other place. Maranhão received the majority of slave imports into Amazonia. Throughout most of the period, Upper Guineans made up the largest single segment of Maranhão's slave population. Almost all Upper Guineans came through two ports – Bissau and Cacheu – and were from a small slice of territory not far from the coast.

Returning to Almeida's 1767 slave holdings from the beginning of this chapter, it is clear that they were typical for the region at the time. He owned two Mandinka men from the Upper Guinea interior, and two slaves – a Biafada and Papel – from the immediate coastal zone near the ports of Cacheu and Bissau. The rest of his African-born slaves were female and not identified by ethnicity but by region – *Guiné*. Given the profile of slaves entering Maranhão, it is likely that these *Guiné* slaves had been born in very close proximity to the Biafada and Papel.[126]

The makeup of Almeida's slave holdings was similar to planters' holdings in Maranhão for about five decades to come. Take, for example, Izabel Ribeiro and her husband Luís José da Costa. In 1794, the couple owned five slaves from the Upper Guinea interior (Mandinkas and Fulas) and seven from the immediate coastal zone near Bissau and Cacheu

---

[126] TJEM, AJ, Inventory of Ventura de Almeida, 1767.

(three Papel, three Bijago, and one Floup). Their two *crioulo* slaves were children, ages eleven and one, who were most likely the products of relationships between Upper Guineans. Only one of their slaves was from elsewhere in Africa – Kongo, a kingdom in West Central Africa.[127] Similarly, in 1800, Anna Maria Roza de Carvalho and her husband, Antonio Henriques Leal, had on their plantation on the Itapecurú River sixty-five slaves who can be indentified by place of birth or ethnicity. Of those from the Upper Guinea coastal zone, five were Balanta, fourteen Bijago, one Papel, and six Nalu. An additional eight were labled Cacheu, likely meaning they had been born in or near the port. Of those from the Upper Guinea interior, there were thirteen Mandinka. In addition, they owned seventeen *crioulos* and one West Central African.[128]

Although West Central Africans would enter Maranhão at an increasing rate after 1815, overall the Upper Guinean population continued to be the largest segment of the African population for some time to come. In the second half of the eighteenth and early nineteenth centuries, Maranhão was, then, a place firmly linked to the Upper Guinea coast. Its colonial population was overwhelmingly Upper Guinean – and most of those Upper Guineans had been born very near Bissau and Cacheu.

Why black slaves became the heart of the labor force belonging to Ventura, the Ribeiros, and other landowners in Amazonia between 1750 and 1815 can be attributed to the facts that Indians died in large numbers from diseases introduced from the Atlantic, and white settlers perceived Indians to be poor workers compared to people of African descent. Also important were Pombal's efforts to develop Amazonia by granting a favorable contract to the CGPM. Why Upper Guineans were the largest single group of immigrants into Maranhão and Pará in the second half of the eighteenth century can be attributed to the nature of Atlantic winds and currents and to Portuguese mercantile policy. Why most of the slaves aboard slave ships from Cacheu and Bissau from 1750 through 1815 hailed from small-scale and politically decentralized societies that occupied the immediate coastal zone near those ports will be explored in the next chapter.

[127] TJEM, AJ, Inventory of Izabel Ribeiro, 1794.
[128] TJEM, AJ, Inventory of Anna Maria Roza de Carvalho, 1800.

2

Slave Production

To supply slaves to its underdeveloped captaincies of Maranhão and Pará, Portugal renewed its interests after 1750 in the Upper Guinea ports of Cacheu and Bissau. Sailing times from these two ports to Amazonia were relatively short. Moreover, Portugal desperately wanted to reassert itself on a stretch of African coastline that it had long claimed. Having dominated trade from Upper Guinea since the mid-fifteenth century, Portuguese merchants found themselves unable to compete with rivals from France and Britain toward the end of the seventeenth. Portuguese administrators and merchants constantly complained that "interlopers" were overrunning "our Guinea." When European conflicts, particularly the Seven Years' War (1756–1763), distracted France and Britain, Portugal saw an opening to reclaim "their" ports.[1]

Just after the mid-eighteenth century, Portugal decided that the cheapest way to control trade from Bissau and Cacheu was to grant a trade monopoly to a private entity – the Company of Grão Pará and Maranhão (CGPM). It would defend Portuguese interests by building forts and pacifying independent-minded coastal peoples and would supply slaves to Amazonia. The monopoly went into effect in 1755 and ended in 1778 with the company continuing to trade in a freer market through 1787. Although interlopers continued to take a portion of the trade that Portuguese merchants considered theirs, the Portuguese trade in slaves from Bissau and Cacheu increased dramatically after 1755, the volume

[1] George E. Brooks, *Eurafricans in Western Africa: Commerce, Social Status, Gender, and Religious Observance from the Sixteenth to the Eighteenth Century* (Athens: Ohio University Press, 2003), 250–61.

remaining at relatively consistent levels through abolition in 1815. Slave exports between 1751 and 1800 were 88 percent higher than from 1701 to 1750.[2] By the 1780s, settler-controlled regions of Maranhão, which only decades earlier had had few blacks, boasted a black majority. Of those blacks, most hailed from Upper Guinea. Although exports from Bissau and Cacheu were never enough to satisfy the insatiable desire of shippers and planters for an ever-increasing flow of slaves, the CGPM succeeded in ensuring a Portuguese presence on the Upper Guinea coast and in substantially increasing Portuguese trade there.

How can the success of the CGPM be explained? Boubacar Barry and Walter Rodney argue that a Fula jihad launched in the hinterland on the Futa Jallon plateau was the biggest producer of slaves carried by the CGPM.[3] The company, they write, established itself at an auspicious time – when a powerful Futa Jallon state was producing captives and when that state's elites were hungry for weapons and luxury goods. In agreement with much thinking about the slave trade in other parts of the continent, Barry and Rodney figure that it was states' leaders who directed large-scale wars that produced the bulk of slave exports. Elites alone, they argue, reaped profits from trading humans.[4] In Rodney's words,

European ... goods contributed nothing to the development of African production. Only [African] rulers benefited narrowly, by receiving the best cloth, drinking the most alcohol, and preserving the widest collection of durable items for prestige purposes. It is this factor of realized self-interest which goes some way towards explaining the otherwise incomprehensible actions of Africans toward Africans.[5]

Barry agrees, writing,

The slave trade and its corollary, warfare ..., were a permanent part of a situation of chronic violence imposed ... by the existence of a military aristocracy reigning above

[2] TSTD2, http://slavevoyages.org/tast/assessment/estimates.faces.

[3] Walter Rodney, *A History of the Upper Guinea Coast, 1545 to 1800* (New York: Monthly Review Press, 1970); Walter Rodney, "Slavery and Other Forms of Social Oppression on the Upper Guinea Coast in the Context of the Atlantic Slave Trade," *Journal of African History* 7, 3 (1966), 431–47; Boubacar Barry, *Senegambia and the Atlantic Slave Trade* (New York: Cambridge University Press, 1998).

[4] A great number of studies focus on state elites directing the slave trade. For an analysis, Martin A. Klein, "The Impact of the Atlantic Slave Trade on the Societies of Western Sudan," in *The Atlantic Slave Trade: Effects on Economies, Societies, and Peoples in Africa, the Americas, and Europe*, eds. Joseph E. Inikori and Stanley L. Engerman (Durham, NC: Duke University Press, 1992), 25–48.

[5] Rodney, *A History*, 251.

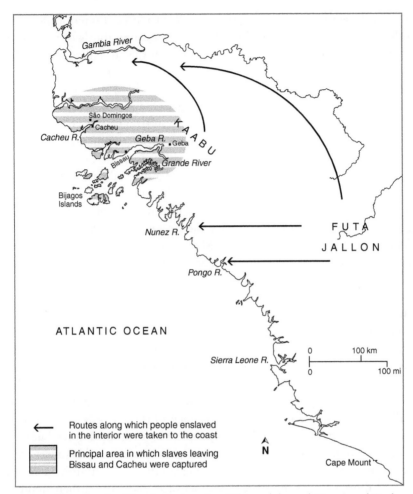

MAP 2.1. Homelands of People Enslaved and Shipped through Bissau and Cacheu, and Interior Slaving Routes to Other Coastal Ports, Eighteenth Century. Courtesy of Jackie Hawthorne.

peasant populations, potential victims of slave raids. Slave trading became a royal monopoly based on violence. As such, it prevented the peasant population working productively under secure conditions. The result was economic regression.[6]

In this chapter, I challenge the applicability of Rodney's and Barry's thinking to all of Senegambia and Upper Guinea. Archival data from Maranhão shows that most of the CGPM's slave exports after the second

---

[6] Barry, *Senegambia*, 107.

half of the eighteenth century were not the products of interior jihads or other wars waged by state elites. Rather, about two-thirds of the slaves shipped from Bissau and Cacheu hailed from the coastal zone. Coastal people were made captive mostly through raids and trials directed by common folk in small-scale, politically decentralized societies. Contrary to the thinking of Barry, the communities that comprised these societies were not "decimated" by any state with "a powerful war machine devoted exclusively to manhunts."[7] Rather, most coastal communities defended themselves, realizing losses of only a small percentage of their populations to enslavement and sale abroad. When combined into ships' cargoes in Bissau and Cacheu, people taken in small numbers from multiple and scattered communities were enough to fill the hulls of CGPM vessels. However, there is no evidence that the overall demographic impact of losses to the slave trade was great. Most coastal communities *controlled and managed* the trade in slaves – marketing people while keeping losses of core community members low.

Further, I argue that it was not "realized self-interest" – selfishness – that motivated most slave raids in the Upper Guinea coastal zone. Coastal communities did not eagerly participate in slave trading. Most took strides to ensure the material equality of their members and feared the pernicious influence of foreign wares, which tempted people to act greedily to realize more gains than their neighbors. Most considered those who profited at the expense of others to be what Balanta called *befera*, Floup called *kusaye*, and Baga called *waser*. Each of these words can be translated as "witches" or "cannibals" – people who consumed others' health, souls, or bodies and undermined community coherence. Kidnappers who seized kin or neighbors in the night and sold them fell into this category, as did European and Eurafrican (mixed race) slavers and their middleman agents.

However, coastal communities found themselves forced to engage with slave purchasers. It was the only way to avoid becoming their victims. It was, as well, the only way to ensure continuing agricultural productivity. In addition to some luxury items, the CGPM offered iron for slaves, and iron was vital for the crafting of weapons and agricultural implements. Communities that possessed iron-tipped spears, swords, hoes, and shovels could defend themselves and prosper. Those who didn't risked annihilation. The CGPM succeeded because coastal communities were compelled to trade with the company – to deal with

---

[7] Ibid. Also, Rodney, *A History*, 109.

witches – to obtain an item that they desperately needed. For that trade item, the CGPM and other Atlantic shippers demanded captives, so it was captives that coastal communities produced. Their challenge was finding ways to keep individuals in their midst from becoming like European and Eurafrican slavers – from becoming avaricious and self-serving witches.

GEOGRAPHY, CLIMATE, AND SOCIETIES

Geography and climate have certainly shaped Upper Guinea's history. The coastal strip, from which most of the slaves sent to Amazonia hailed, was characterized by dense vegetation, winding rivers and streams, and mangrove swamps. The interior region, from which a smaller number of slaves sent to Amazonia hailed, was characterized by woodlands, savannas, and cool, elevated uplands. Differences in geography and climate affected agricultural and trade patterns, social formations and political institutions, and the strategies people adopted for warfare and for defense against threatening enemies.

Geographically, Upper Guinea's coastal zone is "sunken," barely rising above sea level for tens of kilometers inland. This allows brackish water to flood up the region's many rivers at high tide. Where land elevations begin to rise, the sunken coast gives way to a low plateau that begins at about 180 meters (590 feet) above sea level. Here rapids separate inland fresh water from coastal salt water. Southeast of the Guinea-Bissau region, the plateau eventually juts upward to form a massif, which is known as Futa Jallon. Elevations generally range from 370 to 900 meters (1,200 to 3,000 feet) above sea level, shooting as high as 1,500 meters (4,900 feet) in places. High elevations coupled with rain from ocean weather systems make the Futa Jallon the source of many of West Africa's most important rivers.[8]

In the greater Guinea-Bissau region, coastal and interior rainfall patterns begin to deviate at about the point of the inland rapids. This was particularly true during a dry period in West African history, which stretched from 1630 to 1860 with aridity reaching its peak around the mid-eighteenth century. During the dry period, coastal rain forests shrank

[8] Walter Rodney, "Jihad and Social Revolution in Futa Djalon in the Eighteenth Century," *Journal of the Historical Society of Nigeria* 4 (1968), 269; George E. Brooks, *Landlords and Strangers: Ecology, Society, and Trade in Western Africa, 1000–1630* (Boulder, CO: Westview, 1993), 11–26.

and the desert, grasslands, and woodlands shifted south. Also during this time, Guinea-Bissau's coastal zone received less rain but still remained relatively well watered with an average 1,500 millimeters (60 inches) of precipitation annually – most coming between June and September, the height of the rainy season. However, annual average accumulations declined inland and to the north. From 1630 to 1860, the coastal zone from about the Casamance River southward was characterized by rain forests. North of the Casamance was a savanna-woodland region. Still farther north, starting at about the Gambia River, the savanna or "bright country" began. The savanna received less than 1,000 millimeters (40 inches) of rain each year. Inland, from the coastal strip, forests also thinned, becoming savanna-woodlands.[9]

The sunken coastline's edge has long been the approximate dividing line between peoples speaking languages from two broad language groups. Mande languages are spoken in the greater Guinea-Bissau region by Mandinka and related peoples such as the Dialonke, Soninke, and Susu, who have historically occupied territories beyond the sunken coastline's edge. West Atlantic languages are spoken by a range of peoples including Papel, Manjaco, Balanta, Biafada, Bijago, Floup, and Brame, who have historically resided within the coastal strip (Map 0.2).

Language is not the only thing that has differentiated West Atlantic peoples from Mande peoples. Indeed, both groups have long structured their societies in very different ways. Mande tended toward centralized states. West Atlantic peoples favored decentralized, small-scale political systems, many of which maintained an egalitarian ethic that stressed equal rights within groups divided by gender, and age, and the equal distribution of material resources. Political and cultural traditions partially explain this difference. But, too, the natural environment has influenced politics. The coastal zone's dense vegetation, swamps, and winding rivers provided natural defenses against attacks by large, state-based armies. Small groups of West Atlantic people could live there in relative safety, not finding it necessary to unite with many others to form large-scale military units capable of warding off massive attacks. However, in the interior Mande people found fewer natural defenses against threatening enemies, meaning that they often had to come together, subject themselves to the rule of elites who promised protection, and form hierarchies

---

[9] See Rodney, "Jihad and Social Revolution" and Brooks, *Landlords and Strangers*. Walter Hawthorne, *Planting Rice and Harvesting Slaves: Transformations along the Guinea-Bissau Coast, 1400–1900* (Portsmouth, NH: Heinemann, 2003), 41.

capable of directing armies that could fend off powerful outsiders. Elites could, of course, order their armies to attack other groups, to seize people, to take control of trade routes, and to claim resources.[10] At times, Mande elites did just this.

INTERIOR STATES, THEIR ELITES, AND SLAVE PRODUCTION

Long before the arrival of Europeans in sub-Saharan Africa, Mande benefited from their location in the fertile and gold-rich Niger River basin and profited from trade links to the north and south. Wealth facilitated a Mande expansion and the formation of a large empire called Mali. Toward the end of the fifteenth century, Mali's most distant provinces began to split away. Hence, Kaabu, which had previously been a military outpost, emerged as an independent state dominated by Mande-speaking Mandinka. Located to the interior of the greater Guinea-Bissau region, Kaabu straddled important trade routes that moved goods along the Gambia, Cacheu, Geba, and Corubal Rivers. Goods also flowed between northern states and the prosperous southern Futa Jallon plateau controlled by Dialonke, a Mande people. Kaabu was well positioned to exploit new commercial ties with Atlantic merchants in the centuries to come.[11]

The Mande expansion greatly affected large parts of Upper Guinea. George Brooks writes that the Mande language "diffused among conquered groups" and that Mande speakers instituted "tripartite hierarchical social structures comprised of ruling elites and free people, endogamous occupational groups, and domestic slaves." Ruled by a *mansa* chosen from one of three of its most important provinces, Kaabu was a confederation that eventually encompassed a vast territory. Supporting the *mansa* was the military aristocracy, or *nyaanco*. Below them came the provincial rulers, or *korin*, who ruled over castes of craftspeople, or *namaalo*. The *namaalo* made leather products and iron, and they kept oral histories. *Korin* also ruled over free peasant producers. Some in Kaabu subscribed to Islam, but the state was not theocratic. Prominent among the non-Mandinka in Kaabu were Fula. The Fula were non-Muslims in the seventeenth century

---

[10] Hawthorne, *Planting Rice.*

[11] Brooks, *Landlords,* 46. For similar analysis, Carlos Lopes, *Kaabunké, espaço, território e poder na Guiné-Bissau, Gâmbia e Casamance pré-coloniais* (Lisbon: Comissão Nacional para as Comemorações dos Descobrimentos Portugueses, 1999), 79; Barry, *Senegambia,* 8, 21–4, 40; Mamadou Mané, "Les origines et la formation du Kaabu," in *Éthiopiques, revue socialiste de culture négro-africaine* 28 (1981), 96.

and principally pastoralists across much of West Africa in savanna and derived savanna zones. In many places Fula lived, they were taxed by state-based agriculturalists, creating considerable social tension. Slaves occupied another range of social categories in Kaabu. Some slaves held positions of considerable importance, as they were attached to the royal court. Others labored in fields for free owners of a variety of social ranks. Still others were trade slaves who were bought and sold in markets, often for sale to merchants who moved them toward Atlantic ports.[12]

Through the sixteenth, seventeenth, and eighteenth centuries, Kaabu turned its formidable military toward the production of slaves, many of whom it sold to Atlantic merchants, bringing wealth and power to the center. The Frenchman La Courbe, who traveled toward Kaabu as far as Geba in 1687, left the best description of Kaabu's kings' escapades. He reported that the king of Kaabu, who was reputed to be "very powerful, very rich, and very generous," had shipped many slaves to Geba. "He is capable," La Courbe wrote, "of killing a man like a mosquito. He makes war on his neighbors for no cause." For six years, La Courbe reported, Kaabu's king besieged the town of Cantor before destroying it and enslaving its inhabitants. "He sends warriors into the lands of his neighbors to seize all the people they can capture and brands them for sale at the first opportunity."[13] In the early eighteenth century, a map by Jean Baptiste Bourguignon d'Anville contained a notation that the king of Kaabu, Biram Mansaté, died in 1705 and was a "rich and powerful ruler who had established good order in his state."[14]

Biram Mansaté, like other Mandinka kings of Kaabu, offered protection, it seems, to Mandinka followers and waged wars against non-Mandinka elsewhere. Thus, surveys of slave populations in parts of the New World that were supplied by Portuguese ships from the Upper Guinea coast indicate that Mandinka represented an insignificant portion of total slave exports before the mid-eighteenth century.[15] However,

---

[12] Brooks, *Landlords*, 46; David C. Conrad and Barbara E. Frank, eds., *Status and Identity in West Africa: Nyamakalaw of Mande* (Bloomington: Indiana University Press, 1995).

[13] Brooks, *Eurafricans*, 181–2.

[14] Biram Mansaté is written also as Mansa Biram. A. Teixeira da Mota, *Guiné Portuguesa* (Lisbon: Agência Geral do Ultramar, 1954), 156; Sékéné Mody Cissoko, "De l'organisation politique du Kabu," *Ethiopiques* 28 (1981), 195–206.

[15] Frederick Bowser, *The African Slave in Colonial Peru, 1524–1650* (Palo Alto, CA: Stanford University Press, 1974), 39–41; Jean-Pierre Tardieu, "Origins of the Slaves in the Lima Region in Peru (Sixteenth and Seventeenth Centuries)," in *From Chains to Bonds: The Slave Trade Revisited*, ed. Doudou Diène (Paris: UNESCO, 2001), 43–54; Gabriel Debien, "L'origine ethnique es esclaves antillais," *Bulletin de l'IFAN*, B, 27 (1965), 320–3; Jean Mettas, "La traite portugaise en haute Guinée," *Journal of African History* 16 (1975), 353.

in the second half of the eighteenth century, well after Biram Mansaté's death, Mandinka began to appear in greater proportions at Portuguese-, French-, and British-controlled ports, victims for the most part of a series of wars stretching from the mid-eighteenth through the nineteenth centuries.

The surge in Mandinka slave exports is illustrated in the Maranhão Inventories Slave Database (MISD). From the 1760s through the 1830s, it shows that 33.5 percent of all slaves exported through the greater Guinea-Bissau area and to Maranhão were Mandinka – a sizable increase over levels from the sixteenth, seventeenth, and early eighteenth centuries. From 1761 through 1815, this would have been about 415 Mandinka per year exported through Portuguese ports, or about 22,825 individuals.[16] Other Mandinka were exported through English- and French-controlled ports.

Some of those Mandinka were the products of kidnappings and judicial procedures, which are scantly documented for the regions beyond Upper Guinea's sunken coastline.[17] Whether or not abductions and judicial enslavements in the Upper Guinea interior became more common in the mid-eighteenth century is something about which we can only speculate. What is clear is that warfare increased in this period and was the major producer of Mandinka slaves shipped to coastal ports.

The warfare that produced Mandinka captives exported from Bissau and Cacheu and, more broadly, from the whole of Upper Guinea took three forms after the mid-eighteenth century. First, in about 1700, Muslim Fula pastoralists and farmers on the Futa Jallon plateau to the south of Kaabu began to stage a series of small-scale jihads against a Mandinka people known as Dialonke, who were their overlords. In the preceding decades, non-Muslim Fula populations in Upper Guinea had been augmented by the arrival of Muslim Fula from the north. Taxes and restrictions on religious practices raised the ire of Muslim Fula, sparking a series of rebellions. By 1725, these rebellions could be characterized as jihads taking the form of organized military efforts. What resulted was a nascent Fula theocratic state. The Muslim Fula triumph in Futa Jallon came about 1750 with military consolidation continuing until about 1780.[18] In Futa Jallon, Dialonke-Mandinka became, then, the target of Fula attacks.

---

[16] Calculated by combining figures from TSTD2 and MISD.

[17] P. E. H. Hair, "The Enslavement of Koelle's Informants," *The Journal of African History* 16, 2 (1965), 193–203; Philip D. Curtin, "Ayuba Suleiman Diallo of Bondu," in *Africa Remembered: Narratives by West Africans from the Era of the Slave Trade*, ed. Philip D. Curtin (Madison: University of Wisconsin Press, 1967), 17–59.

[18] See Hair, "The Enslavement of Koelle's Informants" and Curtin, "Ayuba Suleiman Diallo of Bondu." Also, David Robinson, *Holy War of Umar Tal: The Western Sudan*

Although religion was a motivator for the Fula jihads, it may not have been the principal motivator over time. Once they threw off the yoke of their Mandinka-Dialonke overlords, many Fula elites continued their jihad so that they could produce the captives needed to garner valuable imports from the coast. Particularly important were guns, which were of great use in the acquisition of wealth and power. European trader Thomas Watt visited Timbo in the Futa Jallon in 1794, later recounting that a Fula leader told him "that the sole object of their wars was to procure slaves, as they could not obtain European goods without slaves, and they could not get slaves without fighting for them."[19]

There can be little doubt that Fula-led wars in Futa Jallon produced sizable numbers of captives. However, there is no evidence that many of those captives were brought along land routes connected to Cacheu and Bissau. Small numbers may have been shipped through these Portuguese-controlled ports, but most moved along routes that connected to the south on the Pongo and Nunez Rivers, with others likely moving along routes that connected to the north on the Gambia River.[20] Bissau and Cacheu were farther from the Futa than ports on the Pongo and Nunez, so transportation costs were a consideration for Fula merchants. Further, the Portuguese paid less for slaves than the British and French, so long-distance merchants had few incentives to travel to the Geba and Cacheu Rivers instead of the Gambia, Pongo, and Nunez.[21] Most often, then, it was the French and British who purchased slaves shipped from the Futa and not the Portuguese (Map 2.1).

A second reason for the proportional increase in Mandinka slave exports from the whole of Upper Guinea after the mid-eighteenth century was stepped up attacks by Futa Jallon's Fula population on Kaabu itself. In other words, some Mandinka slaves were the victims of attacks launched by Fula away from the Futa Jallon plateau. Studies of the interior suggest that after about 1750, Fula were "wreaking havoc" in Kaabu, producing considerable numbers of captives.[22] Corroborating evidence can be

in the Mid-19th Century (Oxford: Clarendon Press, 1985), 49–59; John Ralph Willis, "Jihad Di-Sabil Allah: Its Doctrinal Basis in Islam and Some Aspects of Its Evolution in 19th Century West Africa." *Journal of African History* 8 (1967), 395–415; Amar Samb, "L'islam et le Ngabou," *Ethiopiques* 28 (1981), 116–23.

[19] Robinson, *Holy War of Umar Tal*, 49–59; Willis, "Jihad Di-Sabil Allah," 395–415; Samb, "L'islam et le Ngabou," 116–23; and Rodney, *A History*, 236.

[20] See TSTD2 for data on surges in exports from these locations after 1750.

[21] AHU, Guiné, cx. 9, doc. 71.

[22] Joye Bowman, "Conflict, Interaction, and Change in Guinea-Bissau: Fulbe Expansion and Its Impact, 1850–1900" (Ph.D. thesis, University of California, Los Angeles, 1980), 88–9; Lopes, *Kabunke*, 191; Barry, *Senegambia*, 98–9, 114; Brooks, *Eurafricans*, 203.

found in a late –nineteenth-century Portuguese study of the history of the Fula in the Kaabu region. It concluded that the Fula leader Ibrahima Sori, who consolidated power in Futa Jallon in the 1760s and 1770s, also sent armies that "marched in the direction of the high Gambia, submitting the people that he encountered [Mandinka of Kaabu] during his passage and receiving as vassals some Fula chiefs who maintained their independence."[23] Because of the proximity of Kaabu to routes connected to Cacheu and Bissau, some captives taken by Sori were likely transported to these Portuguese-controlled ports. Some Mandinka made captive by Sori may, too, have followed other routes.[24]

Finally, Mandinka made captive after the mid-eighteenth century were the products of infighting among Mandinka themselves. Some of that fighting occurred periodically within Kaabu among three royal lineages, and some occurred on Kaabu's borders.[25] Given the decentralized nature of some Mandinka-dominated regions outside Kaabu, this is not surprising. Describing the zone immediately beyond the Guinea-Bissau region's coastal strip, Paulo Joze Álvares noted in the 1790s people living in independent cities, each of which had a king and many of which were walled. Fula, he said, had their own populations that lived in settlements called *fulacundas* of about one thousand people, who were under a "despot" who was in turn subject to a "king of the district." "Black Muslims" lived in different populations called "*morocundas*, in which they follow[ed] the law of the Koran." Soninke-Mandinka, too, lived in their own populations, called *tienecundas*.[26] Disputes among rival *morocundas* and *tienecundas* easily turned violent, giving rise to wars that produced captives. It was these wars – many of which often took place only one hundred or so kilometers from Bissau and Cacheu – that produced the bulk of the Mandinka slaves shipped by the Portuguese after 1750.

War was common in times of economic instability. And the period after about the mid-eighteenth century was especially unsettling across

---

[23] Joaquim da Graça Correia e Lança, *Relatorio da provincia da Guiné Portugueza, referido ao anno economico de 1888–1889* (Lisbon: Imp. Nacional, 1890), 52–3.

[24] AHU, Guiné, cx. 10, doc 6-A. Also see, Emmanuel Bertrand-Bocandé, "Notes sur la Guinée-Portugaise ou Sénégambie Méridionale," *Bulletin de la Soc. Géographie* 12, 3a série (1849), 58. Despite Futa-based Fula attacks on Kaabu, there was no widespread Fula uprising within Kaabu until the nineteenth century, when rebellions caused the collapse of the ancient state.

[25] Barry, *Senegambia*, 92. On political fragmentation and infighting in the region, SéKéné Mody Cissoko, "Traits fondamentaux des sociétés du Soudan Occidental du XVIIIe siècle au début du XIXe siècle," *BIFAN* 21, Série B, no. 1 (1969), 23.

[26] AHU, Guiné, cx. 10, doc 6-A.

Senegambia and Upper Guinea, as a series of droughts and natural catastrophes set off struggles for resources in many places.[27] "Never before in this territory has there been such widespread famine," a British observer wrote in 1752. "It rages from Bissau all the way to Galam, and we are having a difficult time indeed finding food for nearly 600 captives."[28] Localized and regional droughts flared in the years that followed. In 1766, for example, the captain major at Bissau reported that a "great scarcity" of food for slaves had forced him to send a ship to the Pongo River to purchase rice.[29] In 1786, a British official said that on the southeast bank of the Gambia River people "were reduced to the horrible necessity of selling each other in order to buy what they needed to subsist." Mandinka "bought slaves for flour and European goods and sold them to white merchants on the coast, which is how a large number of these slaves came into my possession."[30] Of the period, Brooks writes, "The Mandinka-ruled state of Kaabu and Futa almamate in Futa Jallon engaged in almost continuous warfare to acquire captives for sale into the Atlantic slave trade. So did the rulers of numerous states."[31] For this, Muslim Fula often referred to Kaabu and its hinterlands as *darul-harb*, "the land of war."[32]

SLAVE PRODUCTION IN THE DECENTRALIZED COASTAL ZONE: RAIDING AND KIDNAPPING

If the production and trade of slaves in the interior of Upper Guinea was controlled by elites capable of launching large-scale attacks and organizing *jihads*, in the coastal zone things were very different. In the Upper Guinea coastal area, there were no armies composed of horse warriors or large-scale, sustained sieges that resulted in the destruction of towns and wholesale capture of their people – such as the siege that Kaabu sustained at Cantor.

---

[27] Barry, *Senegambia*, 109–13; James F. Searing, *West African Slavery and Atlantic Commerce: The Senegal River Valley, 1700–1860* (New York: Cambridge University Press, 1993), 132–44. For different dating of droughts, Philip Curtin, *Economic Change in Precolonial Africa: Senegambia in the Era of the Slave Trade* (Madison: University of Wisconsin Press, 1975), 110.

[28] Quoted in Barry, *Senegambia*, 110.

[29] AHU, Guiné, cx. 9, doc. 60.

[30] Searing, *West African Slavery*, 133.

[31] Brooks, *Eurafricans*, 203.

[32] Thierno Diallo, *Les institutions politiques du Fouta Dyalon au XIXe siècle* (Dakar: IFAN, 1972), 51.

On the coast, the scale of slaving operations was smaller than those of the interior, because the scale of coastal societies was correspondingly smaller. Compared to Kaabu and Futa Jallon, all coastal communities occupied little territory, and most were politically decentralized. In these societies, the village (or a confederation of villages) was the largest political unit. Although a range of positions of authority often existed within villages and confederations, in most places no one person or group claimed prerogatives over the legitimate use of coercive force. In face-to-face meetings involving many people, representatives from multiple households sat as councils working out decisions affecting the whole. At times, particularly influential people emerged, sometimes wielding more power than others and becoming "big men" or "chiefs." However, in most societies no ascriptive authority positions existed. In most places, consensus was king. Whereas state-based systems concentrated power narrowly in a single ruler or small group of power brokers, in decentralized systems power was more diffuse. Decentralized systems relied on *leaders*, but they lacked *rulers*. In the coastal reaches of the greater Guinea-Bissau region, most societies had gerontocratic forms of governance, which placed elders in leadership positions with youths attaining more power as they passed through age grades on their way to becoming adults. The promise of future power gave youths the incentive to submit to elders' demands.[33]

There were exceptions, however, with some coastal societies having more hierarchical systems than others. As a rule, societies that had, over time, the most contact with Atlantic merchants (principally Papel, Biafada, and Brame societies) possessed what the Portuguese referred to as "kings." Some of these "kings" appear to have wielded great power during certain periods. However, most often they could not act capriciously. They sought to respond to the demands of their followers to avoid being deposed. That is, power flowed from the bottom up rather than top down. Hence, when a Papel "king" took lavish gifts in exchange for agreeing to allow the CGPM to establish itself on Bissau, a council composed of the heads of various households objected. The king's unpopular decision, company officials later discovered, resulted in his death,

---

[33] Hawthorne, *Planting Rice*, 2, 120. On decentralized or "stateless" societies, see, also, Robert Martin Baum, *Shrines of the Slave Trade: Diola Religion and Society in Precolonial Senegambia* (New York: Oxford University Press, 1999); Martin A. Klein, "The Slave Trade and Decentralized Societies," *Journal of African History* 42, 1 (2001), 49–65.

creating a tense environment in the first years of the CGPM's efforts in Upper Guinea.[34]

If the scale of societies and their political configurations made the scale of slaving operations relatively small near the coast, so, too, did other factors. Situated in a densely forested, swampy, and mosquito- and tsetse fly–infested land, communities on Guinea-Bissau's coast were relatively shielded from attacks from the armies of interior states. Further, coastal populations took defensive measures to protect their people. They walled their villages by using tree trunks to create palisades or by planting trees and thorny bushes close together so as to create live fences.[35] They also traveled and worked in fields with weapons at their sides in case strangers should stage surprise attacks.[36]

But no matter how good their communities' defenses were, some coastal people in the Guinea-Bissau region fell victim to slavers. Most often, those slavers were from the coastal region itself. Through what processes were people enslaved on the coast? The answer to this question is threefold – raids, kidnappings, and trials that determined guilt for certain offenses, particularly witchcraft.

Archival sources are replete with references to coastal groups' raids.[37] Writing after his experiences in West Africa in the 1740s, '50s, and '60s, French merchant Antoine Edme Pruneau de Pommegorge said that in the Guinea-Bissau area there was a "very large number of different nations. The people are continually at war among themselves," especially Bijago, Papel, and Biafada.[38] In 1777, Portuguese Ignacio Bayao described Balanta attacks on the Geba River. It was "not possible," he wrote, "to navigate

[34] Hawthorne, *Planting Rice*, 104–5; Rodney, *A History*, 246–7.

[35] Hawthorne, *Planting Rice*, 121; Peter Mark, *A Cultural, Economic and Religious History of Basse Casamance since 1500* (Wiesbaden: F. Steiner, 1985), 54; Chris S. Duval, "A Maroon Legacy? Sketching African Contributions to Live Fencing Practices in Early Spanish America," *Singapore Journal of Tropical Geography* 30, 2 (2009), 232–47.

[36] Philip Beaver, *African Memoranda* (London: Dawsons of Pall Mall, 1968), 327. Also, Walter Hawthorne, "The Strategies of Small-Scale Societies: Defending Communities from Slave Raiders in Coastal Guinea-Bissau, 1450–1815," in *Fighting Back: African Strategies against the Slave Trade*, ed. Sylviane Diouf. (Athens: Ohio University, 2003), 160–4.

[37] André Donelha, *Descrição da Serra Leoa e dos rios de Guiné do Cabo Verde (1625)*, ed. Avelino Teixeira da Mota, trans. P. E. H. Hair (Lisbon: Junta de Investigações Científicas do Ultramar, 1977); André Álvares de Almada, *Tratado breve dos rios de Guiné*, trans. P. E. H. Hair (Liverpool: University of Liverpool, Department of History, 1984); AHU, Guiné, cx. 11, doc. 7, 30, 37, 43, 57; AHU, Guiné, cx. 12, doc. 3A; AHU, Guiné, cx. 14, doc. 31, 62; AHU, Cabo Verde, cx. 73, doc. 429.

[38] Antoine Edme Pruneau de Pommegorge, *Description de la nigritie* (Paris: Chez Maradan, 1789), 132–3.

FIGURE 2.1. "Bijouga War Canoe."
Source: From: George Thompson, *Palm Land, or West Africa, Illustrated* (Cincinnati: Moore, Wilstach, Keys & Co., Printers, 1859), 88.

boats on those parts without some fear of [being made] captive." Bayao also said that Balanta raids on Bissau resulted in the capture of people and seizing of cattle.[39] In the 1790s, British captain Philip Beaver described Bijago islanders, saying, "Unconnected by any ties with the neighbouring nations, whom they generally hold in contempt, they consider the world as their own; and that what it contains they have a right to plunder ...; they war with every body."[40] From observations he made about Bissau toward the end of the eighteenth century, Jean Baptiste Léonard Durand wrote, "The king contrives to preserve peace within his own states; but ... he is continually in hostilities with his neighbours: for when he wants slaves, he makes an irruption amongst the Biafares, the Bissagots, the Balantes, and the Nalons, who live contiguous to his territories."[41]

The oral narratives of a variety of coastal groups also discuss raids. Describing the period of Atlantic slavery, an elder told Robert Baum, "Some people did not want to work [in the rice paddies]. [They wanted to]

[39] AHU, Guiné, cx. 11, doc. 30. Balanta raids for people continued well after the abolition of the slave trade. In the late nineteenth century, Correia e Lança described Balanta attacks on Manjaco and Papel, which included the capturing of people. *Relatorio da Provincia da Guiné Portugeza, 1888–1889* (Lisbon: Imprensa Nacional, 1890).

[40] Beaver, *African Memoranda*, 336. Also, Gaspard Mollien, *Travels in the Interior of Africa to the Sources of the Senegal and Gambia Performed by the Command of the French Government in the Year 1818* (London: Frank Cass, 1967), 336.

[41] J. P. L. Durand, *A Voyage to Senegal* (London: Richard Philips, 1806), 63.

War only." Another elder described what was often done with many captives. They were sold to Afro-Portuguese merchants. "If you sold to these people, perhaps they would give you a musket, perhaps gunpowder."[42] Similarly, Balanta elder Nhafde Sambe told me, "In times past, Balanta were very cruel to other Balanta. Many went to the houses of the weakest Balanta and seized all of their goods and carried the people back to their own homes."[43] Reflecting on the period, another Balanta elder, Fona Benuma, said, "Balanta mistreated their fellow Balanta" because they "did not have a ruler who could reprimand anyone who abused others."[44]

I have argued for Balanta, and Baum has for Floup, that the capturing of people for sale to Atlantic merchants grew out of the practice of nabbing villagers during raids to ransom back to their communities for cattle and other valuables. Raiding distant villages was a quick way to garner wealth and the accepted way for young men to prove their bravery. The ransoming of captives was common in the eighteenth century, but when Europeans, Eurafricans, or middleman merchants from other African societies offered more cattle or more sought-after goods for captives, villagers often eagerly accepted them. Baum reports that the standard ransom for a female captive was six cows and for a male, seven.[45] Balanta informants told me that their standard was "five or six cows" per slave.[46] However, in a report from 1779, the sergeant major of Cacheu, António Vaz de Araújo, said that area merchants were paying fifteen to eighteen cows for a slave.[47] In this case, declining a ransom in favor of sale would have been tempting indeed.

That villagers in a politically decentralized zone sold captives for imported goods might be, for some, unsettling. Why? If we can, as scholars have, finger a class of "greedy" elites as being responsible for the interior wars that produced a flow of captives from the Futa Jallon, we cannot similarly blame elites as being responsible for the raids that produced captives on the coast.[48] In societies that lacked rulers, power was

---

[42] Baum, *Shrines*, 111–2.

[43] Interview with Nhafede Sambe and Abna Dafa, Blimat, January 28, 1995.

[44] Interview with Fona Benuma, Encheia, January 13, 1995.

[45] Baum, *Shrines*, 113–8; Hawthorne, *Planting Rice*, 135. The ransoming of captives continued through the era of Atlantic slavery. For example, Leopold Butscher, *Account of the Mandingoes, Susoos, & Other nations, c. 1815* (Leipzig: Institut fur Afrikanistick, Universitat Leipzig, 2000); Beaver, *African Memoranda*, 55.

[46] Interview with Cabi Na Tamnbá, Mato-Farroba, December 6, 1996.

[47] AHU, Guiné, cx 11, doc 63.

[48] On "greed" of elites, see Barry, *Senegambia*, 181; Rodney, *A History*, 115–6.

diffuse, wielded by people holding many offices and most often buttressed by community consensus. Hence, it was not typically a class of self-serving people who directed the production and trade of captives for foreign manufactures. Rather, it was the heads of multiple families, holders of several titles, and directors of many institutions within a community who called for raids on strangers' compounds.

Was, then, greed – the greed of many within communities – *the* force motivating raids in Guinea-Bissau's coastal zone? Coastal people did, after all, step up the production of slaves in response to European demand in the mid-eighteenth century (Table 2.1). The sale of captives became particularly attractive to coastal people as the prices that Europeans paid for human beings increased steadily in the eighteenth century. Prices rose because demand increased for slaves in the Americas, spurring competition among slave buyers. According to Philip Curtin, prices in Senegambia peaked in about 1780.[49] It is evident, too, that in the Guinea-Bissau region prices escalated through the century, which was something about which Portuguese merchants constantly complained.[50] Clearly wars in the interior produced some of the slaves traded in the eighteenth century. However, only about 34 percent of the Upper Guinean slaves in Maranhão were Mandinka after 1750; 5 percent were from other groups in the Upper Guinea interior. The other 61 percent were from coastal communities.[51]

Despite the fact that coastal communities marketed more slaves for higher prices after the mid-eighteenth century, greed was not *the* motivation behind their actions. Although cloth, guns, gunpowder, and alcohol flowed into Guinean ports, no trade item was more important on the coast than iron, and the word "greed" does not adequately explain why communities wanted it.[52] "Necessity" does. Lacking deposits of iron ore and those skilled to transform it into metal, coastal people in the Guinea-Bissau region have always turned to long-distance merchants. Before sustained contact with traders from the Atlantic, coastal people obtained some quantities of iron from Mandinka. However, the range

---

[49] Curtin, *Economic Change*, 328–34.
[50] ANTT, AHMF, CGPM, Copiadores, Cartas para Pará, livro 97, p. 125; ANTT, AHMF, CGPM, Registo de decretos, Livro 87, fl. 56–58; AHU, Guiné, cx. 12, doc. 24. For an early nineteenth-century complaint about prices: AHU, Guiné, cx. 18, doc. 43.
[51] MISD.
[52] Iron was usually the most valuable item on ships going to the area. ANTT, AHMF, CGPM, Livro das Carregações, 52 H. English interlopers at Cacheu were said to trade "arms and iron" for slaves in 1751. ANTT, Concelho da Fazenda, livro 349, fl. 240.

TABLE 2.1. Slave Exports from the Greater Guinea-Bissau Region, 1701–1843

	Bijagos	Bissau	Cacheu	Casamance	Portuguese Guinea	Cape Verde Islands	Total	Average by year
1701–1705			130				130	26
1711–1715			714			81	795	159
1716–1720		61	593			330	984	197
1721–1725		395	927			27	1,349	270
1726–1730		39					39	8
1731–1735			584			11	595	119
1736–1740		766	1,204			100	2,070	414
1741–1745		331	1,754			300	2,385	477
1746–1750		107	685			465	1,257	251
1751–1755		2,098	1,500			322	3,920	784
1756–1760		1,121	1,787			212	3,120	624
1761–1765		2,238	2,370				4,608	922
1766–1770		3,705	2,421	436		2	6,564	1,313
1771–1775		2,893	2,162	53		558	5,666	1,133
1776–1780		3,882	1,962			7	5,851	1,170
1781–1785		3,473	1,516				4,989	998
1786–1790		3,495	3,070		353	363	7,281	1,456
1791–1795	277	5,516	2,300				8,093	1,619
1796–1800		2,830	1,458		296		4,584	917
1801–1805		4,523	2,103		882	530	8,038	1,608
1806–1810		9,863	2,650			1,060	13,573	2,715
1811–1815		4,237	4,633		492	390	9,752	1,950
1816–1820	640	1,163	1,705	146		488	4,142	828
1821–1825	376	2,114	239	366		734	3,829	766
1826–1830		826	727			1,398	2,951	590
1831–1835		184	174			179	537	107
1836–1840		669				1,809	2,478	496
1841–1843		1,950				1,009	2,959	592
Totals	1,293	58,479	39,368	1,001	2,023	10,375	112,539	

Source: Estimates from TSTD2 (accessed 20 May 2009).

of goods that coastal people produced did not provide them with much purchasing power, so large quantities of expensive iron could not be obtained. The equation changed in the sixteenth century, when Atlantic merchants visited Upper Guinea ports with increasing frequency. Then, as in the seventeenth and eighteenth centuries, merchants brought a range of goods, iron bars prominent among them. For iron and other goods, these merchants most often demanded slaves.[53]

Iron had two principal uses on the coast. It was fashioned into the digging and cutting edges of agricultural instruments and was crafted into effective weapons for hunting and warfare. Long before the arrival of Europeans on Africa's shores, some coastal groups cultivated paddy rice, capturing and conserving rainwater within man-made dikes. These dikes were built in mangrove swamps along the edges of rivers that ran brackish when surges from the ocean came sweeping in as tides rose. Dikes, then, served two purposes – keeping brackish water (which killed rice plants) off fields and keeping fresh rainwater on them. Within diked areas, mangroves, which were isolated from the river, died, later being cut. Fresh rainwater (and rainwater runoff) was captured within the dikes. Once soils were desalinated (by allowing fresh water to sit for some time on the fields enclosed by dikes and then draining off the water), the area was ideal for rice production. Rice could be planted in the diked area in the early rainy season, water captured as rains came, and this water drained off at the end of the rainy season to facilitate the cutting of mature rice stalks.

In the eighteenth century when iron was introduced in large quantities by Atlantic merchants, groups practicing mangrove-rice agriculture expanded their efforts to capture rainwater and runoff. Further, new groups that were not committed to mangrove farming carved paddies of their own along rivers' edges. In previous centuries, many of these groups had practiced "upland" agriculture, growing crops like millet, yams, and "dryland" rice – the latter being produced in areas that did not have standing fresh water. However, as slave raids intensified, mangrove – or "lowland" – agriculture became increasingly attractive. Lowlands were also advantageous places to establish communities, because dense vegetation along rivers' edges provided places for populations to hide and barriers

---

[53] On demand for iron, AHU, Guiné, cx. 8, doc. 48. Merchants also traded for hides, ivory, beeswax, and other items, but the volume of trade of these goods was very small in comparison to slaves. António Carreira, *Os portugueses nos rios de Guiné (1500–1900)* (Lisbon: Privately published, 1984), 27–8.

against attack. Further, communities could gain access to rivers, permitting increased access to the trade that moved along them.[54]

The problem that coastal people faced was that rich, mangrove swamps could not be efficiently cleared and diked without iron-edged tools. Iron was absolutely necessary for *intensive* mangrove-rice production, and it was useful for the expansion of other types of agriculture as well.[55] In 1729, William Charles, who worked for the Royal African Company in Sierra Leone, noted just this. Having returned to an area after a long absence, he was struck that locals complained of a falloff in trade. "The natives of the country," he wrote, "have most need for Iron, to make Axes, Hoes & other tools for cutting down the Woods & Cleaning the Grounds to make Lugares [fields] for rice."[56]

If iron obtained from Atlantic merchants was the catalyst for necessary agricultural transformations, it also sparked a revolution in intergroup relationships. Through a process that I have described elsewhere as the "iron–slave cycle," many coastal communities were compelled to produce slaves to obtain the iron to forge weapons. That is, as some threatening coastal communities obtained increasing quantities of iron that could be crafted into weapons, all coastal communities sought iron so as to avoid being victimized. It was, then, the *need* to obtain iron to forge weapons and agricultural implements that compelled Africans in the coastal reaches of the greater Guinea-Bissau area to produce and market captives. Raids were not often launched out of greed but out of need.[57]

---

[54] Hawthorne, *Planting Rice*, 156.

[55] Edda Fields-Black is skeptical that iron was necessary for swamp rice. In my thinking, though iron may not have been necessary for cultivating the *cabeça* ("head" or top part) of *bolanhas* (mangrove areas), it was necessary for intensive mangrove cultivation beyond a *bolanha*'s *cabeça*. In the top part of *bolanhas*, mangroves are not thick. However, this area is limited. To carry out mangrove cultivation on the scale that is evident in parts of eighteenth-century coastal Upper Guinea, iron was necessary for cutting mangroves. Simply put, people could not intensively cultivate vast swamp rice fields without iron. Marina Padrão Temudo concurs with my analysis. Edda L. Fields-Black, *Deep Roots: Rice Farmers in West Africa and the African Diaspora*, (Bloomington: Indiana University Press, 2008); Marina Padrão Temudo, "From the Margins of the State to the Presidential Palace: The Balanta Case in Guinea Bissau," *African Studies Review* 52, 2 (2009), 64–5.

[56] Quoted in Eltis, Morgan, and Richardson, "Agency and Diaspora," 1346. Of Niumi on the Gambia, Abbé Demanet said in 1764, "Without iron and alcohol one cannot live there, much less trade." Donald R. Wright, *The World and a Very Small Place in Africa* (Armonk, NY: M. E. Sharpe, 1997), 120.

[57] Hawthorne, *Planting Rice*, 97–8.

Although many people in Guinea-Bissau's coastal zone were enslaved during raids, others fell victim to kidnappers. Whereas raids were often sanctioned by a community and involved a sizable group of men striking another group, kidnappings within one's own community were not sanctioned. They were seen as outside the boundaries of acceptable behavior and might involve an individual or small group of people acting out of greed – a desire to accumulate wealth for themselves instead of the entire community. If raiding was one aspect of community productivity, kidnapping undermined productivity by sacrificing present or future producers. Kidnapping, too, weakened social bonds, as neighbors became suspicious of one another when people disappeared in the night.[58] As Baum writes, kidnapping was "a polluting activity" carried out by people who acted in secret and who sought protection from spirits considered evil.[59]

SLAVE PRODUCTION IN THE DECENTRALIZED COASTAL ZONE: WITCHCRAFT TRIALS

Coastal people were also enslaved after trials to determine guilt for a variety of offenses. Unlike raids and wars, which were aimed at those outside communities, trials resulted in community members condemning one of their own to enslavement. That is, they were intracommunity affairs. Unlike kidnappings, trials were recognized as legitimate; they were community sanctioned. Across the coast, loyalty to and selfless hard work for family and community were virtues, deserving of praise. However, disloyalty, disobedience, and greed were "sins" deserving of punishment. Among the crimes seen as challenging the integrity of communities were murder and theft, which could result in sale or exile of the offender. Those exiled often became easy prey for slavers.[60]

Perhaps the most serious of transgressions in coastal areas was witchcraft. What witchcraft was and how it was dealt with in the Guinea-Bissau area was detailed by Philip Beaver, who launched a failed attempt to

[58] Interviews with Tona Na Isna and Suna Na Isna, Cantoné, March 5, 1995; Mariano Martino Natiori, N'foto (Quidet), July 17, 2000.

[59] Baum, *Shrines*, 122.

[60] Beaver, *African Memoranda*, 337; Manuel Álvares, *Ethiopia Minor and a Geographical Account of the Province of Sierra Leone*, trans. P. E. H. Hair (Liverpool: Department of History, University of Liverool, 1990), ch. 11; Olga F. Linares, "Deferring to the Trade in Slaves: The Jola of Casamance, Senegal in Historical Perspective," *History in Africa* 14 (1987), 124; Rodney, *A History*, 114; P. E. H. Hair, "The Enslavement of Koelle's Informants," *Journal of African History* 6, 2 (1965), 193–203.

establish an English colony on the island of Bolama in the late eighteenth century. In his diary, he expressed shock at the degree to which people in the area believed in "witches," or people who attained unnatural wealth or fortune by entering into a contract with a spirit. The spirit aided the supplicant but demanded human souls in return. One evening, Beaver said, two or three of the colony's African workers, who were known as *grumetes* (literally, "cabinboy" but on the coast the word was applied to blacks laboring in any capacity for an employer), visited him to report that one of their colleagues named Francisco "was not a good man." Francisco, they said, "wanted to eat one of them (John Basse) who had been very ill."[61]

By "eating," the *grumetes* meant consuming the health, soul, or body of another, which resulted in the victim becoming sick, dying, or disappearing. The term has been used for centuries to describe witches' actions; witches were thought to sacrifice others clandestinely at night, consuming them as part of their spirit contract. Some witches had the power to shift shapes, assuming the form of an animal and then devouring their prey. When people disappeared in the night – the victims of kidnappers who enslaved and sold them – they had been, in the coastal conception of things, "eaten" by witches. That is, they had been consumed by someone who benefitted from their demise.[62]

For Europeans like Beaver, the notion of witches consuming others was ridiculous. Beaver, indeed, was struck by what he saw as the improbability of a man "eating" another, so he sought explanation from a *grumete* named Johnson, who was fluent in English. Johnson "said that the man

---

[61] Beaver, *African Memoranda*, 177–9.

[62] Diane Lima Handem, "O arroz ou a identidade Balanta Brassa," *Soronda* 1 (1986), 150–61; Roy Van der Drift, "Birds of Passage and Independence Fighters: An Anthropological Analysis of Balanta Migration to Southern Guinea-Bissau and Mobilisation for the Liberation War (1890–1864)," in *Migrations anciennes et peuplement actual des côtes guinénnes*, ed. Gerald Gaillard (Paris: Harmattan, 2000), 157; Scrantamburlo, *Etnologia*, 66–70; Peter Mark, *The Wild Bull and the Sacred Forest: Form, Meaning, and Change in Senegambian Initiation Masks* (New York: Cambridge University Press, 1992), 30–1; Álvares, *Ethiopia*, ch. 6; Baum, *Shrines*, 138. The belief that witches literally and figuratively ate people was common across West Africa in the era of the Atlantic slave trade. John Thornton, "Cannibals, Witches, and Slave Traders in the Atlantic World," *The William and Mary Quarterly* 60, 2 (2003), 273–94; Rosalind Shaw, *Memories of the Slave Trade: Ritual and the Historical Imagination in Sierra Leone* (Chicago: The University of Chicago Press, 2002); Nicolas Argenti, *The Intestines of the State: Youth, Violence, and Belated Histories in the Cameroon Grassfields* (Chicago: The University of Chicago Press, 2007), 93–120; David Pratten, *The Man-Leopard Murders: History and Society in Colonial Nigeria* (Edinburgh: Edinburgh University Press, 2007).

accused of eating the other was a witch, and that he was the cause of John Basse's illness, by sucking his blood with his infernal witchcraft." Although Beaver insisted "that there is no such thing as a witch," Johnson had no doubt that there was, saying that Francisco "is well known to be a witch; that he has killed many people with his infernal art, and that this is the cause of his leaving his own country." Should he return to his people, Johnson said, Francisco "would be sold as a slave." Johnson also told Beaver of another witch among the *grumetes* named Corasmo. He "could turn himself into an alligator" and "had killed many people by his witchcraft." Corasmo had also fled his country so as to avoid being sold to Atlantic merchants. Witchcraft, Johnson insisted again to Beaver, "was never forgiven, and its professors never suffered to remain in their own country when once found out" because "they would either be killed or sold."[63]

Johnson's statement is strikingly similar to others recorded on the Upper Guinea coast over a period of several hundred years. Writing of the late sixteenth century, André Álvares de Almada described how people suspected of being witches on the Upper Guinea coast were sold, along with their relatives.[64] In 1684, Francisco de Lemos Coelho said that Biafada in the Bisegue region of the Grande River "abhor all witches so much that when it is known that someone is a witch, the leader sells him and all of his family." This happened frequently because "there is no lack of witches in the land."[65] In 1686, Spanish Capuchins wrote of how people in Upper Guinea were enslaved for "some offense that they call 'chai.'" A word from a creole language spoken on the coast (Kriolo), *chai* derived from *achaque*, which is Portuguese for "ailment" or "vice," and indicated that someone was a witch. The Capuchins continued, "And they say *tem chai* [he has a vice] to make someone a slave, and this is the same as saying, speaking vulgarly, that they accuse him of some offense." After an elaborate trial, guilt was assessed. "With this, the poor person starts to clamor, saying, 'Senhor, don't kill me, sell me for rum.'"[66] In 1856, a Portuguese administrator was stunned when people on the Bijago island of Orango told him that if those convicted of witchcraft were not

---

[63] Beaver, *African*, 177–9; also see, 183, 395.

[64] Almada, *Tratado*, 70.

[65] Francisco de Lemos Coelho, *Duas descrições seiscentistas da Guiné* (Lisbon: Academia Portuguesa da História, 1990), 198.

[66] Avelino Teixeira da Mota, ed., *As viagens do Bispo D. Frei Vitoriano Portuense à Guiné e a cristianização dos reis de Bissau* (Lisbon: Junta de Investigações Científicas do Ultramar, 1974), 120–33.

sold, they would be killed "because you could not live with witches."[67]
Similar reports had been sent since 1815, the year treaties abolishing the
Atlantic trade in slaves from the region took effect.[68]

Although there were (and are) differences in how various coastal
societies viewed witches, Beaver's account makes clear, as do many studies, that in the Guinea-Bissau area, selfish and self-serving behavior was
evidence of witchcraft. Witches gained fortune and elevated themselves
above their peers by harming those around them, and in societies that
sought to equalize the distribution of wealth and power within gender
and age groupings, this was unacceptable and dangerous. People of the
Cacheu River region of Guinea-Bissau, Eve Crowley writes, believe that
witches focus "excessively on personal achievement and advancement
even at the expense of others." Witches, then, defy sanctions against
"immoderate greed," becoming "ruthless and dangerous and willing to
sacrifice the lives of their kinspeople."[69] Similarly, Eric Gable argues in
a study of the Manjaco of the same region, "Excessive prosperity is evidence of a heinous crime" – a pact with a spirit that could only be forged
at the expense of others in the community. In small-scale, egalitarian
communities, he argues, "wealth is evil," and the rich are thought to be
"morally reprehensible" witches.[70] Among the Ehing, northern neighbors
to the Manjaco, Marc Schloss finds that "a wealthy man never admits
to his fortune to ... avoid raising questions about how the surplus was
obtained."[71] And William Simmons writes that Badyaranke in Senegal
think that "prosperity" is evidence that "a person has engaged in secre-
tive contracts with forest spirits."[72]

Other groups view prosperity the same way. For example, Balanta,
a group with whom I have spent many years, believe that to become
wealthy and powerful requires striking a deal with a spirit. Such contracts are forged with the sacrifice of human lives, which is the price
that spirits demand. For this, when people fall ill or die it is widely suspected that someone in a community must have acted nefariously.[73] And

[67] AHU, Cabo Verde, cx. 73, doc. 73.
[68] ANTT, Junta do Comércio, mç. 63, cx. 203, no. 12.
[69] Eve Crowley, "Contracts with the Spirits: Religion, Asylum, and Ethnic Identity in the
Cacheu Region of Guinea-Bissau" (Ph.D. thesis, Yale University, 1990), 326–7.
[70] Eric Gable, "A Secret Shared: Fieldwork and the Sinister in a West African Village,"
Cultural Anthropology 12, 2 (1997), 213–34.
[71] Marc Schloss, *The Hatchet's Blood: Separation, Power and Gender in Ehing Social Life*
(Tucson: University of Arizona Press, 1988), 118.
[72] William Simmons, *Eyes of the Night: Witchcraft Among a Senegalese People* (Boston: Little
Brown, 1971), 58.
[73] Personal observations.

in a recent study of Baga, Ramon Sarró explains that when members of descent groups excel at something, "they will fear that the *aser* [cannibal witch] of their descent group will try to annihilate them, either as a 'punishment' for their individualism or out of sheer envy." Inversely, they fear that "their own enrichment will also cause other members of their ... [descent group] to suspect that they are themselves *aser*, and deaths and misfortunes of younger members will be related to their success." An elder Baga put this in clear terms in an interview with Sarró. "This is an egalitarian society," he said. "We all keep our heads at the same level; if someone wants to raise their head above the rest of us, they will have it chopped off."[74]

The frequency of raiding after the mid-eighteenth century offered some people increased access to wealth and introduced the possibility of widening social differentiation within egalitarian communities. Of Esulalu, Baum notes that slave raiders and their extended families managed to acquire more cattle and rice fields and took control of important religious shrines. However, because cattle holdings could be wiped out from disease, a rich man could quickly become poor. Further, slavers did not control all shrines, so they were forced to share some of their fortune with other shrine keepers. Similarly, those who reaped gains from slaving "had to be careful how they displayed their wealth or how they wielded power, lest they be accused of using nefarious means to achieve their preeminence." Esulalu were, then, able to limit the influence of those who realized gains from slave raiding and trading and to "preserve a structure of diffuse power."[75] Here, as elsewhere on the coast, witchcraft trials served to maintain the status quo – to prevent some from rising too far above others.

This interpretation runs counter to that of anthropologist Rosalind Shaw. With Walter Rodney's scholarship comprising the historical backdrop of her analysis, Shaw argues that in the era of Atlantic slavery (as after), it "was the growing distinctions of class that constituted the relations of power permeating witchcraft accusations."[76] Her work is based primarily among Temne in Sierra Leone, who she says were dominated after the second half of the sixteenth century by Mane "invaders," who spoke a Mande language and produced most of the slaves sold to Portuguese merchants in the area. In the seventeenth century, some Temne

---

[74] Ramon Sarró, *The Politics of Religious Change on the Upper Guinea Coast: Iconoclasm Done and Undone* (Edinburgh: Edinburgh University Press, 2009), 36.

[75] Baum, *Shrines*, 126–7.

[76] Shaw, *Memories*, 221.

migrated to areas controlled by a different group of Mane, coming under their "political hegemony" in the eighteenth century when the slave trade, still under Mane control, flourished.[77]

The domination of the Temne by centralized Mane groups frames Shaw's analysis, making class and class distinctions central. In the seventeenth century, she argues, it was Temne without "connections, we may suppose, to the ruling Mane elite" who were revealed as witches. Two hundred years later, when Temne continued under Mane hegemony, there were "contrasting trajectories of witchcraft conviction for the well connected and for those lacking such resources." Sticking closely to Rodney's analysis, Shaw concludes that mechanisms of "witchcraft detection" in Africa were under the control of "rulers, big men, and members of elite lineages" who exploited "those with less power and wealth."[78] Witchcraft accusations were not only a product of "growing distinctions of class" but also a means for their "exacerbation and intensification."

Although Shaw's conclusions might fit the Temne case, not all societies in Upper Guinea were structured under the same political hierarchies that she and Rodney describe. In Guinea-Bissau, Mande failed to bring most societies under their control. Most communities remained free from rule by a state's elite. If, as Shaw writes, "witchcraft – driven by such transregional processes as Atlantic trade – had a ... recursive relationship" with forms of hierarchy in Sierra Leone,[79] witchcraft similarly had a recursive connection with forms of egalitarianism in Guinea-Bissau. Witchcraft and witchcraft trials were a means of perpetuating political and economic decentralization. Witchcraft accusations reflected tensions in society, but they did not necessarily intensify class distinctions. In Guinea-Bissau, such accusations eradicated these distinctions. Witchcraft trials were the means through which common folk resisted the emergence of a political elite.

And they long had been. In the early seventeenth century, another period of intensive slaving in the Guinea-Bissau area, the missionary Manuel Álvares wrote that Banhuns discovered witches through the use of "red water." This liquid was prepared by boiling the bark of a tree to create a red-colored poison, which those accused of being witches were forced to consume. If the person vomited, he or she was presumed to be innocent. If the person did not vomit, he or she either died, or lived and was sold to slavers as a punishment for witchcraft. The witch's immediate kin were also sold. Importantly, Álvares said that death or a failure to vomit came "if ... the official who administers it wants it so, or if the accused is such a lonely individual that he lacks friends to save him with antidotes in the form of emetics."[80] That is, those who failed to make connections within their communities – to foster friendships by acting generously rather than selfishly – were necessarily witches. No one came to their aid. Following a trial, community members, Álvares continued, "attack the household of the forsaken wretch and confiscate all his goods."[81] In this way, wealth that should have been the community's was distributed to the population at the moment of a witch's elimination.

Although direct evidence is lacking, we might speculate that as the number of ships arriving in Bissau and Cacheu increased and as coastal groups stepped up the production of slaves to garner imports after 1750, the frequency of witchcraft accusations and trials increased as well. Because imports were more readily available, the acquisition of personal wealth (at the expense of others through the illicit sale of victims or the abandoning of villages for employment in urban areas as *grumetes*) became more tempting. Those who got too close to Europeans or, more likely, Eurafricans, who lived on the coast and served as intermediaries in trade relations, risked disrupting group cohesion by shirking their responsibilities in fields and by elevating themselves above their peers as they accumulated excessive wealth.[82]

Those who engaged too much with Europeans and Eurafricans risked becoming like them – risked becoming witches. And this is precisely how coastal people viewed whites and those associated with them – as witches. Beaver noted this when he wrote that "'all white man witch' is an article of general belief among these people."[83] A few years earlier in Sierra Leone, John Matthews wrote something similar; Africans thought "the white man" carried out the actions of witches with each slave he purchased, using the slave as "a sacrifice to his God, or to devour him as food."[84] On the Upper Guinea coast from as early as the sixteenth

---

[80] Álvares, *Ethiopia*, ch. 7.
[81] Ibid.
[82] This may have been why a chief on Bissau was accused of witchcraft and killed for agreeing to allow the CGPM to build a fort on the island. J. Mendes da Cunha Saraiva, "A Forteleza de Bissau e a Companhia do Grao Para e Maranhão," *Congresso comemorativo do quinto centenario do descrobrimento da Guiné* (Lisbon: Sociedade de Geografia de Lisboa, 1946).
[83] Beaver, *African Memoranda*, 200.
[84] John Matthews, *A Voyage to the River Sierra Leone* (London: White and Son, 1966), 152.

century and through to today, many Africans called Christians (or people who professed Christian- or European-based identities) "white" (*branco* in Portuguese and *branku* in the creole language of the region).[85] Given this, "white man" – as in "all white man witch" – likely applied to a broad spectrum of people associated with Atlantic commerce and Christianity, be they light skinned or not.

Whatever the case, it was clear to all that "whites" often took possession of humans and robbed them of their strength by chaining them, marching them to ports, underfeeding them, and holding them in filthy barracoons where they awaited embarkation on ships. Moreover, "whites" were motivated by selfishness and greed. They controlled great wealth, they sought ever more riches, and excessive personal affluence was evil. Europeans and Eurafricans turned people into profit – slaves into tobacco, alcohol, cloth, and other things – which was witchcraft *par excellence*.[86]

Slaving and witchcraft, then, went hand in hand. Coastal communities saw the seizing and trading of people as necessary for the productivity and survival of the group. But these things brought great risks. Mainly, communities had to engage with evil people – selfish, greedy, "white" witches and the minions they sent out to gather people who would be consumed on the other side of the ocean. Moreover, the manufactures "white" witches offered tempted individuals to sacrifice their own for personal gain. For this, engagement in the slave trade had to be carefully managed. And it was done so by institutionalizing the means of slave production. Kidnapping was recognized as illegitimate and was punished when discovered or when unexplained personal wealth pointed to the possibility of it. Conversely, raids and trials were seen as legitimate and were sanctioned and carried out by established bodies within communities and through standardized practices.

Finally, although links to the broader Atlantic were necessary to gain the items needed for agricultural expansion and for defense against

---

[85] António J. Dias, "Crenças e costumes dos Indígenas da Ilha de Bissau no Século XVIII," *Portugal em Africa* II (1945), 160; Peter Mark, *"Portuguese" Style and Luso-African Identity: Precolonial Senegambia, Sixteenth–Nineteenth Centuries* (Bloomington: Indiana University Press, 2002), 107. On present-day association of lifestyles with whiteness in Guinea-Bissau, Lorenzo Bordonaro, *"Sai fora*: Youth, Disconnectedness and Aspiration to Mobility in the Bijagó Islands (Guinea-Bissau), *Ethnográfica* 13, 1 (2009), 125–44.

[86] See similar analyses in Thornton, "Cannibals"; Shaw, "Production of Witchcraft"; and Ralf A. Austen, "The Moral Economy of Witchcraft: An Essay in Comparative History," in *Modernity and Its Malcontents*, eds. Jean Comaroff and John Comaroff (Chicago: University of Chicago Press, 1993), 89–110.

raiders, many groups sought ways to limit interactions with white merchants. One way of doing this was by working through intermediaries. Hence, Floup and Balanta often traded with merchants from neighboring groups, especially Mandinka, rather than meeting face to face with white men.[87] Further, because young males were particularly valuable in paddy-rice producing societies (performing most of the agricultural work and comprising the units that raided other villages and attempted to ward off foreign attackers), they were shielded from interactions with outsiders. It was often females or older men who conducted trade. The producers of slaves were, then, not the sellers of slaves, making it difficult for them to realize personal gains.[88] In the case of the Balanta, men who left their communities to meet with foreign merchants could be given the penalty of death.[89] Balanta, Floup, and Bijago also discouraged the purchase of luxuries. Marina Padrão Temudo demonstrates that Balanta sought from merchants "limited consumer goods (like tobacco and alcoholic drinks)," their efforts focused on the accumulation of that which was "needed for the process of rice production" – mainly, iron or iron tools.[90] Also, Balanta and Floup often sought cattle – the traditional store of wealth – for captives rather than foreign manufactures.[91] Bijago wanted, one late eighteenth-century observer said, only arms, iron, and brandy, showing disdain for luxury items.[92] Their shunning of cloth was evident to Beaver who wrote that Bijago men wore deer and goatskins and women chose "a thick fringe made of the shred of palm leaves."[93] Although there are indications that Floup sometimes traded rice for cloth in the eighteenth century, Floup women who traded in canoes with merchants in Cacheu

[87] Baum, *Shrines*, 121; Philip J. Havik, *Silences and Soundbytes: The Gendered Dynamics of Trade and Brokerage in the Pre-Colonial Guinea Bissau Region* (New Brunswick, NJ: Transaction Publishers, 2004), 96–7; Diane Lima Handem, *Nature et foctionnement du pouvoir chez les Balanta Brassa* (Bissau: INEP, 1986), 182; Hawthorne, *Planting Rice*, 135.

[88] Hawthorne, *Planting Rice*, 125–8; Philip J. Havik, "Women and Trade in the Guinea-Bissau Region," *Stvdia* 52 (1994), 83–120; A. Teixeira da Mota, *Some Aspects of Portuguese Colonisation and Sea Trade in West Africa in the Fifteenth and Sixteenth Centuries* (Bloomington: Indiana University Press, 1978), 15; Carreira, *Os portugueses*, 27–8.

[89] Temudo, "From the Margins of the State," 50.

[90] Ibid. Of his time spent in the Guinea-Bissau region in 1816, Mollien writes, "The Portuguese have little communication with these cruel and savage people." *Travels*, 342.

[91] Hawthorne, *Planting Rice*; Baum, *Shrines*, 121; Handem, *Nature*, 182; Mark, *Wild Bull*, 124.

[92] Knight-Baylac, from the late eighteenth century, cited in Brooks, *Eurafricans*, 290.

[93] Beaver, *African Memoranda*, 335, 337–8.

area ports were said to travel "scantily dressed."[94] By limiting their desires as consumers – and thus the extent of their involvement as suppliers in the slave trade – to goods viewed as necessary and beneficial, coastal societies controlled and managed the slave trade.

THE ETHNICITIES OF THE SLAVES TRADED THROUGH BISSAU AND CACHEU

Slaving patterns indicate that from year to year, the measures that communities in the Upper Guinea coastal zone took to cope with the trade in slaves were generally effective. Indeed, data shows that populations spread over the coastal zone saw only low-level losses to enslavement in the eighteenth century. When combined into ships' cargoes in Bissau and Cacheu, people taken in small numbers from multiple and scattered communities were enough to fill CGPM vessels. However, neither the CGPM nor independent shippers who came to the coast after the company was dismantled could coax communities to produce ever-increasing numbers of captives. Indeed, the volume of slave exports from the region remained relatively steady from 1761 to 1815.

The most comprehensive dataset for slave exports from Upper Guinea is compiled in Voyages: The Trans-Atlantic Slave Trade Database (TSTD2). For the years from 1701 to 1842 (when the last known slave ship left the region), it lists 102,776 slave exports from the greater Guinea-Bissau region (the Casamance River, Bijagos Islands, Bissau, Cacheu, the Grande River, and the Cape Verde Islands). The overwhelming majority of those were shipped to the Americas, with very small percentages bound for Sierra Leone (less than 1 percent) and Portugal (1.5 percent). Of the total, 79 percent (80,936 people) were embarked on Portuguese ships for Amazonia. Another 10,181, or 10 percent, were embarked on Portuguese ships for other parts of Brazil. Most left the ports of Bissau and Cacheu. Of the 102,776 slaves who were shipped from the greater Guinea-Bissau region after 1700, 77 percent were shipped between 1761 and 1820. Between 1761 and 1805, annual exports were fairly consistent, most years seeing about 1,235 slaves departing from the greater Guinea-Bissau region on ships for the Americas. Between 1806 and 1815, the TSTD2 estimates yearly averages at 2,333 slave departures each year for the Americas. However, my own analysis of the data suggests the TSTD2

---

[94] B. A. Álvares de Andrade, "Informações da Guiné em 1777," *Arquivo das Colónias* (Lisbon: Ministerio das Colonias, 1917), 36.

overestimates slave exports from Bissau and Cacheu for this period, with exports likely holding at about 1,235 slaves per year or decreasing slightly.[95] After 1815, yearly averages dropped off substantially, because Portugal followed England, France, and the United States in abolishing the slave trade north of the equator (Table 2.1).[96]

By combining data from the TSTD2 with data from the MISD, estimates for the numbers of captives from particular ethnic groups (and from, therefore, particular places in the greater Guinea-Bissau area) can be determined. Assuming (from the TSTD2) that about 1,235 slaves were exported from the greater Guinea-Bissau area each year between 1761 and 1815, then (from the MISD) each year an average of 61 percent of slave exports from the region (or 761 people) would have been from small coastal societies and 38 percent from the interior, beyond the coastal forest (or 474 people).

Table 2.2 combines data from the TSTD2 and MISD to derive estimates for the numbers of slaves shipped from Guinea-Bissau each year by ethnicity. As P. E. H. Hair comments, with "very few exceptions," the ethnolinguistic units found on the Guinea coast have "*stayed put,*

---

[95] Based on known ship departures for, arrivals in, and departures from Bissau and Cacheu, the TSTD2 estimates the number of slaves on the ships for which data is not otherwise available. Before about 1805, extant documents are plentiful and generally provided detailed information about embarkations and disembarkations. After about 1805, this is not the case. There are many "holes" in the dataset, documents listing ship arrivals on the Upper Guinea Coast but not stating the number of slaves embarked. For the period 1806–1815, the database *estimates* an average of 530 slaves embarked on ships leaving Cacheu and 390 on ships leaving Bissau. However, based on extant data about embarkations, these figures are clearly inflated. A better estimate would be about 182 slaves embarked on each ship leaving Bissau and Cacheu. My figure is derived from known embarkations in Bissau and Cacheu and arrivals from the two ports in Amazonia. If 182 slaves per ship is assumed to be the average boarded on ships for which we have no embarkation data, then about 1,019 slaves per year left Bissau and Cacheu from 1806 through 1815, which is a small decrease from previous years.

[96] If trans-shipments are considered, there is good reason to think that the TSTD2 undercounts departures from the greater Guinea-Bissau area for the whole of the eighteenth century. Throughout the eighteenth century, and particularly after 1750, Portuguese officials filed many reports noting British and French merchants, and their middleman representatives, arriving on small vessels from other regions. The extent of the undercount is impossible to determine. I would guess somewhere between 10 and 25 percent. Observations about "interlopers" abound. From the 1740s: AHU, Guiné, cx. 7, doc. 53; AHU, Guiné, cx. 8, doc. 8, 11. From the 1750s: AHU, Guiné, cx. 9, doc. 11. From the 1760s: ANTT, AHMF, CGPM, Copiadores, Cartas para Pará, livro 97, fl. 125; AHU, Guiné, cx. 9, doc. 71. From the 1770s: AHU, Guiné, cx. 20, doc. 37; AHU, Guiné, cx. 11, doc. 2, 15, 16, 20. From the 1780s: AHU, Guiné, cx. 12, doc. 24. From the 1790s: AHU, Guiné, cx. 12, doc. 24; Beaver, *Africa Memoranda*, 58, 95.

TABLE 2.2. *Estimate of Numbers of Slaves by Ethnicity Exported from Greater Guinea-Bissau Region by Year, 1761–1815*

Ethnic groups	Number in MISD, 1767–1832	Percentage by coastal and interior zones	Percentage by entire Upper Guinea region	Approx. # exported yearly (assuming slave exports of 1,235 yearly), 1761–1815
Coast				
Baga	4	0.00	0.00	2
Balanta	238	0.16	0.10	121
Banhun	86	0.06	0.04	44
Biafada	39	0.03	0.02	20
Bijago	398	0.27	0.16	203
Bissau	1	0.00	0.00	1
Cacheu	296	0.20	0.12	151
Cassanga	41	0.03	0.02	21
Floup	150	0.10	0.06	76
Jola	1	0.00	0.00	1
Manjaco	12	0.01	0.00	6
Nalu	74	0.05	0.03	38
Papel	126	0.08	0.05	64
Sape	26	0.02	0.01	13
Total Coast	1492	1.01	0.61	761
Bambara	9	0.01	0.00	5
Fula	92	0.10	0.04	47
Gabu	2	0.00	0.00	1
Geba	1	0.00	0.00	1
Jalonke	2	0.00	0.00	1
Mandinka	814	0.87	0.34	415
Mouro	7	0.01	0.00	4
Total Interior	927	.99	.38	474
Total (coast and interior)	2419			1235

Source: Combined estimates from TSTD2 and MISD (accessed 20 May 2009). Percentages rounded.

topographically, over the centuries."[97] That is, if one can determine the ethnicity that a person claimed in the seventeenth century, one can be fairly certain from where that person hailed. If he or she claimed an ethnicity common in the coastal zone of the greater Guinea-Bissau region,

[97] P. E. H. Hair, "Ethnolinguistic Continuity on the Guinea Coast," *Journal of African History* 8, 2 (1967), 268.

then he or she hailed from a relatively small *tchon* (*chão* in the plural) or
ethnic "territory" (Map 0.2).[98]

What is striking about Table 2.2 is how varied and dispersed the *chão*
of those made captive and sent into the Atlantic trade were. All told, people from thirteen coastal Guinea-Bissau-region ethnic groups appear in
Maranhense inventories. No one group comprised more than 27 percent
of all slaves exported from the coastal region, meaning that each year, relatively small numbers of slaves were taken from a variety of places. In other
words, no single group suffered enslavement in coastal Guinea-Bissau at
a disproportionate rate after about 1750. Rather, low numbers of slaves
were taken from multiple groups (and locations) year after year.

The registry from the slave ship *São José*, which departed Cacheu in
1756, confirms this point. Slaves from multiple coastal communities were
imprisoned on the ship – Balanta, Banhun, Brame, Bijago, Floup, and Papel.
Of course, from ship to ship, the numbers of slaves from various places
differed, so we should not expect the representation of ethnic groups on
the *São José* to replicate findings from the MISD. Of captives taken in the
coastal zone who were on the *São José*, Floup (31 percent of the coastal
captives) comprised the largest single group, followed by Balanta (26 percent), Banhun (20 percent), and Papel (17 percent).[99] That there were a
relatively high number of Floup on the *São José* is not surprising, because
Cacheu, the port of embarkation, was situated near their *tchon*.[100]

Most of the coastal groups found on the *São José* were also represented
on the slave ship *Conde de Villa Flor*, which embarked slaves at Bissau
before being seized by antislaving squadrons in 1822. However, because it
left from a different port, the proportion of slaves from particular ethnic
groups was different from that of the *São José*. Bijago comprised almost
half (49 percent) of all slaves born in the coastal zone of the greater
Guinea-Bissau region aboard the *Conde de Villa Flor*.[101]

Bijago, too, comprised the largest coastal group in Maranhão after
about the mid-eighteenth century. Combining data from the TSTD2 and
MISD, it is evident that each year from 1761 to 1815, an average of 203
Bijago (27 percent of all coastal-zone-born slaves) were boarded on ships
for the Americas. Bijago were among the most active slavers in the coastal
region; observers remarked about the frequency with which their warriors

[98] Joshua B. Forrest, *Lineages of State Fragility: Rural Civil Society in Guinea-Bissau* (Athens: Ohio University Press, 2003), 28; Havik, *Silences*, 88.
[99] Bibliotheca Nacional de Portugal, Collecção Pombalina, códice 628, fl. 179–82.
[100] After 1750, 34 percent more slaves were embarked at Bissau than Cacheu. TSTD2.
[101] TSTD2, "Names Database."

attacked coastal communities from canoes.[102] However, data from the MISD indicates that Rodney is wrong in claiming that "the Bijago were relatively immune to enslavement" because they "were not favored as slaves by the Europeans." Though some Europeans disparaged Bijago slaves for what they saw as a propensity for rebellion and suicide, data from Brazilian plantation inventories and from slave ships makes clear that Europeans bought relatively large numbers of Bijago captives.[103]

Bijago cannot, then, be classified as simply a "predatory" society.[104] Like all coastal peoples, Bijago were both predators and prey. All coastal societies lost people to raiders and kidnappers; all sold the deviant and disruptive from their own societies; and all raided others, grabbing people for sale to slavers for iron and other valuable imports. In Guinea-Bissau's coastal zone, there were no neat divisions between "captor" and "source" societies. We cannot distinguish what Patrick Manning calls "the Raided and the Raiders."[105] In Guinea-Bissau, the raiders were frequently raided and some among the raiders were sold by their peers.

How Bijago – and particularly female Bijago – became slaves is not clear. Females accounted for 56 percent of Bijago captives in Maranhão (and 69 percent aboard the *Conde de Villa Flor*), indicating that it was not Bijago male warriors captured during raids on coastal societies who were most often enslaved.[106] It is unlikely that coastal communities often staged attacks on the difficult-to-access Bijagos Islands; and there are no accounts of such raids. It is likely that some Bijago were made captive in clashes among the followers of rival Bijago chiefs on the decentralized archipelago. From his time on the Guinea coast in the late seventeenth century, Captain Jean Barbot reported that Bijago on Casegu Island "are continually at war with the other islanders."[107] In the eighteenth century, Bijago from the island of Orango were especially active slavers, who were contracted by slave purchasers.[108] In raids launched on other

[102] AHU, Guiné, cx. 11, doc. 57.

[103] Rodney, *A History*, 109–10; Mettas, "La Traite" 354–8. Bijago were also the largest single group of slaves from the coastal zone of Guinea-Bissau in a series of censuses taken on slave populations in Bissau, Cape Verde, and Cacheu in 1856. AHU, AUL, GG, lv. 10, 35; António Carreira, *Cabo Verde: Formação e extinção de uma sociedade escravocrata (1460–1878)* (Praia: Istituto Caboverdeano de Livro, 1983), 428.

[104] Rodney, *A History*, 109–10.

[105] Patrick Manning, *Slavery and African Life: Occidental, Oriental and African Slave Trade* (New York: Cambridge University Press, 1993), 39–40.

[106] MISD. In censuses from 1856 in Bissau, Cape Verde, and Cacheu, 56 percent of Bijago slaves were females. AHU, AUL, GG, lv. 10, 35; Carreira, *Cabo Verde*, 428.

[107] P. E. H. Hair, Adam Jones, and Robin Law, *Barbot on Guinea: The Writings of Jean Barbot on West Africa 1678–1712* (London: The Hakluyt Society, 1992), I: 319

[108] Personal communication, Philip Havik, June 13, 2009.

Bijagos Islands from Orango, women and children would have been eas-
ier targets than strong male warriors. Bijago were also "reduced to that
state [of slavery]," Philip Beaver claimed in the 1790s, "for the crimes
of witchcraft and adultery; and then, most likely, instantly sold to the
Portuguese."[109] Because the Bijago were among the most active slavers in
Guinea-Bissau's coastal zone, it is not surprising that some among them
got too close to slave buyers, becoming wealthy as a result and being
expelled for the crime of witchcraft. Indeed, an observer in 1777 noted
that the Bijagos Islands hosted a "big trade in slaves ... because they sell
their relatives for next to nothing."[110]

People from other groups also suffered enslavement. "Cacheus," or
people from the Cacheu area, comprised about 20 percent (151 people)
of the captives exported each year from the Guinea-Bissau region between
1761 and 1805. Balanta comprised about 16 percent (121 people) of the
captives exported each year. Smaller numbers of Papel, Banhun, Nalu,
Cassanga, Floup (who may more often have been counted as Cacheus),
and Biafada were exported each year along with very small numbers of
people from other groups.

Like Bijago, Balanta have been described as a group that "did a good
job of defending themselves." For this, Rodney writes, "few ... must
have appeared on the market."[111] Elsewhere, I describe Balanta success
at defending populations against attacks.[112] That a relatively high percentage of the coastal people enslaved each year were Balanta does not,
however, run counter to my conclusions. Balanta communities did defend
themselves well, producing food sufficient enough to feed growing (not
shrinking) populations.[113] But no matter how good their defenses, many
Balanta communities experienced losses to enslavement. Raiders from

---

[109] Beaver, *African Memoranda*, 337. Beaver also wrote, "There has not, it is said, been
any known instance of these islanders having warred with each other." Lending cre-
dence to Beaver's observations are texts written by the priest Francisco de Pinhel a little
over a century earlier. Avelino Teixeira da Mota, *As Viagens do Bispo D. Frei Vitoriano
Portuense á Guiné e a Cristianização dos Reis de Bissau* (Lisbon: Junta de Investigações
Científicas do Ultramar, 1974), 50. However, there is reason to think that Bijago warred
against one another.

[110] Quoted in Havik, *Silences*, 115.

[111] Rodney, *A History*, 110.

[112] Hawthorne, *Planting Rice*, 121–8.

[113] Late –eighteenth-century observations say Balanta regions were teeming with people,
having great surpluses of rice for consumption and trade. Ibid., 190–5. Correia e Lança,
Relatorio, 9. Population expansion likely began in the early nineteenth century, as Balanta
began occupying new sections of the lower Casamance then. This sparked conflicts with
Floup. Havik, *Silences*, 97–8; Christian Roche, *Histoire de la Casamance: Conquêt et
résistance: 1850–1920* (Paris: Karthala, 1985).

Balanta and non-Balanta groups succeeded in some attacks, grabbing small numbers of victims and carrying them off. Moreover, some Balanta became greedy. Like Francisco and Corasmo, who Beaver encountered, they struck deals with spirits and gained the power to enrich themselves at the expense of others. In communities in which group cohesion was necessary for carrying out large-scale mangrove-rice projects and warding off attacks by outsiders, witches had to be eliminated – sold when possible, killed when not. Their actions challenged an ethos of egalitarianism.

CONCLUSION

In the second half of the eighteenth century, slave exports from Bissau and Cacheu showed dramatic increases over the previous fifty years. Most of the slaves exported from the ports were not, as Barry and Rodney argue, the products of a Fula jihad in Futa Jallon. The fault lines across which coastal conflicts raged did not divide economic classes of people. The majority of slaves exported from Bissau and Cacheu hailed from the immediate coastal zone. They were the products of raids and trials carried out by small-scale, decentralized societies.

Greed was not the principal motivator of these raids and trials. Intense competition coupled with changes in the environment compelled coastal groups to find ways to tap trade routes that connected distant points around the Atlantic to Bissau and Cacheu. Obtaining trade items, particularly iron for tools and weapons, was the only way for communities to survive and prosper. Portuguese merchants were successful in ramping up slave exports from Bissau and Cacheu in the mid-eighteenth century because they offered Africans the items they needed.

However, the conduct of white merchants gave coastal people every indication that they were evil. Many saw merchants as white witches who were motivated by greed to enrich themselves by consuming others. Nonetheless, communities had no choice but to deal with them. Communities that failed to sate the hunger of white witches for black bodies risked being consumed. Every coastal group struggled with the morality of turning people into material objects. All sought to limit the pernicious influences that outsiders had on their people. And, all sought to control and manage the slave trade. Most succeeded.

3

From Upper Guinea to Amazonia

In February 1756, the Portuguese galley *São José* was anchored in the river off Cacheu, the ship's crew filling it with slaves who had been shuttled in canoes a short distance from shore. The *São José* was one of the first ships of the Company of Grão Pará and Maranhão (CGPM) to arrive on the Upper Guinea coast. Since 1755, the CGPM had had a monopoly on trade flowing from Bissau and Cacheu and into the ports of São Luís and Belém, the capitals of the Brazilian captaincies of Maranhão and Pará in the northern Amazonia region. The monopoly was ended in 1778 with the company continuing to trade in a freer market through 1787. As slaves were loaded into canoes, a priest sprinkled each of them with water and spoke a few incomprehensible words. He, too, assigned the slaves Christian names – José, João, Roberto, Sebastián, Maria, Catharina, Brizida, Roza, and so on. Those the Portuguese called *gentio* (which can be translated as "savages" or "pagans") were baptized – introduced to Christianity and Western "civilization."

There was nothing unusual about the manner in which slaves were embarked on the ship. Nothing, that is, except for the fact that a scribe took time to record slaves' baptismal names and ethnicities. Initially, a total of ninety-seven people (seven of whom were infants) were forced onto the vessel. The infants were listed in the ship's records without value and were carried by their mothers as *filhos de peito*, "nursing children." Fifty-seven percent of those whose ethnicities were recorded had been taken from the immediate coastal region of Upper Guinea, only tens of miles from the ports of Bissau and Cacheu. The ethnicities they claimed were Balanta, Bijago, Papel, Floup, Banhun, and Brame. The remaining

43 percent were Mandinka, who were from farther inland.[1] Just before the *São José* departed, another few captives were added to the vessel, bringing the total number of slaves of monetary value to the CGPM to ninety-four.[2] Those who survived the passage to Pará probably spent about fifty days together on the ocean.[3]

Decades ago, scholars such as E. Franklin Frazier and Stanley M. Elkins argued that the horrors of the passage from Africa to the Americas traumatized slaves so much that they were rendered culturally void, becoming receptacles that were filled with their masters' cultural assumptions.[4] Since then others have taken different approaches. Prominent among them are Sidney W. Mintz and Richard Price, who argue that slaves' time "shackled together in the coffles, packed into dank 'factory' dungeons, squeezed together between the decks of stinking ships, [where they were] separated... from speakers of the same language" marked "the birth of new societies based on new kinds of principles." For Mintz and Price, those principles were not re-creations of anything that had come before. They were the creation of something new. "What the slaves undeniably shared at the outset," they write, "was their enslavement; all – or nearly all – else had to be *created by them*."[5] In other words, where Frazier and Elkins saw the passage from Africa to the Americas as a "deculturing" experience, Mintz and Price see it as the opposite. It was on their journey from Africa to the Americas, Mintz and Price argue, that African slaves who came from very different backgrounds laid the foundations for the unique African-American cultures that would emerge on New World plantations.

Tracing the flow of captives from their points of captivity in Upper Guinea across the Atlantic and into the hands of Amazonian masters, I argue in this chapter partly along the same lines as Mintz and Price. That is, descriptions of slaves shipped through Bissau and Cacheu make clear that when people from a variety of ethnic groups were forced together on slaving routes, they looked to one another for support and community,

---

[1] BNP, Collecção Pombalina, codice 628, fl. 179–82.

[2] ANTT, AHMF, CGPM, Memorial, livro 63, no. 65; AHMF, CGPM, Livro de demonstrações, livro 77, 1–2; ANTT, AHMF, CGPM, Diário, livro 1, no. 165, 172, and 2857.

[3] TSTD2, http://slavevoyages.org/tast/assessment/estimates.faces.

[4] E. Franklin Frazier, *The Negro Family in the United States* (Chicago: The University of Chicago Press, 1966); Stanley M. Elkins, *Slavery: A Problem in American Institutional and Intellectual Life* (New York: The Universal Library, 1963).

[5] Sidney W. Mintz and Richard Price, *The Birth of African-American Culture: An Anthropological Perspective* (Boston: Beacon Press, 1992), 18, 42–4.

emphasizing unity in the face of great adversity. For Balanta, Papel, Bijago, Floup, Mandinka, and people from other ethnic groups, their time together in transit on ships like the *São José* was central to their later emphasis of a Guinean identity. For Upper Guineans, the Middle Passage was not a deculturing experience.

However, unlike Mintz and Price, I do not see all aspects of the black culture that emerged in the Americas (in this case, Maranhão and Pará) as wholly new creations. For slaves sent from Upper Guinea to Amazonia, time spent in barracoons and on slave ships did not mark the birth of an entirely new society based on wholly original kinds of principles. Indeed, on their shared journey, Balanta, Papel, Bijago, Floup, Mandinka, and people from other ethnic groups began to discover how much they already had in common.[6] First and foremost, they were all slaves, something that was obvious as they huddled together in squalid holding pens and suffered together beneath the decks of filthy ships. But beyond this, the passage from Africa to the Americas was the first step in a realization that all Upper Guineans embraced much of the same aesthetic appreciation, spiritual beliefs, and approaches to family life. When and where they could in Amazonia, Upper Guineans would re-create what they held in common.[7]

MOVING SLAVES FROM COASTAL VILLAGES IN THE ERA OF THE CGPM

As was explained in Chapter 2, Guinea-Bissau's coastal zone, from which most slaves shipped to Amazonia hailed, was politically decentralized. Because of this fact, slave production was not controlled by any one state or single set of elites. Rather, slaves were produced during myriad small-scale raids launched by bands of young men, kidnappings carried out by "evil-doers" from widely scattered places, and witchcraft trials conducted within countless communities. For the most part, the locations where those exported had been captured could be found in an area stretching

---

[6] My thinking is informed by Joseph C. Miller, "Retention, Reinvention, and Remembering: Restoring Identities through Enslavement in Africa and under Slavery in Brazil," in *Enslaving Connections: Changing Cultures of African and Brazil during the Era of Slavery*, eds. José C. Curto and Paul E. Lovejoy (Amherst, NY: Humanity Books, 2004), 81–124.

[7] For a study of the ways slaves viewed shipmates, see Walter Hawthorne, "'Being Now, As It Were: One Family,' Shipmate Bonding on the Slave Vessel *Emilia*, in Rio de Janeiro and throughout the Atlantic World," *Luso-Brazilian Review* 45, 1 (2008), 53–77.

from the Bijagos Islands to the hinterlands of Geba and Farim, and from the Casamance to the Nunez Rivers.

Once they had captives in their possession, communities or individuals tried to get rid of them as quickly as possible.[8] Holding captives was a dangerous business because they could cause great harm if rebellious. Moreover, keeping captives was expensive because they had to be fed and guarded so as to prevent flight. Most often, the communities and individuals who held captives sold them to merchants who plied area rivers. Of these merchants, the most important were baptized with Christian names and based in Bissau, Cacheu, Farim, Geba, and Ziguinchor. The terms used to describe them changed over time. By the second half of the eighteenth century, they were mostly referred to as *moradores* – free residents of fortified trade towns, or *praças*. They were also called *Cristãos da terra* (Christians of the land), *filhos da terra* (children of the land), and *Kriston* (Christians). No matter where they had been born, they called themselves Portuguese. Some indeed were from Portugal. However, many more were Luso-Africans – brown-skinned, African-born children, grandchildren, and great-grandchildren of Portuguese men and local African women. By the eighteenth century, many would have been the fifth or sixth generation of descendants from Portuguese men. Still others were black African "converts" to Christianity. All claimed a Christian identity, but most mixed Christian and local religious beliefs. "Those of this population, called Christians," an observer noted in the early nineteenth century, "having the right to profess the Roman Catholic Religion, in fact profess nothing."[9] Through connections in trade hubs and rural communities, *moradores* served as intermediaries between Atlantic merchants (ships' captains and/or CGPM administrators) and rural slave-supplying communities. Although many in these communities viewed *moradores* as witches who were driven to enrich themselves at the expense of others, villagers nonetheless dealt with them because doing so was the only way to obtain necessary trade items (Chapter 2).[10]

---

[8] Sieur Michel Jajolet de la Courbe, *Premier voyage du Sieur de la Courbe fait à la coste de l'Afrique en 1685*, ed. Prosper Cultru (Paris: E. Champion, 1913), 257–8.

[9] BNP, códice 1679. *Moradores'* inattention to Christian orthodoxy had long been a topic of discussion in official documents. For example, from 1794, AHU, Guiné, cx. 15, doc. 4; from 1733, AHU, Guiné, cx. 6, doc. 2; from 1664, ANTT, Inquisição de Lisboa, P. 2097.

[10] Philip J. Havik, *Silences and Soundbytes: The Gendered Dynamic of Trade and Brokerage in the Pre-colonial Guinea Bissau Region* (Münster: Lit Verlag, 2004), 53–4; Peter Mark, *"Portuguese" Style and Luso-African Identity: Precolonial Senegambia, Sixteenth–Nineteenth Centuries* (Bloomington: Indiana University Press, 2002).

Moradores' ties to many rural areas were strong, indeed. It was there that they conducted business, and it was there that they fled when times were tough in *praças*. In 1733, a report from Cacheu mentioned that Atlantic commerce had fallen off, making it difficult for many *moradores* to sustain themselves. As a consequence, there were "many Christian people [from Cacheu] living among the pagans with great danger to their salvation."[11] Another report described the Christians of Cacheu "fleeing to live with the heretics," participating in their rites and trading among them.[12] And, in fact, when living in rural areas, *moradores* did not abandon their livelihoods. In 1734, a report noted Christians who had left Cacheu amassing two hundred slaves and "much beeswax," which they were trying to ship to "Cape Verde, Brazil and Portugal."[13]

In 1744, an observer summed up the position of Christian merchants, saying, "The *moradores* ... never lived nor could they live without trading what they got from the commissioners of the ships that come here with goods that they take up the rivers."[14] And in the days of the CGPM, an administrator in Cacheu noted that "few slaves are sold by the pagans, but most by the *Cristãos*, who have correspondence with people on the margins of the Cacheu River ... with Papel and Floup."[15] Although male *moradores* often conducted business through locally born women, using their connections to kin to facilitate trade, many *moradores* in Cacheu and Bissau were locally born women who exploited their own connections for their direct benefit. Hence names like Izabel Friz, Maria Gomes de Barros, Maria dos Santos, Antonia Nunes, Izabel Mendes, Izabel Lopes, and Anna Roza are listed in books of CGPM business transactions.[16]

To assist with their business, *moradores* employed *grumetes*, or black African workers who for the most part professed a Christian identity. Some *grumetes* were free people, and others were domestic slaves. Many

---

[11] AHU, Guiné, cx. 6, doc. 2, 24.

[12] AHU, Guiné, cx. 6, doc. 50. On *moradores* elsewhere, doc. 15.

[13] AHU, Guiné, cx. 8, doc. 15.

[14] AHU, Guiné, cx. 7, doc. 44. Compare to Francisco de la Mota's statement in 1686 that it was the "Christian Creoles of this land" who left ports to purchase slaves and who served as interpreters. Avelino Teixeira da Mota, *As viagens do Bispo D. Frei Vitoriano Portuense á Guiné e a Cristianização dos reis de Bissau* (Lisbon: Junta de Investigações Científicas do Ultramar, 1974), 121.

[15] AHU, Guiné, cx. 11, doc. 57. Many *moradores* had connections in a wide range of villages and small "ports," or canoe docks. A report by Bernardino de Andrades in 1777 detailed activities at several such places. "Informções da Guiné em 1777," *Arquivo das Colónias* I (July–December 1917), 34–9. Also, AHU, Guiné, cx. 8, doc. 51.

[16] ANTT, AHMF, CGPM, Extractos, livro 54, entry 26.

carried out trade for *moradores*, going to rural areas and returning with captives. Sieur de la Courbe wrote in the late seventeenth century, "There are Portuguese who send out black assistants to the villages in order to purchase whatever they can find."[17] And in the late eighteenth century, Philip Beaver noted,

> The merchants of Bissau procure ... slaves by means of a class of natives called grumetes, who have generally been brought up from infancy in their houses.... They navigate all their small craft, whether canoes, or decked schooners and sloops; and carry on, for all their principals, all the commerce of the country. The merchant ... sends them with goods to the value of a certain number of slaves, whether to Zinghicor, Cacheo, Geba, or any other place; where they make their purchases, and then return to their employers.[18]

The most powerful Bissau- and Cacheu-based merchants employed large retinues of *grumetes*. However, the powerful did not monopolize the slave trade. Indeed, dozens of *moradores* actively participated in it. Entries in CGPM accounting books make this clear, listing over 120 *morador* debts in Cacheu in 1769.[19] In 1770, the company dealt with twenty-one *moradores* in Ziguinchor and twenty-five in Farim, and in 1780 there were over sixty in Bissau.[20] Typically, the most powerful *moradores* hailed from Portugal, although some were from Cape Verde, Bissau, and Cacheu. Often, the most powerful held official positions in government or the Church. For example, among the wealthiest slave dealers in Cacheu in 1769 was Governor Sebastião Cunha Sotto Mayor; the *praça*'s captain major, Antonio Lopes; the commander of the *praça* of Farim, Captain Joquim Baptista; and an influential father, Manoel de Graça. Another wealthy slave merchant was D. Joanna Baptista, descendant of a long line of Baptistas who lived in and traded from Cacheu.[21] But many other *moradores* of the *praças* of Cacheu, Bissau, Farim, and Geba traded slaves – slaves being far and away the

---

[17] La Courbe, *Premier voyage*, 205.

[18] Philip Beaver, *African Memoranda* (London: Dawsons of Pall Mall, 1968), 322. *Grumetes* were also called upon to defend *morador* interests as a military force. AHU, Guiné, cx. 14, doc. 62.

[19] ANTT, AHMF, CGPM, Extractos, livro 53, entry 61.

[20] ANTT, AHMF, CGPM, Extractos, livro 53, entry 109; ANTT, AHMF, CGPM, Extractos, livro 54, entry 16.

[21] ANTT, AHMF, CGPM, Extractos, livro 53, entry 61. In 1737, a woman who may have been her grandmother (also named Joanna Baptista) was said to be involved in a sexual relationship with a clergyman (Bernardino de Sena Leytão), the two of them orchestrating the shipment of slaves to Brazil. AHU, Guiné, cx. 6, doc. 95.

largest export from the region in the eighteenth and early nineteenth centuries.[22]

The work of *moradores* and *grumetes* was dangerous; at times, some were captured by interior groups. When this occurred, *moradores* and *grumetes* were either killed, ransomed back to their communities, or sold as slaves, eventually being boarded on ships for the Americas. White and brown *moradores* could fetch high ransoms, but young male warriors could also prove themselves particularly brave by hacking captives to death and then displaying their body parts. (The image of whites as witches may have contributed to the glory bestowed on those who killed them.) Black *moradores* and *grumetes* were usually either ransomed or sold as slaves.[23] However, when they were made captive, *moradores* and *grumetes* used their profession of Christianity as a justification for their release. This strategy often worked with Portuguese shippers. The CGPM frequently met resistance when it tried to export *grumetes* and members of *moradores'* extended families. But this tactic did not often work with the British and French. These "foreigners," observers claimed, purchased "Portuguese" Christians obtained in Mandinka raids on Farim, and they exported them through ports to the north.[24] Portuguese officials claimed in 1751 that the British and French frequently traded "arms and iron not

---

[22] António Carreira, *Os Portuguêses nos rios de Guiné (1500–1900)* (Lisbon: Editorial Presença, 1984), 71.

[23] See, for example, descriptions of captures of *moradores* and *grumetes* in Walter Hawthorne, *Planting Rice and Harvesting Slaves: Transformations along the Guinea-Bissau Coast, 1400–1900* (Portsmouth, NH: Heinemann, 2003), 134–5. Attempts were also made to ransom white sailors on oceangoing vessels when they were captured while visiting the coast. When American Elbridge G. Woodward was captured by Balanta after he left a U.S. flag ship near Bissau, Joze Nozolini arranged his release "by paying the price of two prime slaves only, he being sick." American Seamen's Friend Society, *Sailor's Magazine and Naval Journal* 6 (1834), 243. Similarly, see Brown University Library, Center for Digital Initiatives, "Brig Sally's Account Book," p. 37, for account of redeeming an American sailor in the 1750s. http://dl.lib.brown.edu/repository2/repoman.php?v erb=render&id=1161038386638650.

[24] On ransoming Christians, AHU, Guiné, cx. 10, doc 26; cx. 13, doc. 53. In 1776, an observer described Christians captured outside *praças* being "ransomed by their relatives" and discussed the company's obligation not to trade them overseas. AHU, Guiné, cx. 11, doc. 21. The ransoming of *moradores* had long been the practice, as was done in 1697 when Balanta captured residents of Bissau. AHU, códice 489, fl. 139. On ransoming of *grumetes*, AHU, Guiné, cx. 11, doc. 43. Reports describe the capture of many Christians in Farim. AHU, Cape Verde, cx. 35, doc. 15. On selling of Christians into the slave trade, see AHU, Guiné, cx. 6, doc. 33. In 1793, disturbances racked Bissau when *grumetes* were loaded on a ship. AHU, Guiné, cx. 14, doc. 62. On killing, Hawthorne, *Planting Rice*, 133–39. There is a detailed description of *grumetes* being seized by Manjaco and one of them redeeming himself in the 1790s in Beaver, *Africa Memoranda*, 176.

only to obtain slaves who are still infidels but also who have knowledge of the faith."[25]

The above discussion should make clear that the slave trade linked to Cacheu and Bissau did not operate in the manner that is often depicted in studies of other slaving regions. Ship captains did not deal with African kings who monopolized slave exports and who controlled armies that rounded up large numbers of slaves in wars.[26] Further, large caravans moving slaves from distant points in the interior did not supply the bulk of captives exported from Bissau and Cacheu.[27] Generalizations about the slave trade in Africa requiring very large capital outlays to equip caravans and being "dominated," therefore, "by the political and military leaders of African societies, who controlled the process and the product of military enslavement" cannot be applied to the trade to Bissau and Cacheu.[28] By the early nineteenth century, one caravan route did exist in the region. Traveling through Kaabu from Sumakonda to Seraconda and then to Geba, French explorer Gaspard Mollien described the road as "almost impassable" in the rainy season but "covered with slave-dealers and salt-merchants; the latter came from Geba and were going into the countries situated to the east; the former, on the contrary, were going towards the sea-coast to the west; they drove their slaves, who were fastened together by the neck, with long sticks."[29]

However, as data (Chapters 1 and 2) show, the bulk of slaves exported from Bissau and Cacheu hailed from the immediate coastal zone, west of Geba, not east of it. Near the coast, individual or small groups of slaves

---

[25] ANTT, AHMF, CGPM, Extractos, Concelho da Fazenda, livro 349, fl. 240.

[26] For example, Robert Harms, *The Diligent: A Voyage through the Worlds of the Slave Trade* (New York: Basic Books, 2002), 149–264; Robin Law, *Ouidah: The Social History of a West African Slaving "Port"* (Athens: Ohio University Press, 2004).

[27] Joseph C. Miller, *Way of Death: Merchant Capitalism and the Angolan Slave Trade, 1730–1830* (Madison: The University of Wisconsin Press, 1988), 148.

[28] Quote from Robin Law, "Slave-Raiders and Middlemen, Monopolists and Free-Traders: The Supply of Slaves for the Atlantic Trade in Dahomey, c. 1715–1850," *Journal of African History* 30, 1 (1989), 45. See also, Paul E. Lovejoy and J. S. Hogendorn, "Slave Marketing in West Africa," in *The Uncommon Market: Essays in the Economic History of the Atlantic Slave Trade*, eds. H. A. Gemery and J. S. Hogendorn (New York: Academic Press, 1979), 213–32; Richard L. Roberts, *Warriors, Merchants and Slaves* (Palo Alto, CA: Stanford University Press, 1987), 13. There are exceptions. See David Northrup, *Trade without Rulers: Pre-Colonial Economic Developments in South-Eastern Nigeria* (Oxford: Clarendon Press, 1978), 93–4; Robert W. Harms, *River of Wealth, River of Sorrow: The Central Zaire Basin in the Era of the Slave and Ivory Trade 1500–1891* (New Haven, CT: Yale University Press, 1981).

[29] Gaspard Mollien, *Travels in the Interior of Africa to the Sources of the Senegal and Gambia* (London: Frank Cass, 1967), 316–17.

were filtered through the region's dense forests and mangrove swamps, as *moradores* and their *grumete* employees extracted them from multiple locations and moved them along countless small creeks and into rivers. On rivers, they took slaves to Geba and Farim and then to Bissau and Cacheu – or, they would go directly to these two coastal ports. Most slaves arriving in Bissau and Cacheu could measure the time since they were handed over to *moradores* or their minions in days or weeks, not in months. The majority could measure the distance from Bissau and Cacheu to the places they were made captive in tens of miles, not hundreds.

Along with *moradores* and their employees, a second set of slave buyers operated in the hinterlands of Bissau and Cacheu. Unlike most *moradores*, their skin color was black (and only black), and they had African (not Christian baptismal) names. These were people from coastal rural communities who were intermediaries in the slave trade. Hence, Balanta groups dubbed *bravo* or "wild," because they were "so wicked that they will not allow any whites in their lands," were said to sell captives "to other black neighbors" and "other pagans" who then passed them onto *moradores*.[30] Some Floup, too, disliked engaging with merchants from Bissau and Cacheu, so they sold slaves through area middlemen, especially Brames and Mandinka.[31] However, it should be emphasized that many Balanta and Floup, like people from other groups, dealt directly with *moradores*, whom they met in rural areas and visited in area *praças*. Direct dealings with *moradores* became more regularlized in the mid-eighteenth century, when the prices paid for slaves increased in Upper Guinea, tempting more and more people to enter the market.[32]

Of Upper Guinea ethnic groups, Papel had the most regular and ongoing relationships with *moradores*. This was especially true of Papel based on the island of Bissau, which became the focal point of Portuguese efforts to export slaves from Upper Guinea in the second half of the eighteenth century. But some Bijago, too, regularly met with *moradores*. At times, powerful Bijago warriors took their slaves directly to *praças*. For this, *moradores* competed for the favor of Bijago, often paying large

[30] André de Faro, "Relaçam (1663–1664)," in *André de Faro's Missionary Journey to Sierra Leone in 1663–1664*, trans. P. E. H. Hair (Sierra Leone: University of Sierra Leone, Institute of African Studies, 1982), 69; Mateo de Anguiano, *Misiones capuchinas en África* (Madrid: Instituto Santo Toribio de Mogrovejo, 1950), 116, 143; Havik, *Silences*, 97.

[31] Robert Martin Baum, *Shrines of the Slave Trade: Diola Religion and Society in Precolonial Senegambia* (New York: Oxford University Press, 1999), 109, 115.

[32] Hawthorne, *Planting Rice*, 136; Havik, *Silences*, 90, 97; Baum, *Shrines*, 110–17.

sums in *daxa*, or tribute, to them.[33] In the 1810s, Mollien penned a vivid description of the arrival of Bijago boats in Bissau.

The inhabitants of the Archipelago of the Bissagos visit Bissao for the purpose of selling rice and slaves. On their arrival at Bissao, these Negroes exclaim; "here is a vessel from the Bissagos!" and a market is immediately opened on the beach; they bring fruits the large size of which proves the fertility of the soil in their islands.... I saw three hundred and fifty slaves arrive in one month at the Portuguese establishments.[34]

The *moradores* of Bissau and Cacheu also traveled to the Bijagos Islands to obtain slaves – a writer in 1776 saying that this trade had been going on "as long as can be remembered."[35] On the Bijagos, slaves abounded, but competition for them was often fierce. This was largely because Portugal had no official presence on the islands, so British and French merchants frequented them and drove up prices.[36] Further, *filhos da terra* purchased slaves from the Bijagos Islands, trading them to French and British ship captains. Such was the case with Luis Pessoa, who lived on the Pongo River and sent boats to the Bijagos. These boats returned with slaves for English vessels that anchored near Pessoa's factory. Pessoa also controlled a vessel at Cacheu, which he used to purchase slaves for sale to the English.[37]

Although their dealings with foreign interlopers infuriated CGPM administrators, local *moradores* and *filhos da terra* were heavily relied upon by the company to supply it with slaves. The importance of local merchants for the company became especially apparent in 1766, when Sebastião da Cunha Souto-Mayor, the Portuguese government's chief representative in Bissau, prohibited the circulation of "white merchants in canoes on rivers" and the entrance into *praças* of *grumetes* with trade slaves. A CGPM administrator wrote a letter to the king of Portugal in 1767 describing this prohibition as causing "great harm to this Company." Begging for a lifting of the ban, he said of white merchants and *grumetes*, "that population is very vital to commerce."[38]

---

[33] Havik, *Silences*, 115–16.
[34] Mollien, *Travels*, 336.
[35] AHU, Guiné, cx. 11, doc. 7, 57; AHU, Guiné, cx. 33, doc. 21.
[36] AHU, Guiné, cx. 11, doc. 14; AHU, Cape Verde, cx. 33, doc. 21.
[37] AHU, Guiné, cx. 12, doc. 24.
[38] AHU, Guiné, cx. 10, doc. 28, 30. Why Souto-Mayor posted the ban is unknown. Because he, himself, was deeply engaged in the slave trade, he may have been trying to undercut area rivals.

Souto-Mayor's was not the only attempt to regulate *morador* activities. In 1773, CGPM flirted with expanding what were limited direct connections to rural, black African slave suppliers. In effect, this would have cut out *morador* middlemen (and -women).[39] Further, in 1776, the governor of Cacheu reported that company administrator Pedro Rodrigues had angered *moradores* by attempting to restrict their activities. His actions were widely viewed as "insufferable" and so far afield of what was appropriate that, in the governor's words, he had proven himself to be "a crazy man."[40] And in 1777, fourteen *moradores* of Geba complained that company administrators João da Costa and João Antonio Pereia were impeding the flow of goods into ports, taking "our slaves" only for very low prices, "robbing publically all that we had" on boats of Antonio Franz Martins and others, buying goods directly from African "kings" and not Christians, and interfering in a long-standing salt trade from the coast to the interior.[41] Company officials who stayed on the coast for some time also angered *moradores* by favoring their own "girlfriends" (i.e., local women who supplied slaves to and often served as domestic partners for company officials) in trade relations.[42]

Moradores did not, then, always view the CGPM favorably. Nonetheless, they continued to trade with the company and vice versa. Neither side had much choice. *Moradores* needed a trading partner, and the company was well established in the region. The company needed slaves, and *moradores* had connections to slave suppliers. Further, because administrators came and went – some (but not all) spending only brief periods of time on the coast and many becoming ill from malaria – they had few opportunities to establish long-term relationships of trust with many people.[43]

THE *PRAÇAS* OF GEBA, BISSAU, FARIM, AND CACHEU

Moradores, their *grumetes*, and black African merchants took slaves obtained in communities near the Geba River either directly to Bissau or to "bulking stations" in Geba. Bulking stations were trade houses in which slavers amassed cargoes for shipment downriver to Bissau. Also, in trade houses, merchants conducted exchanges among themselves. In

---

[39] AHU, Guiné, cx. 10, doc. 14.
[40] AHU, Guiné, cx. 11, doc. 21.
[41] AHU, Guiné, cx. 11, doc. 47.
[42] Havik, *Silences*, 233.
[43] AHU, Guiné, cx. 11, doc. 1.

Geba, *moradores* (all of whom had links to Bissau) as well as Mandinka and Fula (many of whom arrived with people enslaved to the east) owned trade houses.[44] The slave trade operated similarly along the Cacheu River. Slaves purchased from communities near the Cacheu were taken either directly to the port of Cacheu or first to Farim and then downriver to Cacheu. Farim, like Geba, was the site of bulking stations and a place where Christians and Muslims met to do business.[45]

In both Geba and Farim, houses typically had enclosed yards (*quintais*) and barracoons, or slave-holding houses (known as *funkus* locally), most often made of thatch and wood.[46] In barracoons, it was typical for slaves who arrived from scattered places to be crammed closely together. Naked, they were kept in irons. Lacking proper sanitation facilities, protection against the elements (particularly rain, which could come in torrents in the wet season), and defenses against mosquito infiltration, barracoons were hellish places where disease could spread easily, and slaves could become sick and weak. Given this, it is understandable (Chapter 2) why slaves saw those who held them as witches. Merchants sapped their captives' energy, gaining wealth and power from their misfortune.[47]

It was in bulking stations that coastal people snatched one by one in raids or kidnappings, or condemned individually in trials found themselves among other enslaved people for the first time. Bulking stations were, then, the first places where many newly enslaved people could forge bonds with others holding a similar fate. It was in these places that captives from different communities and varying ethnic groups began to see themselves as sharing a common state: they were all slaves. Whatever their cultural differences, Floup, Brame, Balanta, Mandinka, Biafada, and Nalu who sat naked, chained, and guarded were now one. They had all been alienated from their communities. They were all in the grip of witches. And they all began a process of forging new human connections with others around them.

---

[44] AHU, Guiné, cx. 9, doc. 60.

[45] AHU, Guiné, cx. 11, doc. 20, 57, 63; AHU, Cabo Verde, cx. 17, doc. 64. However, long-standing conflicts between Muslims and Christians frequently disrupted trade in Farim. Indeed, it was the site of ongoing warfare. AHU, códice 489, fl. 136; AHU, Guiné, cx. 13, doc. 1, 13, 53; AHU, Guiné, cx. 14, doc 1-A; AHU, Cape Verde, cx. 35, doc. 11, 15, 32.

[46] See mention of a *quintal* in ANTT, Feitos findos, Juíz da India e Mina, Juízo das Justificações Ultramarinos, África, mç. 24, n. 8-A, cx. 42. Havik mentions *funkus* in *Silences*, 67, 225, 358.

[47] See description of a barracoon on the area island of Bolama in "Bolama Arbitration," BNA, CO 879/2, p. 23.

Recognizing their shared status, captives in bulking stations sometimes found common cause against those who abused them. This point is illustrated in documents about João Lucas Cordeiro, a white merchant living in Bissau who had family in Portugal. In December 1798, he paid a visit to a trade house called Ganjar, which was outside Geba and was owned by his business partner Joaquim Pedro Giniour. On a day when few *grumetes* were at the trade house, he decided to "walk by the yard where brute slaves were milling rice." When he was among them, the slaves took up large, wooden pestles and "struck blows on his head, leaving him for dead." To assure that they had accomplished their task, they then "cut his throat." Although Cordeiro did not die immediately, the severity of his wounds meant that the "medicine" he received was not effective. He languished for some time before expiring, a report detailing his death later reaching his wife. Most of the slaves who attacked Cordeiro fled, while the others created a diversion by setting fire to some gunpowder. An explosion ensued, killing many. Eventually those who fled were captured by *grumetes*, who proceeded to decapitate some before Giniour stopped them.[48]

Reports about Cordeiro's death make several things clear. First, shortly after their capture, enslaved people in Upper Guinea, no matter what their ethnic backgrounds, recognized themselves as comprising a group with shared interests. Second, newly enslaved people often resisted their oppressors, and they did so not always as individuals but as members of a group. And finally, slaving was a dangerous business because slaves could do great harm to those who held them. For all of these reasons, *moradores* sought to pass slaves in their possession onto the CGPM in Bissau and Cacheu as quickly as possible. Trade slaves, then, rarely spent much time in Geba and Farim. Having been "bulked" in groups large enough to fill boats or canoes, they were transported with haste toward the coast where *moradores* attempted to convert them into a less risky form of wealth or to pass them onto those to whom they owed debts for goods advanced for trade.

Moradores often accepted goods from company administrators in Bissau and Cacheu, promising them that they would pay their debt with captives to be delivered in the future. They then took the goods they

---

[48] ANTT, Feitos findos, Juíz da India e Mina, Juízo das Justifiações Ultramarinos, África, mç. 24, n. 8-A, cx. 42. Upon being informed of his death, Cordeiro's wife arranged to have his assets liquidated in Bissau and his slaves (he owned forty-four) and trade goods shipped to Maranhão for sale. ANTT, Junta do Comércio, mç. 63, cx. 203.

accepted into the interior (hoping that they would not be robbed of them) and traded them for people enslaved by area groups.[49] Once a trade had been made, *moradores*, themselves, realized losses if slaves in their possession died before they were delivered to CGPM officials. Moreover, *moradores* absorbed costs from having to feed, guard, and defend slaves from would-be thieves. Passing slaves off to another owner quickly was the best course of action.

As for CGPM, when it established itself in Cacheu and Bissau, company administrators faced two choices about how to conduct business. The company could take possession of slaves from *moradores after* ships destined for Amazonia arrived in port, or it could take possession of slaves *before* ships arrived for embarkation. The advantage of the former strategy was that the company would not assume the risk of (and profit loss from) slaves dying, being stolen, or fleeing while in its possession. The time between ship arrivals ranged from days to weeks to months. If, then, the company waited to take possession of slaves, it could avoid considerable losses by passing risks onto *moradores*, who would have to wait to unload captives they had.

The advantage of taking possession of slaves from *moradores before* company ships reached port was, as one administrator noted, that the company would be "assured that all of the slaves would be ready," so ships would have to delay "only a little time" in port. Setbacks in embarking slaves slowed the flow of captives to Amazonia and the flow of rice, cotton, and other exports from Amazonia to Lisbon.[50] The faster these ships could get from Lisbon to Cacheu and Bissau and from there to São Luís and Belém and then back to Lisbon, the sooner they could prepare for another circuit. For the CGPM, time lost was money lost. Further, administrators thought that if the company took possession of slaves quickly, independent area merchants would continue to sell it slaves because they would not experience delays in making transactions. In an area in which French and British interlopers frequently broke the CGPM's monopoly and often paid high prices for captives, a willingness to take possession of slaves when they were available would give the CGPM a competitive advantage.

Historian António Carreira notes that ultimately the company decided that it was "most economical and most convenient" to have slaves waiting in its storehouses for ships to arrive.[51] Thus, ship captains sailing

---

[49] On attacks on boats and houses, AHU, Guiné, cx. 11, doc. 20, 30, 43.
[50] ANTT, AHMF, CGPM, Copiadores, Cartas para Cacheu e Bissau, livro 98, fl. 30–1.
[51] Ibid. For analysis, António Carreira, *As companhias pombalinas de navegação comércio e tráfico de escravos entre a costa Africana e o nordeste Brasileiro* (Bissau: Centro de Estudos de Guiné Portuguesa, 1969), 146–7.

for the company were instructed in a manner similar to Captain Joseph dos Santos, who sailed from Lisbon to Cacheu in 1760 on the *N.S. da Esperança*. Once he reached Cacheu, he was to "go personally to the Administrator of the Company, Manoel Ferreira de Oliveira, giving him any letters that he had received for delivery ... and arranging for the disembarkation [of goods carried on board] as quickly as possible." He was then to embark "on the same ship all of the slaves that are of your capacity to transport without delay of time to the port city of São Luiz of Maranhão."[52] And for much time to come, administrators operated in this fashion. "It was always the custom," the governor of the fort of Cacheu wrote in 1776, "for the company to take the slaves that the residents buy from the pagans."[53]

Where the company kept slaves in Cacheu and Bissau is not clear from available sources. Indeed, there is little in any source from the period about the lives of trade slaves in the ports. At the start of its charter, the company had few facilities in Bissau. However, it made efforts to establish itself there and, ultimately, exported more slaves from Bissau than Cacheu. Bissau offered the advantage of being closer to two major slave supply centers – the Bijagos and Geba. In 1755, the company assumed responsibility from the state for finishing a fort that the Portuguese government had begun in 1752. Progress was slow, the project not being completed until 1775.[54] At some point, the company succeeded in building what Carreira says was "an enormous storehouse for slaves."[55] But beyond occasional notes that the slaves of the company were kept in irons, little was ever written about their state while in company possession.[56]

What is clear is that storing slaves together in Cacheu and Bissau for periods stretching from days to months presented problems. First, in company barracoons, slaves had to be guarded against thieves.[57] Second, because the bulk of captives exported from Bissau and Cacheu

---

52 ANTT, AHMF, CGPM, Copiadores, Cartas para Cacheu e Bissau, livro 98, fl. 2–3. Similar orders for another captain are on fl. 5–9, 24, 34–5.
53 AHU, Guiné, cx. 11, doc. 21. In this instance, D. Maria Nunes was complaining that the company was refusing to purchase one of her slaves.
54 Walter Rodney, *A History of the Upper Guinea Coast, 1545 to 1800* (New York: Monthly Review Press, 1970), 246; Avelino Teixeira da Mota, *Guiné portuguesa* (Lisbon: Agência Geral do Ultramar, 1954), 2: 27; Bernardino António Álvares de Andrade, *Planta da praça de Bissau e suas adjacentes*, ed. Damião Peres (Lisbon: Academia Portuguesa da História, 1952); N. Valdez dos Santos, "As fortalezas de Bissau," *Boletim cultural da Guiné Portuguesa* 26 (1971), 481–519.
55 Carreira, *As companhias*, 77.
56 AHU, Guiné, cx. 10, doc. 30.
57 AHU, Guiné, cx. 10, doc. 32; AHU, Guiné, cx. 11, doc. 20.

were taken from the nearby area, many knew the territory and could plot escape. Finally, as slaves sat in barracoons, they were weakened by the spread of illness. Ailments ranged from dysentery to smallpox (one of the worst killers of slaves) to malaria (acquired from mosquitoes, which were ubiquitous on the coast). Needless to say, the sick and weak did not fare well on the passage to Amazonia. Those who did fetched low prices. Illness also led to slaves' deaths in Bissau and Cacheu (and, therefore, to the loss of company revenue). Hence in the 1770s, a series of brief entries in diaries note the monetary losses suffered from "86 slaves who died or fled," "27 slaves who died or fled," and "29 of 36 slaves who fled."[58] Other reports assess losses from a mother and daughter who fled and a woman who died.[59]

All told, losses from the flight and death of slaves in Bissau and Cacheu were great. From 1763 to 1768, about forty-four slaves per year died or escaped after the company purchased them.[60] This was about 4 percent of the total embarked in Bissau and Cacheu for Amazonia over the same period.[61] Between March 1768 and December 1777, the average annual number of slaves lost to flight and death rose to seventy-three.[62] During this period, then, about 7 percent of slaves purchased by the company for shipment

---

[58] ANTT, AHMF, CGPM, Diário, livro 9, no. 516; ANTT, AHMF, CGPM, Diário, livro 11, no. 5349; ANTT, AHMF, CGPM, Diário, livro 12, no. 515.

[59] ANTT, AHMF, CGPM, Diário, livro 12, no. 590; no. 950. In the same report it is written that a soldier was rewarded 4,000 réis for retrieving a female slave who threw herself into the river, indicating that some deaths may have been from suicide. Though not recorded in company records, suicide may have indeed been the cause of some slave deaths. There is one recording of a slave suicide on an American vessel that was boarding slaves on the Rio Grande in the 1750s. On the *Sally*, a slave was said to have "henged [*sic*] herself between the decks." Brown University Library, Center for Digital Initiatives, "Brig Sally's Account Book," p. 69. http://dl.lib.brown.edu/repository2/repoman.php?verb=render&id=1161038386638650.

[60] Calculation: A record places costs of such occurrences from 1763 to 1768 at 14,320,840 réis. Unfortunately the document does not list the number of slaves lost over the period. However, in 1771 records put the loss of a single slave at an average cost of 65,500 réis (cost varying depending on health, age, and gender). Assuming this was the normal cost of a single slave from 1763 to 1768, about forty-four slaves per year died or escaped after the company purchased them. ANTT, AHMF, CGPM, Diário, livro 13, no. 3559. It is likely that 65,500 réis is an overestimate for the period, so it is likely that many more slaves were lost.

[61] TSTD2.

[62] Calculation: In a document, an official put the total losses from slaves dying or fleeing in Bissau and Cacheu between March 1768 and December 1777 at 49,254,000 réis. Assuming a cost of about 65,500 réis per slave for this period, the company lost about 752 slaves to death or flight – an average of 73 each year. ANTT, AHMF, CGGPM, Diário, livro 12, no. 590.

to Amazonia died or fled before they embarked on vessels in Bissau. The increase from the previous period can probably be attributed to an increase in the volume of slave traffic. More slave arrivals raised the chances of disease spreading and made storage and oversight more complicated.[63]

Records also indicate something about the size of the company's slave holdings. In 1769, when Pedro Roiz de Souza left his post as administrator in Cacheu, the company's books were balanced, revealing that it had 150 slaves. Three of them were "in the service of the house," meaning they were not trade slaves but performed duties for the company. The others were awaiting shipment to Amazonia.[64] Later that year, the company held 196 slaves in Cacheu.[65] In December 1772, it held 226 "slaves for embarkation."[66] In Bissau in 1778, company books listed 148 trade slaves.[67]

Despite efforts to mass slaves in company barracoons, it was often the case that adequate numbers of slaves were not available when ships arrived. Indeed, the 148 captives held in company barracoons in Bissau in 1778 would not have comprised a ship's full cargo. Insufficient numbers of slaves led to postponements in ships' departures. Delays, in turn, translated into greater suffering among slaves who sat chained together in barracoons – needing to be fed, kept healthy, and guarded – while more slaves were acquired for waiting ships.

When ships could not acquire full cargoes in Bissau or Cacheu, the company had several options. First, ships could leave Bissau and Cacheu with only partial cargo. This, however, did not often occur because it decreased revenues.[68] Second, if a ship was in Bissau with only a partial load of slaves, it could be sent to Cacheu to complete its cargo. Similarly, ships with a partial load in Cacheu often traveled south to Bissau.[69]

---

[63] In 1770, a report listed total losses to flight and death at seventy-four, so this estimate seems reasonable. In 1768, a report listed seventy-three slaves having died or fled over the course of the year. ANTT, AHMF, CGGPM, Mestre, livro 22, p. 120.

[64] ANTT, AHMF, CGPM, Extractos, livro 53, entry 60.

[65] ANTT, AHMF, CGPM, Extractos, livro 53, entry 111.

[66] ANTT, AHMF, CGPM, Extractos, livro 53, entry 143.

[67] ANTT, AHMF, CGPM, Extractos, livro 53, entry 372.

[68] ANTT, AHMF, CGPM, Copiadores, Cartas para Cacheu e Bissau, livro 98, fl. 34–5.

[69] Among many examples is the *N.S. da Esperança* in 1764. See, ANTT, AHMF, CGPM, Livro mestre, 26, fl. 56; Livro das carregações, 48 D, no. 8; ANTT, AHMF, CGPM, Diário, livro 9, no. 64, 68, and 1028; ANTT, AHMF, CGPM, Livro dos navios, 65, fl. 380; ANTT, AHMF, CGPM, Cartas para o Maranhão, livro 230, fl. 91. And the *N.S. Necessidades* in 1766. ANTT, AHMF, CGPM, Livro das carregações, 48 D, no. 110, 112, and 139; ANTT, AHMF, CGPM, Livro mestre, 26, p. 56; ANTT, AHMF, CGPM, Diário, livro 9, no. 1052, 1297; ANTT, AHMF, CGPM, Diário, livro 10, no. 1493.

This increased the time that slaves spent on vessels, elevating their suffering, and often increasing death rates. But the cruel calculation that administrators made was that the risk of increased death was preferable to sailing without full cargoes. Third, captains could fill out their cargoes by taking on slaves that local residents wanted shipped to Cape Verde. When residents loaded slaves on company vessels, they paid a freight charge. They could also pay freight charges for trade goods (such as beeswax) that they wanted shipped to Lisbon. Often, slaves carried to Cape Verde were "of a quality not suited for shipment to Pará and Maranhão."[70]

Fourth, the company could wait for *moradores* and local African groups to supply more slaves to them. There was a problem with this strategy. That is, when locals knew the company was desperate to get a ship on its way, they often raised their asking prices for trade slaves. The company could refuse to pay the price, resort to threats, or seek other ways to acquire captives. But whatever it did, delays meant costs from feeding and guarding slaves increased, as did the risk of disease spreading and losses mounting from death. The elaborate gamesmanship that went into filling ships' hulls often resulted in increased misery for captives. Floup, Balanta, Papel, Bijago, Mandinka, Nalu, Brame, and Fula slaves, who were held in stinking barracoons, suffered together, desperately plotting escape but finding few opportunities.[71]

Finally, when sufficient slaves were not available to fill waiting ships in Bissau and Cacheu, administrators sometimes sent smaller boats to purchase slaves from points south along the coast or from the Bijagos Islands. In 1776, slaves were purchased on the Bijagos to help fill the hulls of ships leaving for Pará.[72] In 1767, a company boat was dispatched to Sierra Leone "to buy up to forty slaves."[73] And in 1768, another was sent out, retrieving slaves that filled out the cargo holds of the *N.S. Antonio* and *N.S. Pedro* that were docked at Bissau.[74] Further, company records indicate that trade goods were advanced some years to kings and powerful merchants in Sierra Leone with the expectation that they would repay their debt in slaves.[75] However, the problem the Portuguese faced south

---

[70] ANTT, AHMF, CGPM, Copiadores, Cartas para Cacheu e Bissau, livro 98, fl. 45–53.

[71] AHU, Maranhão, cx. 53, doc. 5060.

[72] AHU, Guiné, cx. 11, doc. 14.

[73] AHU, Guiné, cx. 9, doc. 71.

[74] ANTT, CGPM, Livro mestre, 26, p. 233; ANTT, AHMF, CGPM, Diário, livro 10, no. 2415, 2422; ANTT, AHMF, CGPM, Livro das carregações, 48 D, no. 167, 194.

[75] ANTT, AHMF, CGPM, Extractos, livro 54, entry 16.

from Bissau was British competition, and the British, reports claimed, paid much higher prices for slaves.[76]

In addition to sending small boats to purchase slaves to augment ships' cargoes, CGPM at times sent boats to purchase rice and other foodstuffs to sustain captives on their journey across the Atlantic. Such was the case in June 1766 when the *N.S. Marçal* sat in harbor loaded with slaves but without sufficient provisions to reach Amazonia. Rice being unavailable in Bissau, the *N.S. do Rozario* was dispatched south to the Pongo River.[77] Later that same year, an official in Bissau noted that food was lacking because locals frequently refused to trade except at exorbitant prices.[78] Of course, slaves had to be fed on the journey to Amazonia, so insufficient food in company warehouses added to delays that ships faced in port. If food shortages were severe enough, slaves loaded on ships or held in company barracoons went hungry, adding to their misery, weakening them, and heightening the risk of death.

Evidently, the company's strategy of purchasing slaves far in advance of ship arrivals led to relatively unhealthy slaves being boarded on ships for Maranhão and Pará between 1755 to 1778. Over that period (the duration of the company's monopoly), slave deaths on the ocean between Upper Guinea and Amazonia averaged 7.5 percent. However, from 1779 through 1800, they averaged 4.9 percent. It seems likely, then, that once company administrators had slaves in their possession, they sent them off to Pará and Maranhão no matter what their condition. When healthy slaves fell ill in company barracoons, they were, nonetheless, boarded on ships. The company owned them. The only way to redeem costs was to sell them in Amazonia. But once the company's monopoly ended, there was no longer an entity in Bissau and Cacheu from which to purchase slaves far in advance of the arrival of ships. Rather, with the demise of the company, it was coastal merchants who held slaves in barracoons in Bissau and Cacheu. These merchants – *moradores* – waited for ships to arrive so that they could strike deals with captains. Ship captains had little incentive to purchase sick and unhealthy slaves. They might take some at a discount to fill out shipments, but if slaves abounded in port, they could choose those they thought most likely to survive the passage to Amazonia and most likely to fetch high prices.

---

[76] For example, AHU, Guiné, cx. 9, doc. 71.

[77] AHU, Guiné, cx. 9, doc. 60.

[78] AHU, Guiné, cx. 9, doc. 67. Also on food shortages in Bissau AHU, Guiné, cx. 11, doc. 60.

AFTER THE COMPANY

After 1778, then, *moradores* bore increased risks because they often held slaves for extended periods waiting for ships to arrive. They had to feed their trade slaves, try to keep them healthy, and guard them. When slaves died, *moradores* suffered financial losses. This was made clear in 1798 when Antonio Joze Carlos wrote a letter from Bissau to merchant Antonio Esteves Costa in Portugal. Discussing trade with Maranhão, Carlos complained that "slaves are on hand" but "in great danger for a lack of ships." He went on to describe how he "traveled all the rivers that could be found." Having acquired many slaves, he was suffering great financial losses because "it is not possible to have slaves two years and sustain them." He then discussed a failed attempt to board slaves on another vessel that "could not carry as many slaves as there are." He concluded, "If you want to trade with me, I am very ready but you need to send good merchandise for me to supply good cargo." A short time later, Carlos sent another letter to Lisbon, complaining of a "lack of trade goods here [in Bissau], which forced me to send the little that I have to Cacheu to buy trade goods to be used to purchase food to sustain the slaves that I have here for Senhor Carabone." He again complained that he had been trying to sustain slaves for two years but "almost all" had died.[79]

There was, indeed, rarely a perfect correspondence between when slaves were available in Bissau and Cacheu for shipment and when ships were in port to load them. As in the days of the company's monopoly, after 1778 captains sometimes found an abundance of slaves in ports and at other times found a dearth. In 1799, a captain who was on one of five ships that sailed from Lisbon to Bissau related how the vessels were forced to delay fifty-eight days waiting for sufficient slave cargo. Over this time, many crew became sick and some died. The governor of Bissau facilitated trade for the ships, eventually ordering a boat to go to Ziguinchor to inquire if *moradores* there had captives on hand.[80]

After the company's monopoly ended, powerful local merchants continued to use the machinery of the state to buttress their own interests.[81] Around Ziguinchor, individuals with the names Alvarenga, Carvalho, and Carvalho Alvarenga dominated trade and government. Around

---

[79] BNP, Mss. 224, no. 376.
[80] AHU, Maranhão, cx. 107, doc. 8479.
[81] ANTT, Junta do Comércio, mç. 63, cx. 203, no. 12.

Cacheu, it was the Barretos who filled the void left by the CGPM. In the 1770s, João Pereira Barreto, a Luso-African who hailed from São Tiago of the Cape Verde Islands, moved to Cacheu. With a slave woman, he had two sons – João Pereira Barreto and António Teixeira Barreto. The family formed an alliance with the powerful Rosa de Carvalho Alvarenga, giving members influence over trade in the Cacheu–Ziguinchor area. The Barreto sons ascended through the ranks of the military and government, using their posts to further their family's business, which was centered in Cacheu and included property in Maranhão. The most successful of the Barretos was Honório Pereira Barreto, who became a renowned slave trader and, in 1858, governor of the areas Portugal claimed in Guinea.[82]

Farther south, on the Geba, other brokers controlled trade and government. In the 1790s, one of the most powerful traders in Bissau was former governor Ignacio Xavier Baião. He regularly contracted ships to take slaves to Amazonia.[83] Also trading in Bissau was Thomas de Costa Ribeiro, who came to dominate slave traffic in 1807 and 1808.[84] He competed with Joaquim António de Mattos and Caetano José Nozolini, who operated along the Geba. After Ribeiro's death in 1816, Nozolini took advantage of his marriage to influential Bijago Mãe Aurélia Correia to become Bissau's leading merchant. He also established a factory on Bolama, from which he orchestrated slave shipments to Cuba and Maranhão, where he owned property. As for Mattos, he struck a partnership with Mãe Júlia da Silva Cardoso, providing him links to African slave suppliers.[85]

Besides these men, smaller traders competed for business, often taking advances from the wealthy and paying debts in slaves. The nature of such relationships is made clear in Manoel Antonio Claudino's 1805 will. When he wrote it, he was sick in bed in Geba. He said that he had been born in Traz os Montes, Portugal, and was not married. For goods advanced for slave trading, he noted that he owed unnamed amounts to Joze Bento Garcia in Lisbon, Thomas da Costa Ribeiro in Bissau, and Captain João Rodrigues Bicho, who had a trade house in Bissau and went regularly to Amazonia on the *Santo Antonio Vitorioso*. Claudino also

---

[82] Brooks, *Eurafricans*, 285–7; Havik, *Silences*, 200–30.

[83] AHU, Maranhão, cx. 75, doc. 6460.

[84] AHU, Guiné, cx. 19, doc. 10, 58.

[85] On Ribeiro's death, ANTT, Feitos findos, Juíz da India e Mina, Juízo das Justifiações Ultramarinos, África, mç. 8, n. 11, cx. 3. On Nozolini and Mattos, Brooks, *Eurafricans*, 295, 310–11; Havik, *Silences*, 267–88.

claimed to owe Joaquim Antonio de Mattos two slaves for tobacco and Joaquim dos Santos seven slaves for alcohol. And he owned various slaves who worked for him, some *grumetes*, and trade slaves – nineteen males, nine females, and nine children. Further, he had trade goods "in the house of Beatriz, a widow and *moradora* of this population of Geba." Among them were a slave named Julia, alcohol, and kola nuts. With the female merchant Mai Gregoria, he had white cloth and alcohol. Elsewhere he held other slaves – Elefante, Bartholomei, and Cristovão, whom he left to Mai Jeronima and Mai Lourença.[86]

The relationship between wealthy and poor *moradores* in Bissau is also revealed in documents about the seizing of the *N.S. Vitoria* near Bissau by British antislaving vessels in May 1814. The ship was stopped because, the British commander said, it was suspected that slaves on board had come from British possessions along the coast. Records found on the ship indicate that most slaves loaded on it had been supplied by Mattos. However, other *moradores* – D. Anna da Fonseca Pinto, Antonio Leocadio da Costa, Throdozia da Costa, Luís Antonio Estives, Joquim Filipe Telles de Avaellar, and Antonio Leocadio da Costa – supplied some slaves, filling out the load. All told, 424 slaves were boarded for Maranhão.[87]

With the abolition of the slave trade north of the equator in 1815, *moradores* in Upper Guinea continued to ship slaves (in diminished numbers) to Amazonia. They did so by evading British antislaving vessels that patrolled the coast and by exploiting loopholes in international antislaving law. How many dodged antislaving squadrons is not known because by its nature, illegal trading is almost impossible to document. Traders went to great lengths to avoid paper trails. But records taken by British captains and Brazilian and Portuguese port officials in Maranhão hint at the nature of the trade and reveal the continued involvement of Portuguese government officials in it. For example, in 1822 Lieutenant John Mildmay of the ship of war *Iphigena* arrived at Bissau where the *Conde de Vila Flor* was anchored with 192 slaves crammed beneath its decks. The lieutenant seized the vessel, taking its captives to the British colony of Sierra Leone. He wrote, "The voyage commenced at Para and was to have ended at Para." Upon taking the ship, Mildmay planned "to communicate with the Governor at Bissao [Joaquim António de Mattos] but finding that he had a number of slaves on board the detained vessel,

---

[86] AHU, Guiné, cx. 20, doc. 8.
[87] ANRJ, Junta do Comércio, 7x, cx. 371, pct. 1.

it was my opinion that such communication would not be attended with any good effect."[88]

But not all slave shipments from Upper Guinea were considered illegal after 1815. The most exploited loophole in international antislaving law was one that allowed people to move personal (or "domestic") slaves from place to place in the Atlantic. That is, people who owned slaves could ship them to another place for their own use. British observers noted how Africa-based merchants, and especially João Pereira Barreto (who continued to supply Maranhão with considerable numbers of slaves after 1815) took advantage of what were termed "exceptions" to slave-trading prohibitions. Of eleven ship arrivals from Bissau, Cacheu, and Cape Verde to São Luís in Maranhão between 1819 and 1822, a British council wrote of the 1,736 cargo slaves, "All these ... entered as Domesticks, but the whole were openly sold, like any other Slaves."[89]

Hence, in 1819, Antonio Pereira Barreto sailed on the *São João Victorioso* from Cacheu to Maranhão with 228 slaves and his family "with the goal of establishing himself in this captaincy."[90] The vessel was owned by João Pereira Barreto and Caetano José Teixeira. The 203 slaves who survived the oceanic voyage were subsequently sold.[91] Later that year, the *Pombal Feliz* reached Maranhão from Cape Verde with forty-three slaves belonging to Luiz Antonio Estevez Freire. Because the slaves were his personal possession, they were "legitimate for transport," or so local officials argued.[92] A second ship from Cape Verde quickly followed with 125 "domestic slaves" aboard. At least two other ships from Cacheu reached Amazonia the same year (holding a total of 366 of João Barreto's slaves). Each was allowed to disembark captives for sale with no objections coming from local authorities.[93] In 1821, the *Henrique* arrived in Maranhão from Cape Verde. The nineteen slaves on board were the personal property of Joze Antonio Pereira who "comes to establish himself" in the captaincy with his wife and children.[94] Also in 1821, the

---

[88] ANTT, Negocios Estrangeiros, Commissão Mista, cx. 224.

[89] *State Papers* XXVI (21 November 1826–2 July 1827) 2: 109–10.

[90] ANRJ, Ministério do Reino, Maranhão, Registro de Correspondência, IJJ9 42; IJJ9 552; BNA, FO 63/280. Years earlier, João Pereira Barreto was given permission to take his slaves and family to Maranhão. Havik, *Silences*, 208.

[91] TSTD2.

[92] ANRJ, Ministério do Reino, Maranhão, Registro de correspondência, IJJ9 42, Série Interior, AA; ANRJ, Ministério do Reino, Maranhão, Registro de correspondência, IJJ9 552, AA.

[93] *State Papers*, 110; TSTD2.

[94] APEM, Secretaria do Governo, Inventário dos códices, Livro de registro de entradas e saídas das embarcaões no porto, 1820–1822, livro 1320.

Apollo, which was the property of João Pereira Barreto and Antônio José Pinto, reached Maranhão from Cacheu with 231 slaves (239 having been embarked). Antonio Pereira Barreto was aboard the vessel.[95] A ship with eighty-four slaves owned by Joaquim Antonio de Mattos followed months later. And in 1822, Mattos and João Barreto arranged separate shipments of 84 and 224 slaves from Bissau.[96]

In 1823, the brig *Maria* arrived in Maranhão from Bissau with 212 "domestic slaves" belonging to the sixteen-year-old Joaquim Antonio da Silva, "natural of Bissau." Silva was accompanied on the ship by his family. He said that they planned to stay in Maranhão but did not know where they would live. A short time later, Henrique Seasou advertised an auction in Maranhão for "various Cacheu slaves." There can be no doubt that these "Cacheus" had been shipped by Silva.[97] And in 1827, Manoel Pereira Barreto received a license to bring his family and slaves to Maranhão.[98] There are, too, other documented voyages from Upper Guinea to Amazonia (and elsewhere) in the post-1815 period (Table 1.2, Chapter 1; Table 2.1 Chapter 2). All were conducted with the knowledge of government officials on the African coast and in Amazonia. In most cases, officials in Africa – and especially Barreto and Mattos – profited from the voyages.

MIDDLE PASSAGE

Like all slaves exported from Bissau and Cacheu, those sold by Barreto and Mattos faced many horrors once passed off to ship captains.[99] In Bissau and Cacheu, those awful acts sometimes began with branding. In many parts of Africa, Portuguese shippers of slaves branded them before embarkation. Brands provided an easy way to indicate ownership, especially in cases where multiple merchants owned portions of slave cargoes.

---

[95] TSTD2; BNA, FO 63/280.

[96] *State Papers*, 110.

[97] APEM, Secretaria do Governo, Inventários dos avulsos, Oficios do admistrador da alfândega do Maranhão ao governador e capitão-general da capitania do Maranhão, no. 203; *O conciliador*, n. 198, 4 June 1823; *O conciliador*, n. 203, 21 June 1823.

[98] ANRJ, Ministério do Reino. Maranhão. Registro de correspondência. IJJ9 42, Série Interior, AA.

[99] For studies of the slave trade from Africa, see Marcus Rediker, *The Slave Ship: A Human History* (New York: Viking, 2007); Emma Christopher, *Slave Ship Sailors and their Captive Cargo, 1730–1807* (New York: Cambridge University Press, 2006); Stephanie E. Smallwood, *Saltwater Slavery: A Middle Passage from Africa to the American Diaspora* (Cambridge, MA: Harvard University Press, 2007).

In extant documentation about ships sailing from Bissau and Cacheu to Amazonia during the CGPM's monopoly, there is no mention of slaves being branded. Noting this, Carreira wonders if branding took place often in these ports. He records some cases of the branding of company slaves after its monopoly ended in 1778. A total of ninety-five slaves were branded, all between 1783 and 1788.[100]

Although the branding of slaves is rarely mentioned in documents, it is likely that the practice was more commonplace in Bissau and Cacheu after 1777, when independent Portuguese shippers began operating in the ports – multiple merchants often contracting slaves to be carried on ships. To distinguish which merchant owned which slaves, brands were seared into slaves' skin on different parts of their bodies. Brands on a particular place indicated, then, who the owner was. Hence in 1814, nine slaves of Joaquim Antonio de Mattos were branded "on the right chest," forty of Caetano Jozé Teixeira "on the left chest," and seven of João Francisco Carriço "on the right arm." The document listing the locations of brands continues in gruesome detail, slaves having been burned on their backs, bellies, shoulders, and forearms.[101]

When captains were ready to board captives, "the whole of the slaves," an observer noted, "were brought from the shores at Bissau in boats and canoes." The same procedure was used at Cacheu. At neither place was the water deep enough to allow ships to dock. Rather, ships dropped anchor in the deep sections of the Geba and Cacheu Rivers with the crew shuttling goods to shore and slaves to ship. Prior to ships' departures, slaves were taken from barracoons and marched to rivers' banks. Naked and unsure what lay in store, they were pushed into canoes and paddled a short distance to the ships that would be their homes for, on average, a month and a half.[102]

[100] Carreira, *As companhias*, 149–51.
[101] ANRJ, Junta do Comércio, 7x, cx. 371, pct. 1. In Portuguese ports in West Central Africa, it was common for slaves boarding vessels for the Americas to be baptized by a priest. However, in Cacheu and Bissau, the Church hardly had a presence. Further, the baptism of trade slaves is rarely mentioned in sources from Bissau and Cacheu for the period after 1750. In 1697, an order was posted that slaves exported from Cacheu be baptized. But it was noted that few were. AHU, códice 489, fl. 134–7. Many slaves were sold in Maranhão without having been baptized, devout owners later taking them to the Church. See, for example, 1770 baptism of the slave André from Guiné, an adult who was purchased by a priest in Maranhão. APEM, Batismos, livro 107, fl. 35.
[102] On Bissau: Observation of Lieutenant G. W. S. John Mildmay of His Majesty's Ship of War *Iphigena* in ANTT, Negocios Estrangeiros, Commissão Mista, cx. 224. On Cacheu boarding: ANTT, Negocios Estrangeiros, Vária, Papeis Relativos Escravatura, cx. 930, Annexo C, 1834, no. 62.

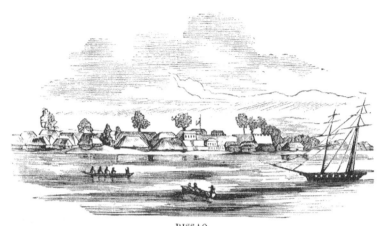

BISSAO.

FIGURE 3.1. Bissau in the mid-nineteenth century.
Source: From: George Thompson, *Palm Land, or West Africa, Illustrated* (Cincinnati: Moore, Wilstach, Keys & Co., Printers, 1859), 87.

Having reached ships, slaves were lifted to deck by crews and then hustled below into areas outfitted for human cargo. There can be no doubt that the trip from Upper Guinea was hell for those locked beneath ships' decks where they were chained, lying or sitting on rough-hewn platforms. Describing typical voyages on Portuguese vessels that left Africa for Brazil in the late eighteenth century, Luiz Antonio de Oliveira Mendes, who wrote from firsthand observations, said, "First of all, with two or three hundred slaves placed under the decks, there is hardly room enough to draw a breath. No air can reach them, except through the hatch gratings and through some square skylights so tiny that not even a head could pass through them." Captains, he continued, brought "a certain number of slaves ... on deck in chains" each day "to get some fresh air, not allowing more because of their fear of rebellion." This, he concluded, accomplished "very little ... because the slaves must go down again into the hold to breathe the same pestilent air." Mendes went on to describe short rations of poor-quality water. Water was heavy and space-consuming and, therefore, costly to transport. For this, shippers did not wish to carry much more than what they anticipated needing. Short supplies of water, then, caused slaves to suffer extraordinarily from "dryness and thirst." Slaves, Mendes said, were also "kept in a state of constant hunger" (food, like water, being costly to purchase and carry).[103]

[103] Conrad, *Children of God's Fire*, 22.

Mahommah Gardo Baquaqua, who was forced onto a Portuguese vessel on the Mina coast and taken to Brazil, later recalled the horrors of his shipboard experience.

We were thrust into the holds of the vessel in a state of nudity, the males being crammed on one side, and the females on the other; the hold was so low that we could not stand up, but were obliged to crouch upon the floor or sit down; day and night were the same to us, sleep being denied us from the confined position of our bodies, and we became desperate through suffering and fatigue.

Only twice, he said, was he brought above deck. He, too, recalled suffering "very much for want to water" and from seasickness. And he recounted the punishment for disobedience. "When any one of us became refractory, his flesh was cut with a knife and pepper or vinegar was rubbed in to make him peaceable." Most barbarous was the crews' treatment of the sick. "Some were thrown overboard before breath was out of their bodies; when it was thought any would not live, they were got rid of in that way."[104] There is no reason to think that slaves aboard vessels leaving Bissau and Cacheu were treated any differently.

However, we have only hints of what life was like on vessels out of these ports. No extant document mentions food allotments for the journey from Bissau and Cacheu.[105] What is documented are the items most often loaded. In the era of the CGPM, those consisted typically of milled rice, water, and palm oil. At times, fruit (especially lemons), vegetables (such as pumpkins), and some meat were purchased for slave ships.[106] But how much food the company distributed to slaves daily is not known. It is clear from records from the *N.S. de Oliveira* in 1774 that African captives received little more than rice and water on Portuguese vessels out of Upper Guinea. The ship's records list cows, chickens, pigs, and palm oil along with 221 slaves boarded at Cacheu. Also listed were "400 alqueires of rice for the slaves." In documentation, rice was the only food item

---

[104] Ibid., 27.
[105] Maria Manuel Torrão attempts to project what allotments might have been in the early years of the trade from Upper Guinea. *Dietas Alimentares: Transferências e Adaptações nas Ilhas de Cabo Verde (1460–1540)* (Lisbon: Ministério do Planeamento e da Administração do Território, 1995), 45–59.
[106] ANTT, AHMF, CGPM, Livro mestre, 26, fl. 56; Livro das carregações, 48 D, no. 70; ANTT, AHMF, CGPM, Cartas para o Maranhão, livro 230, p. 110; ANTT, AHMF, CGPM, Diário, livro 9, no. 567, 1030; ANTT, AHMF, CGPM, Livro mestre, 27, fl. 16; ANTT, AHMF, CGPM, Livro das carregações, 52 H, no. 19; ANTT, AHMF, CGPM, Diario, 12, no. 214; ANTT, AHMF, CGPM, Copiadores, Maranhão, Administadores, livro 220, fl. 18.

specified for slave consumption – it seems that meat was reserved solely for the crew. Assuming a forty-nine-day crossing (the average at the time), each slave would have received about half a liter (two cups) of rice per day. Of course, that is assuming some rice was not withheld for fear of a longer voyage.[107]

After CGPM's monopoly ended, rice continued to be the mainstay of diets on ships leaving the area. The *N.S. Victoria*, seized in 1814 by a British vessel after it left Bissau, had water, 241 sacks of rice, 400 alqueires (340 kilograms, or 750 pounds) of farinha (manioc flour), and 600 sacks of dried beef. Some portion of this was to sustain its slave cargo. Having seized the *Conde de Vila Flor* near Bissau in 1822, British Lieutenant G. W. S. John Mildmay wrote that its "cargo consists of slaves, rice and water."[108]

Slaves taken from Bissau and Cacheu left on ships of more or less the same size from the mid-eighteenth through the early nineteenth centuries. Most were galeras, bergantims, and curvetas. On average, 187 slaves were carried on ships leaving the ports, the average not changing much over the entire period.[109] Nor did the normal duration of oceanic voyages between Upper Guinea and Amazonia change much from 1751 to 1800. The average time of the journey was 49 (n = 6) days under the company's monopoly and 48 days (n = 34) over the two decades that followed.[110] The average number of deaths during the passage from Africa to Amazonia varied from port to port. From 1751 to 1800, 5.1 percent of slaves embarked on ships at Cacheu for Amazonia died. Over the same period, a slightly higher percentage – 6.8 percent – embarked at Bissau died. From West Central Africa (most from Angola, Congo, and Benguela), average deaths in transit to Amazonia were much higher – 15.6 (n = 5) percent for the period 1751 to 1800.

Many factors contributed to slave deaths at sea. Clearly, the longer the voyage, the more deaths one would expect. That is, the more days slaves spent in cramped, filthy quarters, the more likely they were to fall sick and die. However, the nature of winds and currents meant that the voyage from West Central Africa to Amazonia was, in fact, shorter on average than the voyage from Upper Guinea to Amazonia. From 1751 to 1815, the average sailing time from West Central Africa to Amazonia was

---

[107] AHU, Maranhão, cx. 47, doc. 4618.
[108] ANRJ, Junta do Comércio, 7x, cx. 371, pct. 1.
[109] TSTD2.
[110] Ibid.

38.6 days (n = 5; sd = 10.9), about 10 days shorter than from Bissau. A very small sample size for the West Central African voyages makes conclusions tentative, but available data points to sailing times not accounting for differences in average deaths in transit from Upper Guinea and Angola to Amazonia.[111]

Other factors must have been more important. Among the possibilities are differences in the diet, treatment, and health of slaves who were embarked in the two regions. Another possibility is differences in the sizes of the ships that left the two regions. Data does not permit an assessment of how much food slaves received in passage from Upper Guinea to Amazonia compared with West Central Africa to Amazonia. Nor does it allow a study of how slaves were generally treated in the passage between the regions. It is clear, however, that ships leaving West Central Africa were larger than those leaving Upper Guinea – 369 tons versus 238 tons on average between 1751 and 1800. The larger ships leaving West Central Africa carried considerably larger cargoes of slaves than the smaller ships leaving Upper Guinea. On average, 384 slaves arrived on ships reaching Amazonia from West Central Africa and 187 on ships from Upper Guinea. The risk of contagions spreading on ships increased as more slaves were added to it. Moreover, the more tightly packed slaves were on ships, the more likely diseases were to spread among them. And there were fewer slaves per ton on ships out of Upper Guinea than out of Angola.[112]

A final factor contributing to slave deaths at sea was the condition of slaves when they were embarked. Sick and weak slaves, along with old and infant slaves, died in higher proportions than healthy slaves in their teens and twenties. As argued earlier, most slaves boarded on vessels at Cacheu and Bissau had been made captive within tens of miles from the ports. They could measure the time from their capture to their being forced into a barracoon in Cacheu and Bissau in days or weeks. However, slaves forced onto ships at Luanda (a busy port in Angola, West Central Africa, that supplied slaves to Amazonia, among other places) in the eighteenth century, often came from areas hundreds of miles to the interior. Those who survived the trek arrived tired and weak. Moreover, disease was much more commonplace in Luanda than in Bissau and Cacheu. Consequently, slaves were in much worse condition.[113]

---

[111] Ibid.
[112] Ibid.
[113] Miller, *Way of Death*, 148.

Reports of illness outbreaks, especially smallpox, on ships leaving Bissau and Cacheu are relatively scarce.[114] However, onsets of disease on ships leaving Angola were routine. For example, in 1756 the *N.S. da Conceição*, which sailed from Angola to Maranhão, lost a considerable part of the 348 Africans it had embarked to smallpox; some, too, died when the ship ran aground near São Luís. All told, a staggering 193 slaves died.[115] In 1757, the *S. Anna e S. Joaquim* sailed from Angola to Pará. Before the captain boarded any slaves, eighty-four designated for the voyage died. Eventually, the captain loaded 508 slaves, losing 129 to disease before reaching Belém.[116] The following year, slaves on the ships *S. Luís de França* and *N.S. da Atalaia*, both out of Angola for Pará, suffered mightily – about one in five dying in transit and dozens more before embarkation.[117] In a description of slaves on another voyage of the *N.S. da Conceição* (this one from Angola in 1759), an official in Pará said that "of the 500 embarked 122 died during the voyage, the remaining 368 [*sic*.], being the major part of them boys, and all arriving with fevers and so emaciated as to appear like skeletons rather than the living."[118] Large losses of life were also seen on the *S. João Batista* in 1762. The captain acquired 585 slaves in Angola. Of those, ninety-four died before embarkation, and others were too sick to load, so the captain left them. Ultimately, the captain embarked 424 with 111 dying on the voyage.[119] In 1765, the *S. Luiz* reached Maranhão from Angola. The captain lost 20 of the ship's 480 slaves before embarkation and another 54 on the ocean from "an epidemic of smallpox." In São Luís, the captives from the ship were quarantined and continued to die.[120]

---

[114] For a study of smallpox on slave ships bound for Amazonia, see Magali Romero Sá, "A 'pesta branca' nos navios negreiros: epidemias de varíola na Amazônia colonial e os primeiros esforços de imunização," unpublished paper from Anais do III Congresso Internacional de Psicopatologia Fundamental.

[115] ANTT, AHMF, CGPM, Diário, livro 1, no. 378, 379, and 520; BNP, codice 627, F. 318, fl. 120.

[116] AHU, Pará, cx. 72, doc. 6110; ANTT, AHMF, CGPM, livro 63, no. 177; ANTT, AHMF, CGPM, Diário, livro 1, no. 543, 548, and 555; ANTT, AHMF, CGPM, Copiadores, Cartas para Pará, livro 97, p. 120-1.

[117] AHU, Pará, cx. 72, doc. 6110; ANTT, AHMF, CGPM, Livro das carregações, 45 A, no. 21, 14; ANTT, AHMF, CGPM, Diário, livro 1, no. 970, 975; ANTT, AHMF, CGPM, Cartas para Pará, livro 97, p. 6; ANTT, AHMF, CGPM, Diário, livro 1, no. 2052, 2066.

[118] Carreira, *As companhias*, 125-6.

[119] AHU, Pará, cx. 72, doc. 6110; ANTT, AHMF, CGPM, Livro das carregações, 47 C, no. 1; ANTT, AHMF, CGPM, Copiadores, Cartas para Pará, livro 97, p. 309; ANTT, AHMF, CGPM, Diário, livro 8, no. 24, 29; ANTT, AHMF, CGPM, Livro dos navios, 65, 11.

[120] ANTT, CGPM, Livro mestre, 26, p. 56; ANTT, AHMF, CGPM, Livro das carregações, 48 D, no. 67; ANTT, AHMF, CGPM, Cartas para Cacheu e Bissau, livro 98, p. 201;

The ill health of many slaves coming out of West Central Africa meant that they typically sold for less than slaves out of Upper Guinea. Noting this, an observer wrote in 1787, "The common price for slaves in Maranhão is 150,000 réis for those of top quality from Cacheu and Bissau and for those of first quality from Angola 120,000 réis." Price differentials existed, he continued, because slaves from Angola "are less robust and less strong than the others who are more appropriate for the work of the fields. Those from other parts of Africa are sold in proportion to the needs that there are for these Africans, or for their quality."[121]

Poor-quality slaves also arrived on ships from other captaincies in Brazil. In 1785, Governor Teles da Silva wrote from Maranhão that every year ships arrive from Bahia and Pernambuco loaded with slaves "who are the worst that come to this colony and are already refuse, which the planters in Bahia and Pernambuco looked down upon and don't want to buy." They were, he said, "bad and old, the ones no one wants to keep and they send them to this captaincy and to Pará." They arrived on small ships "infected with epidemic illnesses and smallpox and they die in this climate, and they send evil doers who come to exercise their vices and commit crimes." Many of the sick and weak were likely recent arrivals from Angola, whom planters in Bahia and Pernambuco would not buy. For this, they were boarded on different ships and sent to the relatively labor-poor region of Amazonia. However, they were not buyers' first choices. The best slaves, Teles da Silva wrote, "come from Cacheu, and Cape Verde, and Costa da Mina."[122]

This is not to imply that outbreaks of sickness were unheard of on ships leaving Bissau and Cacheu. They did occur. One of the most common problems for slaves out of Upper Guinea was scabies, the itching from which was constant and highly irritating for slaves sitting motionless in dark, dank ship holds. Also, common were eye infections, scurvy, and chicken pox. Slaves, too, boarded with malaria, suffering fevers for the entirety of their voyage. And with poor sanitation, dysentery plagued slaves, leading to dehydration and sometimes death.[123]

ANTT, AHMF, CGPM, Cartas para o Maranhão, livro 230, p. 114; ANTT, AHMF, CGPM, Diário, livro 9, no. 558, 738, and 996. Examples of similarly tragic voyages from Angola abound.

[121] ANTT, Ministério do Reino, mç. 601, cx. 704.

[122] APEM, Códices, Livro de registro das ordens de Sua Magestade, suas respostas e contas dadas pelo cevernador e capitão-geral, 1784–1787, livro 13, fl. 122–23.

[123] APEM, Livro de visita de saude.

But when large numbers of slaves died on ships out of Bissau and Cacheu, the cause was usually smallpox. For example, in 1767, Captain Manoel da Cunha Bitencourt reported a catastrophic outbreak of the contagion on his vessel. After 194 slaves had been designated for his ship (*N.S. do Cabo*) in Bissau, 34 died before they ever set foot on deck. Once embarked, another thirty-five died at sea, their bodies thrown overboard. Company officials in Pará were dismayed by the losses (although it was the monetary value of the dead Africans that they bemoaned, not the tragic loss of human life).[124] In 1770, the *S. Antonio* left Bissau for Pará with 198 slaves, 41 dying in transit. A letter about the ship was sent from administrators in Pará admonishing those in Bissau and Cacheu to take measures to ensure that everything possible should be done to avoid shipping "any slaves infected with smallpox or a bad contagion to avoid the mortality on the *S. Antonio*."[125] Despite this, in 1774, the *N.S. da Oliveira* arrived in Pará from Cacheu with a large number of sick slaves. Of the 221 that had embarked, 12 died and 69 were gravely ill. Two of the sick slaves died before they could be sold and the others were dubbed "refuse" and sold at a price over two-thirds lower than the healthy slaves from the ship.[126]

Stressing the need to keep slave deaths to a minimum, orders given to Captain Francisco de Salley of the *São Francisco de Paula* when he sailed for Bissau in 1778 were for him to take only slaves "that are clean and well conditioned to board." Sick slaves, the instructions made clear, were to be left to avoid the spread of disease.[127] However, such orders were not always followed. Hence, in October 1782, a CGPM administrator in Maranhão complained about the condition of the slaves who arrived on the *São Francisco de Paula* from Cacheu. The journey itself took 100 days and resulted in the deaths of more than 100 slaves of 267 loaded.

---

[124] AHU, Pará, cx. 72, doc. 6110; ANTT, AHMF, CGPM, Livro mestre, 26, fl. 233; ANTT, AHMF, CGPM, Livro dos navios, 65, 11; ANTT, AHMF, CGPM, Livro das carregações, 49 E, no. 36; ANTT, AHMF, CGPM, Copiadores, Cartas para Cacheu e Bissau, livro 98; 262; ANTT, AHMF, CGPM, Copiadores, Cartas para Pará, livro 97, fl. 534, 560; ANTT, AHMF, CGPM, Diário, livro 10, no. 2000, 2037.

[125] AHU, Pará, cx. 72, doc. 6110; ANTT, AHMF, CGPM, Livro das carregações, 49 E, no. 236, 268; ANTT, AHMF, CGPM, Diário, livro 13, no. 2309, 2311.

[126] AHU, Pará, cx. 47, doc. 4618; cx. 48, doc. 4665; ANTT, AHMF, CGPM, Livro das carregações, 50F, no. 289, 304; ANTT, AHMF, CGPM, Cartas aos administradores do Maranhão, livro 215, fl. 139; ANTT, AHMF, CGPM, Diario, livro 11, no. 4668, 4916; Anaiza Vergolino-Henry and Arthur Napoleão Figueiredo, *A presença Africana na Amazônia colonial: uma notícia histórica* (Belém: Governo do Estado do Pará, Secretaria de Estado de Cultura, 1990), 95–9. Often, slaves near death (*moribundo*) at arrival were given away.

[127] ANTT, AHMF, CGPM, Copiadores, Cartas de Bissau, livro 96, fl. 1.

When an unknown contagious disease broke out, the captain, part of the crew, and most of the slaves fell ill, making sailing difficult. Maranhão was only a stopover on the way to Pará. The length of the journey meant that provisions were running low.[128]

Although it was the biggest killer, disease was not the only cause of death on ships. Shippers sometimes reported "suffocation" from lack of air beneath decks.[129] Crew incompetence also resulted in slave deaths. This is best illustrated on the *Madre de Deus Santo Antonio e Almas*, which arrived in Maranhão in May 1741 after an arduous journey of over two years. Having left Lisbon in February 1739, it sailed to Cacheu to purchase slaves for a new sugar mill in Pará. In Cacheu, the captain and pilot died during a months-long wait for slaves. With a partial load of human cargo embarked, the surviving crew decided to forge ahead. The number of slaves aboard the vessel was put at "one hundred and some" in documents. The crew, under the command of master Antonio Joze Vellozo, proved incompetent. They accidentally sailed to Barbados and then backtracked to Terceira, of the Azores Islands, before going to the Island of Madeira. From there they left for Amazonia, arriving in Maranhão with only seven surviving Africans.[130]

IN MARANHÃO

Once in Maranhão, captains sailing for CGPM visited company administrators and arranged to have the slave cargo handed over to them.[131] Administrators then sent slaves to auction. After 1787, shipping agents sold slaves who arrived at ports on noncompany vessels, and most often those sales took the form of auctions. Some public sales were held not far from the port outside an infamous slave house called the Cafuá das Mercês (Cave of the Blessings) that still stands today on Rua Jacinto Maia. Still others were held at the Arazem dos Leilões (Warehouse of Auctions) on the Beco dos Barbeiros (Street of the Barbarians) and the Caza dos Leilões (House of Auctions) in Praya Grande. In the 1820s, auctions were frequently advertised in local newspapers.[132]

---

[128] AHU, Maranhão, cx. 59, doc. 5415.

[129] AHU, Pará, cx. 72, doc. 6110; ANTT, AHMF, CGPM, Livro das carregações, 45 A, no. 21, 14; ANTT, AHMF, CGPM, Diário, livro 1, no. 970, 975.

[130] AHU, Pará, cx. 24, doc. 2263. Whether or not some slaves were sold along the way is unclear. Crown officials on Madeira provided Vellozo a letter that said he had not traded slaves there.

[131] ANTT, AHMF, CGPM, Copiadores, Cartas para Cacheu e Bissau, livro 98, fl. 2–3.

[132] *O conciliador*, no. 106, 17 July 1822; *O conciliador*, no. 203, 21 July 1823.

Toward the end of the eighteenth century, officials in Maranhão established a "hospital" to hold slaves whom they suspected of carrying contagious diseases. Governor José Teles da Silva took credit for this measure, claiming in 1787 that he had found ways to cut down substantially on deaths from smallpox. He wrote,

> I have always taken precautions when slaves from abroad have been brought here to be sold.... [T]hese precautions were directed at any blacks infested with smallpox who had not shown any signs of it at all.... I was vigilant in founding a *Lazareto* [isolated hospital for treating people with infectious diseases] which had never been done here to cure those who had these evil smallpox or any other contagion. The slaves who came infected would be quarantined.[133]

Hence, in 1790, the governor of Maranhão reported that the slaves of two ships from Cacheu and one from Bissau had been quarantined in hospital for twenty days.[134] In 1796, a *lazareto* was proposed for the Island of Bahia de Santo Antônio near Belém.[135]

The health of a slave figured greatly in his or her price at auction. But pricing was more complicated. Slaves sold for different prices depending on their age, gender, health, and strength. For example, in June 1774, the *São Paulo* arrived in Pará, having sailed from Bissau. On board were 120 slaves. Thirty-three white residents bought them, paying a variety of prices. Strong males went for 120,000 réis each. Bernardino Joze Pereira bought three at that price but paid 100,000 for a male perceived to be of a lower quality. Boys were sold for considerably less – 50,000 réis typically, but strong boys fetched 80,000 réis and particularly young boys, 40,000. Luis Antonio de Souza purchased four boys and a "prime" male, spending 320,000 réis. "Prime" women sold for half the price of "prime" men, fetching 60,000 réis; "inferior" and sick women sold at a 10,000-réis discount. Girls were bought for 40,000 réis with city official Miguel Marcelino purchasing one. Young girls were sold at a discount, one going to Agostinho de Couta for 20,000 réis, along with two "prime" and two "lesser quality" men. Finally, came the *refugo* or "refuse" – those very sick from the voyage. Local buyers purchased these slaves at a deep discount, hoping they would stave off death and recover, so that they could be put to work or sold for a tidy profit. Hence, Francisco Roiz

---

[133] Ibid. The *lazareto* was about three miles outside São Luís at a place called Seta or Sota. It had "fifty beds and two infirmaries, one for men and one for women."

[134] AHU, Maranhão, cx. 75, doc. 6460. Also on the *lazareto*, APEM, Secretaria do Governo, Inventários dos Avulsos, no. 203.

[135] Ernesto Cruz, *História do Pará* (Belém: Universidade do Pará, 1963), 2: 786–7.

purchased twenty-five males "of refuse" for 55,000 réis each, along with four healthy males for 120,000 each. The seller threw in another "very sick" slave for free – a woman who was "moribund" and with whom was a *cria*, or baby. *Crias* always went with their mothers at no charge.[136]

As the above analysis of the *São Paulo* makes clear, in Maranhão slaves were not sold in huge lots to a single buyer. Rather, multiple buyers purchased slaves, often in small numbers. Nonetheless, many slaves from one ship were purchased together in small lots and settled on plantations together. From the *São Paulo*, some slaves were sold alone to residents of São Luís and to farmers in the interior. But many went with one, two, or three of their shipmates to the same buyer. Sales records from the *S. Sabastiam*, which reached Maranhão from Cacheu in 1774 with a cargo of 176 slaves (2 having died in transit), reveal a similar pattern. Alfres Jozé Alexadre bought twelve of the *S. Sabastiam*'s slaves; Anna Margarida da Costa bought seven; Joaquim Joze de Moraes bought six; Eugenio de Arouche bought ten; Francisco Xavier de Arouche bought seven; Joze Felipe de São Thiago bought twelve; Joze Carvalho bought nine; and the company kept sixteen. Other slaves went in lots of two, three, and four to purchasers. Only a handful were sold alone.[137]

Having been purchased in São Luís, most slaves were loaded into canoes or small boats and taken upriver to plantations, some small number remaining in São Luís to perform labor for urban owners. On plantations, newly purchased Africans joined other slaves – most of whom were from the Upper Guinea coast – forced to labor for life clearing forests and planting, tending, harvesting, and processing crops.

CONCLUSION

It is a difficult task to discern what life in transit was like for people enslaved in Upper Guinea and shipped through Bissau and Cacheu to Amazonia in the latter eighteenth and early nineteenth centuries. To *moradores*, Portuguese government officials, CGPM administrators, and ship captains, slaves were commodities. Their plight from the point of their capture to their sale in the Americas was not a concern. Keeping slaves alive was a goal, but keeping costs low figured into merchants' calculations. This meant that slaves' comfort was unimportant and that some death was to be tolerated. For merchants, slaves' values were measured

---

[136] AHU, Maranhão, cx. 47, doc. 4618.
[137] AHU, Maranhão, cx. 47, doc. 4638.

in réis. Values varied based on health, gender, age, and strength, so notes were kept about these things, but little was recorded about much else.

In this chapter, I have assembled a picture of slaves' experiences from bits and pieces of information about supply routes that connected myriad Upper Guinean rural villages, to bulking stations, and then to Bissau and Cacheu. And I have drawn on a great range of shipping records to paint a picture – however incomplete – of what life was like aboard vessels that carried human beings from Upper Guinea to Amazonia.

From these sources it is clear that when captives from a variety of Upper Guinea ethnic groups were forced together on slaving routes, they looked to one another for support and community, emphasizing, as they did, unity in the face of adversity. The Balanta, Biafada, Bijago, Papel, Floup, Banhun, Brame, and Mandinka who found themselves aboard the *São José* in 1756 and the ships that followed to Amazonia in the decades to come may have been strangers. But it quickly became obvious that they shared a common plight. They were all slaves; they were all in the possession of people they considered "witches" who wanted nothing more than to exploit them to enrich themselves. Some of the slaves aboard the *São José* may have first met when chained together for a brief period of time in Farim. Others first met in Cacheu, where they sat naked in filthy company barracoons for days or weeks. All ninety-four slaves listed as boarded on the *São José* survived what was likely a month-and-a-half-long journey to Belém. During that time, they were locked hungry and thirsty beneath the ship's decks, rarely being allowed up for a breath of fresh air. Some of the slaves from the *São José* were likely sold together to the same master, taken subsequently to plantations that would become the homes of majority–Upper Guinea populations.

Sources from various places suggest that African slaves in the Americas shared a strong bond with others from the same slaving vessel. Throughout Brazil, slaves out of Angola who arrived on the same ship often called each other *malungo*. This word was derived from the Mbundo *malunga*, which were ancient authority symbols brought by ancestors from the sea. For Mbundo slaves, the association of shipmates with ancestors from the sea made them more than fellow passengers on a vessel. Shipmates were links to a real and mythical past and people who shared a special bond in the present. In Suriname, Africans who endured the oceanic crossing together referred to one another with the affectionate nickname *sippi*. In other parts of the colony *máti* was used, in Trinidade it was *malongue*, and in Haiti, *baitiment*. In Spanish colonies, Africans often called shipmates *carabela*. All of this suggests, I write elsewhere, that "the slave ship was more than a place of suffering.... [It] was a place of rebuilding" – a place where Africans constructed intimate human bonds with others who suffered the same fate.[138] What will become clear in the following chapters is that bonds formed in barracoons and on ships were the foundations upon which Upper Guineans in Maranhão and Pará built communities. Within those communities, slaves exported through Bissau and Cacheu emphasized a common Guinean identity. That identity was rooted in a shared Guinean culture that all Bijago, Balanta, Brame, Floup, Biafada, Papel, Mandinka, Fula, and Nalu brought with them from the hinterlands of Bissau and Cacheu to the hinterlands of São Luís and Belém.

[138] Hawthorne, "Being Now," 56, 71–2. See also Mintz and Price, *The Birth*, 8, 42–4.

PART II

CULTURAL CHANGE AND CONTINUITY

4

Labor over "Brown" Rice

In 1805 in Maranhão, João Diogo de Souza owned a thirty-two-year-old slave named Rita. At the time, the principal crop in the region was rice, so much of Rita's time was devoted to it. Born on Africa's Upper Guinea coast in a Balanta village and under a different name, Rita labored for Souza beside twenty-seven other slaves, most of whom (75 percent) were also Upper Guinean by birth. Those with whom Rita had daily contact were Bijago, Mandinka, and Papel, along with four other Balanta. Of Souza's African-born slaves, only three were from outside Upper Guinea. There were also several Maranhão-born slaves, or *crioulos*, most of whom were the products of relationships among the Upper Guineans owned by Souza. One of the *crioulos* was Rita's one-year-old daughter, Veridina.[1]

We don't know at what age Rita was made captive, but chances are she was in her teens or twenties when she was enslaved and taken across the ocean. If so, her life on the Upper Guinea coast was patterned like the lives of many other Upper Guinean females. Rita grew up in her father's household, and she spent much of her infancy carried on her mother's and sisters' backs, going everywhere they went. The females in her life spent most of their time working over rice, the staple of area diets. Like most aspects of Balanta society, rice work was gendered; females were charged with planting, weeding, milling, winnowing, cooking, and preparing the cereal as the base for a protein-rich sauce that accompanied every meal. As Rita grew, she continued to spend most of her time with females in her community, learning what it meant to be a successful woman – learning, that is, how to grow rice and prepare it for consumption.

[1] TJEM, Relação do Maranhão, Inventory of João Diogo de Souza, 1805.

In 1807, Roberto, a Papel who was about thirty-five years old and had been given a different name on the Upper Guinea coast, labored on Antonio Henriques Leal's plantation on the Itapecuru River in Maranhão. He was married to Roza, a thirty-five-year-old Bijago, who was also from the Upper Guinea coast. Working and living with Roberto and Roza were eighty-six other slaves. Most (53 percent) had been born in Upper Guinea; only 23 percent were from elsewhere in Africa; and 24 percent had been born in Brazil, mostly the products of relationships among Upper Guinean slaves on Leal's plantation. Those with whom Roberto had daily contact were Papel, Bijago, Balanta, Mandinka, Biafada, and Floup, along with some Angolans and *crioulos*.[2]

It is unclear how old Roberto was when he was captured, but it is likely he was in his teens or early twenties when he was forced into slavery and sent to Amazonia. If that was indeed the case, his life on the Upper Guinea coast was very similar to the lives of many other Upper Guinean males. He spent his formative years in his father's household. Roberto accompanied his mother and sisters just about everywhere. In his youth, he was charged with caring for livestock, a job that took him away from females and placed him in a realm that was distinctly male. As he grew, Roberto participated in male rites of passage. With males of the same age, he learned and refined the highly technical skills used in mangrove rice farming and especially the field-preparation techniques used to carve paddies from tidal flats. He also participated in raids on distant groups for captives. By raiding and making fields, Upper Guinea coastal-zone boys became men.

Given that Rita and Roberto both labored over rice in Maranhão, did they apply knowledge gained in the Old World to their work in the New? Did Maranhão's rice plantation system owe its existence to knowledge brought across the ocean from Upper Guinea? These questions go to the heart of what has come to be known as the "black rice thesis." Developed over several decades by Peter H. Wood, Daniel C. Littlefield, Judith A. Carney, and Edda Fields-Black, the thesis posits that skilled rice farmers from Upper Guinea introduced technology useful for the establishment and expansion of the eighteenth-century rice-based plantation system in the lowland of South Carolina and Georgia.[3] Carney extends

---

[2] TJEM, Inventory of Captain Antonio Henriques, 1807.

[3] Peter H. Wood, *Black Majority: Negroes in Colonial South Carolina from 1670 through the Stono Rebellion* (New York: Norton, 1974); Daniel C. Littlefield, *Rice and Slaves: Ethnicity and the Slave Trade in Colonial South Carolina* (Baton Rouge: Louisiana State University Press, 1981); Judith A. Carney, *Black Rice: The African Origins of Rice*

the argument by applying it elsewhere, including Maranhão, Brazil.[4] "An examination of rice," she argues, "reveals how Africans, despite enslavement, transferred an entire knowledge system" to the Americas.[5]

David Eltis, Philip Morgan, and David Richardson challenge the black rice thesis. First, and most broadly, they see advocates of the thesis as overly obsessed with transfers of unchanging knowledge through particular conduits that stretched across the ocean. As an alternative, they propose that historians focus on "overlapping circuits" and transformations in knowledge systems that resulted from migrants (forced and voluntary) acting as improvisers and experimenters.[6] Second, and more narrowly, Eltis, Morgan, and Richardson argue that the innovators who shaped American rice regimes were Europeans – not Africans. "Slaves arrived in the Americas with certain skills," they write, "and some of them contributed ideas about rice cultivation. Nevertheless, planters held the reins of power, had access to capital, experimented keenly, and in essence called the shots."[7]

This chapter builds on the work of contributors to both sides of the black rice debate to forge two arguments. First, I assert that over the long history of exchange and migration across the Atlantic there was both change and continuity in approaches to rice production and consumption. Africans did not transfer an unaltered rice "knowledge system" to Maranhão. After about 1500, rice agriculture on both sides

---

Cultivation in the Americas (Cambridge, MA: Harvard University Press, 2001); Edda L. Fields-Black, *Deep Roots: Rice Farmers in West Africa and the African Diaspora*, (Bloomington: Indiana University Press, 2008). Also see, Reinaldo dos Santos Barroso Júnior, "Nas rotas do atlântico equatorial: tráfico de escravos rizicultores da Alta-Guiné para o Maranhão (1770–1800)," Ph.D thesis: Universidade Federal da Bahia, 2009.

[4] Judith A. Carney, "'With Grains in Her Hair': Rice in Colonial Brazil," *Slavery and Abolition* 25, 1 (2004), 1–27; Judith A. Carney, "Rice and Memory in the Age of Enslavement: Atlantic Passages to Suriname," *Slavery and Abolition* 26, 3 (2005), 325–47.

[5] Carney, "With Grains," 22.

[6] David Eltis, Philip Morgan, and David Richardson, "Agency and the Diaspora in Atlantic History: Reassessing the African Contribution to Rice Cultivation in the Americas," *American Historical Review* 12, 5 (2007), 1329–8.

[7] Ibid., 1357. Also see, S. Max Edelson, "Beyond 'Black Rice': Reconstructing Material and Cultural Contexts for Early Plantation Agriculture," *American Historical Review* 115, 1 (2010), 125–35; Gwendolyn Midlo Hall, "Africa and Africans in the African Diaspora: The Uses of Relational Databases," *American Historical Review*, 115, 1 (2010), 136–50; Walter Hawthorne, "From 'Black Rice' to 'Brown': Rethinking the History of Risiculture in the Seventeenth and Eighteenth Century Atlantic," *American Historical Review*, 115, 1 (2010), 151–64; David Eltis, Phip Morgan, and David Richardson, "Black, Brown, or White? Color-Coding American Commercial Rice Cultivation with Slave Labor," *American Historical Review* 115, 1 (2010), 164–71.

of the Atlantic changed in response to multiple factors. Where rice was introduced, climate and physical environment affected decisions about when, where, and how to farm it. Moreover, in Maranhão and across Brazil, rice agriculture owed a great deal to the cultural traditions of multiple groups – Africans, Europeans, and American Indians. In my analysis, rice as it was known in Maranhão was neither black nor white. It was brown.

Second, I argue that proponents of the black rice thesis have not delved adequately into how Maranhão's plantation system gave male and female slaves different opportunities to shape rice production, processing, and cooking. Indeed, I demonstrate that the labor that Rita and other Upper Guinean females performed in Maranhão owed much more to knowledge acquired on the Upper Guinea coast than did the labor that Roberto and other Upper Guinean males performed. Both Rita and Roberto labored over rice, but the gendered division of labor common to work regimes in Maranhão gave considerably more space to females for cultural creativity. In Maranhão, as elsewhere, planters did not and could not call all the shots. They allowed, by choice or necessity, slaves to shape some aspects of their lives and labor, and women had more leeway to do this than did men.

EARLY ACCOUNTS OF RICE CULTIVATION IN THE LUSO-ATLANTIC

Brazil's rice history begins well before explorers claimed the territory for Portugal. Indeed, rice is indigenous to South America and was consumed by native peoples before the arrival of Europeans. On the first Atlantic voyage to South America in 1500, Portuguese sailors reported taking "some rice" and other items from a Tupiniquin Indian village.[8] As they were not agriculturalists, Tupiniquin did not cultivate rice, but they did gather and consume it.[9] The rice with which they were familiar was one of a variety from the *Oryza* genus. In Brazil, these include *O. glumaepatula*, *O. grandiglumis*, *O. latifolia*, *O. alta*, and *O. rufipogon*.

---

[8] Tarciso S. Filgueiras and Ariane Luna Peixoto, "The Flora and the Vegetation of Brazil in Caminha's Letter, Written in 1500, to the Portuguese King, D. Manoel I," *Acta Botanica Brasilica* 16, 3 (2002), 263–72; *Arquivo Portuguese Oriental* 1, 1 (1936), 118–19.

[9] Area Tupinambá did practice agriculture, planting manioc and other tubers, beans, squash, and maize. Alfred Métraux, "The Tupinamba," in *Handbook of South American Indians*, ed. Juliann H. Stewart (Washington: Smithsonian Institution, 1948), 99–103.

When milled, these rices appear dark in color. In Brazil, the Portuguese term *arroz de terra*, or "rice of the land," was applied to wild rice.[10]

Today, there are two cultivated species of *Oryza*, one native to Asia (*O. sativa*) and one native to West Africa (*O. glaberrima*). Around the world, *O. sativa* is the best known, as it is cultivated widely and traded in international markets. Most varieties appear white when milled, but some have a light red hue. Produced since long before Europeans arrived on the African coast, *O. glaberrima*, which is called "black rice" in some African societies, appears dark after milling, making it less appealing in global markets. Also, the flavor is unfamiliar to those used to *O. sativa*. By 1500, Portuguese knew both types of rice from trade with Arabs, black Africans, and Italians.[11]

However, until the eighteenth century, rice was not central to the Portuguese diet. This is not to say that Portuguese did not have a long history of engagement with the cereal. Rice was introduced to the Iberian Peninsula under Moorish rule from the eighth to the twelfth centuries and was cultivated there in the late thirteenth and early fourteenth centuries before being abandoned for reasons unknown.[12] From then until the eighteenth century, imported rice was marketed in Portugal most often as a luxury. It was not a staple but was used in sweet desserts, particularly in the sixteenth century.[13] By the early sixteenth century, much of Portugal's rice came from Africa. Portuguese on the Cape Verde Islands purchased *O. glaberrima* on Africa's coast and regularly sent it to Lisbon.[14] In 1552, João Brandão observed Africans on Lisbon's streets selling *arroz-doce*

---

[10] Te-Tzu Chang, "Crop History and Genetic Conservation in Rice – A Case Study," *Iowa State Journal of Research* 59 (1985), 405–55; Manuel Barata, *A antiga producção e exportação do Pará, estudo historico-economico* (Belem: Typ. da Livraria Gillet de Torres & Comp., 1915); José Almeida Pereira, *Cultura do arroz no Brasil, subsídios para a sua história* (Teresina: Embrapa, 2002), 40–3.

[11] Andrew M. Watson, *Agricultural Innovation in the Early Islamic World* (Cambridge: Cambridge University Press, 1983), 83.

[12] Victor Hehn, *Cultivated Plants and Domesticated Animals in their Migration from Asia to Europe* (Amsterdam: John Benjamins B. V., 1976), 379–83; R. J. Forbes, *Studies in Ancient Technology* (Leiden: E. J. Brill, 1955), II: 46–7; Manuel Vianna e Silva, *Elementos para história do arroz em Portugal* (Coimbra: Nova Casa Minerva, 1955), 7.

[13] "Um tratado da cozinha portuguesa do século xv," http://www.cervantesvirtual.com/servlet/SirveObras/05810518790525195209079/index.htm; António Henrique R. de Oliveira Marques, *Daily Life in Portugal in the Late Middle Ages* (Madison: University of Wisconsin Press, 1971), 24–5; Joana Monteleone, "Manjar branco, uma história portuguesa," *História Viva* (10 March 2008), no page numbers.

[14] Teixeira de Sousa, *Alimentação e saúde nas ilhas de Cabo Verde* (Lisbon: Imprensa Nacional, 1957), 7; Christiano José de Senna Barcellos, *Subsidios para a história de Cabo Verde e Guiné* (Lisbon: Imprensa Nacional, 1899), I: 72.

(sweet rice).[15] Because Africans, who had been shipped to Portugal as slaves, comprised a sizable portion of Lisbon's population, they may have been attracted to O. *glaberrima* to preserve their culinary traditions in diaspora.[16]

In 1538, Portugal began sending small numbers of slaves across the Atlantic to work in what would be named Bahia. Although sugar quickly became central to Bahia's social and economic order, colonists experimented with other crops, including rice. In the late 1540s, ships brought rice shoots to Bahia from Cape Verde for the purpose of beginning a rice industry.[17] Those shoots were likely of the O. *glaberrima* variety, obtained from Upper Guinea. From the mid-sixteenth century, observers left notes about rice in Brazil. In the 1550s, Gaspar Madre de Deus wrote of the sale of unmilled rice near Rio de Janeiro. In 1568, Pêro de Magalhães Gândavo mentioned the cereal in Bahia.[18] This rice was cultivated rather than harvested from wild fields. Planter Gabriel Soares de Sousa, writing of the 1570s and 1580s, noted, "The rice of Bahia is better than in any other known part, because they plant it in swamps and on inundated lands."[19]

There is no way of knowing if the bulk of rice consumed in Bahia was by this time O. *glaberrima*, O. *sativa*, or an indigenous variety. Although O. *glaberrima* was likely introduced to Brazil in the 1540s, O. *sativa* may have been introduced in subsequent decades. Further, historian Roberto Simonsen argues that indigenous "*arroz vermelho* [red rice], or *arroz da terra*, was adopted by colonists, becoming the basis of their nourishment."[20] Carney disputes this claim, asserting that

---

[15] Daniela Buono Calainho, *Metropole das Mandingas: religiosidade negra e inquisição portuguesa* (Ph.D. diss., Universidad Federal Fluminense, 2000), 20, 52.

[16] Barcellos, *Subsidios*, 69–76; A. C. de C. M. Saunders *A Social History of Black Slaves and Freedmen in Portugal* (New York: Cambridge University Press, 1982), 20–1.

[17] T. Bentley Duncan, *Atlantic Islands: Madeira, the Azores and the Cape Verdes in Seventeenth-Century Commerce and Navigation* (Chicago: The University of Chicago Press, 1972), 167–8; Ilídio Cabral Baleno, "Povoamento e formação da sociedade," in *História geral de Cabo Verde*, eds. Luís de Albuquerque and Maria Emília Madeira Santos (Lisbon: Centro de Estudos História e Cartograpfia Antiga, 1991), 134; Maria Manuel Ferrz Torrão, "Actividade comercial externa de Cabo Verde: Organização, funcionamento, evolução," in *História geral de Cabo Verde*, eds. Luís de Albuquerque and Maria Emília Madeira Santos (Lisbon: Centro de Estudos História e Cartograpfia Antiga, 1991), 276–9, 336.

[18] Carney, "With Grains," 7–10.

[19] Gabriel Soares de Sousa, *Tratado descritivo do Brasil em 1587* (São Paulo: Companhia Editora Nacional, 1971), 182.

[20] Roberto Simonsen, *História ecconômica do Brasil* (São Paulo: Cia. Editôra Nacional, 1938), II: 207.

Upper Guinean slaves selected *O. glaberrima* seed because the taste was familiar. Soares de Sousa's 1587 description of Bahia's rice as having "come to Brazil from Cape Verde" might be read as evidence supporting Carney's assertion [21]

However, there are two reasons to doubt that Upper Guinean slaves in Bahia selected *O. glaberrima* in the sixteenth or seventeenth centuries. First, there were not many Upper Guineans anywhere in Brazil during this period. Merchants on São Tomé, who drew slaves from Angola, supplied Brazil, and few if any Angolans knew rice before they reached the Americas.[22] It is possible that small numbers of Upper Guineans influenced others in Brazil, persuading them of the superiority of *O. glaberrima*.[23] But there is no evidence for this. It is equally plausible that white settlers selected a variety of rice because they liked its taste. In the second half of the sixteenth century, Upper Guineans in Brazil did not have a monopoly over rice knowledge. Rice was known in Portugal. Moreover, in Brazil, whites and Indians knew the grain as did locally born blacks. Over the long history of trade in the Mediterranean and South Atlantic, rice knowledge spread, people from multiple places embracing rice as a food and shaping the ways it was farmed and integrated into dishes.

Second, rice farming in early colonial Brazil required little skill, meaning that if a few Upper Guineans selected *O. glaberrima* seed, they did not apply any sophisticated technologies from their homelands to it. In 1618, Ambrósio Fernandes Brandão, who had owned a sugar plantation in Paraíba, said that planters liked rice because it was "easily grown anywhere; on the marshlands, which are good for nothing else, it grows best of all." Moreover, he emphasized rice "is produced in great abundance, at the cost of little labor." Ease of planting and harvesting meant slaves were not taken away for long from other tasks. In Paraíba, slaves did not carry out the time-consuming task of replanting rice after harvest. Once cut, the stalks of rice plants regenerated grain naturally, he noted. Although

---

[21] Frederico Carlos Hoehne, *Botanica e agricultura no Brasil no seculo XVI* (São Paulo: Companhia Editora Nacional, 1937), 187.

[22] Duncan, *Atlantic Islands*, 195–238, 204–5; Eltis, Morgan, and Richardson, "African Agency," 1343–4; Baleno, "Povoamento," 169–70; Maria Manuel Ferraz Torrão, "Rotas comerciais, agentes económicos, meios de pagamento," in *História Geral de Cabo Verde*, ed. Maria Emília Madeira Santos (Lisbon: Centro de Estudos História e Cartografia Antiga, 2001), II: 19, 58; Linda M. Heywood and John K. Thornton, *Central Africans, Atlantic Creoles, and the Foundation of the Americas, 1585–1660* (Cambridge: Cambridge University Press, 2007), 293.

[23] Eltis, Morgan, and Richardson, "Agency and Diaspora," 1330.

yields were not particularly high, the labor demands of this type of rice gathering were low.[24]

Through the seventeenth and into the eighteenth century, rice gained popularity in Brazil as a food for slaves, very few of whom were Upper Guineans. At the end of the seventeenth century, Francis Froger purchased rice to provision his ship in Rio de Janeiro, noting that the area was "very fertile in rice, maize and manioc." At São Salvador, too, he described rice.[25] And in the early eighteenth century, Sebastião da Rocha Pitta said rice was central to Brazilian diets. "Immense is the production of rice in Brazil.... In the Province of Bahia, the units that they collect are not countable."[26] By Pitta's time, rice was indeed an important staple of Brazilian diets (second only to manioc). But, as earlier, this was because the manner in which it was produced required little labor, meaning slaves could devote their full energies to sugar and other export crops.

RICE IN MARANHÃO AND PARÁ BEFORE
THE MID-EIGHTEENTH CENTURY

As with the rest of Brazil, the link between Upper Guinean and Amazonian rice production is tenuous before the mid-eighteenth century. White planters, using almost exclusively Indian laborers, experimented with rice in Maranhão and Pará long before Upper Guineans were there. In 1619, Symão Estacio da Sylveira arrived in Maranhão, later writing that the province had "much maize and very good rice in quantity."[27] From extant documents, it is impossible to know what type of rice he was describing. The French were the first Europeans to colonize Maranhão Island in the early seventeenth century. It is unlikely that the French introduced rice, as Claude d'Abbeville left descriptions of their agricultural efforts but said nothing about the grain.[28] It is possible that the Portuguese introduced

---

[24] Ambrósio Fernandes Brandão, *Dialogues of the Great Things of Brazil*, trans. Frederick Holden Hall, William F. Harrison, and Dorothy Winters Welker (Albuquerque: University of New Mexico Press, 1987), 197–8.

[25] Francis Froger, *Relation of a Voyage Made in the Years 1695, 1696, 1697* (London: M. Gillyflower, 1698), 53–60.

[26] Rocah Pita, *História da américa portuguesa* (São Paulo: Livraria Itatiaia Editora, Ltda., 1976), 27–8.

[27] Symão Estacio da Sylveira, *Relaçaõ sumaria das cousas do Maranhão* (Lisbon: 1624), 26.

[28] Claude d'Abbeville, *História da missão dos padres Capuchinos na Ilha do Maranhão* (São Paulo: Livraria Martins Editôra, 1945), 158–80.

rice, particularly in 1618 and 1619, when 500 Azorean colonists arrived on Maranhão Island.[29] Whatever the case, Carney's conclusion that early seventeenth-century settlers in Maranhão cultivated *O. glaberrima*, which had "diffused" from Bahia, is wholly unsupported. Rice was never produced on the Azores. However, officials in Lisbon may have directed the ships that brought Azoreans to Amazonia to bring rice seed. Or, Portuguese colonists may have cultivated or gathered wild varieties of the cereal, which grew in abundance in swampy areas.[30] But if white settlers grew (or gathered) rice for local consumption, they did so without African know-how, the first shipment of African slaves arriving in the 1660s or 1670s (Table 1.1, Chapter 1). Indeed, if Azoreans relied on the rice knowledge of some other group, that group was composed of Indians, whom settlers began to enslave shortly after their arrival.[31]

For almost a century after Sylveira's observations, extant documentation makes no mention of rice cultivation or consumption in Maranhão. Throughout the period, the settler population of the region was small and exports miniscule. Rice was not exported, but it may have been a food source. It was in 1712 that an inventory taken in Alcântara listed among a planter's possessions 220 gallons (833 liters) of rice valued at 24,000 réis, which was one-quarter of the cost of a good Indian slave.[32] The planter owned no African slaves, who were scarce in the territory, but had thirty-three Indian slaves, demonstrating again the degree to which some level of rice knowledge was shared widely in the Luso-Atlantic.

Other evidence also points to rice being consumed locally before the mid-eighteenth century and to considerable Portuguese experimentation with the grain. Indeed, planters were innovators. They sought to master and profit from crops that they knew nothing about before arriving in the Americas. In 1716, Manuel de Madueira Lobo asked permission from the crown to establish "a factory to mill rice" in Pará.[33] Whether he

[29] Simonsen, *História*, 110; Carlos de Lima, *História do Maranhão* (São Luís, Instituto Geia, 2006), 59.
[30] Sebastião da Rocha Pitta, *História da américa portuguesa* (São Paulo: Livraria Itatiaia Editora, Ltda., 1976), 27–8.
[31] On Azoreans, Stuart B. Schwartz, "Colonial Brazil, *c.* 1580–*c.* 1750: Plantations and Peripheries," *The Cambridge History of Latin America*, ed. Leslie Bethell (Cambridge: Cambridge University Press, 1984), II: 475.
[32] Francisco de Assis Leal Mesquita, *Vida e morte da economia algodaoeira do Maranhão: Uma análise das relações de produção na cultura do algodão, 1850/1890* (São Luís: Universidade Federal do Maranhão, 1987), 328–9.
[33] AHU, Pará, cx. 6, doc. 557.

planned to mill wild or cultivated rice is not known. In 1738, the priest Antonio de Oliveira Pantoja petitioned to take a rice mill from Lisbon to Maranhão.[34] In 1739, João Pinto Rosa, Diogo Manem, and Manuel José petitioned to establish factories to process rice and timber in Pará. There was, he said, "an abundance of rice of good quality in the land and it would be of good use to Portugal." To provide labor for the mills, he requested a ship with slaves be sent "from *Guiné*." None were.[35]

In 1749 in Amazonia, José Gonçalves da Fonseca noted the harvesting of rice on plantations. It was, he said, of "good quality, in the size of the grain and the flavor is not inferior to that of *Veneza*." *Arroz veneza* or "Venetian rice" from Italy was well known in Portugal at the time. Fonseca distinguished cultivated rice from wild rice, which, he thought, was not appetizing "and only out of necessity would one submit to its use."[36] From Fonseca's description, there is no way of determining what types of cultivated rice he encountered. Nor does he explain the technologies applied to rice production. They were surely not technologies transplanted directly by Upper Guineans, as there were no slave-ship arrivals from anywhere in Pará in the first half of the eighteenth century.[37]

João Daniel's observations from 1741 and 1757 complement Fonseca's. Daniel wrote that rice "is a foodstuff that is very abundant in Amazonia." He implied that locals ate wild varieties but also noted that in some places he saw *arroz manso* – domesticated rice – that, he said, "is rice from Europe, that has a larger grain, and cleaner, which many residents cultivate."[38] It was not, then, *O. glaberrima*. Whatever was produced was the result of Indian labor, Africans still being scarce in the region.[39] And whatever was produced was consumed locally because rice was not yet a viable export. In Maranhão (as in the rest of Brazil) before the second half of the eighteenth century, rice was a staple because it required minimal labor and little technological sophistication and also because it flourished on swampy lowlands that were good for no other crop.

---

[34] AHU, Maranhão, cx. 51, doc. 4970.

[35] AHU, Maranhão, cx. 25, doc. 2538, 2568.

[36] Quoted in Hoehn, *Botanica*, 36.

[37] As late as 1766, some plantations in Pará were producing rice and other crops with exclusively Indian labor. AHU, Pará, cx. 87, doc. 7075, 7076.

[38] João Daniel, *Tesouro descoberto no máximo Rio Amazonas* (Rio de Janeiro: Contraponto Editora, 2004), 1: 529, 2: 184.

[39] Marcos Carneiro de Mendonça, *A Amazônia na era pombalina* (Rio de Janeiro: Instituto Histórico e Geográfico Brasileiro, 1963), 2: 498. Shortly after mid-century, one observer noted a trade by Indians in rice. João Lúicio Azevedo, *Os Jesuitas no Grão-Pará* (Lisbon: Livraria Editora, 1901), 338–42.

In the seventeenth and early eighteenth centuries, settlers in Pará and Maranhão produced other things as well. Some emulated planters in other parts of Brazil by cultivating sugar. However, because labor was scarce, little came of the industry.[40] Settlers also cultivated cotton, which was spun and made into cloth. This cloth was *the* local currency. For this, Maranhense recoiled at the thought of exporting cotton. However, Lisbon had other ideas. In 1739, two settlers received a license to open a factory that was to produce "calicos like those of India" for export. Nothing came of the enterprise.[41] Two decades later, the wealthy planter Lourenço Belfort raised the ire of locals by shipping two bags of cotton to Lisbon. Fearing for his life, he fled to Portugal but quickly returned with the promise of protection from the crown. In 1760, the region recorded its first significant cotton exports.[42]

Settlers also grew manioc (cassava), which was the foodstuff of choice in most of colonial Brazil.[43] Native to the continent, manioc is a woody shrub that produces an edible tuber. Europeans introduced it to Africa, where it quickly became a staple of coastal diets. Indeed, most Upper Guineans transported to Maranhão in the eighteenth century would have known the crop. Some varieties (dubbed "sweet") can be eaten raw, but others (dubbed "bitter") contain high levels of cyanide. The toxin keeps pests away and can be removed by soaking the tuber in water or by boiling it.[44] In Brazil, manioc was often soaked, peeled, grated, pressed, and then forced through a sieve, so as to create a pulp, which was then roasted over a fire. The result was a flour known as *farinha de mandioca*. Manioc reaches an edible size after six to twelve months in the ground and an optimal size after eighteen.[45] In Maranhão, slaves planted manioc in December and January. Because manioc was not exported, no statistics were kept about its production, but many referred to it as a staple of Maranhense diets.[46]

[40] AHU, Maranhão, cx. 13, doc. 1375; cx. 19, doc. 1955; AHU, Pará, cx. 7, doc. 593; cx. 11, doc. 951.

[41] Osvaldo da Silva Neves, and others, *Cultura e adubação do algodoeiro* (São Paulo: Instituto Brasileiro de Potassa, 1965), 63.

[42] J. Lucio Azevedo, *Estudos de Historia Paraense* (Pará: Typ. de Tavares Cardos & C., 1893), 105; Manuel Nunes Dias, *Fomento e merchantilismo: A Companhia Geral do Grao Pará e Maranhão (1755–1778)* (Belém: Universidade Federal do Pará, 1970), 430.

[43] Froger, *Relation*, 53–60; Hoehne, *Botanica*, 36–7.

[44] Hoehne, *Botanica*, 103–4; Thomas Astley, *A New General Collection of Voyages and Travels* (London: Printed for Thomas Astley, 1743–1745), 90; Philip Beaver, *African Memoranda* (London: C. and R. Baldwin, 1805), 232–3.

[45] William O. Jones, "Manioc: An Example of Innovation in African Economics," *Economic Development and Cultural Change* 5, 2 (1957), 97–117; Hoehne, *Botanica*, 103–5.

[46] For example, APEM, Códices, Secretaria do Governo, Livro 45.

RICE PRODUCTION IN MARANHÃO AND PARÁ AFTER 1755

With earlier development schemes leading nowhere, Portuguese policy makers renewed their interest in Amazonia in the mid-eighteenth century. Officials extended in 1755 a monopoly to the Company of Grão Pará and Maranhão (CGPM) to bring African, and particularly Upper Guinean, slaves into Amazonia and ship commodities from São Luís and Belém to Lisbon. About the same time, Indian slavery was abolished.[47] As Upper Guineans became the backbone of the region's labor force, rice, followed by cotton, became the leading exports from Maranhão. To both crops, new technologies and considerable labor were applied.

With respect to both rice and cotton exports, things played out differently in Pará and Maranhão. In Pará, neither rice nor cotton production was sustained at particularly high levels. Under the CGPM's monopoly, Pará's annual cotton exports were usually far below Maranhão's. After 1777, when the monopoly ended, cotton exports from Pará decreased dramatically, as slave imports into the distant province dropped. In turn, settlers, who were few in number compared to those in Maranhão, focused on cacao. As for rice, most years after 1777, Pará's exports were one-half to three-quarters less than Maranhão's. By century's end, no rice was exported at all from Pará, observers blaming a lack of black slave laborers (Table 4.1).[48]

With far more slaves going into Maranhão, rice agriculture succeeded in comparison, and as it did, it met the demands of Portuguese consumers. In Portugal, demand for rice increased in the eighteenth century because domestic wheat was in short supply and an expanding urban middle class wanted to serve rice with fish on Catholic holy days. In 1769, a CGPM official said, "Rice is the most popular and greatest staple in the kingdom" and encouraged its increased production in Maranhão.[49] In 1772, officials in Lisbon said that Iberian Portuguese consumed more than 18 million pounds of rice each year – about half an ounce per person

---

[47] "Directorio que se deve observar para o governo dos Indios do Maranhão," 17 August 1758, in *Collecçaõ das leys, decretos, e alvaras, 1750 a 1760* (Lisbon: Miguel Rodrigues, 1761), I: no page numbers.

[48] AHU, Pará, cx. 87, doc. 7078. On Pará's small population, João Filippe da Fonseca, "Decreto a favor do comercio dos negros para o Pará," 22 October 1798, ANTT, Junta do Comércio, mç. 62, cx. 204, n. 123. On Pará's economic woes, Colin M. MacLachlan, "African Slave Trade and Economic Development in Amazonia, 1700–1800," *Slavery and Race Relations in Latin America*, ed. Robert B. Toplin (Westport, CT: Greenwood Press, 1974), 112–30.

[49] ANTT, CGPM, Cartas para o Maranhão, livro 230, fl. 162–3.

TABLE 4.1. *Rice and Cotton Exports from Maranhão, Pará, and Rio de Janeiro, 1761–1810*

	Annual rice exports in millions of pounds			Annual cotton exports in millions of pounds	
	Maranhão	Pará	Rio de Janeiro	Maranhão	Pará
1761–1765				0.2	0.1
1766–1770				0.6	0.5
1771–1775	1.7	0.3	0.1	0.8	0.8
1776–1780	4.1	1.9	0.8	1.2	0.4
1781–1785	5.9	3.1	1	1.7	0.2
1786–1790	8.9	3.2	0.6	2.2	0.1
1791–1795	9.2		0.8	2.9	
1796–1800	9.1	2.2	2	4.3	
1801–1805	6	1.7	0.7	5.3	
1806–1810	9.1			7.3	

Sources: Alden, "Late Colonial Brazil," 637, 640; AHU, Maranhão, cx. 67, doc. 5843; cx. 68, doc. 5938; cx. 70, doc. 6112; cx. 73, doc. 6288; cx. 75, doc. 6429; cx. 77, doc. 6567; cx. 79, doc. 6718; cx. 81, doc. 6868; cx. 84, doc. 7042; cx. 86, doc. 7178; BNP, Mss. 213, n. 1.

per day.[50] Before the turn of the nineteenth century, one observer said that in Portugal, rice "is present in all of the meals."[51] It featured prominently as a side dish and in many recipes in eighteenth-century cookbooks. Some of those recipes are still popular today.[52]

Italy was Portugal's primary supplier of rice until about 1730 when the English colony of South Carolina supplanted it.[53] Attempting to free his country from reliance on foreign rice, King Dom José I pursued two strategies. First, he encouraged rice cultivation along several of Portugal's rivers in the third quarter of the eighteenth century. However, labor was not adequate for harvests.[54] Second, he encouraged rice production in the colonies, mainly Amazonia, where his efforts were largely successful.

[50] Dias, *Fomento*, 144; Pereira, *Cultura*, 27.
[51] Joseph Barthelemy François, *Voyage en Portugal et particulièrement à Lisbonne* (Paris: Deterville, 1798), 207; Carlos Veloso, *A alimentação em Portugal no século XVIII nos relatos dos viajantes estrangeiros* (Coimbra: Menerva História: 1992), 58.
[52] Veloso, *Alimentação*, 141–55.
[53] Dauril Alden, "Late Colonial Brazil, 1750–1808," *Colonial Latin America*, ed. Leslie Bethal (Cambridge: Cambridge University Press, 1984), 639–40.
[54] Rosa Elizabeth Acevedo Marin, "Agriculture no delta do Rio Amazons: Colons produtores de alimentos em Macapá no período colonial," *Novos cadernos NAEA* 8, 1 (June 2005), no page numbers; Pereira, *Cultura*, 27.

By 1781, rice imports from Brazil, and particularly Maranhão, were sufficient enough that Portugal could ban foreign imports.[55] A little over a decade later, Portugal began shipping rice to Spain and Hamburg.[56] Exports from Maranhão grew steadily in the 1770s, leveling at about 9.1 million pounds per year from 1785 to 1810.[57] Lesser amounts were exported from Pará and Rio de Janeiro. Rice was also a staple of the rapidly growing colonial population of Maranhão. Considerable amounts were often shipped to other parts of Brazil – those shipments not always being counted in official export data. For this, production levels were above official export levels by some unknown amount.[58]

To be sure, government officials and planters in Amazonia were instrumental in shaping the agricultural system that freed Portugal from reliance on foreign rice imports. In February 1759, Pará's governor sent a letter suggesting to the Portuguese secretary of state that rice agriculture be developed in Amazonia. Given that rice was already being cultivated there and grew wild in abundance, the region seemed ideal for meeting Portugal's food needs. The secretary was persuaded.[59] In 1761, the crown decreed that for ten years after 1763, rice exported from Brazil had to go to Portugal and would not be subject to duties.[60]

Immediately, Maranhense planters responded to this incentive. Credit is often given to Lourenço Belfort exporting the first sacks of rice from São Luís in 1763.[61] But officials in Portugal were unimpressed with the dark-grained rice they received (probably *arroz de terra*). Its color and flavor were not appealing to a Portuguese palate used to *O. sativa* rices

---

[55] J. Mendes da Cunha Saraiva, *Companhias gerais de comércio e navegação para o Brasil* (Lisbon: Sociedade Nacional de Tipografia, 1938), 47; Dauril Alden, "Manoel Luis Vieira: An entrepreneur in Rio de Janeiro during Brazil's Eighteenth Century Agricultural Renaissance," *Hispanic American Historical Review* 39, 4 (1959), 534–5.

[56] Veloso, *Alimentação*, 58.

[57] Calculated from Gayozo, *Compendio*, 182; Barata, *Antiga producção*, 3; Dias, *Fomento*, 430; Corsino Medeiros dos Santos, "Cultura, indústria e comércio de arroz no Brasil colonial," *Revista do Instituto Historico e Geografico Brasileiro* 318 (1978), 6–20; Alden, "Late Colonial Brazil," 601–60.

[58] AHU, Maranhão, cx. 45, doc. 4458; AHU, Pará, cx. 43, doc. 4245, 1769; ANTT, CGPM, Cartas para o Maranhão, livro 230, p. 162–163; ANRJ, Junta do Comércio, 7X, cx. 448, pct. 1.

[59] Saraiva, *Companhias*, 45–6.

[60] Arquivo Nacional, *Documentos históricos* (Rio de Janeiro: Braggo and Reis, 1928), 2: 309–10.

[61] BNA, London, England, FO 63/149; BNP, Collecção Pombalina, PBA 627; PBA 630; ANTT, Lisbon, Portugal, Ministério do Reino, mç. 500, cx. 624; AHU, Pará, cx. 21, doc. 1967. Other powerful families disputed this claim in the nineteenth century.

imported from South Carolina.[62] Attention, therefore, turned to encouraging the planting of *O. sativa* in Amazonia. As noted above, settlers may have planted *O. sativa* in parts of Pará before 1750. There are, too, reports that Manoel Benardo de Mello Castro experimented with it in 1761 in Macapá, Pará. In the years that followed, Pará's governor, João Pereira de Caldas, distributed white rice seed to others in the area.[63] And in 1766, CGPM administrator José Vieira da Silva gave white rice seed from South Carolina (called *carolina*) to Maranhense planters. The same year, José de Carvalho arrived in Maranhão with equipment for the construction of a mechanical rice mill, which he established on the Anil River.[64] These efforts paid some dividends. In 1767, the CGPM recorded its first significant exports of rice from São Luís to Lisbon, a total of about 7,000 pounds.[65]

However, in the short term, production grew slowly for a host of reasons. First, from the 1750s through the 1770s, Maranhão had a shortage of laborers, as blacks were slow to replace Indians in fields.[66] Second, droughts in 1769, 1771, and 1776 constrained the growth of rice plantations.[67] Third, planters everywhere in the Amazonian interior faced difficulties moving rice and other exports to São Luís and Belém. Throughout the second half of the eighteenth century, there were hardly any roads in Amazonia, so the region's rivers were its highways. However, a dearth of boats made navigating those highways impossible for some.[68] Fourth, the company faced transport problems, ships sometimes not coming regularly enough to take rice to Lisbon.[69]

Further, despite efforts to encourage the planting of *O. sativa* seed from South Carolina, Maranhão's governor, Joaquim de Mello e Póvoas,

---

[62] César Augusto Marques, *Dicionário histórico-geográfico da província do Maranhão* (Rio de Janeiro: Editôria Fon-Fon e Seleta, 1970), 28; Jerônimo de Viveiros, *História do Comércio Maranhão, 1612–1895* (São Luís: Associação Comercial do Maranhão, 1954), 1: 76; Raymond Jozé de Souza Gayozo, *Compendio historico-politico dos principios da lavoura do Maranhão* (Paris: Officina de P.N. Rougeron, 1818), 181.

[63] Marin, "Agricultura no delta."

[64] Gayozo, *Compendio*, 181; Marques, *Dicionário*, 91.

[65] Dias, "Fomento," 470.

[66] ANTT, CGPM, Cartas para o Maranhão, livro 230, p. 211.

[67] AHU, Maranhão, cx. 43, doc. 4245, 4264; cx. 45, doc. 4407; ANTT, CGPM, Cartas para o Maranhão, livro 230, 182–3; APEM, Secretaria do Governo, Livro de registgro da correspondência do governador e capitão-geral com o Conselho Ultramarino e diversas autoriades da metrópole, 1799–1804, livro 286; ANRJ, Maranhão, Ministerio do Reino, IJJ9–534, AA.

[68] APEM, Códices, livro 13; AHU, Maranhão, cx. 50, doc. 4874.

[69] APEM, livro 12.

complained in 1772 that "some farmers continue to cultivate rice called *da terra* and it comes to the storehouses of the Company for sale mixed with the Carolina variety." *Arroz de terra*, he said, was "very red and difficult to mill," its grains often breaking. That and a continuing Portuguese distaste for anything but white rice meant Maranhão could not compete with South Carolina. Nonetheless, many in Maranhão liked *arroz de terra* because it was longer grained and heavier. To discourage the continued planting of *arroz de terra*, Mello e Póvoas posted a ban on the production of rice other than *carolina*. Whites who grew anything else were subject to one year in prison and a fine of 100,000 réis. Slaves who cultivated other rices were subject to two years in prison. Under the ban, rice other than *carolina* was to be seized and burned.[70] After 1772, the export of *carolina* rice from Maranhão increased dramatically, at the same time that slaves from Upper Guinea rapidly replaced Indians as the colony's most important workers.

In this period, Lourenço Belfort held his place as the leading rice planter in Maranhão. As early as 1770, his plantation produced large quantities of high-quality rice. Having begun experiments in the 1760s, Belfort had a factory that milled rice with admirable precision, with grains emerging unbroken from his machine. The CGPM paid Belfort up to 2,000 réis per quintal (about 129.5 pounds) of rice, while other planters fetched 20 percent less for unmilled rice.[71] It was more economical to ship milled rice, as the cost of labor was lower in Amazonia than in Lisbon. Further, space was at a premium on ships, so transporting rice with worthless husks made little sense. Hence, the company sought ways to encourage milling in Brazil.

However, for decades, rice milling presented problems. Most of the slaves arriving in the region in the second half of the eighteenth century were from Upper Guinea, and Upper Guinean females knew how to mill rice with wooden mortars and pestles. For domestic consumption, slave women in Maranhão made use of mortars and pestles, and initially, plantation owners put slaves to work hand milling rice for export. However, labor was scarce in Amazonia, and hand milling took slaves away from other tasks. Further, whites complained that hand milling produced an undesirable product, as the grains that emerged from pestles were often broken into little pieces.[72]

---

[70] AHU, Maranhão, cx. 46, doc. 4528.
[71] Marques, *Dicionário*, 91.
[72] AHU, Maranhão, cx. 45, doc. 4458; APEM, livro 12, letter of 24 December 1770. *Pilões* are noted in plantation inventories. TJEM, Inventory of Caetano Rodrigues, 1804.

FIGURE 4.1. "Women milling rice with mortar and pestle in Guinea-Bissau."
Photo by Walter Hawthorne.

Given this, the CGPM encouraged mechanical mill construction, but the company's efforts met with uneven results. In 1768, CGPM administrators ordered a mill built at Igarapé da São José (in Pará near Belém) and paid an engineer to design it. The machine, powered by one horse, vibrated so much as to shear the teeth off its gears.[73] The following year, company officials reported their satisfaction with one of three horse-powered mills in Maranhão, which was partly modeled on Belfort's.[74] The other two mills produced a less desirable product because, administrators speculated, they were made entirely of wood and did not use millstones, which Belfort's mill used.[75] For this, the company encouraged the adoption of Belfort's millstone innovations elsewhere and paid him to visit area planters for discussions. In the meantime, Belfort experimented with wind power.[76]

[73] Marques, *Dicionário*, 91; Marin, "Agricutlura no delta"; Santos, "Cultura," 42.
[74] AHU, Maranhão, cx. 43, doc. 4245, 4264; cx. 45, doc. 4460; ANTT, CGPM, Cartas aos Administradores do Maranhão, livro 215, 15–23.
[75] ANTT, CGPM, Cartas aos Administradores do Maranhão, livro 215, 15–23.
[76] Santos, "Cultura," 42.

Despite these efforts, new mill construction proceeded at a slow pace.[77] By 1772, there were five major mills in Maranhão.[78] However, these were not enough, as "many, many planters have made great fields of rice," but after harvest, it sat in storage waiting for milling.[79] In 1773, officials complained that there was no rice mill in one of the most productive rice-producing regions – Alcântara, which was across the bay from São Luís. Loading unmilled rice onto boats, taking it across the bay, unloading it, transporting it to São Luís–based mills, and then taking it back to ports was "extremely costly."[80] For this, in Alcântara and most other places, masters ordered slaves to mill rice with mortars and pestles on their plantations.[81]

However, hand milling continued to be inadequate, so orders went out for the construction of more mills – fifty being the short-term goal for Maranhão.[82] As these mills were slowly assembled, it became clear that many did not meet minimum standards.[83] Indeed, as late as 1807, an observer from Lisbon said that there were twenty mills in Maranhão that "do not pay any attention to quality."[84] And in 1817, Antonio Julião da Costa Cavalheiro petitioned for the exclusive right to build new "machines to clean and mill rice" in Amazonia. His reason for doing this was that rice from South Carolina was more valued in the European market "since it is cleaner and because its grains are whole, whereas grains from Brazil come with all the grains broken due to the method of milling."[85]

In sum, Portuguese experimented keenly with rice, but their experiments did not always meet with desired results. In Maranhão, Portuguese

---

[77] AHU, Pará, cx. 69, doc. 5913.
[78] AHU, Maranhão, cx. 46, doc. 4514.
[79] APEM, livro 12, letter of 24 December 1770; AHU, Maranhão, cx. 45, doc. 4458; Marques, *Dicionario*, 91.
[80] APEM, livro 12.
[81] AHU, Maranhão, cx. 45, doc. 4458.
[82] AHU, Maranhão, cx. 45, doc. 4458, 4460; ANTT, CGPM, Cartas aos administradores do Maranhão, livro 215, 58–9.
[83] AHU, Maranhão, cx. 48, doc. 4671. For Pará, Alexandre Rodrigues Ferreira, *Viagem filosófica ao Rio Negro* (Belém: Museu Paraense Emilio Goeldi, 1983), 132–7; AHU, Maranhão, cx. 52, doc. 5025. If a more competitive shipping sector raised planter hopes, the regulation of other aspects of the economy squashed them. After 1778, planters complained about the overregulation of the milling market. To encourage mill construction, the government mandated where small producers of rice had to take rice for milling. However, planters complained that quality varied greatly from mill to mill. AHU, Maranhão, cx. 59, doc. 5410, 5462; ANTT, CGPM, Pará, Copiador dos administradores, livro 216, 65–70.
[84] AHU, Maranhão, cx. 154, doc. 11057.
[85] ANRJ, Junta do Comércio, cx. 385, pct. 02.

planners were successful in their attempts to force farmers to grow *O. sativa* from Carolina. Once dark rices were purged from Maranhense fields, Portuguese consumers accepted imports from Maranhão. Planners were less successful, however, in their efforts to design and encourage the construction of mechanical rice mills. In the late eighteenth and early nineteenth centuries, a dearth of quality mills hindered the growth of the rice sector.

MAKING FIELDS

If planters grappled with milling, they also struggled with other aspects of a rice-export economy. Many were recent immigrants and demonstrated complete ignorance of the basics of rice agriculture. In Macapá in the early 1770s, for example, planters failed to retain enough seed from the previous year's crop to begin a new planting.[86] Experiment they did, but Portuguese who knew rice as a food were not experts at producing it on a large scale. The rice system that they created was unsustainable. It destroyed huge sections of forest and transformed much of Maranhão into scrub plain. The system relied little on the skills of the expert rice planters – Upper Guineans – who began to arrive on Maranhão's shores after 1755 and who knew much about producing surpluses of rice without destroying ecosystems.

The first stage of the annual rice cycle was field making. In much of Upper Guinea and in Maranhão, field making was men's work. However, from descriptions of field-making techniques in Maranhão, it is clear that for Upper Guinean males, the labor of carving fields in Amazonian forest was deskilled and decultured. Field making took place in the context of the two types of rice agriculture – wetland and upland. Occasionally, slaves planted rice in freshwater wetlands. In 1771, Maranhão's governor, Joaquim de Melo e Póvoas, noted this while writing that Lourenço Belfort described to him how slave owners in the interior "plant rice on fields that are marshy." Belfort assured the governor that rice grown on wetlands "produces well and that the grain is a perfect size, better than that grown on the upland fields."[87] And a 1787 report noted planters cultivating "wetlands" along the Itapecuru, Mearim, and Monim Rivers. The same planters cultivated cotton on dry lands.[88]

---

[86] Marques, *Dicionário*, 91–3.
[87] APEM, Livros de registro das ordens, livro 12.
[88] ANTT, Ministério do Reino, mç. 601, cx. 704.

Nonetheless, few planters embraced wetland rice. The Portuguese minister for the colonies complained in 1772 that despite the fact that Amazonia had "humid and swampy" lands, little rice was produced there.[89] Discussing the more popular upland form of cultivation, Melo e Póvoas wrote elsewhere, "Here, the only way they farm the land is by cutting the jungle and when it is dry they set it on fire. If there have been no rains, it burns well, and the land is well prepared. However, if it burns badly ... it will never yield much."[90] And F. A. Brandão Júnior's descriptions of field preparation in Maranhão indicate that little changed through the first half of the nineteenth century. Published in the 1860s, his account was based on memories from decades earlier. Brandão Júnior linked the work that was performed to particular seasons. In Maranhão, there are two seasons, one called *tempo de chuva* (or "time of the rain") that stretches from January to July, and one called *tempo sem chuva* (or "time without rain") that lasts from August to December.[91] "The first assignment of the [agricultural] cycle is the chopping down of the forests for the next year's planting, using a scythe to hack down smaller trees," he wrote. This work typically commenced in September or October, mid-dry season, and lasted about two months. Next, in November or December, came the "destruction of the large trees" with iron axes. Once trees were downed, slaves "set fire to the devastated jungle, and then they cut and stack the branches and smaller tree trunks which have escaped the fire and which, occupying the surface of the earth, could hinder development of the crop." The stacks were burned, leaving a field "ravaged by fire and covered with ashes."[92]

The slashing and burning of brush and trees was and is an often-used method for preparing fields in tropical environments the world over. In hot and humid regions, plant matter decays quickly, meaning there are few nutrients in soils to sustain crops. However, upon burning, the stock of nutrients in a forest's biomass is released, becoming ash that settles

[89] AHU, Pará, cx. 67, doc. 5793.

[90] APEM, Livros de registro das ordens, livro 12. Similar description in BNA, FO 63/149; Antonio Bernardino Pereira do Lago, *Estatistica historica-geografica da provincia do Maranhão* (Lisbon: Academia Real das Sciencias, 1822), 54–6.

[91] Description of the seasons is in ANRJ, Diversos códices, códice 798. Rains on the Mearim and Itapecuru Rivers, the center of rice production, became heavier by March. AHU, cx. 45, doc. 28. Also on agricultural cycle, Matthias Röhrig Assunção, *Pfanzer, sklaven und kleinbauern in der brasilianischen provinz Maranhão, 1800–1850* (Frankfurt: Vervuert, 1993), 409.

[92] F. A. Brandão Júnior, *A escravatura no Brasil precedida d'um artigo sobre agricultura e colonisação no Maranhão* (Brussels: H. Thiry-Vern Buggenhoudt, 1865), 31–8.

onto the ground and serves as fertilizer for, usually, one to three plant-ing seasons.[93] To be sure, slash-and-burn – or shifting – agriculture was not unheard of in some of Upper Guinea's forested areas, but Africans in forests everywhere, as well as many Indians in Brazil, approached forest agriculture the same way.[94] Across Brazil, the slash-and-burn approach to field preparation was so widespread that it had its own name – *coivara*, or "the burning of the land."[95] Because there was nothing particularly Upper Guinean about *coivara* in Maranhão, planters showed no prefer-ence for Upper Guinean slaves for field preparation.[96]

Indeed, *coivara* as practiced in Maranhão differed so profoundly from slash-and-burn agriculture as practiced in parts of Upper Guinea that much of the field-making knowledge that Upper Guineans brought with them across the ocean was useless. Mandinka, who comprised a large portion of Maranhão's slave population, came from Upper Guinea's savanna-woodland zone. In 1818, Gaspard Mollien described it as "composed of plains only, covered in several places by thick forests" with inhabitants cultivating "[upland] rice, millet, and maize, and a little indigo and cotton." The high salinity of soils necessitated the shifting of fields, but most farmers burned plots on grasslands, not in forests, creat-ing a space to plant for a year.[97]

[93] Karen Dvoràk, "Resource Management by West African Farmers and the Economics of Shifting Cultivation," *American Journal of Agricultural Economics* 74, 3 (1992), 809–15; Warren Dean, *With Broadax and Firebrand: The Destruction of the Brazilian Atlantic Forest* (Berkeley: University of California Press, 1997), 26–7.

[94] On Indians: Gilberto Freyre, *The Masters and the Slaves: A Study in the Development of Brazilian Civilization*, trans. Samuel Putnam (Berkeley: University of California Press, 1986), 88. On Bahia: Stuart B. Schwartz, *Sugar Plantations in the Formation of Brazilian Society: Bahia, 1550–1835* (New York: Cambridge University Press, 1985), 107. On Central Africa: Paul L. Woomer, Jean Kotto-Same, Mateete A. Bekunda, and J. Robert Okalebo, "The Biological Management of Tropical Soil Fertility: Some Research and Development Priorities for Africa," in *Soil Quality and Agricultural Sustainability*, ed. R. Lal (Boca Raton: CRC Press, 1998), 113. Africa generally: Harold K. Schneider, "Traditional African Economies," in *Africa*, eds. Phyllis M. Martin and Patrick O'Meara (Bloomington: Indiana University Press, 1986), 186. Other regions of Brazil: BNA, FO 63/149; Sandra Lauderdale Graham, *Caetana Says No: Women's Stories from a Brazilian Slave Society* (Cambridge: Cambridge University Press, 2002), 151; Dean, *With Broadax*, 26–27; Hoehne, *Botanica*, 77, 103–5.

[95] B. Madari, V. de M. Benites, and T. J. F. Cunha, "The Effect of Management on the Fertility of Amazonian Dark Earth Soils," in *Dark Earths: Origin Properties Management*, ed. Johannes Lehmann (Dordrecht: Kluwer Academic Publishers, 2003), 411; APEM, Livros de registro das ordens, livro 12, letter of 24 December 1770.

[96] From *Maranhão Inventories Slave Database* (MISD).

[97] Donald R. Wright, *The World and a Very Small Place in Africa: A History of Globalization in Niumi, The Gambia* (Armonk, NY: M. E. Sharpe, 2004), 43–4.

The areas to the west and south, which was the coastal zone from which most Upper Guinean slaves in Maranhão came, was composed partly of dense forest and partly of tidal floodplain in the eighteenth and early nineteenth centuries. For vegetables, tubers, and rice nurseries, coastal-zone farmers sometimes slashed and burned sections of forest, cultivating plots for a year or two before letting them fallow.[98] However, by the second half of the eighteenth century, forest agriculture was of secondary importance for many coastal-zone farmers, and particularly Balanta, Floup, Papel, and Brame, who concentrated efforts on planting rice in mangrove-covered tidal flats.

In mangrove areas, field preparation was particularly demanding and required highly refined knowledge that males acquired over lifetimes. Mangroves had to be cleared, dikes built and maintained with specialized tools, salt leached from soil, paddies carved out of the land, and freshwater levels managed. As nutrient levels in soils diminished, water from rivers had to be introduced and, sometime later, soils desalinated again. Mangrove rice farming was technologically demanding, perhaps more than any other staple of eighteenth-century Atlantic-rim diets. Males who mastered field-preparation techniques gained the respect of their neighbors and the spirits who lived among them. Boys became men in part by learning to produce bounty from saltwater swamps. So successful were coastal farmers at managing salt and soil-nutrient levels that they were able to root villages in the same places for generations. Mangrove rice farming was, then, an equilibrium agricultural system that transformed natural environments but brought no long-term deterioration of them.[99]

The farming of Upper Guinea uplands did not require the same amount of labor or level of technological sophistication. Nonetheless, in Upper Guinea where farmers cleared uplands, they often used strategies to manage environments so that they would support communities over time.

---

[98] Andrew D. Ward, and others, *Environmental Hydrology* (Boca Raton: CRC Press, 2003), 311–12.

[99] Walter Hawthorne, *Planting Rice and Harvesting Slaves: Transformations along the Guinea-Bissau Coast, 1400–1900* (Portsmouth, NH: Heinemann, 2003), 151–76; J. M. Blaut, *The Colonizer's Model of the World* (New York: Guilford Press, 1993), 73; James Fairhead and Melissa Leach, *Misreading the African Landscape: Society and Ecology in a Forest-Savanna Mosaic* (Cambridge: Cambridge University Press, 1996), 79. None of this is to imply that West Africans did not, in some places, drastically alter their environment. See, George E. Brooks, *Landlords and Strangers: Ecology, Society, and Trade in Western Africa, 1000–1630* (Boulder, CO: Westview Press, 1993), 173–4; A. Endre Nyerges, "Ethnography in the Reconstruction of African Land Use Histories: A Sierra Leone Example," *Africa* 66, 1 (1996), 132–4.

One way of doing this was by encouraging forest regeneration. Forests were, after all, vital for community survival, providing protection from enemies as well as game and fruit to supplement diets. Farmers ensured water retention in soils by mounding dirt into which they planted seed and by working organic matter into mounds. As a result, when fields were abandoned, trees established themselves quickly. Also, most farmers cut trees at waist height and took measures to avoid damaging root masses. Consequently, after farmers harvested crops, trees coppiced back, quickly reconstituting forest. To allow nutrients to build up in soil and weeds to be fully shaded out, farmers often did not reuse forest fallows for about thirty years.[100]

In Upper Guinean forests and mangrove swamps, man-made ecological disasters did not force wholesale relocations of populations. Communities did not move because they overfarmed the lands around them. Indeed, in the second half of the nineteenth century, an observer was struck that in Guinea-Bissau "everything denotes ... a country very rich in natural products, low lands and uplands literally covered with ostentatious vegetation that was the most lasting and varied."[101] Another described "virgin jungle extending from the Casamance to the Geba Rivers."[102] This despite the fact that the Mansoa and Geba Rivers contained "the greatest densities of population" in West Africa.[103]

But in Brazil, the *coivara* system was terrifically destructive of the natural environment. In his reflections on Maranhão, Brandão Júnior emphasized that *coivara* "exhausted the soil, which in many places now produces nothing but grasses suitable for grazing cattle."[104] Others left similar descriptions. Robert Hesquith noted how *coivara* coupled with heavy rains led to a "want of cultivation."[105] According to Antonio Pereira do Lago, fields in Maranhão were productive for only one year. In the second, yields fell off considerably. "And in the third," he wrote, the area "was already called *roça velha*," or "old field." This "*destructive*

---

[100] James C. McCann, *Green Land, Brown Land, Black Land: An Environmental History of Africa, 1800–1990* (Portsmouth, NH: Heinemann, 1999), 62; Nyerges, "Ethnography," 124.

[101] Francisco Travassos Valdez, *Africa occidental: Noticias e considerações* (Lisbon: Imprensa Nacional, 1864), 305.

[102] Henrique de Arpoare, "Exploração agronomica em Cabo Verde e Guiné," *Boletim da Sociedade de Geographia de Lisboa* 3a series, 1 (1882), 366.

[103] Joaquim da Graça Correia e Lança, *Relatorio da provincia da Guiné Portugueza* (Lisbon: Imprensa Nacional, 1890), 50–1.

[104] Brandão Júnior, *A escravatura*, 96–9.

[105] BNA, FO 63/149.

and negligent agricultural system," he argued, left farmers with "a lack of land," something that seemed impossible in such a large territory.[106] Others confirmed Lago's observations. Raymundo Jozé de Souza Gayozo, who lived in Maranhão in the late eighteenth and early nineteenth centuries, wrote that rice production decreased after 1807 because of "a lack of forests, as there had been in the past, on the edge of rivers and near great [population] centers." Lands along the Itapecuru River, which had been central to rice farming, were "tired" or nutrient deficient.[107]

One indication of just how land-hungry Maranhense planters were can be found in lists of *sesmarias*, or royal land grants. Best estimates are that under Dom José I (1750–1777), about ninety-five such concessions were given to planters, each for an astonishing fifty square miles. In the last quarter of the eighteenth century, about 505 *sesmarias* were issued. Extant documentation is insufficient to estimate the number of *sesmarias* granted from 1800 to 1822, when the practice was ended.[108] After decades of white planters consuming jungles on their *sesmarias*, Hesquith wrote, "All the land on the banks of the rivers [of Maranhão] is more or less cultivated." The interior, he said, "is much more cultivated and inhabited than is generally supposed." Indeed, a passage to Bahia by way of the Itapecuru River was "cultivated all the way."[109]

Maranhense forests were consumed at a rapid rate because, unlike Upper Guinean farmers, white planters were interested in producing something other than food to sustain local populations. They produced crops for export, proceeds from which lined their pockets. With capital from Lisbon and labor from Africa, planters fully exploited the lands around them. With no thought for long-term consequences, whites pressed blacks to clear jungles as fast as they could and to reclear them as soon as possible. Maranhão's system for claiming fields was not, then, transplanted from Africa. Male slaves' work preparing fields was void of any African-based cultural significance. It was deskilled and decultured drudgery. If boys became men in part by making fields on the Upper Guinea coast, in Maranhão field making made male slaves little more than cogs in a great machine that converted virgin forests into fields and then scrub plains.

---

[106] Lago, *Estatística*, 50–6. Emphasis in original.
[107] Gayozo, *Compendio*, 222–3, 228.
[108] Calculated from APEM, Secretaria do Governo, Códices, livro 9; APEM, Livros de registro das ordens, livro 12. Planters also obtained land by claiming it without a royal grant.
[109] BNA, FO 63/149.

PLANTING, HARVESTING, AND PROCESSING
RICE AND COTTON

Upper Guineans did, however, apply some limited skills and knowledge to other stages of the agricultural cycle in Maranhão. Male and female slaves planted rice and cotton in January, at the start of the rainy season. Male slaves worked *roças novas*, or "new fields" with long-handled hoes, which were modeled on fulcrum shovels from coastal Upper Guinea.[110] Male and female slaves planted seed by using sticks with iron points to make holes. For cotton, they deposited about a dozen seeds in each hole, which was three to four inches deep and spaced five to six feet from the next. Rice holes were made closer. Slaves covered holes by moving dirt over them with the heel of a foot, in the same way Upper Guineans did across the ocean.[111] Doubtless, experience with rice planting made Upper Guineans efficient workers in Maranhão – but not, it seems, efficient enough to make them more valuable than slaves of the same gender and age from other parts of Africa. Indeed, valuations of slaves by African region of origin (Angola, Mina, and Guinea) show no difference once slaves had become acclimated to life in Maranhão.[112] Upland planting skills, then, must have been easy to learn.

After rains came, upland fields of cotton and rice needed to be weeded frequently. Where forest canopies had not become thick before lands were reburned, weeds were not shaded out so seed stocks were heavy. Male and female slaves weeded with iron hoes, tilling soils around sprouting rice and cotton so as not to disrupt their roots, while upending invasive plants that might shade out crops. The work of weeding continued for "as long as it takes for the plants [rice or cotton] to fully establish themselves."[113]

The next step in the agricultural cycle was harvesting. Male and female slaves harvested rice from the end of May through July, the end of the *tempo de chuva*. By this time rice was knee or waist high. Slaves harvested it by moving in lines through fields, each worker holding "a small knife, cutting the stems one by one."[114] The knife was likely

---

[110] Carney, "With Grains," 15; Hawthorne, *Planting Rice*, 162.

[111] Mello e Povoas's description in APEM, Livros de registro das ordens, livro 12.

[112] From 1767 to 1800, the average inventory valuation of slaves in Maranhão who had been born in the Upper Guinea coastal zone was not different from that of slaves from the Angola-Congo region. Calculated from MISD. Calculations made for groups delineated by age and gender and adjusted for inflation over time in the price of slaves.

[113] Brandão Júnior, *A escravatura*, 31–8.

[114] Ibid., 96–9.

FIGURE 4.2. Working fields in Guinea-Bissau with a fulcrum shovel.
From: Hugo Adolf Bernatzik, *Äthiopen des Westens: Forschungsreisen in Portuguiesisch-Guinea* (Wien: Verlag von L. W. Seidel & Sohn, 1933), 79. Image courtesy of Kevin Conru.

modeled on one used in Upper Guinea for the same purpose (known as *cubom* among Balanta). The variety of cotton that was cultivated in the eighteenth and nineteenth centuries was harvested from September through November, eight to ten months after planting.[115] Slaves picked cotton from shoulder-high plants, dispersing "themselves over a certain part of the field, collecting the pods and depositing them in a basket or sack which each slave carries for this purpose attached to his waist."[116] In addition, they dug and processed manioc from September through December, and, during these months, began again the process of making new fields by clearing forest.[117]

Once harvested, rice and cotton needed to be processed. Rice was taken in large bundles to threshing stations. Observers said that the threshing of rice was done in the same manner as in Upper Guinea – "with a branch to loosen the grains" from grasses.[118] Rice was then gathered for milling.

---

[115] Octavio da Costa Eduardo, *The Negro in Northern Brazil* (New York: J. J. Augustin Publishers, 1948), 21. Alden says the harvests of cotton began in October and November in Maranhão. Alden, "Late colonial Brazil," 638; Arno S. Pearse, *Cotton in North Brazil* (Rio de Janeiro: Taylor Garnett Evans and Company, 1923), 120–1.

[116] Brandão Júnior, *A escravatura*, 31–8.

[117] APEM, Livros de registro das ordens, Livro 12; *Journal de lavoura* 9 (São Luís: Typ. do Paiz, June 1875/December 1876).

[118] Brandão Júnior, *A escravatura*, 31–8.

As explained earlier, slaves from Upper Guinea who were skilled at using mortars and pestles often milled rice. When mechanical mills were available in an area, the work was done by machine.[119] If the hand milling of rice was laborious, so, too, was the processing of cotton. Because mechanical devices modeled on Eli Whitney's gin were not experimented with in Maranhão until 1826 (and not widely used until about 1850), slaves processed cotton by hand, separating lint from seed.[120] Lint was then sacked in bundles, which were taken by cart to storage houses and then to riverboats.[121] Despite the difficulty of removing cottonseed from lint, Maranhão's governor claimed in 1775 that planters preferred cotton to rice because it required less work.[122]

In Maranhão after 1755, rice was the product of black labor.[123] Clearly some of the tools and techniques used for rice planting and processing had their origins in Upper Guinea. But the deep roots of rice agriculture in Maranhão stretched in many directions. They sprang from long histories of Upper Guinean involvement with the crop, Indian rice gathering, Indian slave labor, Portuguese experimentation, and European capitalist production.

WORK'S PHYSICAL TOLL

No matter what knowledge Upper Guineans brought to agriculture in Maranhão, rice, like cotton, was a cruel crop. "At six o'clock in the morning," Brandão Júnior wrote, "the overseer forces the poor slave, still exhausted from the evening's labors, to rise from his rude bed and proceed to his work." An old man, who in the early twentieth century recalled his days as a slave in Maranhão, described a day beginning at four o'clock, "when a bell was struck and the overseers knocked at the houses of the slaves to be sure they awakened." Work, he said, continued until five in the evening.[124] In September and October, slaves' work consisted of twelve or more hours of slashing forest undergrowth. After the initial burn, they worked in shadeless fields, cutting and moving heavy trees to large piles. Of all the work in Maranhão, clearing fields was the

---

[119] AHU, Maranhão, cx. 45, doc. 4458.
[120] Mesquita, *Vida e morte*, 114.
[121] Alden, "Late colonial Brazil," 638.
[122] APEM, Livros de registro das ordens, Livro 12.
[123] Though in scattered places, free Indians produced it and took it to mills. AHU, Marnahão, cx. 59, doc. 5452.
[124] Brandão Júnior, *A escravatura*, 31–8; Eduardo, *The Negro*, 16.

most dangerous, often "fatal for a worker." Fires sometimes got out of control, resulting in some being burned alive and others being crushed by falling trees. "Rarely escapes some disgraced slave from becoming a victim," Brandão Junior wrote.[125]

Although less dangerous, weeding brought little relief. A constant chore throughout the early part of the rainy season, weeding was "painful labor for slaves, who, with nothing to work with but a weeding-hook, are forced to stand in a stooped position during the entire day, cutting the shoots of other native plants, and enduring a temperature in the sun of 40 Celsius [104 Fahrenheit]."[126] And harvesting brought no less discomfort. Slaves endured hot, shadeless twelve-hour days, standing bent over to cut rice and upright with a heavy basket as they picked cotton.

The physical toll that labor in fields took on slaves is obvious from plantation inventories, many of which justify lower-than-average values for slaves by listing injuries. Although there is no way of knowing how particular injuries occurred, we can assume that because plantation slaves spent twelve hours each day, six or seven days each week working for their masters, most injuries were directly related to their labor. Overworked and exhausted slaves could not avoid losing focus and accidentally cutting themselves or others with machetes, axes, scythes, planting sticks, and hoes. Sent into forests and fields without the protection of shoes or clothing beyond a loincloth or coarse cotton wrap, slaves suffered scrapes, cuts, and punctures to their extremities. Hazards were everywhere – from falling trees that could kill a man or break his bones, to sharply cut limbs and vines that could gouge an eye or slice a limb, to rice milling machinery that could catch a finger or whole arm in turning gears. Wounds that today would be considered minor often festered, becoming major health risks. Although many wounds healed with the application of slaves' home remedies, some resulted in the loss of fingers, toes, arms, legs, and eyes, and others brought death.[127]

Careful inventory takers made notes of slaves who were *aleijado* (crippled), *coxo* (lame), suffered *feridas* (wounds), or were *cego* (blind). On Antonio da Silva's plantation in 1824, seven slaves were blind in one or both eyes (and another had a seriously wounded eye), one had a "crippled" arm and one had a "crippled" foot, another had a "lame" leg, and another

---

[125] Brandão Júnior, *A escravatura*, 31–8.
[126] Ibid.
[127] Many plantations had slave *barbeiros*, who specialized in healing. See TJEM, Inventory of Antonio da Silva, 1824; Inventory of Antonio da Souza, 1802; Inventory of D. Anna Maria Rapoza, 1804.

was listed as "sick in the legs."[128] On Felippe de Barros Vasconcellos's plantation in 1831, nine slaves were blind in one or both eyes (including several who were missing eyes), and ten slaves had "crippled" limbs. In addition, eight were *ruim* ("defective" in a way that left them unable to work). Sometimes seriously wounded limbs were amputated and occasionally replaced with prosthetics.[129] Hence in 1813, Adão, a Bijago, was "crippled for not having a foot," and in 1810 an inventory taker noted that Julião had a "wooden leg."[130] Other possible work-related injuries recorded in inventories included broken ribs and shoulders and cuts on various parts of the body.[131]

One of the most common injuries from which slaves suffered was a *quebradura na verilha* – "rupture in the groin" or hernia of the inguinal or femoral variety.[132] Inguinal hernias are most often brought on by heavy lifting, which can result in the failure of an embryonic closure around the abdomen. When the embryonic closure herniates, the contents of the intestines descend into the hernia, causing a noticeable bulge. Hernias are not necessarily painful but can be uncomfortable. Moreover, if the intestines are pinched in the hernia, an obstruction can occur, resulting in strangulation followed by gangrene and death. Marçal, a fifty-year-old Mandinka on Leonel Fernandes Vieira's plantation, may have suffered from a strangulated intestine as he was said to have a *quebradura na verilha* and obstruction. On the same plantation, sixty-year-old Nastacio from Cape Verde also had a hernia.[133] And hernias are noted in many other inventories from the early nineteenth century. For example, in 1831 on Felippe de Barros Vasconcellos's plantation, five male slaves ranging in age from twenty to sixty had "bulges" or "ruptures" in their groins.[134] In 1807, on Antonio Henriques Leal's plantation, two male slaves had hernias, and in 1824 on Antonio da Silva's plantation, three male slaves had them.[135]

The seriousness of some slaves' injuries is evidenced by the fact that after descriptions of wounds in inventories, notes were sometimes penned later in the margin stating *morto*, or "dead," and *falecido*, or

[128] TJEM, Inventory of Antonio da Silva, 1821.
[129] TJEM, Felippe de Barros Vasconcellos, 1831.
[130] TJEM, Inventory of Antonio Joze Mesquita, 1813.
[131] TJEM, Inventory of Sargento Mór Manoel Joquim do Paço, 1823.
[132] See description of Miguel, in TJEM, Inventory of Jozefa Joaquina de Berredo, 1808.
[133] TJEM, Inventory of Leonel Fernandes Vieira, 1816.
[134] TJEM, Inventory of Felippe de Barros Vasconcellos, 1831.
[135] TJEM, Inventory of Antonio Henriques Leal, 1807.

"deceased." On Vasconcellos's plantation, forty-year-old Caetano, a Mandinka who was "crippled in an arm and leg," and twenty-four-year-old Silvestre, a Bambara who was "crippled in the right leg," died shortly after notes were taken about them.[136] Similarly, in 1807 twenty-eight-year-old Jacinto was listed in an inventory as "defective for having a wound on a leg." In the margin was later written "*falecido*."[137] In an 1813 inventory, fifty-eight-year-old Leonora was "sick with an illness of the foot." A short time later someone wrote beside her name, "This slave is dead."[138] In 1806, fifty-year-old Alberto was said to have "an incurable illness in his right foot." Sometime later, *morto* was scrawled next to his name.[139]

THE CULTURAL AND GENDERED DIMENSIONS OF LABOR

Although they performed dangerous work over long days for their masters, slaves in Maranhão generally received some time to tend their own crops. An observer noted in the 1780s that many slave owners "gave a little land to slaves, ordinarily with time allotted to them on Sundays, and from which to raise crops for subsistence."[140] This practice continued for decades to come. A visitor noted in the early 1820s, "Some *senhores* give their slaves every week a *dia de fazer* [day to do things] to work for themselves ... for the better part ... this is Sundays."[141] Planters liked this arrangement because it was cheaper than giving food to slaves. Moreover, slaves often liked cultivating their own crops, as they could shape their diets. Indeed, in Maranhão, Upper Guinean slaves produced rice for themselves, replicating as best they could diets from their homelands. It was so common for slaves to grow rice on their plots that in 1772, when Mello e Póvoas mandated planting of *carolina*, he felt it necessary to decree a special punishment for slaves who continued to grow *arroz de terra*.[142] The severity of the punishment – two years in

[136] TJEM, Inventory of Felippe de Barros e Vasconcellos, 1831.
[137] TJEM, Inventory of Dona Anna Joquina Baldez, 1807.
[138] TJEM, Inventory of Jorge Gromuel, 1813.
[139] TJEM, Inventory of Anna Joaquina Gromuel, 1806.
[140] ANTT, Ministério do Reino, mç. 601, cx. 704. However, some slaves worked some hours on Sundays for their masters. See, APEM, AAM, cx. 20, doc. 883; Livro 214.
[141] Francisco de N. S. Dos Prazeres, "Poranduba maranhense ou relação histórica da província do Maranhão," *Revista trimensal do Instituto do Histórico e Geographico Brazileiro* 54 (1891), 139.
[142] AHU, Maranhão, cx. 46, doc. 4528.

FIGURE 4.3. Man collecting unmilled rice that has dried in the sun, Maranhão. Photo by Walter Hawthorne.

prison – indicates that slaves may have been loath to grow white rice, perhaps because *arroz de terra* bore more similarities to the *glaberrima* they knew in their homelands.

Rice-based meals often included protein from slaves' holdings of animals and from "stealing and hunting."[143] A report from 1767 described slave diets in Maranhão on the plantation of S. Bras as consisting of rice,

---

[143] D. J. G. de Magalhaens, "Memoria historica da revolução da provincia do Maranhão (1838–1840)" *Opusculos historicos e litterarios* (Rio de Janeiro: Livraria de B.L. Garnier, 1865), 8.

farinha, and dried meat.[144] Traveling in Amazonia in the early nineteenth century, an observer said of black slaves, "Their sustenance was based on rice and manioc flour and sometimes a piece of meat."[145] That meat often consisted of beef – cattle being prevalent in parts of Maranhão. However, where beef was not plentiful, slaves sought protein from "shellfish, small fish and some game."[146] They, too, consumed beans and manioc leaves, which are particularly high in protein.

Although slaves harvested much of their own food, they did not always produce all of it. In some cases, masters supplemented slave diets. "It was not unusual," Governor Silva wrote in 1787, for a master to give slaves "a basket or an *alqueire* [3.7 gallons] of *farinha* every month." Moreover, some provided protein, giving them on occasion two *libras* (32 ounces) of fresh meat and "an *arrouba* [32 pounds] per month of dried meat." How many slaves this was supposed to sustain is unclear.[147] In the early nineteenth century, wealthy planter Antonio José de Souza killed some number of livestock each week to feed his 350 slaves. Also, 1,310 *alqueires* (18,340 liters, or 4,847 gallons) of rice were stored specifically for consumption by slaves.[148] Planter Joze Ferreira da Costa had 110 *alqueires* of rice marked for consumption by his slaves, along with twelve head of cattle.[149] However, on poorly producing plantations, food was often lacking with some slaves becoming so hungry that they resorted to "dirt eating."[150]

But when they were given plots, Upper Guinean slaves grew rice for themselves in Maranhão. This is hardly surprising. Rice was, after all, *the* staple of Upper Guinea coastal diets and was central to interior diets. To this day, Upper Guinea coastal people cannot conceive of a meal that does not involve rice. If rice is sometimes a food for most of us, for Upper Guineans food *is* rice. In addition to being the sustenance of Balanta, Papel, Floup, Brame, and others, during the high point of Atlantic slavery, rice was a store of wealth, a trade good in

---

[144] ANTT, Ministério do Reino, mç. 601, cx. 704.

[145] Quoted in Zelinda Machado de Castro e Lima, *Pecados da gula: Comeres e beberes das gentes do Maranhão* (São Luís: CBPC, 1998), I: 6.

[146] Lago, *Estastíca*, 25.

[147] ANTT, Ministério do Reino, mç. 601, cx. 704. Another description of slave diets is in BNA, FO 63/149.

[148] TJEM, Inventory of D. Luiza Maria de Souza, 1805.

[149] TJEM, Inventory of Joze Ferreira da Costa, 1808.

[150] TJEM, Inventory of Felippe de Barros Vasconcellos, 1831. Also on slave hunger, see, ANTT, Ministério do Reino, mç 601, cx 704; AHU, Maranhão, cx. 41, doc. 4050; Magalhaens, "Memoria historica," 8.

bartering arrangements, and treasure offered to spirits of the deceased. For Upper Guineans, rice was, following David Evan Sutton's examination of food's meaning in societies around the world, "about identity creation and maintenance." It was a "boundary marker," distinguishing – like dress, language, and many other things – those who were part of a group from those who were not.[151] But rice was even more than that. Food, Sutton argues, can evoke powerful memories, making meals the times when "past becomes present."[152] And, indeed, there can be no doubt that meals around calabashes filled with rice and a protein-rich sauce evoked memories for Upper Guineans in Maranhão of the land of their birth.

Females from Upper Guinea certainly attempted to re-create meals from a place they remembered. They favored darker, long-grained rices that resembled *glaberrima*, they milled rice by hand with mortars and pestles like those they had grown up using, and they winnowed rice in flat baskets that they weaved as they had across the ocean.[153] Rice-cooking techniques used in Maranhão also point to an Upper Guinean origin. In Africa, rice was cooked so as to become a product that separated on the plate or in the bowl. That is, Africans cooked "loose" and not sticky rice. To achieve this, African women brought water in a pot to a rapid boil before adding rice. After a short time, they drained off excess water and removed the pot from high heat, allowing grains to absorb moisture from steam. This method of rice preparation differs from those of European traditions. For risottos, paellas, and pilafs, oil or animal fats are added to rice during cooking. Upper Guineans, to the contrary, did not add animal fat or oil to rice while cooking it.[154] And in Maranhão, the preferred way to cook rice is rooted in the African, rather than European, tradition. Indeed, cookbooks have long instructed that for *arroz maranhense* (Maranhão rice), rice should be added to rapidly boiling water, "then the water drained, leaving a little." Finally, the pot is left to sit covered until the remaining water has turned to steam and been absorbed.[155]

[151] David Evan Sutton, *Remembrance of Repasts: An Anthropology of Food and Memory* (New York: Berg Publishers, 2001), 5.
[152] Ibid., 159.
[153] Eduardo, *The Negro*, 16, 19–25.
[154] Carney, *Black Rice*, 114–15.
[155] Recipes are explored in Castro e Lima, *Pecados*, II: 6; Luis da Camara Cascudo, *História da alimentação no Brasil* (São Paulo: Companhia Editora Nacional, 1968), 126.

Upper Guinean women on both sides of the ocean topped rice prepared this way with sauces made from vegetables and protein from wild
game, fish, shellfish, small animals they kept, and beef. The topping of
rice with sauces is not part of a Portuguese culinary tradition in which
rice is served beside meat or as part of a soup (rice having been cooked
with the other ingredients). Today, the popular Maranhense dish *arroz
de caranguejo* – rice topped with a sauce made from crab – especially
replicates Upper Guinean culinary sensibilities. So, too, does *moqueca de
peixe*, a fish stew made with palm oil (common in West African cuisine),
which is dished on top of *arroz maranhense*. And *arroz de cuxá* also
appears to have been adapted from West African traditions. Also called,
caruru de Guiné, which hints at its origin, *arroz de cuxá* is dried shrimp
(popular on the Upper Guinea coast) mixed with a range of spices, all
served on top of rice. Hibiscus leaves give the dish its distinctive flavor,
and these have long been used in dishes throughout Upper Guinea. The
word *cuxá*, which is not Portuguese, is most likely from *kutxá*, which is
Mandinka for hibiscus (*Hibiscus sabdariffa*).[156]

As they had across the ocean, Upper Guinean women on Amazonian
plantations served rice-based meals in calabash gourds, gathering around
them with their families and plantation mates. They remembered, perhaps, communities lost while forging different sorts of community bonds
under slavery.[157] The meals African women prepared were not identical
to those known in Upper Guinea. After a long day of fieldwork, female
slaves likely had little energy to prepare food the way they might have
wished. Moreover, they had to work with the limited foodstuffs available
to them. Nonetheless, Upper Guinean females prepared dishes the only
way they knew how. That is, they prepared them as they had learned to
in their homelands. Although they had little control over what they did
in their masters' fields, they did have some control over how they nour-
ished their families, and they shaped their families' meals the way their
mothers had taught them. As they made meals, they remade Guinea in
Amazonia.

---

[156] Antonio Carreira, *As Companhias Pombalinas de Grão-Pará e Maranhão e Pernambuco
e Paraíba* (Lisbon: Editorial Presença, 1983), 102–3. Matthias Röhrig Assunção,
"Maranhão, terra Mandinga," *Comissão maranhense de folclore* 20 (2001), 5; Cascudo,
História da alimentação, 125–6. Others have placed the origins of the word *cuxá* elsewhere. Zelinda Machado de Castro e Lima "Pescados da gula," in *Comeres e beberes
das gentes do Maranhão* (São Luís: Centro Brasileiro de Produção Cultural, 1998), 22.
On "caruru de Guiné," Raul Lody and Raul Giovanni da Motta, *Dicionário de arte
sacra & técnicas afro-brasileiras* (Rio de Janeiro: Pallas Editora, 2003), 46.
[157] Eduardo, *The Negro*, 29.

CONCLUSION

For the *crioulo* children of Upper Guineans in Maranhão, Africa was a woman. Little of what *crioulos* knew of Africa came from work in fields. Much came from observing women milling rice with mortars and pestles, winnowing it in straw baskets, and cooking it over high heat. It came while sitting around calabashes that contained rice-based meals. Slaves controlled few aspects of their working lives in Maranhão, but masters did see fit to allow them to have a say in what they grew for themselves and how they prepared it for consumption. Hence, the meals that Upper Guinean women made closely resembled the meals they had known in their homelands. Slaves like Rita, whose story opened this chapter, led lives in Upper Guinea that were patterned like those of their mothers and grandmothers. In Maranhão, Rita and her female plantation mates from Upper Guinea found it possible to emulate part of their working lives as they had been fashioned before. Hence, slaves like Rita passed knowledge of Upper Guinean cuisine to children like Veridina, the result being a culinary tradition that spans the ocean and links people of African descent in two very distant places.

Although slaves like Roberto, whose story also opened this chapter, came from rice-producing societies, they had few opportunities to shape their work over rice in Maranhão. After 1755, white masters, driven by the desire to make quick profits, pressed black male slaves to clear massive amounts of primary forest for the planting of rice and cotton. With no thought for the future and no knowledge of tropical agriculture, planters' strategies were devastating – both for slaves and forests. Planters' approaches bore little resemblance to those pursued for field making in Upper Guinean mangrove swamps or interior savanna-woodlands. Few of the skills Upper Guinean slaves brought with them across the ocean were valuable in field making in Maranhão. If boys became men by making fields in Upper Guinea, they gained no glory by working them in Maranhão. The work was deskilled and decultured.

This is not to imply that Upper Guineans did not shape any aspect of the rice regime in Maranhão. That regime grew out of a long, Atlantic-wide engagement with rice. It was shaped by Indian, Portuguese, and Upper Guinean knowledge of agriculture and tastes for food. In Maranhão, planters put considerable thought into how to transform a crop that had been a staple into a viable export. They substituted Upper Guineans for Indian slaves, mandated the planting of *carolina*, experimented with mechanical mills, and invested in transportation. Upper Guinean slaves labored under a task system, which gave them some incentive to work efficiently. They crafted tools for the planting, weeding, harvesting, and milling of rice as they had across the ocean. Further, many Upper Guinean techniques for planting and harvesting crops were applied in Maranhão. In Maranhão, then, rice was neither metaphorically black nor white. It was brown. That is, it was the product of inputs from people from three corners of the Atlantic.

5

Violence, Sex, and the Family

In 1799, a white woman living in Maranhão named Maria de Bairros complained in divorce proceedings that her husband, Antonio de Bairros, "regularly raped and violated his female slaves and those of others." She also claimed that for "years he has lived publicly and scandalously with a concubine who is his slave and is called Jeronima."[1] Maria made mention, as well, of another slave with whom Antonio had had a sexual relationship – Barbara. Called before a priest, Antonio confessed to the sins of which his wife had spoken. However, in the heat of the divorce proceedings, he turned the tables on Maria, recounting how jealousy had driven her to commit a horrendous act. Antonio said that Maria became so enraged at his escapades, and particularly those with his favorite black concubine, that she took an iron poker and heated it in fire before "burning the private parts of his slave named Barbara, martyring her and leaving her in a miserable state." A short while later and "to escape justice, it was necessary to sell the slave out of the district."[2] Neither Antonio nor Maria would have to pay an earthly penalty beyond a small fine for the torture and subsequent sale of Barbara.

This heart-wrenching account is recorded alongside notes about other episodes in the lives of slave women and men in Church books of divorce and denunciation found in Maranhão's state archive. Most of the slaves mentioned in those books were from the Upper Guinea region of Africa or were the *crioulo* (Afro-Brazilian) descendants of Upper Guineans. Taken together, entries in Church records show that people of color were

---

[1] APEM, AAM, cx. 129, doc. 4415.
[2] Ibid.

incredibly constrained by complex gendered and racial hierarchies in Maranhão. In this racist and patriarchal society, the state rarely intervened in matters concerning white masters and their slaves. White power over people of color, and especially slaves, was immense. It was so in Maranhão's frontier period – which stretched from the early seventeenth through the mid-eighteenth centuries, when Indian slaves were the captaincy's principal workers and economic production was very limited. And it was so in Maranhão's plantation period – which began after the mid-eighteenth century, when Portuguese policy makers encouraged the importation of large numbers of African slave laborers, and rice and cotton exports rose dramatically.

But despite the fact that whites reigned over them, Africans in Maranhão managed to shape some aspects of their lives. This is particularly true of their family lives. Though there were a number of impediments to slaves' forming families in the captaincy, many slave women managed to escape the horrific fate of Barbara and to find long-term African and *crioulo* male companions, and, at times, white male companions. Many married and raised children who, themselves, lived to marry and have children. Moreover, most Africans made conscious, culturally shaped decisions about whom to marry. Indeed most marriages involving African slaves in Maranhão took place between Africans from the same region of the continent. That is, African slaves favored companions who were from the same broad African cultural zone. Through these relationships, African slaves found it possible to pass cultural knowledge accumulated across the ocean to their *crioulo* children. Slave children on plantations in Maranhão grew up in houses that were, in some ways, defined by cultural patterns their parents had known. When and where they could, African slaves, and particularly the Upper Guinean majority, shaped Maranhão's cultural landscape. As slaves in Maranhão, Upper Guineans re-created some aspects of the lives they had known in Upper Guinea.

This is not to imply that in domestic matters all of Maranhão's cultural roots stretched in one direction. Not all long-term sexual relationships involving slaves had them coupling with each other. Some slaves coupled with whites – even with their own masters. If Maria de Bairros described her husband's actions accurately, he raped some of his slaves, forcing himself upon them in violent and humiliating short-term encounters. However, he also took at least two slave women – Barbara and Jeronima – as concubines, "living with them" for extended periods of time.

When taken as a whole, notes about slave concubines that are recorded in Church books of divorce and denunciation indicate that slaves sometimes took advantage of their masters' desires for them to better their lot in life. Clearly Barbara, Jeronima, and others like them were limited in their ability to navigate within Maranhão's slave system. Slave women had few good options when men like Antonio pursued sex. If sex was unwanted, physical resistance could (and in many cases did) bring harsh reprisal. Further, because white men wielded great power on their plantations, slave women in Maranhão often had no one to whom to appeal when wronged by their masters.[3] And, slaves' sexual relationships with white men who were married raised the ire of white wives, resulting, in Barbara's case, in an unspeakably agonizing attack. Nonetheless, some slaves managed to exploit cracks in the colonial system by maneuvering themselves to realize some gains when masters wanted sex, short-term companionship, or long-term domestic partnerships.

In this chapter, then, I examine the range of domestic relationships in which African and *crioulo* women found themselves in Maranhão. Most often, women from Upper Guinea who were slaves in Maranhão fostered long-term sexual relationships with Upper Guinean men, re-creating patterns they had known across the ocean. However, Upper Guinean women and their *crioulo* descendants also fostered relationships with white men, doing their best to advance their material and social conditions and those of their children.

SLAVE FAMILY LIFE

From the arrival of the first slave ship from Africa in the seventeenth century through the early nineteenth century, the ratio of black males to black females in Maranhão was skewed. It was particularly so after the mid-eighteenth century, when, following the chartering of the Company of Grão Pará and Maranhão, African slaves began arriving in greater numbers than ever before. From plantation inventories taken between 1767 and 1800, it is evident that 56 percent of the black slave population was male, a percentage that remained unchanged from 1800 to 1830 (Tables 5.1 and 5.2). Among *crioulo* slaves over both periods, there was one female for every male. But the African portion of the slave population was about two-thirds male because, overall, more males than females were shipped from African ports. Examining African slaves by the region

---

[3] In other Brazilian settings, women found ways to appeal against injustices. See, particularly, Sandra Lauderdale Graham, *Caetana Says No: Women's Stories from a Brazilian Slave Society* (New York: Cambridge University Press, 2002).

TABLE 5.1. *Regions of Origin and Gender Ratios of Slaves in Maranhão Plantation Inventories, 1767–1800*

	Gender		
	Female	Male	Total
West Central	19	30	49
	38.80%	61.20%	
Africa, unknown	0	4	4
	0%	100%	
Brazil (*crioulo*)	48	48	96
	50%	50%	
Mina coast, Africa	4	4	8
	50%	50%	
Upper Guinea, unknown	1	1	2
	50%	50%	
Upper Guinea coast/rice	43	47	90
	47.80%	52.20%	
Upper Guinea interior/mixed	9	26	35
	25.70%	74.30%	
Total	124	160	284
	43.66%	56.34%	

Sources: Hawthorne, MISD.

from which they hailed, great variations in gender ratios are evident. From 1767 to 1800, 74 percent of slaves from the interior of the Upper Guinea region (most of whom were Mandinka) were male. From West Central Africa, 61 percent of slaves were male. However, the population of slaves in Maranhão who hailed from the Upper Guinea coastal zone displayed a near-even gender ratio (52 percent male).[4]

In Maranhão, gender ratios along with decisions that slaves, masters, and the state made about sexual relationships shaped male–female interactions both within and outside the institution of marriage. Focusing first on the decisions African slaves made, it is clear that they favored marriage and sexual partners from their own broad cultural group – that is,

---

[4] Surveys of the population of Ribeira do Itapucurú from 1803 to 1805 make the skewed gender ratio clear. Of the slave population, there were 6,025 males and 4,685 females in 1803, 6,302 and 5,195 females in 1804, and 6,600 males and 5,175 females in 1805. That is, about 56 percent of the slave population was male. Of the free population, in 1803, adults numbered 676 men and 318 women. Raymond Jozé de Souza Gayozo, *Compêndio histórico-político dos princípios da lavoura do Maranhão* (Paris: P. N. Rougeron, Impressor, 1818), 164.

TABLE 5.2. *Regions of Origin and Gender Ratios of Slaves in Maranhão Plantation Inventories, 1801–1830*

	Gender		
	Female	Male	Total
Angola-Congo	549	803	1352
	40.60%	59.40%	
Africa, unknown	37	79	116
	31.90%	68.10%	
Brazil (*crioulo*)	1532	1475	3007
	50.90%	49.10%	
Cape Verde	4	4	8
	50%	50%	
Mina coast, Africa	173	391	564
	30.70%	69.30%	
Mozambique	29	122	151
	19.20%	80.80%	
Portugal	2	1	3
	66.70%	33.30%	
São Tomé	0	9	9
	0%	100%	
Upper Guinea, unknown	15	34	49
	30.60%	69.40%	
Upper Guinea coast	655	748	1403
	46.70%	53.30%	
Upper Guinea interior	311	592	903
	34.40%	65.60%	
Total	3307	4258	7565
	43.70%	56.30%	

Sources: Hawthorne, MISD.

from their region of Africa, but not necessarily from their more narrow ethnic group. I should also emphasize that in rural areas of Maranhão, *casar na amizade*, or "marrying in friendship" – marrying "informally" and not in the Church – was common for both blacks and whites. These arrangements were also called *mancebía* or *amigação* and often involved partners living together in the same house over a long term.[5] But whatever

[5] Octavio da Costa Eduardo, *The Negro in Northern Brazil* (New York: J. J. Augustin Publishers, 1948), 29–38; Matthias Röhrig Assunção, "Popular Culture and Regional Society in Nineteenth-Century Maranhão, Brazil," *Bulletin of Latin American Research* 14, 3 (1995), 273.

form marriages took, Africans most often made their own decisions about whether or not to marry and whom to marry. Their choices, then, reveal something about how they saw themselves.[6]

A wealth of information about marriage patterns can be culled from postmortem inventories taken in Maranhão. When a property owner died there, the state made record of his or her slaves and other possessions. Typically, inventory takers asked slaves a standardized list of questions, which included to whom they were married, how many children they had, and from what "nation" they hailed. To the question, "What is your nation?" Upper Guineans usually responded with an ethnonym – Balanta, Bijago, Papel, Banhun, Brame, Mandinka, and Floup, for example. Such responses reveal (see the Introduction to this volume) who slaves thought they were – what identities they thought were important. They make clear that African ethnic or national identities often survived the Atlantic crossing and held meaning for slaves in the Americas.[7]

But ethnic identities were not the only identities that Upper Guineans possessed. Like all people, Upper Guineans saw themselves as holding multiple and overlapping identities that changed over time. In Upper Guinea, members of particular ethnic groups identified themselves by the place they lived, a language they spoke, the histories they told, the clothes they wore, the foods they ate, and the ancestral spirits they called on for help with earthly matters. But, members of particular ethnic groups were often multilingual; some people spoke a regionwide language of trade called Kriolo; people changed their clothes depending on the setting in which they found themselves; some moved to different places to take up residence; and they recognized the power of spirits that had regionwide significance to the members of many ethnic groups. Further, migrants from one ethnic community were often absorbed into another one. And most Upper Guineans saw rice as the most important life-sustaining food. That is, all Upper Guineans, regardless of their ethnic group, came from a common cultural zone. All Upper Guineans shared a broader regional identity.[8]

The importance of that regional identity is shown through marriage patterns. In Upper Guinea, marriage patterns varied across ethnic groups.

---

[6] The arrangement of slave marriages by slave owners is not discussed in extant documents. It may have occurred, but I have no evidence that it did.

[7] Gwendolyn Midlo Hall, *Slavery and African Ethnicities in the Americas: Restoring the Links* (Chapel Hill: The University of North Carolina Press, 2005), 52.

[8] Boubacar Barry, *Senegambia and the Atlantic Slave Trade* (New York: Cambridge University Press, 1998), 35; Hall, *Slavery and African Ethnicities*, 52.

However, generally speaking, most people married endogamously – within their own ethnic group and often within their own village. At times, villages forged linkages with villages of people from other ethnic groups and with merchants in ports and trade towns through exogenous marriages. Indeed, it was common for black merchants from coastal and interior entrepôts and for white settlers and Afro-Portuguese traders in Bissau and Cacheu to marry women from rural groups. Exogenous marriages helped facilitate exchange and broadened communities' kinship networks. Nonetheless, many more people married within their ethnic group than married people from other groups.

In Maranhão, Upper Guineans fostered the endogamous marriage norms they had known across the ocean, but the nature of the group in which they married endogamously changed. That is, there is nothing in records describing marriages to indicate that Upper Guineans most often married others from the same ethnic group – the pattern that was most common across the ocean. Rather, records recounting marriages in Maranhão point to Upper Guineans most often marrying others from the same cultural zone – regardless of ethnicity. Upper Guineans usually married Upper Guineans. In Maranhão, endogamy was defined by regional – not by ethnic – affiliation. Through their marriages, Upper Guineans re-created a regional identity in Maranhão; they did not re-create ethnic identities. A regional preference can also be seen in marriages involving women from Angola and Mina.[9]

Though sources for the period are scarce, it appears that a regionally defined pattern of African endogamous marriage was established in Maranhão well before the Portuguese policy changes that ushered in a wave of African slaves after 1755. From the early seventeenth through the mid-eighteenth centuries, African imports into Maranhão were few, numbering less than 3,500. Scattered over a vast territory, life for African slaves in Maranhão was, then, difficult and lonely. Most Africans were purchased from ships by owners who could afford only one or two slaves. Therefore, in this period, most Africans were not clustered on plantations

---

[9] Comparisons can be made to Bahia, where Linda Wimmer shows high rates of endogamous marriage within broad African regional zones of origin. "Ethnicity and Family Formation among Slaves on Tobacco Farms in the Bahian Recôncavo, 1698–1820," in *Enslaving Connections: Changing Cultures of Africa and Brazil during the Era of Slavery*, eds. José C. Curto and Paul E. Lovejoy (Amherst, NY: Humanity Books, 2004), 149–62. Also, on African marriage preference, Stuart B. Schwartz, *Sugar Plantations in the Formation of Brazilian Society: Bahia, 1550–1835* (New York: Cambridge University Press, 1985), 391–2.

with others from the same cultural zone. Many lived in isolation with their masters and a few Indian slaves on small frontier farms.[10] However, some managed – on farms and in towns – to find others from the same broad region of Africa. Hence, in 1687, Jesuits recorded the marriage of two of their slaves, Miguel and Luiza, both "of the pagans of Guinea," a designation indicating that each had been born in Africa's Upper Guinea region.[11] Further, in 1745, the will of João da Cunha, a resident of Maranhão, listed two married slaves from Africa: Manoel and Maria, both from the Mina coast, who had a son named João.[12] And in 1752, Jacinho and Anna, both from Upper Guinea and slaves of the merchant Antonio Luis Abreu, were married in São Luís.[13] Other records for the period are frustratingly less conclusive. For example, in 1735, Ignaçio and Jozepha, both listed simply as "black" in Church records, married in the São Luís parish of Nossa Senhora de Vitória. Also married in 1735 were Raymundo and Thereza, "black" slaves who lived in São Luís.[14]

Data for the period after the mid-eighteenth century is much richer and points to a clear pattern of Africans choosing regionally defined endogamous marriage. The first source is Church books of marriages. Combining hundreds of listings over several parishes, it is evident that 80 percent of Upper Guineans who married in Maranhão did so with other Upper Guineans; and 65 percent of Angolans married other Angolans. Very clear preferences indeed! Unfortunately, marriage records do not permit a finer breakdown of from where exactly these Africans hailed. That is, priests who recorded marriages generally designated the region of birth of Africans – *Guiné* (for Upper Guinea), *Mina* (for Lower Guinea), *Angola* (for West Central Africa), and *Moçambique* (for East Africa). They did not, generally, write down ethnonyms – Balanta, Bijago, Floup, Banhun, Cacheu, Papel, etc. – like the recorders of postmortem inventories did.[15]

---

[10] AHU, Maranhão, cx. 8, doc. 869.

[11] BNL, Collecção Pombalina, no. 4, f. 18.

[12] Antonia da Silva Mota, and others, *Cripto maranhenses e seu legado* (São Paulo: Editora Siciliano, 2001), 61–5.

[13] APEM, AAM, Livro de registro de casamentos da freguesia de N.S. da Vitória (Sé), 1748–1759, livro 85.

[14] APEM, AAM, Livro de registro de casamentos da freguesia de N.S. da Vitória (Sé), 1748–1759, livro 84.

[15] From analysis of 1,841 marriages recorded in APEM, AAM, Livro de registro de casamentos da freguesia de N.S. da Vitória (Sé), 1748–1759, livro 85; APEM, AAM, Livro de registro de casamentos da freguesia de N.S. da Vitória (Sé), 1759–1773, livro 86; APEM, AAM, Livro de registro de casamentos da freguesia de N.S. da Vitória (Sé), 1773–1790, livro 87; APEM, AAM, Livro de registro de casamentos da freguesia de N.S. da Vitória (Sé), 1790–1798, livro 88; APEM, AAM, Livro de registro de casamentos da Igreja de Santaninha, 1805–1844, livro 91.

The second set of sources is composed of those postmortem inventories – recorded from 1767 to 1832 (Table 5.3). Those who compiled them were, over time, consistent in how they kept their books. However, a review of hundreds of inventories makes clear that some inventory takers were more thorough than others. A few did not bother to record marriages, while some made frequent corrections, making notes when they heard or wrote something incorrectly.

As with Church books of marriage, inventories indicate that Upper Guinean slaves in Maranhão expressed a clear preference for marriage partners from the same broad cultural group. Upper Guinean women from the coastal zone married men from the coastal zone in 39 percent of their marriages. They married Upper Guinean men from the interior in 26 percent of their marriages. That is, 65 percent of Upper Guinean coastal women who married from 1767 to 1832 married other Upper Guineans. Upper Guinean women from the interior displayed a similar tendency. Of all Upper Guinean interior women who married between 1767 and 1832, 40 percent married men from the Upper Guinea interior zone and 27 percent married men from the coast. That is, 67 percent married other Upper Guineans. Nothing indicates that Balanta favored marriages to Balanta, Bijago tended to marry other Bijago, or that Papel most often married other Papel. But data does point to a clear regional preference, slaves who identified themselves as Balanta, Bijago, and Papel choosing, most often, to marry Upper Guineans.

Marriage trends for Mina slaves are similar. From 1767 to 1832, 42 percent of Mina women recognized as married in plantation inventories were married to males from the same region of Africa. Considering that there were few Mina in Maranhão, this percentage is impressive indeed. That is, typically there were not all that many Mina slaves on plantations, yet Mina slaves still gravitate toward one another for marriage. The other 58 percent of Mina slaves were married to slaves from a variety of backgrounds – 13 percent of whom were from the Upper Guinea coastal strip, 17 percent of whom were from the Upper Guinea interior, and 15 percent of whom were from West Central Africa. Many Mina slaves during this period would have been Muslim, and they may have sought out marriage partners sharing their religion. This may also explain why Mina married Upper Guineans from the interior (most of whom were Mandinka and many of whom were Muslims) at the next highest rate. Other Mina slaves were from Yoruba groups who, in this period, recognized a pantheon of gods. West Central African and Brazilian-born slaves show similar patterns in their choice of partners – marrying, most often, endogamously with regard to region of origin.

TABLE 5.3. *Black Slave Marriage Patterns by Region of Partner Birth, Maranhão, 1767–1832*

Region of wife's birth		Region of Husband's Birth									
		West Central Africa	Africa, unknown	Brazil	Cape Verde	Mina	Mozambique	Upper Guinea, unknown	Upper Guinea coast	Upper Guinea interior	Total
West Central Africa		49 37.12%	5 3.79%	11 8.33%	1 0.76%	16 12.12%	3 2.27%	0 0%	22 16.67%	25 18.94%	132
Brazil		27 22.88%	1 0.85%	40 33.90%	0 0%	8 6.78%	2 1.69%	0 0%	23 19.49%	17 14.41%	118
Mina		8 15.38%	0 0%	5 9.62%	0 0%	22 42.31%	1 1.92%	0 0%	7 13.46%	9 17.31%	52
Upper Guinea coast		33 15.21%	0 0%	19 8.76%	0 0%	21 9.68%	1 0.46%	1 0.46%	85 39.17%	57 26.27%	217
Upper Guinea interior		16 14.55%	1 0.91%	4 3.64%	0 0%	15 13.64%	0 0%	0 0%	30 27.27%	44 40.00%	110

Source: MISD.

In his study of African identities in Portuguese colonies, James Sweet argues that for Africans, endogamous marriage was "a first step in the attempt to recreate specific social and cultural forms in the Americas."[16] For Africans in Maranhão, those cultural forms were not ethnically based. They were regionally based. This is not to say that Upper Guineans rejected marriages to people from their own African ethnic group. Marriages like the one between Antonio and Izabel, both of whom identified themselves as Banhun, did occur. Both were slaves of Bento da Cunha in 1788.[17] But they did not occur more often than marriages between Banhun and people from other Upper Guinea ethnic groups.

Why African slaves did not more often gravitate toward slaves from their specific ethnic (rather than regional) group is a matter of speculation. It is clear that on any given plantation, the number of males and females of about the same age and from the same ethnic group was often small compared to the number from the same region of Africa. However, I suspect more was at play than demographic realities. Marriage patterns paired with sources from Africa make clear that Africans in Maranhão did not see themselves only in ethnic terms. They saw themselves as possessing broader, regional identities as well. Those identities were forged in Africa through common regional approaches to spirituality, food, child rearing, and much more. They were reinforced through a common and shared Middle Passage experience – one that brought Balanta, Biafada, Mandinka, Banhun, Papel, Floup, Fula, and other Upper Guineans together in the hulls of ships. There, no matter what their ethnicity, slaves shared the same suffering. And these identities were strengthened under enslavement in Maranhão, where slaves worked together. When, where, and how slaves worked was not determined by ethnicity; it was determined by a shared slave status.

For Upper Guineans in Maranhão, re-creating regional approaches to child rearing, food production and preparation, and religion was more important than re-creating ethnic approaches to these things. More narrow ethnic approaches might, after all, have been divisive. Such approaches could have raised tensions in Maranhão that were rooted across the ocean and that resulted in violence among different ethnic communities and in the production of captives. This is not to say that

---

[16] James H. Sweet, *Recreating Africa: Culture, Kinship and Religion in the African-Portuguese World, 1441–1770* (Chapel Hill: The University of North Carolina Press, 2003), 47.

[17] Arquivo Judiciário of the Tribunal de Justiça do Estado do Maranhão (hereafter TJEM), Inventory, Bento da Cunha, 1788.

ethnic hostility did not, in some cases, carry over from Africa. Evidence from elsewhere in Brazil indicates that at times it did.[18] It is to say that in Brazil, social forces within African communities often mitigated these tensions. For Upper Guineans in Maranhão, endogamous marriage was a step toward re-creating specific African social and cultural forms. But Upper Guineans chose from among a range of cultural forms, and they chose to re-create one that was regionally – not ethnically – based.[19]

There is no evidence that ethnically based dress, scarification practices, religious practices, or rites of passage were re-created in Maranhão. Though recently disembarked slaves who did not speak Portuguese probably spoke ethnic languages to others who understood them, there is no evidence that any Upper Guinean ethnic language was spoken widely over time in Maranhão. Rather, Upper Guinean slaves sought to foster a larger Upper Guinean regional identity. Among themselves they spoke a creole (which may have sprung from the widely spoken Kriolo language of trade centers in Upper Guinea at the time). And among themselves they married most often other Upper Guineans, while simultaneously forging kinship linkages through marriage to fellow slaves from other places. With endogamous marriages, Africans who shared cultural understandings passed knowledge to their *crioulo* children. Meals around calabash gourds filled with rice, protein, and sauce could be, then, times for remembering a *Guiné* lost and for forging a different sort of *Guiné* under slavery.

Over a meal with rice-filled gourds, African men, particularly, might have recounted the tremendous loss they felt in Maranhão. As demonstrated in Chapter 4, the nature of work in Maranhão denied men one marker of manhood. And demographics coupled with racial hierarchies denied them another. That is, in Maranhão many African men were not able to find marriage or sexual partners – the way they could across the ocean. There were two reasons for this. First, as noted above, there were considerably fewer African females in Maranhão than African males. Second, free Indian females rarely chose to look down the social ladder for male companions. After 1755, Indian enslavement was banned, so African slaves were, by Maranhense social norms, inferior to free Indians.

But before 1755, things were different. Then, African men sometimes found female companions (for marriage and sexual relationships outside

---

[18] João José Reis, *Slave Rebellion in Brazil: The Muslim Uprising of 1835 in Bahia*, trans. Arthur Brakel (Baltimore: The Johns Hopkins University Press, 1993), 110, 157.
[19] Sweet, *Recreating*, 47.

marriage) from among the Indian population. During this period, Indians comprised the vast majority of enslaved people in Maranhão, so it was among Indian populations that African slaves found themselves before the mid-eighteenth century. African male–Indian female relationships produced a growing body of people dubbed *cafuzos* or *cafuzes*, and there are numerous references to them in a variety of texts. For example, the list of marriages performed at the Church de San Francisco Xavier notes the marriage in 1703 of Vital, a *cafuzo* slave, with Catharina, a free Indian from a nearby village. In 1720, the *cafuza* Izabel married an Indian named Caethano.[20] In 1751, Matheos, a black man from a place unknown, married Ignacia, a *cafuza*.[21] Other examples are legion.

All told, before 1755 parish records from Maranhão show that 82 percent of marriages between Africans and Indians involved African males marrying Indian females, only 18 percent being African females marrying Indian males.[22] This reveals, again, that African women most often chose to marry African men and that men's choices of marriage partners were more limited, because African men far outnumbered African women. Hence, African men looked, when possible, to other groups for marriage partners. However, African–Indian marriages became increasingly rare after 1755, when Indian enslavement was abolished and Africans began to take the place of Indians as the most important laborers in Maranhão. Indeed, very quickly plantations emerged upon which only African and *crioulo* slaves worked.

But there was for African men after 1755 a growing group of non-African women from which they could find marriage and sexual partners. That group was made up of Afro-Brazilian women – *crioulas*. And, indeed, *crioula* women did not express that much of a preference for *crioulo* men. From plantation inventories, it is evident that from 1767 to 1832 Brazilian-born slave women chose to marry Brazilian-born slave men 33.9 percent of the time. The same percentage chose to marry men from Upper Guinea (interior and coast) – and this despite the fact that gender ratios among the *crioulo* population were even. For other parts of Brazil, historians have argued that Brazilian-born blacks were "caught between Western and African ways of life," possessing "much linking

[20] BNL, Coleção Pombalina, no. 4, f. 20–1.
[21] APEM, AAM, Livro de registro de casamentos da freguesia de N.S. da Vitória (Sé), 1748–1759, livro 85.
[22] APEM, AAM, Livro de registro de casamentos da freguesia de N.S. da Vitória (Sé), 1748–1759, livros 85–91.

them to the white man and to the New World."[23] However, marriage patterns indicate that in Maranhão, *crioulas* often sought to foster ties to the Old World through their choice of marriage partners. On Maranhense plantations, most *crioulas* were the products of relationships between Upper Guinean men and women, and many gravitated toward Upper Guineans for their marriage partners.[24]

Specific examples of these relationships are rare, and inventories and church records do not often make it possible to determine who the parents of postpubescent Afro-Brazilians were. That is, inventories most often list *crioulo* children with their African parents, but inventory takers did not usually note the parents of adult *crioulos*. But I have run across one example from another source. In 1809, Miguel, who was listed in a marriage record as a slave from Guinea, married a woman named Ignacia, a *crioula*. Notes that followed said she was the daughter of João and Clara, "both blacks of the pagans of Guinea."[25] In this case – and likely many others – the diaspora-born child of Upper Guineans gravitated toward an Upper Guinean for marriage.

Despite the fact that some African men in Maranhão found marriage partners from among the Afro-Brazilian population, many African men found themselves on plantations with unbalanced gender ratios. African men in Maranhão came from societies that encouraged polygynous marriages. In Upper Guinea, Mandinka, Banhun, Balanta, Papel, and Floup men, for example, expected to have multiple wives over the course of their lives. Among Balanta, it was common for older men to have several wives who ranged greatly in age. The youngest wives frequently had young male lovers in other villages and could run away to them, leaving their children and starting a new life as a first bride after some arrangement was made with the older first husband. Mandinka came from a region in which the gender ratio was skewed because more males were exported as slaves into the Atlantic than females. That is, there were more females in Mandinka territories, which encouraged a pattern of

[23] Reis, *Slave Rebellion*, 142–3.
[24] The children of Upper Guineans also gravitated toward one another for marriage. In 1757, for example, Onofre and Gertrudes, both *crioulos*, married in São Luís. In the book of marriages in which their union was recorded, Onofre was listed as the slave of Joze Correya da Costa and son of Maria Vieyra "of unknown parents of the pagans of Guinea." Gertrudes was a slave of Guitina Maria Capella and daughter of Thomazia "also of the pagans of Guinea." APEM, AAM, Livro de registro de casamentos da freguesia de N.S. da Vitória (Sé), 1748–1759, livro 85.
[25] APEM, AAM, Livro de registro de casamentos da Igreja de Santaninha, 1805–1844, livro 91.

polygynous marriage. Angolan men also came from societies where they had increasing access to multiple wives.

In Maranhão after the mid-eighteenth century, the situation was reversed, which posed a serious challenge to notions of masculinity. If fostering a large and productive family was a culturally constructed goal to which most Angolan and Upper Guinean men strived in their homelands, many of these males could not hope to find a lifelong female companion, much less have multiple female partners, in Maranhão. That is, in Angola and Upper Guinea, one of the ways males proved that they had made the transition from childhood to adulthood – from being a boy to being a man – was by marrying one or more women, having multiple children with them, and fostering a large and productive household. In Maranhão, however, few African males married at all.[26]

Of course, many factors shaped slave marriage and sex patterns in Maranhão. Important among them was the fact that slaves came into contact with a limited number of people over the course of their lives and, hence, had a limited pool of people from which to find partners for marriage and sex. Rural slaves were most often in contact with other slaves who lived on the plantations on which they lived and worked. So, it was most common for slaves to find mates on the same plantation. Urban slaves, on the other hand, were often given duties that took them throughout São Luís. Moreover, in São Luís, whites typically held small numbers of slaves, so marriages between slaves of different masters were common. Further, a variety of things that had nothing to do with African cultural identities shaped slave sex and marriage patterns: from particular notions of beauty that were constructed in Brazil to differentials in the skills slaves acquired, the wealth they commanded, and the power they wielded as overseers or lacked as common field hands. Indeed, male slaves holding important positions on plantations (and, therefore, having access to more material resources) were more likely to be married than slave field hands. Plantation inventories make it possible to quantify this difference. From 1767 to 1832, 63 percent of male slave overseers were married, compared to 24 percent of the male slave population between the ages of 21 and 40. Overall, the 37 percent of the female slave population between 21 and 40 were married – 13 percent more than men in the

---

[26] We should not rule out the possibility that some African men in Maranhão chose to enter sexual relationships with other men from oppressed groups. James Sweet has evidence for slave–slave homosexual relationships in other parts of Brazil. Sweet, *Recreating*, 50–8. Also, Luiz Mott, *A Inquisição no Maranhão* (EDUFMA: São Luís, 1995), 37–8.

same age range. (Sloppy inventory takers surely missed some marriages, so the exact figure of marriage rates was likely higher.)

Marriage is only one way to examine African preferences for relationships with people of the opposite sex in Maranhão. Sex, too, occurred outside marriage. Indeed, it is evident that Africans and their *crioulo* descendants did not always choose to marry in the Church but carried on sexual relationships, some of which were long term in nature. Unfortunately, few records exist of such unions, but we do have hints of them. For example, in 1741 in the Santo Antônio do Sorubin parish of Maranhão, an African slave woman named Maria de Simao was denounced for being "in concubinage" with a slave named Antonio, who was from Africa's Mina coast.[27] Further, plantation inventories from Maranhão are replete with references to unmarried African and *crioulo* women who had children. For example, in 1800, Anna, a forty-year-old Nalu from the Upper Guinea coast, had four children – Brazilia, Gertrudes, Joanna, and a still unnamed nursing infant. On the same plantation, Rita, an unmarried twenty-year-old Bijago, had an infant daughter named Apollonia.[28] The same year, the unmarried Antonia from Cacheu was listed as having a seven-year-old daughter named Raymunda.[29] In 1802, the twenty-five-year-old unmarried slave named Sebastiana, who was a Banhun from the Upper Guinea coast, had a one-year-old daughter named Julia. And in 1803, the slave Thereza, a thirty-year-old unmarried Bijago, had an unnamed nursing infant.[30] Other examples abound.

However, in inventories most slave women in Maranhão who had children were married, and most were listed as living on plantations with their husbands. Usually, then, families stayed together. Though rare, it was not unheard of on Maranhense plantations for children to know their grandparents. For example, in 1804, the fifty-year-old Valentim from Mina and fifty-year-old Ignez, who was Mandinka, were listed as having two children – Benedita, who was nineteen, and Monica, who was seventeen. The unmarried Benedita had a son, Francisco, who was less than a year old. Similar was Valentino, a sixty-six-year-old slave from Mina, who in 1818 was owned by Bacharel Henrique Guilhon. Valentino lived with his daughter Benedita and her five children: twin boys who were fourteen years old, another boy who was eight, a girl who was four,

[27] APEM, AAM, cx. 20, doc. 877.
[28] TJEM, Inventory of D. Anna Maria Roza de Carvalho, 1800.
[29] TJEM, Inventory of Alexandre Fereira da Crus, 1800.
[30] TJEM, Inventory of Antonio Jose de Souza, 1802.

and a girl who was eighteen months.[31] Also, in 1823, Antonio, a sixty-year-old slave from Benguela, was married to Bonifacia, a sixty-year-old slave born in Brazil. The couple lived with their twenty-eight-year-old daughter, Aguida, and her daughter, the twelve-year-old Libania. The couple also lived with their twenty-five-year-old daughter, Eufrauzina, and her three-year-old daughter, Efigenia. On the same plantation, the fifty-five-year-old Domingos, who was from Angola and was a widower, lived with his daughter Rosa, who had three children – all girls between one and seven years old. Also, Domingos lived with his daughter Esmeria, who was twenty-two and had two daughters, one three years old and the other one year old. Part of the same household were four other of Domingos's children – Jezuina, Miguel, Maria, and Angela. Recorded next in the inventory was Paulo, a sixty-year-old widower from Angola who lived with his thirty-year-old daughter, Putencianna, and her one-year-old son, Tiburcio. And on the same plantation was Pedro, an eighty-year-old slave from Benguela, who was married to Clara, a sixty-year-old *crioula*. They had three daughters, two of whom had children.[32]

Given the number of Afro-Brazilians in Maranhão by the late eighteenth century, it is not surprising that some knew their grandparents. There were indeed many *crioulo* children in Maranhão. "It is important to observe," Governor José Teles da Silva wrote in 1787, "that in all of the Villas and Locations in the Captaincy the number of births is greater than the number of deaths." For this he credited actions taken to stem the effects of smallpox in slave communities. As the disease was brought under control, slave children lived longer, adding to the number of laborers in rice and cotton fields.[33]

Teles da Silva's point is made clearly through inventories taken from 1767 to 1800, which show that some 34 percent of slaves in Maranhão were *crioulos*. Given that before the mid-eighteenth century there were few Africans in the captaincy and mortality rates were high, the overwhelming majority of those *crioulos* had to have been the product of relationships between Upper Guinea–born slaves who arrived after the mid-eighteenth century.[34] It is important to note that inventory figures are only for slaves. In the period, there was a substantial population of free *crioulos* as well. The growth of the black population through

[31] TJEM, Inventory of Bacharel Henrique Guilhon, 1818.
[32] TJEM, Inventory of Antonio Gomes Pires, 1823.
[33] ANTT, Ministério do Reino, mç. 601, cx. 704.
[34] MISD.

reproduction in Maranhão is impressive because few other places in Brazil demonstrated a positive black-population growth rate at the time. Maranhão was unusual, then, in that it had a high concentration of slaves from Upper Guinea, and its Upper Guinean slaves reproduced at a much faster rate than slaves in most other parts of Brazil.

In addition to bearing children in Maranhão, African women sometimes arrived on slave ships with children under their care. That is, some slave families in Maranhão spanned the Atlantic culturally and physically. Among Maria Freire's slaves in 1810, for example, an unmarried Angolan named Francisca lived with her Angolan-born son, four-year-old Bernardo.[35] Similar is the case of the unmarried sixty-year-old Bijago named Violanta. Frail and listed as nearly worthless in the 1804 inventory of Anna Maria Rapozo, Violanta had a twenty-five-year-old daughter named Francisca who was healthy and valued very highly by her master. Francisca had known the Bijagos Islands of the Upper Guinea coast, having been born there and enslaved with her mother.[36] And, too, there is the case of Ignacia, a fifty-year-old Mandinka, who in 1814 was listed in an inventory with her seventeen-year-old Mandinka son, Thomas, who accompanied her from their point of capture somewhere near Farim or Geba to the plantation of Francisco de Oliveira Bolhao.[37]

It was not unusual for infants and small children to accompany their mothers on slave ships. Data indicates an average of 3.3 percent of the slaves on ships sent from Upper Guinea to Amazonia were children under about ten years old.[38] In Portuguese records, small children were not counted among the slaves inventoried on ships, but notations about them were made beside their mothers – *com filho de peito*, or "with a nursing child" and *com filho de pé*, or "with a child who could stand." In Maranhão, infants and small children who survived the Middle Passage were usually sold with their mothers. Older children were listed separately from their mothers in ships' records and, if not physically reliant on their mothers for care, could be sold separately. Violanta, then, likely arrived in Maranhão with Francisca about twenty-five years before the 1804 inventory, and Ignacia likely arrived with Thomas some seventeen years before the 1814 inventory.

[35] TJEM, Inventory of Izabel Maria Freire, 1810.
[36] TJEM, Inventory of D. Anna Maria Rapoza, 1804.
[37] TJEM, Inventory of Antonio Joze de Mesquita, 1813.
[38] Voyages: The Trans-Atlantic Slave Trade Database, http://slavevoyages.org/tast/assessment/estimates.faces.

Like Francisca, Thomas was listed with a very high value and no injuries, meaning Ignacia had managed to raise a healthy son in the midst of over two decades of incredible suffering. A short, simple note in Bolhao's inventory reveals that in 1814, Thomas bid farewell to his mother through some unknown ceremony. That year, an inventory taker wrote *morta*, or "dead," after notes about Ignacia's age, ethnicity, value, and child. She had been recorded some days earlier as living, but she died while the inventory was still being assembled. The few words about Ignacia that the inventory taker penned tell us much about white attitudes toward black slaves. Black slaves were valued monetarily, and for this, 90,000 réis (Ignacia's monetary value when she was alive) was deducted from the bottom line of the inventory. But Ignacia's callous "biographer" left, too, a history that reveals something about what Upper Guineans who were held in captivity valued. They valued family. Despite great hardships, they chose to forge and maintain families that were often modeled on ones they had known across the Atlantic.

IMPEDIMENTS TO AFRICAN FAMILIES
IN MARANHÃO BEFORE 1755

One of the impediments to slave family life in Maranhão was explored in Chapter 4. It was work – long, hard days in fields. A second impediment was white male power. From its colonial founding through the abolition of the slave trade and beyond, Maranhão, like most of the Americas, was male dominated and racially stratified. Men wielded more power than women, and whites exercised more power than blacks, Indians, and *mestiços*. The latter term meant people of "mixed race," referring broadly in Maranhão to people in one of three categories – *mulato* (mulatto), *cafuzo* (descendant of Indian and black parents), and *mameluco* (descendant of white and Indian parents).

In Maranhão, white men sat atop the captaincy's hierarchy, and women of multiple colors were at the bottom. The few white women who settled or were born in Maranhão had legal, cultural, and social protections not shared by people of color. But they still had less power than white men and particularly less power than their husbands. Because the state was weak in Maranhão, laws meant to protect rights most often went unenforced. The Church attempted to curb abuses of power, denouncing those who it thought acted immorally. But before 1755, settlers and priests often feuded over the use of Indian slave labor, raising resentment of the Church among the lay population. After 1759, when the crown evicted the Jesuits, priests were few in colonial towns and almost never seen in rural areas.

Given the power that white men had, it should not be surprising that many engaged with frequency in sexual relationships with women of color, and especially with slave women. Decades ago, scholars argued that male slave owner–female slave relationships resulted from the particularities of Portuguese culture. Portuguese males, Gilberto Freyre proposed, had open attitudes toward sexual relationships with women from other cultural groups. In his words, they had "an obvious inclination ... for free union with" Indians and Africans.[39] More recently Freyre's scholarship has been questioned by some using demographic data. That is, a newer group of scholars argues that crossracial sex was more prevalent where gender ratios were particularly skewed. In colonies in which white men outnumbered white women, racial mixing was more likely to occur, no matter what the supposed cultural assumptions of the white men in power.[40]

In Maranhão, there were far more white men than white women – particularly in the seventeenth and early eighteenth centuries but also in the decades after 1755. So did a lack of white women in Maranhão make white men more prone to consorting with women of other races? Jennifer M. Spear sees this question as limiting because underlying it is the assumption that "European men's sexual desires were naturally disposed toward European women."[41] For Spear, in colonial settings crossracial sex was not necessarily the product of white males' "natural" urges. It occurred because white men wielded great power. That is, sex was not only about desire. It was also about politics.[42] And, indeed, in Maranhão

---

[39] Gilberto Freyre, *The Masters and the Slaves: A Study in the Development of Brazilian Civilization*, trans. Samuel Putnam (Berkeley: The University of California Press, 1986), 84; Carl N. Degler, *Neither Black nor White: Slavery and Race Relations in Brazil and the United States* (New York: Macmillan, 1971).

[40] Gary Nash, *Red, White, and Black: The Peoples of Early America* (Englewood Cliffs, NJ: Pearson Prentice Hall, 1992), 280. Winthrop D. Jordan, *White over Black: American Attitudes toward the Negro, 1550–1812* (Chapel Hill: The University of North Carolina Press, 1968), 136–78; W. J. Eccles, "Sexual Mores and Behavior: The French Colonies," in *Encyclopedia of the North American Colonies*, ed. Jacob Ernest Cooke and others (New York: C. Scribner's Sons, 1993), 699; Ira Berlin, *Masters without Slaves: The Free Negro in the Antebellum South* (New York: Pantheon, 1974), 108–9.

[41] Jennifer M. Spear, "Colonial Intimacies: Legislating Sex in French Louisiana," *The William and Mary Quarterly*, 60, 1 (2003), 79.

[42] Also, Ann McClintock, *Imperial Leather: Race, Gender, and Sexuality in the Colonial Conquest* (New York: Routledge, 1995); Anne Laura Stoler, "Tense and Tender Ties: The Politics of Comparison in North American History and (Post) Colonial Studies," *The Journal of American History*, 88, 3 (2001), 829–65.

sex between white males and their slaves – male and female – reinforced colonial hierarchies of gender and race. It revealed who was in control and who was subjugated. White men (particularly the rich) were clearly dominant in Maranhão – having considerable ability to choose sexual partners, both female and male, from among other racial groups. Through their relationships with slaves, white men also produced children, adding to the size of the colonial household.

If evidence of white male relationships with women of color tells us much about power, it also reveals something about the nature of formal, Catholic marriage. In Maranhão (as elsewhere in South America), marriage (and especially elite marriage) was not a gauge of partners' sexual desires. Rather, marriage was the institution through which legitimate heirs were produced and the basis for elite economic and social continuity. Marriage, too, conveyed social prestige – honor. It demonstrated a "family's stability and respectability within the community."[43] Whites, particularly powerful and wealthy ones, were expected to marry within their class (to marry well), and the social sanctions for not doing so could be severe. Given this, it was not uncommon for white men who had married well to break their marriage vows and to engage in relationships forbidden by the Church. That is, it was not unheard of for white men to look to women other than their wives to fulfill sexual desires that they could not necessarily have met within the confines of socially advantageous marriages.

To be sure, women of color in Maranhão faced few choices when white men expressed sexual desires for them. When a master sought sex, defiance was often futile and could bring severe retribution. For this, many women submitted to relationships – both fleeting and long term – that they found repugnant. However, in many cases women of color stood to gain from sexual relationships with white men. These elite males could provide sustenance, shelter, luxuries, and protection for their concubines and their concubines' children. Such advantages were sometimes fleeting but were sometimes long lasting – coming as the product of long-term, regularized relationships. We should not, then, discount the possibility that some women of color in Maranhão sometimes sought out regularized sexual

---

[43] Katherine Holt, "Marriage Choices in a Plantation Society: Bahia, Brazil," *International Review of Social History* 50 (2005), 25–41. Also, Ann Twinam, *Public Lives, Private Secrets: Gender, Honor, Sexuality, and Illegitimacy in Colonial Spanish America* (Palo Alto, CA: Stanford University Press, 1999); Lyman L. Johnson and Sonya Lipsett-Rivera, eds., *The Faces of Honor: Sex, Shame and Violence in Colonial Latin America* (Albuquerque: University of New Mexico Press, 1998).

relationships with white men, exploiting cracks in the colonial system to gain as much as they could given a very limited range of possibilities. Making the most of these opportunities brought great risks, as the case of Barbara, which opened this chapter, demonstrated. Nonetheless, women of color found it possible to forge long-term relationships not only with men of their same racial group but also with whites.

Before the mid-eighteenth century, long-lasting patterns in relationships between white men and women of color became clear. Then, most of Maranhão's slaves were Indians. On colonial farms and in towns, Indian slaves frequently married one another, which was something encouraged by the Church. And notes about Indian ceremonies dominate books of marriages from Maranhão for the period before the mid-eighteenth century.[44] But Indian female–white male sex (outside formal marriage) was also common. These relationships took several forms. Some were long term and others were short term; some brought advantages to women while others brought disgrace and suffering. Whatever the case, Indian female–white male sexual relationships replicated and reinforced colonial hierarchies of gender and race.

Details about the nature of these relationships in Maranhão before 1755 can be found in a variety of sources, the most revealing of which are books of denunciations that priests kept. No matter what the form, priests considered sex out of wedlock to be sinful. When such relationships were reported to them, they made notes that hint at the range of sexual relationships between white males and women or men of multiple oppressed groups, including Indians. Priests often mentioned white females' "disgust" at the dishonor that their husbands brought upon their legitimate households by engaging in sex and fathering children with slave and free Indians. It is clear that some of these relationships were ongoing and regularized, Indian women serving as "concubines" of white men. But rarely did priests say anything about the effect of these relationships on Indian women themselves. For example, in 1727, a priest wrote that in the the town of Alcântara, Joseph Mendes de Amorim was said to "treat illicitly" several of his Indian female slaves "with whom he is in concubinage." Through these relationships, he produced "some children." In the same town, Joseph Soares was said to keep a slave concubine named Rita with whom he had several children. The relationship so upset his white wife that she moved out of their house and in with her parents. The same

---

[44] APEM, AAM, Livro de registro de casamentos da freguesia de N.S. da Vitória (Sé), livro 84, 85.

year Joseph Ricardo Coelho was said to keep one of his slaves, who was named Antonia, as a concubine.[45]

In 1734 on the Mearim River in a parish called Nossa Senhora de Nazareth, Ambrozio da Costa, "a man married to a woman with children," was said to keep an Indian concubine named Diodata, "which gave disgust and bad treatment to his wife." Not far away, a married man named Henrique Coelho was said to be in a sexual relationship with Maria, an Indian servant of a Simão Fernandes.[46] In 1749 in São Luís, Antonio Pinheiro kept Rita, an Indian slave of Pedro Reis, as a concubine, which "had given his wife a bad life." Eugenio Frazão also kept one of his Indian slaves as a concubine. And Francisco da Costa Guelarne had bought a slave named Bernarda for the expressed purpose of keeping her as a concubine. Clearly, in the Maranhão frontier period, Indian slave women were much more than field workers. White men valued Indian women because they could provide sex, bear children, and perform domestic tasks, often within the context of long-term relationships.[47]

The offspring of white–Indian relationships – *mamelucos* – often tried to pass as white. Those who could not do so were, like Indians, discriminated against. Lacking power in a racist, male-dominated society, *mamelucas* (the "as" ending indicating females), like their Indian mothers, were often involved in relationships that assumed various forms with white men. Some relationships were clearly exploitative. However, some *mamelucas* seem to have pursued relationships with white men, seeking benefits that might be accrued. Lourença, a *mameluca* who "assists in the house of Andre de Souza" in Maranhão on the Rio Itapecuru, likely fell into the latter category. In 1734, she was said to be the long-term "concubine" of Francisco de Brito with whom she lived in a house and with whom she had had several children. This relationship was, then, regularized and ongoing, a "marriage of friendship" that was not sanctioned by the Church but that served as the foundation for a family.[48]

Though few in number before 1750, African and *crioula* women in Maranhão also had a range of relationships with white men. As with white–Indian and white–*mameluca* relationships, white–black relationships were often kept hidden from public view. But word sometimes got

---

[45] APEM, AAM, cx. 20, doc. 873.
[46] APEM, AAM, cx. 20, doc. 874.
[47] APEM, AAM, cx. 20, doc. 878.
[48] APEM, AAM, cx. 20, doc. 875.

out. For this, it is recorded in 1727 in a Church book of denunciations that a white man named Domiliano Lopes was said to have had a sexual relationship with a black slave of another local man. In 1734, Ambrozio da Costa, who lived on the Mearim River in Maranhão, was said to be having sex with a black woman named Maria, unsuccessfully hiding the fact from his dishonored wife. In the same parish, priests reported that Joseph da Costa was involved with a black slave of a local padre and that Joseph Correira, who was married, kept one of his black slaves as a concubine "in his home."[49]

In 1741, in the Villa de Tapuitapera in Maranhão, Francisco de Campos was denounced for "treating his wife badly" by having a sexual relationship with a black slave named Gertrudes, who belonged to de Campos's mother. Not far away, Verancio de Lemos was "in concubinage" with a black slave of Captain Cardozo named Margarida. And in the same parish, a white man named Eugenio had "carnal knowledge" of a black slave of the Church named Andreza. In 1744, Eugenio Frazão, who lived in the parish of Nossa Senhora da Vitória in São Luis, was denounced for keeping one of his black slaves as a "concubine." Not far away, Bernardo de Souza had a continuing sexual relationship with a black woman named Jozefa. And in the same parish, Father Francisco da Costa Gularza was said to keep Bernarda, a black slave whom he had purchased, as a "concubine."[50]

If some white men attempted to hide their relationships with black women, others made theirs relatively public, perhaps finding it difficult to keep hidden something that assumed a permanent form. For example, in 1727 in the Vila of Alcântara in Maranhão, Joseph Soares was said to have been in a long-term sexual relationship with the black slave of his father. He had children with her and had "never made a life with his wife" from whom he was estranged, spending most of his time with his black partner and their children. It is clear that this "marriage of friendship" brought benefits to Soares's concubine – a house, sustenance, and protection from a range of dangers in a poor and distant outpost of the Portuguese empire. Not far away, Joseph Ricardo Coelho had in his house a black "concubine" named Antonia with whom he had had a child, a fact known by many. Similarly, in 1734 in Maranhão on the Rio Mearim in the parish of Nossa Senhora de Nazareth, a single man named Ignacio da Pelerma was said to have a black "concubine" named Anna,

49 APEM, AAM, cx. 20, doc. 873, 874.
50 APEM, AAM, cx. 20, doc. 876, 878.

who was the slave of his brother-in-law. He lived with her in the same house, not hiding the fact from neighbors.[51]

From these relationships were born *mulatos*. Some *mulatos* were freed and willed property by their master-fathers, as was the case with the *mulata* Eufemia, daughter of Suzana, in 1741. Similarly, in 1744, a white resident of São Luís, Gaspar dos Reys, declared in his will that he had "raised two little *mulatas*, one called Felicia and the other Angelica, and with great love I leave each of them through the love of God three-hundred cows ... [and] ten mares." In other wills, masters implied, without stating outright, that they produced children with black slaves. For example, in 1676, Bartolomeu Pereira de Lemos wrote that upon his death, "a child by the name of Andre son of a black of mine by the name Monica" was to be freed.[52]

Though sometimes favored by masters, *mulatas* and *mulatos* were also discriminated against and victimized in a society dominated by white men. Portuguese males pressed *mulata* women into unwanted relationships but frequently lived with them as concubines in relationships resembling marriages. Thus, in 1741 in the parish of Santo Antônio do Sorubin, Fernando Brandão, a single man, was denounced before Church officials for keeping an unnamed *mulata* who was his slave as a concubine; and Manoel de Souza Aranha, also single, was said to be in concubinage with his *mulata* slave named Filipa.[53]

Cafuzes, the offspring of black–Indian relationships, were also discriminated against and frequently abused by whites. Mistreatment was so bad that in 1721, Governor Bernardo Pereira de Berredo felt it necessary to inform the public that "*Cafuzes* who have been emancipated live in their liberty and serve who they wish and who offers them the better treatment."[54] But opportunities for men and women from racial groups at the bottom of Maranhão's racial hierarchy were few. And for *cafuzas* and other women of color, "service" for white men often meant more than performing labor. "Service" meant sex. Sometimes that sex was for direct payment – taking the form of prostitution. For this, *cafuza* Comelia was denounced in 1749 in São Luís.[55] Other *cafuzas* found themselves in long-term relationships with white men. For example, in 1734 on the

[51] APEM, AAM, cx. 20, doc. 873, 874.
[52] Mota, *Cripto*, 37, 52, 67.
[53] APEM, AAM, cx. 20, doc. 877.
[54] "Livro grosso do Maranhão," v. 2, in *Anais da Biblioteca Nacional* 60 (Rio de Janeiro: Imprensa Nacional, 1948), 182.
[55] APEM, AAM, cx. 20, doc. 878.

Rio Itapecuru, Luciano de Britto was said to have kept the *cafuza* slave Clara as his concubine "for many years" and to have had several children with her.[56] That same year, Mathieus Maciel, a single man who lived on the Mearim River, was said to be having a long-term sexual relationship with Jozepha, a free *cafuza* who was also unmarried. Nearby, Innocenço Perez, a single man, had a free *cafuza* concubine.[57] Three decades later, Gregorio Joze Rebello, a married man in Aldeias Altas, was said to "live in sin with one of his *cafuza* slaves."[58]

Before the mid-eighteenth century, black, Indian, and *mestiça* women engaged in a range of sexual relationships with white men; so, too, did their black, Indian, and *mestiço* male counterparts. Sitting atop the racial and gendered hierarchy of Maranhão, white men were in a position to demand sexual favors from their male slaves. However, the fact that white men were powerful made entering into sexual relationships with them advantageous for some men of color. The complex nature of white male–Indian male sexual relationships is hinted at in notes from a denunciation in 1669. Then, three white men in Maranhão accused Francisco Coelho of *sodomia* (sodomy). Coelho was a white man born in São Luís who owned a large farm upon which his Indian slaves grew cassava. He was accused of "cohabitating" and "committing the sin of sodomy" with an Indian named Rodrigo. His accusers said that they had seen the pair "many times in the hammock together nude and all of the slaves said they went everywhere together." In Coelho's house, Rodrigo was always naked, and the pair were said to have been seen "holding one another's members and measuring them to see which was the largest." It can't be known what Rodrigo thought of the relationship. To rebuff Coelho's advances would have been difficult. But Rodrigo clearly gained something from his relationship with a relatively wealthy white man. Rodrigo ate with Coelho at his table and slept with him in a comfortable house, while other Indians toiled in fields, went without regular meals, and lived in squalled huts. One observer said that for Coelho, Rodrigo "served as a wife."[59]

There are also examples of white men in Amazonia using their power to cajole males of color into sexual relationships that were likely much more exploitative. In 1686, a friar named Manuel de Santa Catharina was

---

[56] APEM, AAM, cx. 20, doc. 875.
[57] APEM, AAM, cx. 20, doc. 874.
[58] APEM, AAM, cx. 20, doc. 879.
[59] Mott, *Inquisição*, 38–40.

accused of *sodomia*, having been seen several times in the company of an Indian boy named Domingos, who was reported to be between eight and fourteen years old and attached to the friars' convent in some capacity. A slave from Cape Verde said it was well known among the convent's slaves that Manuel was a *sodomita*.[60] Another early description of a white man being denounced for *sodomia* with a man of color came in 1749. Then, Bento Graça, a white resident of São Luís, was said to have committed the "sin of bestiality" for a sex act with a goat. Another person said that he also "had carnal knowledge" of a male *mulato* slave, and still another said that he had had sex with a black male. One of the men with whom Bento had engaged in sex was a slave named Quintiliano.[61]

During Maranhão's frontier period, women and men of color were, then, vulnerable to attacks from white men. However, women and men of color also engaged in long-term relationships with white men, acquiring some limited advantage in a harsh colonial setting.

IMPEDIMENTS TO THE FORMATION OF AFRICAN FAMILIES IN MARANHÃO AFTER 1755

As African slave imports into Maranhão rose after the mid-eighteenth century and plantation slavery became the norm, details about white male–African female relations increasingly appeared in parish denunciation records. They demonstrate that as Maranhão's economy expanded in the late eighteenth century, social and political hierarchies remained unchanged. Maranhão continued to be racially stratified and dominated by males. Within Maranhão, sex continued to reflect and reinforce the nature of power in colonial society. African men often failed to have relationships of any sort with women, but white men – married and unmarried, rich and poor – often had numerous sex partners. White male relationships with black women ranged from brief to long term, and from exploitative to beneficial for the women involved.

Clearly some relationships were exploitative. Evidence of this can be found in Maria de Bairros's claim, which opened this chapter, that her husband "regularly raped and violated his female slaves and those of others."[62] It can also be found in reports to priests made in 1757 that João Simões used one of his black slaves as a concubine but did not provide her

---

[60] Ibid., 42–4.
[61] APEM, AAM, cx. 20, doc. 878.
[62] APEM, AAM, cx. 129, doc. 4415.

with sustenance.[63] Further, in 1764, a priest named João Antônio Baldez "illicitly treated and deflowered" Dona Maria, a black slave of the widow Anna Graces.[64] And in 1767, Policena de Barros hinted in divorce proceedings that her husband, Rodrigo Malone, acted with malice by "using badly one of his female slaves named Florinda, who he had deflowered."[65] Further, in 1797 in divorce proceedings, Leonor Lopes da Silveira accused her husband Manoel Rodrigues Ferreira of buying females from ships arriving from Africa for the sole purpose of turning them into sex slaves. She said that he was known for "always being alone with his slave women in private in scandalous concubinage." His behavior with "his female slaves was," she continued, "depraved, and when ships with blacks arrive at the port, he goes there to buy brute female blacks and pagans and then uses them and commits adultery."[66] And in 1794, Leonor Maria de Santa Anna requested a divorce from her husband Francisco de Paula da Cunha Rapozo because he was *adulterios*, having sex with a slave named Luzia, who belonged to a man named Manoel. Franscico, Leonor Maria claimed, paid Manoel for these "services."[67]

Accounts like these raise questions about contentions that scholars should focus first on work when trying to get at the nature of slave's lives.[68] Female slaves in Maranhão, it is clear, were not valued only – or in some times and places mostly – for the labor they performed. In this society, white males often purchased black women for sex. They dominated slave women because they could, their actions reflecting and emphasizing colonial hierarchies of race and gender.[69]

However, some white master–black female slave relationships assumed an ongoing, regularized form after 1755 (as they had before with white masters and their Indian slaves). And though forbidden by the Church, many of these relationships assumed the form of "marriage of friendship." In these "marriages," women were called "concubines" but filled many of the social roles of wives. For example, in 1753, Pantaleão Pinheiro, who

---

[63] APEM, AAM, cx. 21, doc. 913.
[64] APEM, AAM, Autos e Feitos de libelo crime, cx. 116, mç. 559, doc. 4240.
[65] APEM, AAM, Autos de justificação de sevícias, cx. 91, mç. 458–9.
[66] APEM, AAM, cx. 129, doc. 4411.
[67] APEM, AAM, cx. 128, doc. 4407.
[68] Ira Berlin and Philip D. Morgan, "Labor and the Shaping of Slave Life in the Americas," in *Cultivation and Culture: Labor and the Shaping of Slave Life in the Americas,* eds. Ira Berlin and Philip D. Morgan (Charlottesville: University of Virginia Press, 1993), 1.
[69] Slave women's value being derived, in part, from their sexual and reproductive capacities is explored by Jennifer L. Morgan, *Laboring Women: Reproduction and Gender in New World Slavery* (Philadelphia: University of Pennsylvania Press, 2004).

was a married man, kept a slave named Roza as a concubine "for many years," living with her in the same house and sharing much of his life with her.[70] Elsewhere in 1757, Domingos Barboza Carneyro, who was single and from Portugal, was denounced for having had a sexual relationship with a black slave named Thereza, who was the property of João Simoens da Fonseca. It was public knowledge that for more than ten years they had lived in the same house.[71] In 1759 in the parish of Nossa Senhora do Desterro do Poti, Antonio da Costa Bezerra kept a slave concubine, which caused a great scandal because he had a wife in Portugal. Further, Jose Affonso Barboza had in his house a *preta*, or "black female." The same year in Santo Antônio do Serubin, Francisco Pereyra Ribeyro was said to have been in concubinage with his slave Roza Maria "for many years" and to have had children with her. Ignacio Luis, a white tender of cattle on the plantation of Major João de Araujo Costa, kept a slave named Laura as a concubine. Elsewhere in 1760, two brothers, Ambrozio and Antonio de Araeyo, were condemned for keeping two different slave women who worked on a Church farm as concubines.[72] In 1773, it was reported Padre Manoel Joze de Arayo had a long-term sexual relationship with Anna Maria, a *cafuza* and slave of Ignacio Fernades Vianna. He visited her every night at nine or ten o'clock to take her back to his house.[73] That same year, Gregrio Joze Rebello, a white married man, "lived in sin" with one of his African female slaves.[74] In divorce proceedings in 1794, Mônica Tereza said that her husband, Jozé Anastácio de Oliveira, "committed adultery freely" with his slave Luiza "inside the house, saying that for him it was better with the slave than with her [his wife]." The relationship had lasted sometime because Luiza had had two of Jozé's children.[75]

And in Amazonia's plantation society days, white men also engaged in sexual relationships with black men – as some had since the colony's founding. Though we cannot discount the possibility that some black men in Maranhão derived benefits from these relationships (as had the Indian slave Rodrigo who "served as a wife" for Coelho in 1669), often slave men found such relationships humiliating. In the 1760s in Pará, for example, an Angolan slave named Joaquim Antonio told a

[70] APEM, AAM, cx. 20, doc. 879.
[71] APEM, AAM, cx. 21, doc. 913.
[72] APEM, AAM, cx. 20, doc. 880–2.
[73] APEM, AAM, Livro e registro de denúncias, livro 212, no page numbers.
[74] APEM, AAM, cx. 21, doc. 913.
[75] APEM, AAM, cx. 128, doc. 4400.

representative of the Inquisition that he had been sodomized by a white man. He said that his master was Domingos Serrão de Castro, who had moved with his slaves and family to Pará from Maranhão. One day on the rural estate of Boa Vista, Serrão de Castro's son, Francisco, ordered the slave to enter a house. After he did, Francisco locked the door and then ordered Joaquim Antonio to lie down on a bed with his "back facing up." Francisco then removed both of their pants and "introduced his viral member into" Joaquim Antonio's anus. During what the slave described as a "depraved" and "intolerable" act, Francisco ejaculated. He then told him never to tell anyone and gave him a small amount of money, saying that if he kept quiet more would follow. Further investigation revealed that Francisco regularly raped the men his father owned. Stories were recounted by the Kongolese slaves Joaõ Primeiro, Joaõ Valentim, Garcia, and Domingos Joze; and by the Angolan slaves Joze, Domingos, Manoel Bexiga, Florencio Domingos Antonio, Miguel Joze, and Miguel da Costa. They had had, however, no one to whom to complain. It is for this – and, perhaps, for shame – that accounts of similar rapes rarely made it into the historical record in Amazonia or elsewhere.[76]

RESISTANCE AND PUNISHMENT

Though whites held great power over blacks in Maranhão, slaves often resisted their oppressors' actions. The form of resistance that most often appears in historical sources is flight. In Maranhão, some slaves managed to flee to the interior and establish maroon communities, or *mocambos*. This prompted complaints from whites. In 1734, Pará's governor, José da Serra, reported the capture of black slaves from *mocambos*.[77] In 1741, 1750, and 1751, laws were passed to brand slaves who had fled to *mocambos*.[78] In 1750, there were more reports of raids on *mocambos* to which black slaves had fled.[79]

Other evidence of flights can be found in plantation inventories. For example, in 1788, a Mandinka named Domingos was listed without value because he had fled. On an inventory from 1800, Matheos from Angola was listed similarly, as was the Mandinka Simao in 1804, Angolan Domingos in 1804, Mina Antonio Aoussa (Haussa) in 1804, and

---

[76] ANTT, Tribunal do Santo Ofício, Inquisição de Lisboa, livro 785, MF 5221.
[77] AHU, Pará, cx. 16, doc. 1522.
[78] AHU, Pará, cx. 33, doc. 3151.
[79] AHU, Pará, cx. 31, doc. 2977.

Angolan Domingos in 1805. Other examples abound. The vast majority of runaways listed in inventories were unmarried African males. Most left alone, though at times slaves left in groups. Such was the case with the Angolan Francisco, Benguelan Francisco, and Mina Mano, who were listed in an 1815 inventory beside one another with the notation *fugido*, or fled.[80]

Of course, fleeing brought dangers. Africans did not know the jungles of Maranhão. Subsisting in them alone was difficult. Establishing *mocambos* was no easy feat, and they were, as noted above, frequently attacked by the state. Hence, other forms of resistance such as feigning ill, working slowly, breaking equipment, and stealing livestock were probably more common.[81] However, these everyday forms of resistance are rarely mentioned in documentation. What is certain is that slaves who resisted masters risked punishment, which was usually swift and most often severe. And the brutality of slave life in Maranhão was yet another impediment to slave family formation.

Here again, documentation is limited. Most white men in Maranhão could not write, and those who could did not often record how they abused their slaves. But evidence does come from one source: complaints waged by *white women* against their white husbands for beating them. In 1767 in Villa de Vianna, for example, Julia Soares told how her husband of twelve years, Francisco Xavier, was cruel from time to time "treating her like his slave and not his wife by giving her many beatings and bringing her near death." The same year, Policena de Barros said that her husband, Rodrigo Malone, "treated [her] like a slave" with incessant beatings.[82] In 1779, neighbors complained that Eleuterio de Freitas treated his wife "like a slave" because she was "always under his blows."[83] A similar report followed in 1792 from Francisca Maria de Alexandria. Her husband, Manoel Pires, "treated her like a slave submitting her to many beatings over her entire body." She had wounds to prove it.[84]

Books of denunciations and divorce proceedings from late-eighteenth-century Maranhão abound with similar accounts, all including the

---

[80] TJEM, Inventory of Bento da Cunha, 1788; TJEM, Inventory of Alexandre Ferreira da Crus, 1800; TJEM, Inventory of Carlos Antonio de Aguiar, 1804; TJEM, Inventory of Anna Maria Rapoza, 1804; TJEM, Inventory of Joze Joaquim da Silva Roza, 1805; TJEM, Inventory of Maria Barboza Lisboa, 1815.

[81] For theft of livestock, APEM, Livro de registro de alvarás por D. Maria I, livro 30.

[82] APEM, AAM, cx. 91, mç. 458–9.

[83] APEM, AAM, cx. 128, doc. 4397.

[84] APEM, AAM, cx. 91, mç. 458–9.

passage "he treats me like a slave."[85] Taken as a whole, these complaints make several things clear. First, domestic abuse was commonplace in Maranhão with white women frequently suffering beatings from their white husbands. Second, the beating of white women was discouraged – frowned upon by the Church, which denounced men who treated their wives poorly. Finally, the beating of slaves was *expected* – normalized and not discouraged by any authority. Before priests, white women made clear distinctions between themselves and black slaves. White women were not to be "treated like slaves" – not to be beaten. Beatings, it was assumed, were for slaves – Africans and their *crioulo* descendants. And, unsurprisingly, there is not one case in hundreds of denunciations from the eighteenth and nineteenth centuries of a white male master being denounced for beating a slave.

State authorities did intervene at times when they learned that masters punished slaves so severely that death ensued. However, in such instances pardons followed. For example, in 1777, the crown excused Manoel Duarte for killing one of his slaves named Izabel. In 1778, Manoel de Pinto e Silva was pardoned for beating to death one of his slaves named Antonio. In 1779, Jose Pereira da Rocha was forgiven for killing one of his slaves named João. In 1791, Antonio de Araujo was exonerated for particularly severe violence against a slave, as was Francisca Raymunda Machadinha in 1792. And in 1793, Alferes Balduino Jozé was pardoned for killing one of his slaves.[86]

Other records also reveal much about black slaves' treatment at the hands of their masters during Maranhão's plantation period. In the 1780s, a priest wrote of the treatment of slaves in Amazonia, "Those miserable slaves! There are *Senhores* who treat them like dogs. I have seen slaves crippled in the hands and feet, others with backs and lower parts covered with scars, the effects of punishment."[87] In a 1788 report from São Luís, Fernando de Foyoz emphasized "the horror" he felt when confronted with "the inhumanity with which slaves were treated" in Maranhão. Despite the fact that "slaves are very expensive," they were subjected to "great hunger, much work, greater punishments; everything consists of work without end or limit."[88] From observations made in

[85] For example, APEM, AAM, cx. 128, doc. 4410; APEM, AAM, cx. 129, doc. 4419.
[86] APEM, Secretaria do Governo, Inventário dos códices, Livro de registro de alvarás passados por D. José e D. Maria I, 1776–1789, livro 29, fl. 7, 36, 48, 65.
[87] Quoted in Eduardo Hoornaert, *História da igreja na Amazônia* (Pretrós: Vozes, 1992), 233.
[88] ANTT, Ministério do Reino, mç. 601, cx. 704.

FIGURE 5.1. "Nègres ào Tronco," or "Blacks in a *Tronco*."
Source: From: Jean Baptiste Debret, *Voyage Pittoresque et Historique au Bresil* (Paris: Firmin Didot frères, 1834), vol. 2, plate 45, p. 139.

1819 and 1820, Friar Francisco de N. S. Dos Prazeres wrote that many slaves who arrived from Africa died each year from "mistreatment and sadness from knowing that they are separated forever from their country and relatives."[89] And D. J. G. de Magalhaens noted after his time in Maranhão in the 1830s that slaves "are treated with such barbarous rigor and when it is necessary to sustain them, they [the owners] don't: an ear of corn is lunch, rice and *farinha* [manioc flour] dinner; anything else they have is from stealing and hunting; they walk nude or covered with a small loincloth."[90] In the early nineteenth century, Antonio Pereira do Lago wrote that it was common for slaves to receive beatings from masters. The lives of slaves in Maranhão, he said, could be described in three words: "*misery, vice, and punishment.*" "There is not a population," he continued, "more disdained and miserably treated and that suffers punishments more severe and capricious." "Punishment," he concluded, "is always and only corporal and painful."[91]

In addition to whippings and beatings, a frequent punishment for slaves was time in a *tronco* (stocks). In Maranhão, *troncos* were most

[89] Francisco de N. S. Dos Prazeres, "Poranduba maranhense ou relação histórica da província do Maranhão," *Revista trimensal do Instituto do Histórico e Geographico Brazileiro* 54 (1891), 140.
[90] D. J. G. de Magalhaens, "Memoria historica da revolução da provincia do Maranhão (1838–1840)" *Opusculos historicos e litterarios* (Rio de Janeiro: Livraria de B. L. Garnier, 1865), 8.
[91] Antonio Bernardino Pereira do Lago, *Estatistica historica-geografica da provincia do Maranhão* (Lisbon: Academia Real das Sciencias, 1822), 25.

often made of wood (though in parts of Brazil they were iron). A *tronco simples* locked around a slave's ankles. A *tronco duplo* locked around the ankles and wrists, leaving the slave hunched forward in an excruciatingly uncomfortable position.[92] *Troncos* appeared in plantation inventories, along with whips, or *chicotes*. On the Itapecuru River, Alferes Francisco Correiro Homem owned what was described as "a *tronco grande* with its hardware." Henreques Leal had a particularly valuable "*tronco* of wood with an iron lock and hinge." Joze Joaquim da Silva Rosa, who had extensive holdings of land and Upper Guinean slaves, had a "small *tronco* with a lock" along with whips, all listed with values in the inventory in neat columns just after the columns that listed slaves. Similar was plantation owner Jose da Souza's inventory, which listed his more than three hundred slaves and then a "large *tronco* of wood" valued at 4,000 réis.[93]

CONCLUSION

Regardless of the threat of torture, beatings, and rape; despite having few rights in a white male–dominated society; and even with being forced to work long days under the hot equatorial sun, many African slaves in Maranhão found it possible to forge long-term relationships with members of the opposite sex. Many married and raised children who, themselves, lived to marry and have children. White male power defined some of those relationships. White men could, and did, force themselves on their slaves, raping them and cajoling them to perform humiliating acts. But, too, the nature of white male power and white marriages meant that some African women found it possible to seek out long-term sexual relationships with whites, becoming concubines in "marriages of friendship" that served as the bases of families.

Other African women made conscious and culturally patterned decisions about whom to take as a partner. Indeed, most marriages involving African slaves in Maranhão took place between Africans from the same region of the continent. Upper Guineans, then, most often married other

---

[92] For a description of *troncos*, see Mendes, Luiz Antonio de Oliveira, "Discurso Academico ao Programma," in *Memorias economicas da Academia Real das Sciencias de Lisboa* IV (Lisbon: Academia Real das Sciencias de Lisboa, 1812), 222.

[93] See TJEM, Inventory of Antonio Jose de Souza, 1802; TJEM, Inventory of Alferes Francisco Correiro Homem, 1817; TJEM, Inventory of Domingos Martres Fernandes, 1810; TJEM, Inventory of Guilherme Francisco da Silva, 1810; TJEM, Inventory of Antonio Henriques Leal, 1807.

Upper Guineans, re-creating as they did endogamous marriage patterns common across the ocean. They also recast a broad regional identity – remaking *Guiné* by creating families. When and where they could, African slaves – particularly the Upper Guinean majority – shaped Maranhão's cultural landscape. One place they could do this was through their choice of marriage partners.

Many marriages produced children, and within families headed by Upper Guineans, children heard about the place from which their parents had come. They learned of certain Upper Guinean agricultural practices, foods, and core religious beliefs. Some of the patterns of *crioulos'* lives were informed, then, by aspects of a culture transported across the ocean. Thus, the children of Upper Guineans often gravitated toward Upper Guineans or the children of Upper Guinean parents for marriage partners.

6

Spiritual Beliefs

In Grão Pará and Maranhão in the 1760s, a thirty-year-old slave named Joze, who was a Mandinka from Upper Guinea, used what locals called *feitiçaria*, or "magic," to cure many people. Fearing that his actions were sinful, some of Joze's neighbors reported him to a Portuguese representative of the Inquisition, who was visiting the captaincy. One of Joze's clients, someone told the inquisitor, was a black female slave named Maria, who was a Bijago from Upper Guinea. Joze had been summoned to Maria's side because she was "gravely ill, expelling from her vagina various vermin and animated parasites." When Joze arrived, he examined one of the vermin and said that "she still had some inside her." He then "spoke words" that no one in the room was able to understand and "with some herbs that he had secretly taken with him and water that he took from a pot, he made a soup without allowing anyone to watch." Joze gave some of it to Maria who drank it while he again spoke "words that no one understood." He returned later having prepared another medicine in secret and then made more the following morning and afternoon, "each time saying words that no one understood." After having given her the last of his herbal soup, Joze took an ear of corn and a hoe and handed them to Maria, saying the corn should be buried in the yard. After some time, Maria expelled more vermin from her vagina – all contained in a "thing like a sack," which looked like a bladder made of skin. The vermin were said to have resembled a small alligator, small hairy lizard, and small frog – each a different color.[1]

[1] ANTT, Tribunal do Santo Ofício, Inquisição de Lisboa, Livro 785, MF 5221. The Case is transcribed in full in Amaral Lapa, ed., *Livro da visitação do santo oficio da Inquisição ao estado do Grão-Para, 1763–1769* (Rio de Janeiro: Vozes, 1978), 137–40, 153–4.

Inquisitorial notes about Joze's "sinful" act of using "magic" to cure Maria provide a glimpse at how Upper Guineans, who were a majority among slaves in most Portuguese-controlled areas of Amazonia in the late eighteenth century, viewed the relationship between physical health and spirituality. That a Bijago in Amazonia looked to a Mandinka healer to provide a cure for what ailed her should not be a surprise. Indeed, Maria was acting like she would have back in Upper Guinea. There, Bijago, like all people, regularly sought out Mandinka who were recognized as gifted in harnessing the supernatural power of natural objects. Many gifted Mandinka were itinerant Muslim merchant-scholars known as marabouts, or *bexerins*. These individuals made a living as master herbalists and crafters of *guarda di kurpu*, or "body protectors," that when worn on the body kept particular evils at bay. From their actions, it is clear that Maria and Joze were re-creating some aspects of a broad Upper Guinean culture in Amazonia. That is, they were re-creating some of the spiritual beliefs that they had held – and held in common – across the ocean. They found it possible to do this because in Amazonia not the Church, state, or slave masters exercised much control over what slaves believed. Hence, Upper Guineans fashioned spiritual beliefs common throughout the whole of *Guiné*.

In this chapter, I explore Upper Guinean spiritual beliefs – as they existed in Africa and Amazonia. Elements of Upper Guinean spiritual beliefs and aspects of rituals differed over space and changed over time. However, I argue that all people of the Upper Guinea coast, regardless of the community, ethnic group, or occupational group to which they belonged, held a relatively unchanging set of what James Sweet calls "core beliefs." These core beliefs can still be identified in parts of the Upper Guinea coast and are lasting, as Sweet writes, because they are "central to ... personhood and identity."[2] Core beliefs are the elements of culture that Jan Vansina argues show "long-term continuities which lasted ... for millennia."[3] They may have been what Wyatt MacGaffey

[2] James H. Sweet, *Recreating Africa: Culture, Kinship and Religion in the African-Portuguese World, 1441–1770* (Chapel Hill: University of North Carolina Press, 2003), 132, 158; James H. Sweet, "Male Homosexuality and Spiritism in the African Diaspora: The Legacies of a Link," *Journal of the History of Sexuality* 7, 2 (1992), 184–202.

[3] Jan Vansina, *Paths in the Rainforests: Toward a History of Political Tradition in Equatorial Africa* (Madison: The University of Wisconsin Press, 1990): 249–51. Also, Jan Vansina, "Towards a History of Lost Corners of the World," *Economic History Review* 35, 2 (1982), 165–78. Thornton makes a similar distinction, arguing that certain elements of peoples' cultures "change rapidly" while others are "more fixed and change slowly." John Thornton, *Africa and Africans in the Making of the Atlantic World, 1400–1680* (New York: Cambridge University Press, 1992), 206.

had in mind when he wrote, "Change ... must be change in something that itself continues."[4]

In simplest terms, Upper Guineans' spiritual beliefs were composed of four elements. First, all believed that there was one creator, who was distant and did not interfere often in the affairs of humankind. Second, all believed that spirits inhabited the earth, interacted regularly with humans, and affected them for better and worse. These spirits were of two kinds. "Natural spirits" had always existed in forests, streams, and the sea; "ancestral spirits" (or "the living dead") were the souls of deceased relatives or important community members. Third, Upper Guineans thought that certain material objects and natural substances, be they derived from plants, animals, or minerals, contained supernatural powers. These powers could be released only by the uttering of specific words and performing of specific ceremonies. Finally, all held that some people, like the Mandinka Joze, were "gifted," knowing better than most how to receive messages from spirits, to please them with gifts in the form of sacrifices, and to manipulate the supernatural powers of natural substances and material objects.[5]

The embrace of the same core spiritual beliefs was one of the things that united the people of the Upper Guinea coast into a single cultural group.[6] This is not to say that all Upper Guinean spiritual beliefs were unchanging or identical from place to place. What differed over space and altered over time were the spirits that comprised local pantheons, the nature of their interactions with humans, and aspects of the rituals used to communicate with them. Eventually, as coastal people came into contact with different merchants, invaders, and evangelists from both the African interior and Atlantic Ocean, they recognized the power of new gifted people and new spirits, and they learned about the power of myriad natural substances and material objects. As they did so, Upper Guineans

---

[4] Wyatt MacGaffey, "Dialogues of the Deaf: Europeans on the Atlantic Coast of Africa," in *Implicit Understandings*, ed. Stuart B. Schwartz (New York: Cambridge University Press, 1994), 254–7. Also, Ann Hilton, *Kingdom of Kongo* (New York: Oxford University Press, 1985), x, 9.

[5] For other outlines of Upper Guinean beliefs in the supernatural, António Carreira "Símbolos, ritualistas e ritualismos ânimo-feiticistas na Guiné Portuguesa," *Boletim Cultural da Guiné* 16 (1961), 505–41; George E. Brooks, *Landlords and Strangers: Ecology, Society, and Trade in Western Africa, 1000–1630* (Boulder, CO: Westview Press, 1993), 36.

[6] Thornton examines "cultural zones" in *Africa and Africans*, 184–7; Paul E. Lovejoy, "Ethnic Designations of the Slave Trade and the Reconstruction of the History of Trans-Atlantic Slavery," in *Trans-Atlantic Dimensions of Ethnicity in the African Diaspora*, eds. Paul E. Lovejoy and David V. Trotman (New York: Continuum, 2003), 34–7.

learned to speak the spiritual language of Muslims and Christians. That is, they made the foreign familiar by accepting aspects of other belief systems as their own.

It would, then, be incorrect to say that Upper Guinea coastal people's beliefs were "Europeanized" in the seventeenth and eighteenth centuries. Linda Heywood and John Thornton adopt this term in their studies of Central African Christians. As elites in Kongo and Angola interacted with missionaries, Central Africa, they argue, experienced a "religious transformation," which is "best represented by the profession of Christianity."[7] On the Upper Guinea coast, however, few people "became Catholic" – and this despite centuries of Church efforts to evangelize on the coast. Unlike in Kongo and Angola, in the areas around Bissau and Cacheu there were few African elites who could influence a large number of people to embrace Christianity and its religious/cultural program. That is, compared to Kongo and Angola, Upper Guinea was much more politically decentralized. In the few places in Upper Guinea where "big men," or chiefs, held sway over people, their followers were few.[8] Further, unlike in Kongo and Angola, where Christian conversion was influenced by a host of political and economic factors, on the Upper Guinea coast few saw any advantage to becoming Christian. Indeed, the overwhelming majority rejected the notion that there was a Heaven and Hell and that good Christians ascended to one place and non-believers and the evil descended to the other. The spirits of both the good and the evil, most all thought from the seventeenth through the nineteenth centuries, continued to live on earth, affecting the living on a daily basis. [9]

This is not to imply that Upper Guineans rejected all things Christian. In Africa *and* Amazonia many accepted saints alongside their own spirits, priests alongside their own gifted spiritual leaders, and Christian relics

---

[7] Linda M. Heywood and John K. Thornton, *Central Africans, Atlantic Creoles, and the Founding of the Americas, 1585–1660* (Cambridge: Cambridge University Press, 2007), 67, 169. Thornton makes the point that Christianity did not flourish in Sierra Leone as it did in the Kongo in "Perspectives on African Christianity," in *Race, Discourse, and the Origin of the Americas*, eds. Vera Hyatt and Rex Nettleford (Washington, DC: Smithsonian Institution Press, 1995), 183–5.

[8] Heywood and Thornton, *Central Africans*, 62.

[9] Balthasar Barreira wrote in the early seventeenth century of Upper Guineans: "They evaluate all points about the next world in terms of things of this world, believing that the former are also material, and hence that they will employ in the other life what they used in this one. They cannot be persuaded of the existence of hell ... [I]n troubles they commend themselves to the dead, ... and make them offerings." Quoted in Brooks, *Landlords*, 26–7.

alongside material objects they had long recognized as having particular power. But the acceptance of some things Christian did not mean the rejection of preexisting beliefs. Indeed, in Amazonia in the eighteenth and early nineteenth centuries, Upper Guineans continued to embrace the same core beliefs that they had known across the ocean. In Amazonia, Upper Guineans looked to each other – and, at times, to other Africans – for spiritual solace in physically and mentally challenging times. The gifted among them provided that comfort in the only way they knew how. They gave it by drawing on knowledge and ritual practice cultivated for many generations on the other side of the ocean.

ONE CREATOR, MANY SPIRITS

The first element of shared Upper Guinean spiritual beliefs was that there was one creator, who made all things natural and supernatural. His name differed from society to society. Balanta called him *Nhala*, Floup used *Emitay*, Manjaco called him *Nalí Batí*,[10] Mancanha referred to him as *Nasi Baci*,[11] Baga used *Kanu*,[12] and Bijago named him *Nindo*.[13] Generally, the creator god of coastal societies was detached from everyday affairs and was not, therefore, a supernatural force with which people interacted daily.[14] All associated the creator with the sky, and indeed *Nasi Baci* means "chief of the sky," *Emitay* means "sky,"[15] and *Nhala* is derived from *nihala*, which, too, means "sky."[16] Like the sky, the creator

---

[10] Eve Crowley, "Contracts with the Spirits: Religion, Asylum, and Ethnic Identity in the Cacheu Region of Guinea-Bissau" (Ph.D. thesis, Yale University, 1990), 390.

[11] Domingos da Fonseca, *Os Mancanha* (Bissau: Ku Si Mon Editora, 1997), 74.

[12] Ramon Sarró, *The Politics of Religious Change on the Upper Guinea Coast: Iconoclasm Done and Undone* (Edinburgh: Edinburgh University Press, 2009), 146.

[13] Luigi Scantamburlo, *Etnologia dos Bijagós da Ilha de Bibaque* (Bissau: Instituto Nacional de Estudos e Pesquisa, 1991), 66; Robert Martin Baum, *Shrines of the Slave Trade: Diola Religion and Society in Precolonial Senegambia* (New York: Oxford University Press, 1999), 37–42; Brooks, *Landlords*, 36.

[14] Robin Horton developed a model like this for Africa generally. "African Conversion," *Africa* 41 (1971), 101. With variations, scholars studying the Upper Guinea coast have applied it. Diana Lima Handem, *Nature et fonctionnement du pouvoir chez les Balanta Brassa* (Bissau: Instituto Nacional de Estudos e Pesquisa, 1986), 143; J. David Sapir, "Kujaama: Symbolic Separation among the Diola-Fogny," *American Anthropologist* 72 (1970), 1331; Peter Mark, *Cultural, Economic and Religious History of the Basse Casamance since 1500* (Stuttgart: F. Steiner, 1985), 84–5. Baum argues that *Emitay* intervenes in human affairs "when conditions warrant it." *Shrines*, 42.

[15] Fonseca, *Os Mancanha*, 74; Baum, *Shrines*, 39.

[16] I speak the Balanta language. Also, Inger Callewaert, "The Birth of Religion among the Balanta of Guinea-Bissau." (Ph.D. thesis, University of Lund, 2000), 50; Roy van der

was always there but always untouchable.[17] It was because of this belief in a creator that Francisco Travassos Valdez said in the mid-nineteenth century that the people "inhabiting the seaboard" of Upper Guinea were "theists." "They acknowledge," he wrote, "but one God," but their theism was "mixed with" what he called "fetichism." That is, coastal people, he noted, had places to which they made offerings to "souls of the departed" and "spirits."[18]

Indeed, all coastal people believed that spirits, both natural and ancestral, regularly interacted with humans, affecting them positively and negatively. All believed that the world of these spirits was coterminous with the physical world. That is, spirits occupied the same physical space as human beings, there being no clear boundary between the spiritual and physical realms. For Upper Guineans, death was not followed by the ascension of the soul into a distant Heaven or descension into a far-off Hell. Rather, the souls of the dead continued to hold a place on earth among the living. For this belief, those who inhabited the Upper Guinea coast in the seventeenth, eighteenth, and early nineteenth centuries can be seen as "spiritists." In other words, they were people who believed that a range of invisible supernatural entities affected relationships and events in the visible natural world around them, and their broader belief system can be defined as "spiritism."[19]

Every coastal language group had a general word for spirit and a range of words for specific spirits occupying complex pantheons. Among Balanta, a spirit was known as *kusasse*;[20] among Mancanha, *n-cai*;[21]

Drift, *Arbeid en alcohol. De dynamiek van de rijstverbouw en het gezag van de oudste bij de Balanta Brassa in Guinea Bissau* (Leiden: Centrum Voor Niet-west-erse Studies Rijksuniversiteit Leiden, 1992), 224.

[17] See especially, Scantamburlo, *Etnologia*, 66. Some thought about the creator in times of social stress, especially in the nineteenth and twentieth centuries, when Christian influences under European colonialism were felt strongly. Baum, *Shrines*, 130–53; Francisco Travassos Valdez, *Africa occidental: Noticias e considerações* (Lisbon: Ministerio da Marinha e Ultramar, 1864), 364–5.

[18] Francisco Travassos Valdez, *Six Years of a Traveller's Life in Western Africa* (London: Hurst and Blackett, 1861), 215–16.

[19] Especially, Crowley in "Contracts," 1–6; Eve Crowley, "Institutions, Identities and the Incorporation of Immigrants within Local Frontiers of the Upper Guinea Coast," in *Migrations anciennes et peuplement actuel des côtes guinéennes*, ed. Gérald Gaillard (Paris: L'Harmattan, 2000), 123–4; Peter Mark, *The Wild Bull and the Sacred Forest: Form, Meaning, and Change in Senegambian Initiation Masks* (New York: Cambridge University Press, 1992), 26.

[20] Mark, *Cultural*, 79–80; Handem, *Nature*, 144; Brooks, *Landlords*, 36.

[21] Fonseca, *Mancanha*, 74.

among Bijago, *unikán*;[22] among Ehing, *esul*;[23] among southern Floup, *ekin*; and among northern Floup, *enaati*.[24] In Kriolo, a trade language that emerged on the Upper Guinea coast in the era of Atlantic slavery, spirits were called *irans*. Though the specific spirits with whom coastal groups interacted were often different, each group shared with others the same general approach to spiritism.

The structures of the Upper Guinea coast's belief system reflected the organization of its political systems. The region was not dominated by one powerful state. Rather, political structures were small-scale, egalitarian, and controlled locally at the village level or within a conglomeration of villages. Within villages, individual families (or households) had some autonomy, controlling land and claiming rights over family members' labor and reproductive capacities. However, the communities that families were a part of also exercised control over individuals. Most obviously, those holding places in village-level political institutions directed work groups to carry out large-scale agricultural projects and to engage in wars with other villages. Likewise, within communities, individual households controlled the shrines at which some spirits could be contacted, and the village at large tended to the shrines of other spirits. In sum, every family had ancestors that it honored, and every village had spirits to which people made sacrifices.[25] As Jean Baptiste Léonard Durand wrote of Bissau from his observations at the end of the eighteenth century, "The principal idol is a small figure.... The deity however is not exclusively adored: for every individual adopts for his god whatever his imagination presents to him."[26]

Coastal people had a range of spirits with which to cope. First, there were "natural" spirits that occupied things in the physical world. Often, they were associated with water, trees, anthills, and serpents.[27] Forests, especially, were places where natural spirits who could cause harm to village insiders dwelled.[28] Because of this, people often walled their

---

[22] Scantamburlo, *Etnologia*, 66.

[23] Marc R. Schloss, *Hatchet's Blood: Separation, Power, and Gender in Ehing Social Life* (Tucson: University of Arizona Press, 1988), 3.

[24] Mark, *Wild Bull*, 24–5.

[25] The decentralized nature of Upper Guinean cosmology was noted by Manuel Álvares, *Ethiopia Minor and a Geographical Account of the Province of Sierra Leone* (Liverpool: Department of History, 1990), pt. I, ch. 11.

[26] J. P. L. Durand, *A Voyage to Senegal* (London: Richard Philips, 1806), 62.

[27] Across the coast, silk-cotton trees are associated with spirits. Personal observations. Also, Avelino Teixeira da Mota, *Guiné Portuguesa* (Lisbon: Agência Geral do Ultramar, 1954), I: 286.

[28] Sarró describes villages situated in a "landscape of fear." Sarró, *Politics*, 2, 37.

communities in an effort to keep out evil of all sorts.[29] But forests also were a place of protection because the spirits that inhabited them kept foreign raiders at bay, devouring those who entered them unknowingly. Upper Guineans lived, then, in what Ramon Sarró aptly describes as a "religious landscape," a place where the natural and supernatural coexisted and interacted. Villagers took strides to forge alliances with the sprits of their landscape by properly honoring them.[30]

The other broad group of spirits can be called "ancestral." Most Upper Guineans believed that after a person's death, the spirit followed a particular path. It first became a child – which was weak, needy, and vulnerable – and then grew into an angry adolescent before maturing as an adult. Over time, spirits like humans acted in a complex and sometimes irrational or incomprehensible manner that was at once the product of age, personality, individual pasts, and perceptions of the actions of others. To persuade ancestors to act in the interest of the community rather than to exercise power whimsically or negatively, Upper Guinea coastal people have long carried out rituals aimed both at understanding ancestors' desires and at appeasing, praising, thanking, rewarding, cajoling, and even scolding them.[31] Ancestors, then, should not be seen as guardians of the moral and social order.[32] Rather, as Eric Gable argues in his study of Manjaco, ancestors have long been seen "like Nietzchean 'blond beasts' who exercise power because it is in their nature to do so." Ancestors often made their presence felt, he writes, "by making children sick, by killing cattle, or most dramatically, by setting fire to the thatched roofed huts that comprise the house compound, and by burning the rice in the granaries beneath the thatched roofs." The challenge was realizing why they did these things and persuading them to act constructively.[33]

---

[29] Walter Hawthorne, *Planting Rice and Harvesting Slaves: Transformations along the Guinea-Bissau Coast, 1400–1900* (Portsmouth, NH: Heinemann, 2003), 75.

[30] Sarró, *Politics*, 66–7.

[31] Personal observations; Eric Gable, "Women, Ancestors, and Alterity among the Manjaco of Guinea-Bissau," *Journal of Religion in Africa* 26, 2 (1996), 104–21; Crowley, "Institutions," 125; Scantamburlo, *Etnologia*, 70–3; Baum, *Shrines*, 45.

[32] Benjamin Ray, *African Religions: Symbols, Ritual and Community* (Englewood Cliffs, NJ: Prentice Hall, 1976), 146; Eugene L. Mendosa, "Elders, Office-holders and Ancestors among the Sisala of Northern Ghana," *Africa* 46, 1 (1976), 57–65; C. Calhoun "The Authority of Ancestors: A Sociological Reconsideration of Fortes's Tallensi in Response to Fortes's Critics," *Man* 16 (1980), 304–19; C. Calhoun, "Correspondence," *Man* 16 (1980), 137–8.

[33] Gable, "Women, Ancestors," 105, 114. Many Upper Guineans believed that no matter where they died, their spirits returned to their ancestral homelands. This was one reason, Coelho wrote in the late seventeenth century, that some captives committed suicide.

OFFERINGS TO AND FAVORS FROM SPIRITS

What ancestral and natural spirits most wanted was recognition through offerings, especially in the form of sacrifices. In the seventeenth and eighteenth centuries, some sacrifices included people.[34] But across the coast, most sacrifices to spirits involved animals, and especially cattle. Cattle were sacrificed during male initiations, funerals, marriages, and ceremonies honoring births and important spirits. Spirits especially favored cattle because they were associated with wealth and power.[35] In all coastal societies, the cutting of a bovine's neck was cause for great celebration because spirits were pleased to consume the blood that spilled on the ground. To this day, Balanta will comment at the immolation of a cow, "*Bewule ne kpang yid ksaham*," or "The spirits of the compound took the blood."[36] But spirits also appreciated other offerings – the blood of chickens, pigs, and goats, as well as palm oil and alcohol.[37]

If spirits could be pleased through sacrifices, they might be persuaded to act to help a community, family, or individual gain wealth, power, and health. Across the coast, any individual who gained fortune quickly was suspected of having carried out a heinous crime such as sacrificing family members to a spirit (see Chapter 2).[38] There were a variety of spirits whom people from the Upper Guinea coast's various groups called on to enrich themselves in an antisocial way. Among Manjaco, *udjúnpor* (the python), *nandjángurum* (a spirit of the forest that kept wild animals), and *pitchír* (also a spirit of the forest) were thought to make agreements with select individuals.[39] Balanta, too, held a range of nefarious spirits – and

Francisco de Lemos Coelho, *Description of the Coast of Guinea (1684)*, ed. P. E. H. Hair (Liverpool: University of Liverpool, 1985), ch. 7, p. 10.

[34] Sacrifices of people were most common in societies with some political hierarchy. P. E. H. Hair, Adam Jones, and Robin Law, *Barbot on Guinea: The Writings of Jean Barbot on West Africa, 1678–1712* (London: Hakluyt Society, 1992), 320–1. For similar descriptions, Álvares, *Ethiopia*, pt. I, ch. 8. A. Teixeira da Mota and P. E. H. Hair, ed., *Jesuit Documents on the Guinea of Cape Verde and the Cape Verde Islands, 1585–1617* (Liverpool: Department of History, University of Liverpool, 1989), ch. 9, p. 4.

[35] Scantamburlo, *Etnologia*, 30; Hair, *Barbot on Guinea*, 320; Gaspard Mollien, *Travels in the Interior of Africa to the Sources of the Senegal and Gambia Performed by the Command of the French Government in the Year 1818* (London: Frank Cass, 1967), 338–41; Interview with Mam Nambatcha, Cufar, March 3, 1995.

[36] Personal observations. Also, Callewaert-Sjöberg, *The Birth*, 75.

[37] Personal observations. Also, examples in Mota, *Jesuit Documents*, ch. 22, p. 7.

[38] Mark, *Wild Bull*, 26; Eric Gable, "A Secret Shared: Fieldwork and the Sinister in a West African Village," *Cultural Anthropology* 12 (2), 213–33; M. Schloss, *The Hatchet's Blood*, 118; William Simmons, *Eyes of the Night: Witchcraft Among a Senegalese People* (Boston: Little Snyder, Francis, 1971), 158.

[39] Crowley, "Contracts," 333–9.

especially *unikán coratacó* – responsible for death, infertility, illness, and other misfortunes. Jealous and envious Balanta who struck contracts with spirits to harm others became *befera* (*afera* in the singular), or witches, who attacked at night and ate the souls of the living.[40] Among Diola it was the *kusaye*, or "cannibal witches," who preyed on innocent victims.[41] And among Baga, *waser* were witches who ate humans instead of rice.[42] Witches often killed victims, but their actions could also cause those upon whom they preyed to fall ill. Indeed, in the seventeenth and eighteenth centuries (and in places today), coastal people did not see health, illness, and death as resulting from things of the material world, such as microbes and antibodies. Rather, illness and death were seen as resulting from supernatural forces – often from people doing evil things to enrich themselves, which brought harm to others, generally a relative or someone close.[43]

If illness was caused by evil-doers, health was something that could be sustained with spiritual assistance that came with the help of those gifted few who worked for the betterment of the community. They did so by calling on spirits to heal the sick, protect people in war, and root out evil. These clairvoyants, mediums, diviners, prophets, and healers were known by a variety of names. In historical documents, outsiders often recorded the Kriolo word *jambacous* (also *jabacouce, djambakús,* and *djambakos*).

A central role of the *jambacous* was determining why people became sick or died. Because the spiritual realm affected health, medicine focused necessarily on the link between the body and spirit. Determining how spirits were harmed was crucial to maintaining health and order in a community.[44] Hence, in the early seventeenth century, the Jesuit Guerreiro said that in Cassanga territories, "when any black dies, the *jabacouce* or diviner says that so-and-so killed him, and 'ate' him or removed his soul." The accused was "seized as a murderer and witch."[45] Similar accounts can be found in archival sources from the seventeenth, eighteenth, and

[40] Personal observations; Handem, *Nature*, 150–61; Van der Drift, "Birds of Passage," 157; Scantamburlo, *Etnologia*, 66–70.

[41] Mark, *Wild Bull*, 30–1.

[42] Sarró, *Politics*, 36.

[43] For example, Álvares, *Ethiopia*, ch. 5; Beaver, *African Memoranda*, 177. Contemporary examples in Toby Green, *Meeting the Invisible Man: Secrets and Magic in West Africa* (London: Weidenfeld & Nicolson, 2001).

[44] Handem, *Nature*, 150; Callewaert, "Birth," 50; personal observations. Diola/Floup called "good people" *bukan bujak*. Mark, *Cultural*, 86–7.

[45] Mota, *Jesuit Documents*, doc 4. For a similar statement, Álvares, *Ethiopia*, ch. 6.

nineteenth centuries.[46] For example, Valdez said that when someone on the Upper Guinea coast is "attacked by sickness," people think an "evil spirit caused it. Under these circumstances they have recourse to the Jambacoz, or sorcerer, who is considered to have great influence with, and control over, the demon."[47]

POWERFUL THINGS AND POWERFUL SHRINES

In addition to seeing and communicating with spirits, the *jambacous* could harness and direct supernatural powers of material objects. Sometimes a *jambacous* did this by mixing a variety of things found in nature into potions and empowering them with words. Words were crucial, for it was with words that ritual specialists released the supernatural power of the natural world. It was, too, with words spoken aloud that they struck contracts with spirits.[48] Any number of objects contained supernatural powers, which a special few knew how to tap.[49] And when combined in the right way, herbs in particular were thought to have powerful supernatural effects. Mandinka healers were famed for making "magic medicines" from herbs "in the same way as in Moorish geomancy."[50] Fula healers were also "expert in the herbs used in their rites," which made them, for the Portuguese, "witches and sorcerers."[51] And Brame healers were "expert herbalists" who "perform cures like doctors and surgeons."[52] In Kriolo, gifted people who offered herbal cures were known as *curandeiros* and *curandeiras*. In the early nineteenth century, it was noted that *curandeiras* around Bissau made "broths, medicines, enemas, and remedies of herbs, barks, roots and diverse medicinal plants" that could "cure perfectly illnesses."[53]

From powerful natural substances and material objects, gifted people also crafted talismans (*nominas* in Portuguese), which were known

---

[46] See examples in Baum, *Shrines*, 161.

[47] Valdez, *Six Years*, 216. Other sorts of rituals also determined what evil was responsible for illness and death. See Baum, *Shrines*, 138; Schloss, *Hatchet's Blood*, 59; André Alvares Almada, *Brief Treatise on the Rivers of Guinea* (Liverpool: Department of History, University of Liverpool, 1984), 68–70.

[48] Álvares, *Ethiopia*, ch. 1; Baum, *Shrines*, 44.

[49] For example, Álvares, *Ethiopia*, ch. 10; Mota, *Jesuit Documents*, doc. 31.

[50] Álvares, *Ethiopia*, ch. 7, p. 9.

[51] Ibid., ch. 2, p. 3.

[52] Ibid., ch. 6. Throughout Upper Guinea, people used herbs in "love-potions," which were consumed or carried on the body. Ibid., ch. 24, p. 1.

[53] José Conrado Carlos de Chelmicki, *Corografia cabo verdiana* (Lisbon: Typ. de L.C. da Cunha, 1841), II: 305.

locally as *grisgris* (or *grigri*) and *guarda di kurpu*. *Grisgris* contained any range of things, from paper containing writing of a known or unknown language to pieces of the horns of animals to other powerful material objects. They sometimes took the form of leather pouches and for this were called *bolsinhas* (literally "little pouches") by Portuguese.[54]

Grisgris could be used for defensive purposes: to protect the wearer from a spell, physical attack, or illness. Or they could be used for offensive purposes: to win affection or to harm an enemy.[55] Whatever their contents, *grisgris*, like potions made from herbs, were sometimes referred to as medicine (or *medicina* in Kriolo) because of their protective and healing powers.[56]

Often *medicina* was empowered by a spirit. Across the coast, communication with spirits generally happened at shrines, many of which resembled little grass-roofed houses. Though spirits did not necessarily occupy shrines permanently, they could be summoned there through rituals.[57] In Kriolo, grass-roof shrines were called *balboa* (also, *balouba* and *valboa*), and the individual gifted in communications with spirits at the shrine was a *balobeira* (or *balobeiro*).[58] Balanta refer to grass-roofed shines as *fram*. And Floup referred to them by a variety of names. In Fogny, they were *sinaati* (*enaati* in the singular). In Kasa, *bekin* (*ukin*). Elsewhere, *boekine* (*ukine*). The latter terminology was also used by Manjacko, Papel, Cassanga, and Kriolo speakers in the sixteenth century.[59]

In shrines were ritual objects called *chinas* (or *xinas*) in Kriolo that represented spirits.[60] It was in front of *chinas* that sacrifices and offerings

---

54 Mota, *Jesuit Documents*, ch. 1, 3; Álvares, *Ethiopia*, ch. 1; Francisco de Lemos Coelho, "Descrição da costa da Guiné desde o Cabo Verde athe Serra Lioa com todas as ilhas e rios que os brancos navegam," in *Duas descrições seiscentistas da Guiné*, ed. Damião Peres (Lisbon: Academia Portuguesa da História, 1953), ch. 2; Hair, *Barbot*, 85, 221–2.

55 Brooks, *Landlords*, 36; George E. Brooks, "The Observance of All Soul's Day in the Guinea-Bissau Region: A Christian Holy Day, and African Harvest Festival, and African New Year's Celebration, or All of the Above?," *History in Africa* 11 (1984), 14. Barbot noted the large range of uses of *grisgris*. Hair, *Barbot*, 86.

56 For example, Álvares, *Ethiopia*, ch. 1.

57 Baum, *Shrines*, 43; Mark, *Cultural*, 79.

58 See, Avelino Teixeira da Mota, *As Viagens do Bispo D. Frei Vitoriano Portuense à Guiné e a cristianização dos reis de Bissau* (Lisbon: Junta de Investigações Científicas do Ultramar, 1974), 127; António Brásio, *Monumenta missionaria africana. Africa occidental* 2 serie (Lisbon: Agência Geral do Ultramar, 1958), 7: 28; Dias, "Crenças," 161.

59 Mark, *Cultural*, 80. On ubiquity of shrines, see Baum, *Shrines*, 43; Crowley, "Contracts," 254–5; Callewaert, *Birth*, 50. Shrines sometimes took the shape of natural objects, especially enormous silk-cotton trees, and were sometimes man-made. Mota, *As Viagens*, 106–9; Crowley, "Contracts," 255. For Diola/Floup, Mark, *Wild Bull*, 25.

60 Álvares, *Ethiopia*, ch. 11.

FIGURE 6.1. A shrine, or *balboa*, in Guinea-Bissau.
Source: From: Hugo Adolf Bernatzik, *Äthiopen des Westens: Forschungsreisen in Portuguiesisch-Guinea* (Wien: Verlag von L. W. Seidel & Sohn, 1933), 65. Image courtesy of Kevin Conru.

were made. Descriptions of shrines and *chinas* abound in the historical record. In the early seventeenth century, Manuel Álvares said that a Papel *china* was "a bundle of sticks, anointed with the blood of birds, such as hens, and the blood of goats and cows, and with the feathers of a cock over the blood." The *china* sat in a shrine or what Álvares called a "chapel," which he said Papel called a *funco*.[61] Of Papel in the 1690s, Francisco de Santiago wrote, "As for beliefs, imagining that there are ... spirits and that these can reveal to them the future and make real their wishes, they make sacrifices, to what are called 'Chinas,' which are [in shrines] in the form of sun umbrellas covered with grass."[62] In the late eighteenth century, Philip Beaver observed that when a stranger arrived, Bijago "sacrifice one or more cocks" near a *china*.[63] And in the mid-nineteenth century, Valdez wrote of the Biafada, "They ... speak of a

[61] Ibid. See, too, Brásio, *Monumenta*, 6: 199. Earlier description in 1: 719, 729–30.
[62] António J. Dias, "Crenças e costumes dos Indígenas da Ilha de Bissau no Século XVIII," *Portugal em Africa* II (1945), 160. In 1697, King Azinhaté threatened residents of the Portuguese fort with "diabolical ceremonies that he has the custom to make with his *chinas*." AHU, Guiné, cx. 4, doc. 12.
[63] Beaver, *Africa*, 338.

divinity that they call *Hiram* [*Iran*], and they have huts that they call (like the Papel) *babloubs* or *xinas*, where they worship."[64]

THE INCORPORATIVE NATURE OF UPPER GUINEAN SPIRITUALITY

Upper Guineans often visited shrines for help with matters of very local concern. And, indeed, in the seventeenth and eighteenth centuries, much about people's lives on the Upper Guinea coast was rooted in events in their local communities. However, coastal people were well aware that folks from outside their communities affected them. Because of this, coastal people needed their set of core beliefs to explain events both within and outside the confines of the small group of people with whom they most often had exchanges. That is, coastal people were not concerned exclusively with things that happened in their villages. They looked outward to the world, interacted in various ways with people from far-off lands, and sought trade goods from those places. And key to the manner in which coastal people coped with "the larger world" was one assumption: coastal people believed that they did not monopolize communications with things outside the known, natural realm. In other words, they were accepting of the ways that people who were not of their communities drew power from the supernatural.

Hence, coastal people sometimes left their communities to travel to other villages (even those of other ethnic groups) to make offerings and requests at shrines. Because Europeans did not often observe such pilgrimages, we have few records describing them. However, we do have some, and more contemporary pilgrimages point to lasting historical patterns. In the Cacheu region, Eve Crowley describes what has historically been a hierarchy of shrines, from the very local (household shrine) to the regional (provincial shrine). Powerful provincial shrines, she writes, have long attracted pilgrims from multiple ethnic groups and faraway lands. Pilgrims paid for services rendered, and payments brought considerable wealth (often in the form of cattle) to communities controlling provincial shrines.[65] The best known of these multiethnic shrines is that of the spirit Mama Djombo in Caboi. António Carreira noted that pilgrims long visited Mama Djombo's shrine from Manjaco, Papel, Balanta, Cassanga, Banhun, and Brame communities to seek protection

---

[64] Valdez, *Africa Occidental*, 364.
[65] Crowley, "Contracts," 215–89; personal observations.

and health.[66] Pilgrimages illustrate the degree to which beliefs about the power of spirits cut across ethnic divides – all coastal people embracing the same general conception of the relationship between the natural and supernatural and even recognizing the power of specific spirits over all people's lives.[67]

Coastal people also believed that strangers from outside their villages could harness the power of local spirits, summoning them to a shrine and directing them to perform fantastic feats. In the early seventeenth century, Álvares made note of just this sort of thing. Visiting a drought-stricken Mandinka village, he witnessed the arrival of a pilgrim "dressed as a poor man." Locals "rushed ... to ask him for help in this very great disaster.... As if he had the favours of heaven at his command, he ordered those in need to provide him with a good meal." Promising that it would rain, the pilgrim then took a bowl of water to a nearby anthill. "He tipped the water over ... making mud, and anointed himself with this, then made a wooden cross and fixed it on the mound." After spending the night "shrieking and calling out" odd words, the stranger disappeared. When the people awoke, they were thrilled that "such a quantity of rain fell." They spent the day celebrating the gifted stranger's deed.[68]

Another indication that coastal people looked outward from their villages for spiritual power can be found in their embrace of itinerant Mandinka from areas north and east who offered powerful *grisgris*. Most of these Mandinka were Muslim merchant-scholars, or marabouts, who were known locally as *bexerins* (or *bixirins*), *cacizes*, and *mozes*.[69] All coastal people recognized them as possessing unique abilities to negotiate with the supernatural realm. Marabouts were connected to powerful trade networks that stretched deep into the interior and north across the Sahara desert. Marabouts, too, knew of the magic of writing, something that set them apart from coastal people and gave them mystique.[70]

There are numerous accounts of Mandinka *bexerins* visiting coastal communities. In 1625, Donelha wrote that they "bring to sell ... fetishes in the form of rams' horns and amulets and sheets of paper with writing

---

[66] António Carreira, "A etnonímia dos povos de entre o Gambia e o estuário do Geba," *Boletim cultural da Guiné Portuguesa* 19, 75 (1964): 233–75.

[67] Crowley, "Institutions," 132–3. She shows how initiations into secret societies make crosscutting ties especially clear.

[68] Álvares, *Ethiopia*, 3. The man had done the same thing in other villages.

[69] Mota, *Jesuit Documents*, ch. 1, 3; Álvares, *Ethiopia*, ch. 1; Coelho, "Descrição," ch. 2.

[70] André Donelha, *Descrição da Serra Leoa e dos rios de Guiné do Cabo Verde, 1625* (Lisbon: Junta de Investigações Científicas do Ultramar, 1977), 121–3.

FIGURE 6.2. *Grisgris* worn in Guinea-Bissau.
Photo by Walter Hawthorne.

on them, which they sell as [religious] relics."[71] In the late seventeenth century, Santiago wrote of Papel in Bissau, "There are among them, as among all of the nations of that coast, the great sorcerers called Mandinkas, Ethiopian blacks, foreigners of the interior of Africa."[72] In the early eighteenth century, Jean Barbot said that most talismans in Upper Guinea "contain a number of scraps of paper covered with characters either in Moorish or Arabesque script."[73] By the end of the eighteenth century, marabouts regularly interacted with people on the Bijagos Islands, where they were seen as "very holy men." According to Beaver, a Bijago thought that marabouts

'talk with God.' Wherever they go they are ... welcome to remain as long as they please; their merchandise consists of some paper, a reed to write with, and some ink, with which they manufacture their charms, or spells; and they generally continue their residence at each place, so long as there is any demand for the sale of their *gris-gris*. These ... are nothing more than sentences of the Koran neatly

---

[71] Ibid., 161.
[72] Dias, "Crenças," 159–61.
[73] Hair, *Barbot*, 85. Beaver said that many Mandinka marabouts "can speak, yet cannot write Arabic, and are therefore incapable of giving to their gris-gris that form in which alone consists their virtue; that is, the form of some sentence from the Koran." For this, they wrote "odd scrolls and figures" instead. *Memoranda Africana*, 324.

sewed up in leather, or cloth, and attached to the neck, arms, wrist, or ankles of the people; who firmly believe in the efficacy of their virtue.[74]

Muslim religious symbols were also integrated into important coastal rituals. Peter Mark presents an analysis of remarkable Floup bovine-horned initiation masks. These date from the eighteenth and nineteenth centuries and are covered with parchment, on which is written Arabic characters meant to combat sorcery. For Mark, the "incorporation of Arabic script into the decorative program of the honed mask graphically illustrates the fact that the literate tradition of Islam could enrich local ritual symbols without obliterating them."[75]

Given all this, it is clear that in the seventeenth and eighteenth centuries, the belief system of people on the Upper Guinea coast was outward-looking and incorporative. It operated differently, then, from African belief systems described by Robin Horton. For Horton, premodern African societies were "insulated" from the "world as a whole." Events affecting individuals occurred "within the microcosm of the local community," so belief systems were necessarily focused inward, centered on local (or "lesser") spirits rather than a distant creator god. Modern societies, he writes, are different in that they are concerned with "macrocosmic" events – matters of the world. With an outward focus, they need a god who is omnipresent – who is there no matter where community members travel and who has influence over those who live in far-off places. For Horton, people in premodern African societies adjusted their thinking about the relationship between the natural and supernatural when interactions with the world outside the microcosm of the community broadened. That is, they turned from the spirits of the microcosm and to the creator god. Christians and Muslims, then, did not introduce monotheistic religions to Africa. The monotheism evident in places today resulted from interactions on a larger, macrocosmic scale. Christianity and Islam were "catalysts – i.e., stimulators and accelerators of changes which were 'in the air' anyway."[76]

---

[74] Beaver, *Africa*, 324. Similarly, see Valdez, *Africa Occidental*, 385; National Records Service (Banjul, The Gambia) "The Laws and Customs of Mandingos of the North Bank Territory of the Gambia Protectorate," CSO 2/94, 1906.

[75] Mark, *Wild Bull*, 132–3.

[76] Horton, "African Conversion," 101. Also, Robin Horton, "On the Rationality of Conversion," *Africa* 45, 3 (1975), 219. For similar approaches, Victor Turner, *The Ritual Process: Structure and Anti-Structure* (Chicago: Aldine, 1969); Marcel Griaule, *Conversations with Ogotemmeli* (London: Oxford, 1965). For a critique of Horton's approach, J. D. Y. Peel, *Religious Encounter and the Making of the Yoruba* (Bloomington: Indiana University Press, 2003), 2–9.

In my view, Horton's analysis cannot be applied to the Upper Guinea coast for two reasons. First, to apply Horton's analysis would be to mischaracterize premodern Upper Guinean societies as being focused solely on the local – the microcosm of the village. Upper Guinea coastal communities engaged regularly with merchants, warriors, and settlers from beyond. This was not only true of people in urban trade hubs but also of people in rural agricultural communities.

Second, though Horton should be applauded for arguing that change could take place within the logic of African spiritual systems, he underestimates the resilience of premodern core spiritual beliefs. As they entered into ongoing relationships with people from the macrocosm of the larger world, Upper Guineans did not turn away from local or "lesser" spirits and to a creator god. Rather, they supplemented their collection of spirits with those introduced by outsiders. They also supplemented their collection of "gifted people" by recognizing the power of some outsiders to manipulate the supernatural. As they did so, the scope of their spiritual system changed, but their core beliefs remained intact. Coastal people developed an appreciation of the power of Muslim and, as will be examined in the next section, Christian symbols and spiritual leaders *without becoming* Christian or Muslim themselves.

CHRISTIANS ON THE UPPER GUINEA COAST

Over a four-hundred-year period beginning in the mid-fifteenth century, people calling themselves Christians (*Cristãos* in Portuguese) frequented Upper Guinea's coastal zone. Most were not holy men. The first Christians to arrive on the coast were among a group dubbed *lançados*. The word *lançado* means "lanced" or "thrown," so these were men who either "threw" themselves or "were thrown" into Africa – people who left Europe behind to live for a protracted period of time in a foreign land. The earliest were sailors and outcasts. Among them were Jews fleeing the Inquisition. *Lançados* lived among Africans, adopting in many cases African ways of life and participating in African social and spiritual rituals. In the sixteenth and seventeenth centuries, Catholic priests expressed disdain for *lançados*.[77] Take Manuel Álvares's early-seventeenth-century description: "They are evil itself, they are idolaters,

---

[77] António Carreira, *Cabo Verde: Formação e extinção de uma sociedade escravocrata (1460–1878)* (Praia, Cape Verde: Instituto Caboverdeano de Livro, 1983), 53–92.

perjurers, defiers of God ..., and also traitors."[78] Clearly *lançados* put no effort into evangelization. Indeed, they were influenced by coastal cultures and spiritual beliefs much more than they influenced those around them. They were, one priest said, "Portuguese by nation and Christian by religion and baptism" but "live as if they were neither Portuguese nor Christian," as if they "might be blacks themselves and the heathen of the land."[79]

The first sustained efforts to evangelize on the Upper Guinea coast and to save the souls of Portuguese who lived there came in the early seventeenth century. Then, the Jesuits sent seventeen missionaries to Santiago of the Cape Verde Islands for the purpose of converting Africans on the mainland. Of those, only two spent much time off the islands – one from 1604 to 1609 and the other from 1612 to 1617.[80] Others died quickly from illness or fled when sick or threatened by locals. In the latter half of the century, the Franciscans followed; and in the eighteenth century, other missionaries attempted to root themselves on the coast. However, few priests stayed in Upper Guinea for long, most preferring the comfortable and malaria-free confines of Santiago.[81]

Nonetheless, communities of people who were identified as Christian did exist on parts of the coast. Christians were particularly concentrated in the fortified towns, or *praças*, of Ziguinchor, Cacheu, Farim, Bissau, and Geba. They also manned small trading facilities on myriad rivers stretching south through Sierra Leone.[82] By the eighteenth century, free Christian residents of *praças* were referred to as *moradores*. No matter where they had been born, *moradores* called themselves Portuguese. Some, indeed, were from Portugal. However, most were Luso-Africans – brown-skinned, Africa-born children, grandchildren, and great-grandchildren of Portuguese men and local African women. Still others were black Africans who claimed a Christian identity.

But Christians were never many. Indeed, the number of recognized Christians in Upper Guinean *praças* changed little over centuries of Portuguese involvement in the Bissau-Cacheu area. In the 1620s, Cacheu's

---

[78] Manuel Álvares, *Ethiopia Minor and a Geographical Account of the Province of Sierra Leone*, trans. P. E. H. Hair (Liverpool: University of Liverpool, Department of History, 1990), chap. 4.

[79] Quoted in Mota, *Jesuit Documents*, doc. 4.

[80] P. E. H. Hair, "Heretics, Slaves, and Witches – as Seen by Guinea Jesuits, c. 1610," *Journal of Religion in Africa* 28, 2 (1998), 131–44; Henrique P. Rema, *História das missões católicas da Guiné* (Braga: Editorial Franciscana, 1992), 100.

[81] Rema, *História*, 100.

[82] Ibid., 80.

Christian population was 1,500. In 1694, reports estimated Cacheu's population had fallen to 700, with 700 Christians in Bissau, 1,200 in Geba, and 600 in Farim. That is a total of only 3,200 people. In 1777, there were 700 Luso-African and black Christians in Bissau (a number unchanged over eight decades) and 1,000 in Geba (a decrease from decades earlier). Priests did not reside in either community, and no priest had set foot in Geba for six years. By 1841, there were 2,000 Christians in Bissau, 3,000 in Geba, 150 in Cacheu, and 300 in Farim. All told, the Christian population had increased by only 2,250 since the 1690s.[83] Clearly less headway was made in spreading the faith outside *praças* – in the countryside. That is, people who called themselves Christian comprised only a very small fraction of the coastal population in the seventeenth, eighteenth, and early nineteenth centuries.

For hundreds of years, *praça* dwellers had complex relationships with folk in the countryside. At times, they clashed with conflicts erupting into open warfare. And *praça* dwellers were often kidnapped and killed when conducting business on the region's many rivers.[84] However, Christians also shared familial relationships with rural folk and relied on their kin for trade in goods and slaves. They, too, counted on them for protection when times were bad. But the protection they sought was often from more than obvious physical threats. Christians also turned to people outside *praças* for help negotiating with things supernatural. That is, Christians who inhabited *praças* (whether they had been born in Portugal or on the Upper Guinea coast and whether they were black, white, or brown skinned) often embraced the spiritual practices that were dominant throughout the region, visiting local spirit shrines and turning to gifted people – clairvoyants, healers, diviners, and prophets, or, that is, *jambacous* and *bexerins*.

The nature of the religious practices of the residents of Portuguese *praças* is revealed in a document from Inquisition proceedings against Crispina Peres, Genebra Lopes, and Izabel Lopes, who were arrested in Cacheu in 1660. Inquisitors described each as "brown" in appearance and Christian. Despite this, the trio visited *chinas*. Indeed, Catholic priests were appalled to hear accusations that Genebra Lopes took "palm wine and the blood of chicken to one of these shrines which is only a gunshot

[83] Brooks, *Landlords*, 243; António Carreira, *O crioulo de Cabo Verde: Surto e expansão* (Lisbon: Gráfica Europam, 1982), 32; Scantamburlo, *Dicionário*, 21–22.

[84] AHU, Guiné, cx. 4, doc. 18; AHU, Guiné, cx. 11, doc. 63; AHU, Guiné, cx 12, doc 13; AHU, Guiné, cx. 5, doc. 49; AHU, Guiné, cx. 6, doc. 33, 90; ANTT, Concelho da Fazenda, lv. 349, fl. 240.

away from this settlement, which she has heathen Negroes and Negresses pour over it." Genebra was not alone in her sins. An inquisitor wrote that "most of the blacks and some of the whites of this settlement keep these idols and other wrongs in their houses, in which they have more faith than in God."[85]

As for Crispina Peres, she came from a well-established Christian family, having been born of baptized parents and grandparents. Her mother was Banhun, and her father was a Portuguese from the Azores. Nonetheless, she was said to send money to healers or diviners in area Banhun villages. She also sought supernatural assistance in her quest to marry Captain Jorge Gonçalves Francês, a wealthy Portuguese resident trader and former governor of Cacheu. Further, once married, Crispina was said to have put a spell on her husband to make him sick and keep him from traveling. Francês, in turn, attempted to free himself of the spell by visiting a different Banhun healer. Mandinka healers also visited the couple's house and the houses of other important *moradores*. Among those was Armbrósio Gomes, a Portuguese who would eventually become a governor of Portuguese coastal possessions. He was the wealthiest trader in the region and employed a Mandinka woman as a personal healer. He, too, was said to wear *guarda di kurpu* obtained from Mandinka healers. The use of *guarda di kurpu* was widespread among black, white, and brown residents of Upper Guinean *praças*.[86]

Other examples of Christian coastal residents and visitors making offerings at spiritist shrines, seeking help from healers, and participating in local spiritist ceremonies abound.[87] In 1733, a report from Cacheu mentioned that "many Christian people ... die among the pagans without confession or the sacraments, and they further adopt the rites of the same pagans or the superstitions that are contrary to our Catholic faith."[88] Similar reports were filed decades later. In 1753, a priest visiting the coast from Cape Verde said that "Christians" had "lives and customs like those of the local pagans."[89] In the 1770s, Bernardino de Andrade said that on the Nunez River there were "some Christians" who lived "without spiritual guidance almost like savages."[90] Further, in 1780, a Portuguese official bemoaned the state of Christianity in Geba, saying that "*moradores*

[85] Havik, *Silences*, 151.
[86] Ibid., 145–65, 187.
[87] See, Hair, *Barbot*, 320.
[88] AHU, Guiné, cx. 6, doc. 2. Also, doc. 24.
[89] AHU, Cabo Verde, cx. 24, doc. 24.
[90] "Informções da Guiné em 1777," *Arquivo das Colónias* I (1917), 34–9.

depend on their pagan relatives for their passage and sustenance." Getting more from rural folk than Portugal, *moradores* participated in "pagan sacrifices" and went to shrines "with more willingness than they carry out the work of the divine cult" of Christianity.[91]

The Church disapproved, but it hardly had a presence on the coast, so it had little influence. In 1734, the Portuguese priest Antonio Henrique Leitão visited Cacheu, writing, "The Churches are all in ruins and appear ready to fall."[92] In 1753, a priest on the Cape Verde Islands said that on the coast there were "few Churches" and hardly any people received the sacraments.[93] With the coming of the Company of Grão Pará and Maranhão, little changed. In 1767, an observer wrote of the "sadness of Christianity" in Guinea. The religion was "losing ground because of a lack of priests."[94] In 1778, an administrator in Bissau described the Portuguese fort's chapel as being in ruins. There wasn't a priest, and no Catholic received the sacraments. The same was true of Cacheu, where many Catholics died without receiving last rites. Around 1800, the captain of Cacheu, Manuel Pinto Gouveia, said he had not met with a priest for three years. Moreover, the few religious men who at times lived on the coast often dedicated their time to slave trading and womanizing instead of evangelizing.[95]

If the residents of Portuguese *praças* did not much profess Roman Catholicism in the seventeenth, eighteenth, and early nineteenth centuries, coastal people outside *praças* did not either. This is not to say that no one outside *praças* was exposed to Christianity. Coastal people near *praças* sometimes enthusiastically participated in Christian rites and often recognized missionaries as gifted, spiritual people. However, for coastal people, submitting to baptism, attending mass, taking communion, joining in religious celebrations, and marrying in the Church did not often mean abandoning preexisting spiritual beliefs.[96] For example, in the late seventeenth century, Father Francisco de Santiago noted that Papel on the island of Bissau had a "propensity for the Catholic Religion" but sought baptism for reasons of which he disapproved. Frequently, he said,

[91] AHU, Guiné, cx. 12, doc. 3-A.

[92] AHU, Guiné, cx. 6, doc. 50.

[93] AHU, Cabo Verde, cx. 24, doc. 24. Also, André de Faro, "Relaçam (1663–4)," 69.

[94] AHU, Guiné, cx. 9, doc. 71.

[95] Rema, *História*, 217–51. Records note trade activities of priests Francisco Lobo de Andrade, Pedro Fialgo, and Manoel da Graça, and *vizitador* Luiz Gomes Barboza in 1769. ANTT, CGPM, Extractos, livro 53, entry 61.

[96] On popular participation in Christian celebrations, Brooks, "The Observance of All Soul's Day."

they were baptized only because elaborate celebrations followed. But, the "usual motivation" for "pagans" to submit to their own baptism or that of their children "is so that after the baptism they can marry and live among the Christians, which brings great honor and reputation. And this they call *cunhadio* [in-lawship] or kinship with the white, for the custom, in those parts, being that all the blacks use the word 'whites' for those who are black Christians, to differentiate them from the non-Christian blacks."[97] Papel, then, saw baptism as a way to foster close ties with merchants of the *praça* of Bissau and not, in Santiago's eyes, as a path to salvation. At baptism, Africans received a Christian name but, Santiago thought, experienced no change in their world view.

Similarly, an observer in 1780 said that in the Geba area, "pagans" at times "give them [Christians] their children to raise," and "some stay here in this population and are baptized, which they call wash the head." Those who had had their heads washed did it "more for the grandeur than for the knowledge that they will be better." Indeed, afterward all "want to live in their natural paganism rather than subject themselves to the precepts of the Christian religion."[98] For this, most African Christians were *cristãos por ceremónia,* or "ceremonial Christians." Many *cristãos por ceremónia* lived in "wards" built onto fortified *praças.* In wards, they were often called *povo,* or "people," in official documents and were distinguished from the *gentio* – "pagans," "idolaters," or "savages" – who lived in the countryside. Yet because they made sacrifices at spirit shrines, visited *jambacous,* married polygynously, wore *grisgris,* rejected the idea of a Heaven and Hell, and embraced the notion that some around them were witches, the beliefs of *povo* were much the same as those of *gentio.*[99]

So why did some blacks seek baptism and call themselves Christians? They did so largely because the profession of a Christian identity brought clear advantages. First, as noted above, becoming Christian (or sending children to be baptized) was a way to attach one's family to a merchant community. Those who were part of such communities increased their access to trade goods and employment opportunities. They also received legal rights not allotted to *gentio.*[100] Second, people who claimed to be

---

[97] Santiago transcribed in Dias, "Crenças," 161.

[98] AHU, Guiné, cx. 12, doc. 3-A.

[99] Havik, *Silences,* 131. For similar early accounts, Mota, *Jesuit Documents,* 31.

[100] Important was the right of Christian women to inherit their husband's property. See ANTT, Feitos findos, mç. 1, n. 11, cx. 3. Also, ANTT, Feitos findos, mç. 8, n. 11, cx. 3. Baum argues that in the nineteenth century, calling oneself Christian was a way to associate oneself with metropolitan Portugal. Baum, *Shrines,* 134.

Christian were often protected against enslavement and sale abroad because Christians in *praças* posted ransoms for white and black Christians taken by *gentio*.[101] The value of this protection is evident from records of illegal slave ships that boarded at Cacheu and Bissau and were seized on the ocean by antislaving squadrons in the 1820s and 1830s. Two of those ships (the *Conde de Villa Flor* in 1822 and *Vingador* in 1829) were diverted to Freetown, Sierra Leone, when taken by the British navy. Another one (the *Caridad Cubana* in 1839) was diverted to Havana, Cuba. In both places, the names of the captives on board were recorded. Of 533 named Africans from the Bissau and Cacheu region who were on the three ships, only 32 identified themselves by Christian baptismal names. The rest had non-Christian, local names.[102]

Finally, Upper Guineans thought Christian priests and relics offered them protection *in the same way* that *jambacous* and *bexerins*, and *grisgris* and *chinas* did.[103] Many Christian rituals and their elements were similar to Upper Guinean spiritism, making it easy for Upper Guineans to embrace aspects of the religion that the Portuguese introduced. In appearance, Christian icons were not all that different from African *chinas*. Many *chinas* were fashioned from forked or "Y"-shaped pieces of wood (like cow horns), so the resemblance to the Christian cross was a close one indeed. Further, some coastal people carved *chinas* in the image of ancestors or natural spirits, in much the same way Europeans carved images of saints, Christ, and Mary. Added to this was the fact that priests and settlers displayed relics in shrines called reliquaries (*oratorios* in Portuguese), some of which looked like the *funcos, bolobas, valboa, enaati, bekin, boekine*, and *fram* in which some coastal groups kept *chinas*. Christians knelt before their *oratorios* spending much time asking for relief from physical pain and psychological torment. They, too,

---

[101] Examples of ransoming Christians are in AHU, Guiné, cx. 10, doc. 26; AHU, Guiné, cx. 11, doc. 21; AHU, códice 489, fl. 139; Beaver, *African Memoranda*, 176.

[102] Calculated from *Voyages: The Trans-Atlantic Slave Trade Database*, http://slavevoyages. org/tast/assessment/estimates.faces, "Names Database." Some of the men among those thirty-two had distinctly British names, meaning that they had probably not been baptized in the Catholic Church. Those were slaves named Thomas, Jonaton, John, Thomas, Jack Ross, and Jean Jones. It seems likely that some of the names among the thirty-two may not have had baptismal names. That is, scribes may have written down African names in a way that sounded familiar (Western) when they heard them. Too, it is likely that some of those with baptismal names had not been baptized but had been given the names by their "pagan" parents at birth.

[103] On overlap of Christian and local beliefs, see Brooks, "The Observance of All Soul's Day"; Baum, *Shrines*, 148–50.

consulted priests who – like *jambacous* – controlled the places where relics resided and had skills negotiating the supernatural realm.[104]

Examples are numerous of Upper Guineans equating Christian icons with *chinas*. For example, in 1609, the Jesuit Guerreiro wrote, "Just as we call our god 'God,' so they call what they consider their god, and what they worship as such, '*china*.' Hence, when they see our images of Christ or Our Lady, they call them 'whiteman's *china*' or 'Christian *china*,' meaning the god of the Christians, or what the Christians care for or greatly love."[105] Similarly, Álvares described how when Africans on the Rio Grande "see our images of Christ and Our Lady [Mary], they say that these are the *china* of the Christians." Upper Guineans also made sacrifices and gave offerings before images of saints and the Virgin, just as they did before *chinas*. As Álvares wrote, "The sacred image of the Mother of Jesus" was so revered that "the savage … keeps her feast each year by offering a cow."[106] And in the very late seventeenth century, Francisco de Santiago reported that Papel in Bissau, both those baptized and those not, adored the image of Nossa Senhora de Candelária and made her offerings of palm oil. At the time, the small church in which the image was housed was covered in grass, much like *bolobas* on the island.[107]

The integration of Catholic icons into local belief systems would continue for many decades. In the mid-eighteenth century, Hyacinthe Hecquard wrote of Ziguinchor inhabitants, "They have a great veneration for images, the medals and the Christs, to which they associate a wide power to protect them from all accidents." The same belief, he said, "is widespread among the Floups and the Bainounk, the Portuguese traders having made these images, medals and cruxifixes, an object of commerce, and trade them for slaves." A Floup, he said, who purchased small copper images of Christ, "carried them among his gris-gris."[108] And in the early twentieth century, Father António J. Dias, the vicar of Guinea, noted that Papel called the image of the Virgin Mary "*irân de branco*," or "spirit of the whites," and that they frequently brought her offerings.[109]

All of this should make clear that as Upper Guineans entered into ongoing relationships with people from the Atlantic, they did not turn away from local spirits and to a creator god. Rather, they supplemented

---

[104] Mota, *Jesuit Documents*, doc. 41.
[105] Ibid., doc 28.
[106] Álvares, *Ethiopia*, ch. 20, 6.
[107] Santiago transcribed in Dias, "Crenças," 229.
[108] Baum, *Shrines*, 134–5.
[109] Santiago in Dias, "Crenças," 229.

their collection of spirits with those introduced by outsiders. Hence, saints and relics assumed a place beside *chinas* and *irans*. Also, many Upper Guineans accepted that priests had powerful abilities, but they saw them in the same light as *jambacous* and *bexerins*. Upper Guineans did not, then, reject all things Christian. Nor did they become Christian "converts." Some incorporated Christian symbols into their own belief system, developing an understanding of the religion but not the understanding priests hoped to cultivate.

RE-CREATING UPPER GUINEAN CORE BELIEFS IN AMAZONIA

If most people on the Upper Guinean coast had little engagement with Christianity in the eighteenth and early nineteenth centuries, most Upper Guineans sent to Maranhão to labor as slaves continued to have minimal exposure to the religion. Residing in Maranhão in the late eighteenth century, one frustrated priest dubbed the region *Terra do Diabo*, or "Land of the Devil."[110] After crown actions to expel the Jesuits from Maranhão in 1759 (Chapter 1), the region had had few priests, so no one – not Portuguese settlers and certainly not Africans and Indians – participated often in Christian rites.[111] In 1764, Vicar Francisco Xavier Nogreira wrote of "a lack of Churches and Chapels in the whole of our diocese [Maranhão] and the great distances over which our flock is spread without being able to be succored and to hear the mass ... and to receive the sacred communion."[112] From observations made in 1819 and 1820, Friar Francisco dos Prazeres wrote that rural people "attend only one or two masses each year for lack of priests."[113] Similar complaints were voiced throughout the eighteenth and into the nineteenth centuries, one priest noting in 1825 that there was "great relaxation in the praise of God and the Divine Cult since it was rare that parishioners hear mass and receive

---

[110] Mott, *Inquisição*, 15.
[111] Matthias Röhrig Assunção, "A formação da cultura maranhense, algumas reflexões preliminares," *Comissão Maranhense de Folclore* 14 (1999), 8–12; Matthias Röhrig Assunção, "Popular Culture and Regional Society in Nineteenth-Century Maranhão, Brazil," *Bulletin of Latin American Research* 14, 3 (1995), 273. Even before the expulsion, planters had regularly failed to baptize their slaves. APEM, Arquivo da Arquidiocese do Maranhão (AAM), cx. 127, doc. 4377.
[112] APEM, AAM, Livro 195, fl. 26.
[113] Francisco dos Prazeres, "Poranduba Maranhense ou relação histórica da província do Maranhão," *Revista Trimensal do Instituto do Histórico e Geographico Brazileiro* 54 (1891), 139.

the sacraments."[114] It was common for children to go without baptism, people to go without receiving last rites, and bodies to be buried without Church involvement. In addition, chapels throughout the region were falling down or standing unused in a desperate state of disrepair.[115]

Rural black slaves, particularly, had little involvement with the Church. There are several reasons for this. First, though some rural plantations had chapels (many of which had been built before the mid-eighteenth century), they were not necessarily used after 1759 for prayer. For example, in 1816 on Leonel Fernandes Vieira's and D. Francisca Maria Belfort's expansive plantation (on which were over three hundred slaves), there was an old chapel, but it housed a relative of Francisca's.[116] Second, slaves rarely (if ever) saw priests because the latter were few, and most masters did not seek religious instruction for those they owned. Noting this, a priest wrote in the 1780s, "Those miserable slaves! There are many *Senhores* who treat them like dogs.... About their salvation, they absolutely do not care; they are kept at times their entire lives without baptism, and if they are baptized, they never give confession, for there is negligence in the teaching of the Doctrine to them."[117]

Third, rural slaves had no time for Christianity because they worked most Sundays and holy days. Some slaves labored on Sundays for their masters and some for themselves on provision grounds upon which they grew crops to sustain themselves (Chapter 4).[118] That slaves labored without end did not bother the region's governors. "Some *moralistas* have declared themselves opposed to work on Sundays and other sacred days of the Church," Governor José Teles da Silva wrote in the 1780s. "But on this and other points," he continued, "America has a morality that is different from that of Europe."[119] Priests, however, were bothered by Sunday work, one instructing his flock in 1811, "It is incredible but true that one of the commandments of the law of God that is perhaps the most important and without doubt the easiest to observe is among us the

---

[114] APEM, AAM, cx. 20, doc. 887.

[115] APEM, AAM, cx. 20, doc. 888; doc. 892. Prazeres said that plantations had their own cemeteries – priests not participating in burials. "Poranduba maranhense," 139.

[116] TJEM, Inventory of Leonel Fernandes Vieira, 1816. Marques gives examples of chapels built on plantations. César Augusto Marques, *Dicionário histórico-geográfico da província do Maranhão* (Rio de Janeiro: Editôria Fon-Fon e Seleta, 1970), 201, 365.

[117] Quoted in Eduardo Hoornaert, *História da igreja na Amazônia* (Pretrós: Vozes, 1992), 233.

[118] APEM, AAM, cx. 20, doc. 883; Livro 214; ANTT, Ministério do Reino, mç. 601, cx. 704; Prazeres, "Poranduba maranhense," 139.

[119] ANTT, Ministério do Reino, mç. 601, cx. 704.

least observed and most broken. God expressly commanded us to guard Sundays and religious holidays, or, that is, he commanded that no work should be performed on these days."[120] But if any rural slave masters heard this sermon, there is no evidence they heeded its message, particularly with regard to their slaves.

Finally, when given free time on Sundays and holy days, slaves preferred to conduct their own spiritual celebrations rather than attend those of the Catholic Church. Noting this, Prazeres wrote, "To lessen their sad condition, they [black slaves] perform on the days to be guarded [Sundays and holy days] and on the eves of these days a dance called *batuque*, which is called this because they use a type of drum that has the same name. This dance is accompanied by raucous singing that can be heard for very far."[121] Though nothing is known about what happened at *batuques* in the early eighteenth century (or before), they were later associated with black spiritual ceremonies involving healing and communications with the supernatural. Starting in the 1830s, authorities took actions to end *batuques* in scattered parts of Amazonia. However, it is evident from Parzeres's comments that in the 1810s (and likely before), masters tolerated slaves' non-Christian celebrations on Christian religious days.[122]

This is not to imply that the Church played no role in the lives of those who lived in Amazonia. In and near São Luís, slave and free often married in and had their children baptized in the Church (Chapter 5). In and near São Luís, slave and free also celebrated holy days, and many belonged to religious brotherhoods (*irmandades* or *confrarias*), which sponsored religious celebrations. Evidence of black involvement in the Church in São Luís can be found in a 1721 letter to Portuguese King João V written by the officers of Nossa Senhora do Rosário dos Homens Pretos (Our Lady of Rosary of Black Men, the society being composed of Africans and *crioulos*). The officers complained that Governor Berredo would not permit them to stage a festival. The king sided with the black brothers, telling Berredo to allow celebrations as long as they were not disruptive.[123] The brotherhood was represented by a "king," who in 1717 was "the black Luís João da Fonseca."[124] By the 1740s, the brotherhood

---

[120] APEM, AAM, Livro 214.
[121] Prazeres, "Poranduba Maranhense," 138. Efforts to outlaw *batuques* began in the 1830s. Assunção, "A formação da cultura," 8–12.
[122] Assunção, "Popular Culture," 279. Batuques were banned in the Villa de S. José in 1841. See Lei no. 139 de 16 de October de 1841, Camara Municipal da Villa de S. José, p. 344.
[123] AHU, códice 269, fl. 202.
[124] Projecto Vida de Negro, *Frechal terra de preto* (São Luís: 1996), 34.

had built a church for their saint, which stands to this day in São Luís.[125] Later, a black brotherhood dedicated to Saint Benedict emerged in the city.[126]

However, things were different in the countryside. True, many Africans who reached rural plantations had been baptized – often in African ports before ships set sail for the Americas. But for trade slaves, baptisms were not profound religious experiences. Terrified, confused, and often naked slaves were sprinkled with holy water and forced to hear a white stranger mutter a few incomprehensible words. This was hardly the stuff of conversion.[127] Moreover, for many Africans shipped to Maranhão, neither priests nor the Church would, after baptism, ever again play a role in their lives. Indeed, many slaves never attended mass. As Fernando de Foyoz wrote of African slavery in Maranhão in 1788, "Everything consists of work without end and without limit ... and without religious instruction."[128] In Maranhão, the Church offered no solace to most for the physical and psychological pain of slavery, so in the eighteenth and early nineteenth centuries most slaves sought comfort from their Upper Guinean spiritist beliefs.

Unfortunately, there are few records detailing slave spiritual practices in Amazonia before 1830. African slaves in Amazonia kept no written records of their own. Further, their mostly illiterate owners did not record much about slaves' lives. Nor did travelers. As for government bureaucrats, they kept detailed records about slaves when they were imported, when their masters died (in the form of postmortem inventories), and when they reported for censuses. However, in none of their official reporting before the mid-nineteenth century did bureaucrats record observations about slaves' spiritual beliefs. Slaves' beliefs, after all, weren't important to the efficient running of plantations.

[125] Raymond Jozé de Souza Gayozo, *Compêndio histórico-político dos princípios da lavoura do Maranhão* (Paris: P. N. Rougeron, Impressor, 1818), 144. In Maranhão, the brotherhood continued to recruit members into the nineteenth century. White residents of the city sometimes willed money to the church of Nossa Senhora do Rosário dos Pretos. Antonia da Silva Mota, and others, *Cripto maranhenses e seu legado* (São Paulo: Editora Siciliano, 2001), 51.

[126] Prazeres, "Poranduba maranhense," 130–1.

[127] Heywood and Thornton, *Central Africans*, 5–6; Joseph C. Miller, *Way of Death: Merchant Capitalism and the Angolan Slave Trade, 1730–1830* (Madison: University of Wisconsin, 1988), 402–4. Many slaves were sold in Maranhão without having been baptized, devout owners later taking them to the Church. See, for example, 1770 baptism of the slave André from Guiné, an adult who was purchased by a priest in Maranhão. APEM, Batismos, Livro 107, fl. 35.

[128] ANTT, Ministério do Reino, mç. 601, cx. 704. Also, APEM, AAM, cx. 20, doc. 883.

But a handful of notes about slaves' beliefs were penned. In Maranhão they can be found today in records priests kept from *visitas pastorais*, or "pastoral visits." During these visits, priests based in São Luís acted as *visitadores*, or "inspectors," venturing to rural towns and recording information about Catholics' sinful activities. When *visitadores* arrived in rural areas, residents met with them privately to confess their sins and to report on the sins of others. Area residents whose acts were particularly egregious were called before *visitadores*, who took notes in books that are today housed in the Archivo Público do Estado do Maranhão. Because area residents most often denounced the weakest members of society, black slaves appear in records from visitations. Though the notes that *visitadores* took are frustratingly brief, they reveal something about what slaves in Maranhão, the majority of whom were Upper Guineans and their descendants, thought about their relationship with the supernatural. Added to these local records is a collection of records from the *visitação* of Giraldo José de Abranches, who was sent from Portugal to Grão Pará and Maranhão as part of the Inquisition. He stayed in the captaincy from 1763 to 1769.[129] Also, inquisitors investigated a variety of other cases in Amazonia during other periods.

In Maranhão, as in other parts of the Catholic world, priests objected especially to laypeople practicing magic, or *feitiçaria*. Objections arose because magic – the ability to elicit a result that appeared beyond the realm of what would be expected through natural means – could only be achieved by calling on a powerful supernatural agent. For the Church, that agent had to be the Devil or some demon. That is, according to the Church, *feitiçaria* was only possible through a pact celebrated with the Devil or some other evil force. This was true of *feitiçaria* aimed at harming, and it was true of *feitiçaria* focused on protecting or curing. Because "popular" or "folk" healing took place outside the church and relied on magic, the Church saw folk healers' actions as inherently maleficent.[130]

Priests in Maranhão recorded notes about blacks who were said to be practicing *feitiçaria* and were, therefore, *feiticeiros* or *feiticeiras* (male or female magicians). From notes kept in books from visitations, it is evident that Upper Guineans in Amazonia held onto many of the same spiritist beliefs that they had known across the ocean. That is, it is apparent that Upper Guineans in Amazonia believed that some people were

[129] ANTT, Tribunal do Santo Ofício, Inquisição de Lisboa, Livro 785, MF 5221.
[130] José Pedro Paiva, *Bruxaria e superstição num país sem "caça às bruxas," 1600–1774* (Lisbon: Notícias Editorial, 1997), 38.

"gifted" – having knowledge of how to receive messages from spirits, to please them with gifts in the form of sacrifices, and to manipulate the supernatural powers of natural substances and material objects. Further, they believed that gifted people acted in two ways – to better and to harm those around them. Those who acted for the common good used powers as clairvoyants, healers, diviners, and prophets to convince spirits to aid the sick and protect people from any number of harms. The gifted who meant to harm others were witches, who were possessed with jealousy and envy, using their powers to advance themselves at the expense of neighbors and kin. Finally, Upper Guineans continued to believe that certain material objects and natural substances derived from plants, animals, and minerals contained supernatural powers. Those powers could only be released through the uttering of specific words and conducting of specific acts. It was gifted people – those whom Portuguese priests viewed as *feiticeiro* and *feiticeiras* – who knew how to do these things.

Priests, indeed, recorded examples of blacks acting like witches to harm others in the community. In 1759, in Maranhão's parish of Santo Antônio do Serubin, José, whose place of birth was not recorded, was said to "have general fame for his *feitiçaria*." One resident "had heard it said that" José used his powers to kill a black slave of Sergeant Major João de Ararejo. Another said that he had sought to harm a different black slave of the same plantation by "bewitching him."[131] Also in 1759, in Maranhão's parish Nossa Senhora do Desterro do Poti, the African slave Antonio, who was the property of Antonio Fernades de Araujo, was said to have used *feitiçaria* to "kill many people." However, others in the area knew him as a great *feiticeiro* who made "various cures" – his power evidently cutting two ways.[132] In 1774, in Alcântara, Maranhão, a slave named Francisco, who was the property of Manuel Lopes de Sá, was investigated by Church officials for "many harms and evils," including the killing of five people with his *feitiçaria*.[133]

Though in no official writings was it said that any of these men "ate" their victims, it is easy to imagine that Upper Guinean slaves saw these men as acting in much the manner that evil-doers had across the ocean. As we have seen, in Upper Guinea, witches sapped the souls of victims and made them weak – "bewitching" them and, in the process, gaining strength and power. In Maranhão, these witches appear to have done the

[131] APEM, AAM, cx. 20, doc. 880.
[132] *Ibid.*
[133] Luiz Mott, *A Inquisição no Maranhão* (São Luis, EDUFMA: 1995), 15.

same thing. Because Upper Guineans often sold "witches" as slaves, we should expect to find in Maranhão a relatively large number of Upper Guineans who were skilled practitioners of "witchcraft." That is, it should not be surprising that some slaves in Amazonia knew how to kill others by "bewitching" them.

In 1788, the African slave Antonio, who lived in Maranhão's parish of Nossa Senhora do Rosário da Ribeira do Itapecuru, certainly thought that some evil-doer had "bewitched" him. That year, neighbors reported to a visiting priest that Antonio, who was physically ill, had been using "superstitious words saying that he had been bewitched by someone." That is, he blamed his illness on another person – a witch, who presumably was "eating" him. Not finding anyone who could help, Antonio improvised a cure for himself, perhaps drawing on observations he had made of healers when he lived across the ocean. Three residents called him a *feiticeiro* including one who claimed to see Antonio throw rocks into a bowl of rum and that from the rocks arose a strange whistling sound. A neighbor, Francisco de Souza e Antonio de Almeida, said that Antonio "was eager for a magical cure" for his troubles.[134]

Though Antonio could not find a gifted healer, there are examples of blacks in Amazonia acting like the *jambacous* of Upper Guinea to heal and protect supplicants. In 1759, Goete, a black slave of João de Souza Coetinho (whose farm was near where the *feiticeiro* José de Lisboa), was a well-known healer. It was "public knowledge" that Goete visited a *mulata* named Anna Maria, who owned a sick slave girl "for the purpose of performing magic [to cure the slave], which he did." He offered similar (and undocumented) supernatural cures to others. Nearby, a black slave named Manoel Gomes was said to have used *feitiçaria* to cure a black man named Joze by "casting from his body some vermin, which is said to have cured him." And Antonio, a slave of João de Sousa Coutinho was also accused of *feitiçaria* for placing "a spell" on a black woman named Anna Maria, which was supposed to cure her of her ills.[135]

As was noted in the opening of this chapter, in the 1760s in Pará, the Mandinka Joze was said to cure many people by using a variety of magical cures. Like *bexerins* in Upper Guinea, Joze was skilled at manipulating the power of certain herbs by mixing them and speaking specific words over them. Joze used herbs that he combined into a soup and empowered

---

[134] APEM, AAM, cx. 20, doc. 883.
[135] APEM, AAM, cx. 20, doc. 880.

with "words that no one understood" to cure the Bijago Maria, who was "gravely ill, expelling from her vagina various vermin and animated parasites." Further, at times, he burned herbs to fumigate spiritually unhealthy places. One of his clients was a white attorney named José Januário da Silva, who suffered from debilitating headaches. During his consultation, Joze directed the smoke from burning herbs toward the suffering man's head. While blowing on Silva, Joze spoke words that no one understood. Though we cannot know for certain, it is possible that he spoke in Mandinka, using words he had used in Upper Guinea to release supernatural powers from the plant matter he had gathered.[136] Joze, too, cured a white planter named André Fernandes of his fevers and shivering by taking one of Fernandes's hands and "sucking hard and vehemently with his mouth on said hand." Immediately, Fernandes felt better, claiming a full recovery a short time later."[137]

A contemporary of Joze was an African slave healer named João, who was also a master herbalist. He was called to heal Catarina Machado, a white woman and the wife of a boatman in São Luís. João put water in some shallow basins and mixed in herbs and a stone. He then dripped some of the potion into the eyes of those who were present to help them see an apparition that was to appear. Into another basin, he mixed unknown things with water for the sick woman to drink. He covered the second basin with a plate and then twisted a rope out of black and white strands. He tied the rope to the head and foot of the bed on which Machado rested and said that if anyone touched the rope, he or she would die. João then moved around the room holding a gourd and murmuring words that no one understood. As the healing ceremony proceeded, children were running into and out of the room. One accidentally brushed one of the ropes and shouted, "Here I have touched the ropes, and even so I did not drop over, nor did I die!" Machado, however, died a short while later.[138]

In addition to healing, gifted Africans in Amazonia used their powers to help people in other ways. For example, in 1693, a Mandinka slave named Sebastião was able to divine evil-doers who committed crimes. In one case, he did so by rubbing herbs inside a cup of water while speaking

---

[136] Laura de Mello e Souza, *The Devil and the Land of the Holy Cross, Witchcraft, Slavery, and Popular Religion in Colonial Brazil* (Austin: University of Texas Press, 2003), 101.

[137] Lapa, *Livro da visitação*, 137–40, 153–4. The practice (conducted by specialists) of sucking on parts of the body is thought to be a way to cure someone who has been dealt a misdeed by sorcery in parts of the Casamance today. Personal communication, Toby Green, 15 July 2009.

[138] Mello e Souza, *The Devil*, 107.

the names of various people. At the point at which the herbs suddenly turned the water into a thick sauce, the name that was spoken was that of a thief who had stolen a knife.[139] Like the Mandinka Joze, the Mandinka Sebatião was accepted in Maranhão as a skilled herbalist, re-creating through his practices the spiritism common throughout Upper Guinea.

African *feiticeiros* also offered people protection from harm. For over a century, Church officials expressed worry that in Maranhão many wore protective *bolsas de mandinga*, which they described in terms identical to those used across the ocean on the Upper Guinea coast for *grisgris* and *guarda di kurpu*. They were often sewn shut and contained something inside – generally, as in Upper Guinea, a passage from the Koran or Bible – that was meant to keep the wearer safe from a particular harm. Accounts of people wearing *bolsas* abound in the African-Portuguese world – on the Upper Guinea coast, in Brazil, on Madeira Island, on the Cape Verde Islands, in Angola, in Portugal, and even in India. Sweet argues that though there are accounts of Portuguese wearing similar *bolsas* in medieval Iberia, "the proliferations of *bolsas* in the Portuguese world during the eighteenth century can be attributed primarily to Africans.... The use of the term *bolsa de mandinga* makes clear that African *bolsas* were to be distinguished from those that might be more familiar to the Portuguese."[140] Laura de Mello e Souza, also notes the wide use of *bolsas*

[139] Sweet, *Recreating Africa*, 129.
[140] Ibid., 181. In the eighteenth century, the term *bolsa de mandinga* was also applied to *bolsas* worn by blacks and whites in Portugal and Angola. On the use of the term in Portugal, Daniela Buono Calainho, *Metrópole das Mandingas: Religiosidade negra e Inquisição portuguesa no antigo regime* (Ph.D. thesis, Universidade Federal Fluminense, 2000), 89–95. In an interesting case from 1716 (ANTT, Tribunal do Santo Ofício, Inquisição de Lisboa, Processo 5477), a solider in Angola made what was described as a *mandinga*. The charm was placed on a dog, who was unscathed when shot twice, proving to some its effectiveness. The case is mentioned in John K. Thornton, "Central Africa in the Era of the Slave Trade," in *Slaves, Subjects and Subversives: Blacks in Colonial Latin America*, eds. Jane Landers and Barry Robinson (Albuquerque: University of New Mexico Press, 2006), 99. It is examined at length in Selma Pantoja, "Inquisição, degredo e mestiçagem em Angola no século XVIII," *Revista lusófona de ciência das religôes* III, 5–6 (2001), 117–36. Pantoja shows how the term *mandinga* became common in the Kimbundu language of Angola, appearing in Portuguese–Kimbundu dictionaries in the late nineteenth and twentieth centuries. In my estimation, this shows the influence of Mandinka practices on whites and blacks in the Atlantic World. Whites and Africans influenced by Mandinka in Africa, Europe, and Brazil, took *bolsas* across trade routes and introduced their use widely. The contents of *mandingas* changed as gifted people in various corners of the Portuguese empire placed particular natural objects containing supernatural powers in them to protect and cure. Angolans and Upper Guineans arriving in Maranhão in the late eighteenth century may, then, have had a shared understanding of the power of *mandingas*. Moreover, the origins of *mandingas* used in Maranhão

de mandinga, arguing that compared to the rest of Brazil, "Mandinga pouches seem to have been most popular in northern Brazil, that is, in the regions corresponding to the states of Grão Pará and Maranhão."[141]

Of course, the widespread use of "Mandinga pouches" in Amazonia should not be a surprise because Mandinka were a sizable percentage of the Maranhense population. As we have seen, the gifted among them peddled protective pouches in Africa. And they, too, peddled them in Amazonia, re-creating Upper Guinean cultural practices as they did. From 1750 to 1775, Church officials recorded nineteen offenses involving blacks using "Mandinga pouches" in Amazonia, a clear indication that the practice was commonplace.[142] Similar pouches were ubiquitous in black rural communities in Maranhão in the 1940s. Then, the anthropologist Octavio da Costa Eduardo noted "charms" being used "for good." "Such are those seen on small children. A little bag containing a tarantula or crocodile's tooth is usually suspended from a cord around children's necks to avoid the pains of teething or to stimulate a child's appetite."[143]

In Maranhão, whites also made use of protective *bolsas de mandinga*. One case involved Manuel João, a sixteen-year-old white boy who had been born in Maranhão and moved to live with his grandfather in Pará in 1668. Shortly after his arrival, Manuel had conflicts with an uncle and sought supernatural protection in the form of amulets that he wore around his neck. When the boy was taken before the Church, the *bolsas* were ripped apart and found to contain a paper; another piece of torn paper; yet another paper with an image of Jesus as a lamb; garlic; two stalks of rue; and a bone about the size of a fingertip, which was wrapped in paper and "appeared to belong to some dead man."[144] Further, in 1777 in Ribeira do Mearim, Maranhão, a white man named Antônio Brito Tavares had around his neck a *bolsinha*, or little pouch, in which was a "diabolical" oration.[145]

might be traced to multiple places – Upper Guinea, Angola, and Portugal. Nonetheless, Upper Guineans were a majority of Maranhão's colonial population in the eighteenth century, so their influence was likely great. Also, Upper Guineans arriving in Maranhão would have understood *mandingas* in a particular cultural context.

[141] Mello e Souza, *The Devil*, 130, 257.

[142] Ibid., 130.

[143] Octavio da Costa Eduardo, *The Negro in Northern Brazil* (New York: J. J. Augustin Publishers, 1948), 66.

[144] Mello e Souza, *The Devil*, 222–8.

[145] Mott, *A Inquisição*, 16.

Indians also wore *bolsas*. In Pará in the 1760s, in the towns of Benfica and Beja, there were reports of Indian youths stealing communal wafers and pieces of altar stone around Easter to make *bolsas*. When one of the thieves was caught, he said that the items would make him stronger – immune from harm by swords, knives, and sticks. "They were," he said, "protective medicine, to have [in a] *Mandinga* and excommunication could do him no harm." Others complicit in the crimes later agreed, saying that "*mandingas*" with wafers, fragments of altar stone, and a variety of other items from the Church "served to assure that arrows, knives or gunshots would not enter the body of whoever carried it with him."[146]

Decades later, Prazeres noted the continued widespread use of *mandingas* in Amazonia. There, he said, people "have little instruction about religion and for this are very inclined to superstition. Many carry on their chests a *bolsinho* with words of the saints and relics of saints or similar things." Rural folk – white, black, and Indian – had "such great faith" in these "little pouches" that they thought they "had the power to kill and wound and to protect them from the same, judging them impenetrable." They "call the *bolsinho patuá*, and sometimes sell them for much money."[147]

Among other things, reports of Maranhense *feitiçaria* point to the degree to which Europeans in Brazil melded African beliefs with their own. As they did in Africa, Portuguese wore *mandingas* and consulted black healers in Amazonia.[148] This is not to say that the wearing of talismans and use of magic "folk" medicines were unheard of in Portugal at the time. It is to say that in Maranhão, a "local" or "popular Catholicism" emerged – particularly after the Jesuits were expelled in 1759. This Catholicism operated outside Church control. For those who adhered to it, there was, Matthias Röhrig Assunção writes, "a direct relationship between man and the supernatural, which could be considered a personal kind of Catholicism." That is, it was a Catholicism that did not rely on priests – priests being nonexistent in rural areas of Amazonia. It was a Catholicism that allowed for the easy incorporation of overlapping beliefs of non-European peoples – Africans and Indians.[149]

Practitioners of Maranhão's brand of popular Catholicism directed particular devotion to saints and cherished saintly images and religious relics that could facilitate communication with the supernatural. Hence,

---

[146] *Livro da Visitação: Estado do Grão-Pará*, 214–18.
[147] Prazeres, "Poranduba Maranhense," 139.
[148] Ibid.; Souza, *The Devil*.
[149] Assunção, "Popular Culture," 273–4.

many built rural chapels and kept *oratorios* in which they had images of saints who suited their own likings.[150] For example, on the Itapecuru River in 1802, Antonio Jose de Souza and his wife D. Anna Rita owned over three hundred slaves and in their house had "a large cross with the crucified Christ;" two smaller images of the same; another of the same in an *oratorio*; two images of the Virgin; and images of Saint Joseph, Saint John, and Saint Sebastian.[151] In 1806 in Viana, Bernardo dos Santos, who owned seven slaves, had a large *oratorio* in which were three images of saints. In addition, he had carved images of the Virgin; Christ crucified on a cross; and Saints Benedict, Ann, Francisco, Sebastian, and Goncalo.[152] Listed on the inventory of Guilherme Francisco da Silva in 1810 (along with more than twenty slaves) was a large "image of Christ."[153] In 1811, Alfres Joze Gabriel and D. Francisca Thereza, who owned over fifty slaves on the Rio Itapecuru, had a wooden *oratorio* in which was housed a crucifix, image of Saint Francisco, image of Christ, and two images of the Virgin.[154] And in 1816, Leonel Fernandes Vieira and D. Francisca Maria Belfort had a great variety of religious images, mostly of saints and Christ.[155]

It is easy to imagine that Upper Guineans would have viewed saints in Amazonia in the same way they viewed *irans* in Africa. Though we have no documentation for the eighteenth and early nineteenth centuries, Octavio da Costa Eduardo's notes from the 1940s might allow us to project backward. Then, he wrote of rural blacks in Maranhão: "[T]hough holding the saints to be ... supernatural beings ..., [they] attribute to them human motives and desires and act on this belief to gain their favors." If rains did not come, blacks punished images of saints by removing them from their sanctuaries or by tying them up, cajoling them to act for the good of the community. Blacks also made "contracts" with saints, offering them gifts and sacrifices in return for a request. In other words, blacks in Maranhão did not make pleas to saints but struck deals. "In essence," Eduardo wrote, blacks "exert pressure on the saints because they attribute to these supernatural beings selfish motives and thus offer them something in return for what they may do to satisfy man's wishes." Hence, blacks in

---

[150] For an analysis, see Assunção, "Popular Culture," 273–4.
[151] TJEM, Inventory of Antonio Jose de Souza, 1802.
[152] TJEM, Inventory of Bernardo dos Santos, 1806.
[153] TJEM, Inventory of Guilherme Francisco da Silva, 1810.
[154] TJEM, Inventory of Alfres Joze Gabriel, 1811.
[155] TJEM, Inventory of Leonel Fernandes Vieira, 1816.

FIGURE 6.3. Carved figures inside a shrine in Guinea-Bissau.
From: Hugo Adolf Bernatzik, *Äthiopen des Westens: Forschungsreisen in Portuguiesisch-Guinea* (Wien: Verlag von L. W. Seidel & Sohn, 1933), 223. Image courtesy of Kevin Conru.

Saint Joseph of Ribamar petitioned in Eduardo's time: "My Saint Joseph, if you will help me obtain my wish, I'll give you a gift, I'll light you a candle." Suppliants who failed to make proper offerings for favors granted were visited by "these super natural beings" who found ways to express "their displeasure" for promises not kept.[156]

---

[156] Eduardo, *Negro in Northern Brazil*, 52–3.

FIGURE 6.4. Carved figures inside an *oratorio* in Maranhão.
Photo by Walter Hawthorne.

CONCLUSION

The punishing, rewarding, and cajoling of saints and the elaborate processes through which blacks in Amazonia forged contracts with them
might be viewed as essentially Catholic (or essentially medieval Catholic)
practices. However, these black approaches to saints, Eduardo wrote, "as
well as the attitude that underlie them, can be understood only when similar attitudes and practices of West African[s] … are taken into account."[157]
And, indeed, I have argued along the same lines in this chapter.

[157] Ibid.

In previous chapters, I asserted that Upper Guineans in Amazonia were constrained in their abilities to reproduce many aspects of a broad Upper Guinean culture in Maranhão. But because neither planters nor the state exercised much control over what slaves thought, Upper Guinean slaves succeeded in re-creating many spiritual beliefs from their homelands. These beliefs were composed of four elements. Across the Upper Guinea coast, all believed that there was one creator; all held that spirits inhabited the earth and interacted regularly with humans; all thought that certain material objects and natural substances contained supernatural powers; and all believed that some people were gifted. These gifted individuals knew better than most how to receive messages from spirits, to please them with gifts in the form of sacrifices, and to manipulate the supernatural powers of natural substances and material objects.

Upper Guinean spiritual beliefs were not unchanging or uniform over space. Indeed, as coastal people came into contact with outsiders – merchants, invaders, and evangelists from the African interior and Atlantic Ocean – they recognized the power of new spirits, gifted people, and natural substances and material objects previously unknown to them. In other words, Upper Guineans learned to speak the spiritual language of Muslims and Christians by incorporating aspects of other belief systems into their own. But as they made the foreign familiar, they did not fundamentally transform their own worldview – their own core spiritual beliefs.

In Amazonia, things played out much the same. There, Upper Guineans accepted the saints represented in their masters' chapels and *oratorios* alongside their own spirits. They acknowledged priests alongside their own gifted spiritual leaders, and they welcomed Christian relics alongside material objects they had long recognized as having particular power. But the acceptance of some things Christian did not mean the rejection of preexisting beliefs. In Amazonia, Upper Guineans continued to embrace much of what they had believed before their enslavement. In this new land, Upper Guineans looked to each other – and, at times, other Africans – for spiritual solace under the incredible hardships of plantation slavery. The gifted among them provided that relief in the only way they knew how – by drawing on knowledge and ritual practices cultivated for many generations on the other side of the ocean.

Conclusion

This book is one of a handful of studies about Upper Guineans in diaspora and is the only book-length examination of African slavery in Maranhão before the early nineteenth century. In it, I have traced the flow of tens of thousands of Upper Guineans from their points of capture, to the ports of Bissau and Cacheu, across the Atlantic to the ports of São Luís and Belém, and finally onto Brazilian plantations. I have explored the reasons planters in the Amazonian captaincies of Maranhão and Pará demanded African slaves. This was because Indian slaves died in tremendous numbers from European diseases and because the state's encouragement of rice and cotton production in the late eighteenth century brought planters enough capital to afford the import of Africans. Africans, planters thought, were "more robust and capable" than Indians.[1] Also, I have argued that the reason Upper Guineans – as opposed to people from other regions of Africa – came to comprise a majority on most Maranhense plantations can be attributed to the nature of Atlantic winds and currents and to policies aimed at strengthening Portugal's hold on the African ports of Bissau and Cacheu. Policies linking these ports to São Luís, it was thought, would bolster Portuguese efforts on both sides of the ocean.

Turning my attention to the hundreds of thousands of Upper Guineans whose lives were affected by the Atlantic demand for slaves, I have made two broad arguments. First, I have asserted that inventories recording ethnonyms of slaves in the New World can be used to show with great specificity from where slaves hailed within the Old World. With data

[1] ANRJ, diversos códices SDH, códice 807, vol. 11, NP, fl. 9–44.

from inventories recorded in Maranhão, I have challenged long-standing assumptions that scholars have made about slave production in Upper Guinea. Most slaves exported from the ports of Cacheu and Bissau were not usually transported over long distances from the African interior and were not often the products of large-scale wars among states. Rather, they were enslaved through small-scale raids, kidnappings, and witchcraft trials that occurred in Upper Guinea's politically decentralized coastal zone. Slaves exported through Bissau and Cacheu most often came from places tens – not hundreds – of miles from these ports.

Second, knowing from where slaves came within Upper Guinea, I have proposed new directions for scholarship debating whether Africans re-created existing or created new cultural forms and identities in the Americas. By focusing on different realms of African life – labor, family, and spirituality – I have argued that New World slavery produced both continuities and ruptures in Africans' lives. Masters' power imposed mightily into most aspects of slave life but not into all. Upper Guineans in Amazonia had little control over their working lives. They were forced to spend long days producing a crop – rice – that they had known well in their homeland. However, masters directed slaves to make fields in a way that was very different from the way they had done so back in Africa. Upper Guineans did apply their own technologies to some facets of rice planting and processing. But the Amazonian rice system, as designed by Portuguese settlers, was devastating for forests and for slaves, whose bodies were often broken by "work without end."[2]

Though they suffered greatly under slavery in Amazonia, Upper Guineans still had much control over a few aspects of their lives. Where they were able to re-create cultural forms, they did. But they chose carefully the cultural forms that they re-created. Though their ethnic identities continued to be important in Amazonia, Upper Guineans looked back across the ocean for cultural forms that were held in common across ethnic divides – forms that united them as Guineans. The unity of cultures in Upper Guinea was apparent in common approaches to processing and cooking rice and to the preparation of rice-based dishes. Because Amazonian masters cared little about what slaves ate, slave women were able to reproduce much of their shared culinary tradition in Amazonia. There today, rice-based dishes with rich sauces made from meat and vegetables are commonplace, continuing evidence of the region's past links to Upper Guinea, which broke when the Atlantic slave trade died off.

[2] ANTT, Ministério do Reino, mç. 601, cx. 704.

The unity of Upper Guinean cultures also was evident in shared approaches to marriage. In their homelands, Upper Guineans most often married endogamously within groups defined by ethnic affiliations. In Amazonia, skewed gender ratios coupled with social and legal sanctions that relegated blacks to the bottom of the region's hierarchies of power, made it impossible for many Upper Guinean men to find long-term female partners. For Upper Guinean women, things were different. Despite facing many hurdles, they were often able to establish stable families and to foster the endogamous marriage patterns they had known across the ocean. However, they most often married within a group defined by regional – not ethnic – affiliation. In other words, for marriage partners, Upper Guinean women in Maranhão looked usually to other Upper Guineans but not necessarily to Upper Guineans who were of the same ethnic group.

Crossethnic ties were certainly common in Upper Guinea, people having identities rooted in pan-ethnic religions and pan-ethnic occupational groups. Crossethnic bonds were reinforced in the slave trade. As enslaved people were moved from place to place in Upper Guinea and eventually onto slave ships, they found themselves with others from multiple ethnic backgrounds. What became obvious in barracoons and beneath the decks of stinking ships was that all who were enslaved shared the same fate. This reality became a unifying force, reifying an Upper Guinean identity and making it possible for slaves from multiple backgrounds to occasionally rise up together in revolt. This Upper Guinean identity would be further reinforced in Amazonia where Upper Guineans re-created together foods they had all known across the ocean, ate together from the same bowls, and reshaped endogamous marriage patterns within a regionally defined group.

In Amazonia, the oneness of Upper Guinean cultures was also strengthened when religious and healing rituals were conducted. Across Upper Guinea, people from multiple ethnic backgrounds had a shared understanding of the relationship of people with natural spirits and deceased ancestors. They all believed that certain natural substances held supernatural powers. And they all held that a few who were gifted had the ability to communicate with and manipulate the powers of the supernatural realm – one that was coterminous with the realm occupied by humans. Though the spirits they recognized differed over space and time and though ritual forms were never uniform, an Upper Guinean embrace of the same core spiritual beliefs was one of the things that joined them as a single cultural group.

Over time, as Upper Guineans came into contact with different merchants, invaders, and evangelists from both the African interior and Atlantic Ocean, they recognized the power of new gifted people and new spirits. They learned about the power of myriad natural substances and material objects. Upper Guinean spirituality had no orthodoxy. It was incorporative, accepting of new spirits, new sources of supernatural power, and new priests. As Upper Guineans integrated ideas from places beyond their villages, they learned to speak the spiritual language of Muslims and Christians. In so doing, they became Atlantic people.

This is not to say that Upper Guineans became "Europeanized." Indeed, I have argued that over the course of their long engagement with the Atlantic, Upper Guineans did not fundamentally change their worldview. In Africa *and* Amazonia, many Upper Guineans accepted Christian saints alongside their own spirits, Christian priests alongside their own gifted spiritual leaders, and Christian relics alongside material objects they had long recognized as having particular power. Despite this, few rejected pre-existing core beliefs. In Amazonia in the eighteenth and early nineteenth centuries, Upper Guineans – whose lives were shaped in countless ways by an oppressive slave system – continued to embrace the same essential beliefs that they had known across the ocean. In Amazonia, Upper Guineans looked to each other – and, at times, to other Africans – for spiritual solace in physically and mentally challenging times. The gifted among them provided that comfort by replicating knowledge and ritual practices cultivated for many generations across the Atlantic.

If Upper Guinean slaves in Amazonia found greater freedom in the realm of religious belief and practice than they did in other realms of their lives, is Amazonia's Upper Guinean link evident in religious belief and practice today? Scholars of spiritual beliefs devote much attention to the popularity throughout the twentieth century of "Youruban and Dahomean beliefs and rituals" in Amazonia. In many places, *terreiros da mina*, or Mina vodun houses, have become centers of much black spiritual life. In them, dances called *tambor de mina* are held. In them, elements of rituals from multiple traditions – Yoruban/Dahomean (Mina), Upper Guinean, West Central African, Indian, and Catholic – can be identified.[3] For this, scholars often describe *terreiros da mina* as places where

---

[3] Octavio da Costa Eduardo, *The Negro in Northern Brazil* (New York: J. J. Augustin Publishers, 1948), 46–124; Mundicarmo Ferretti, "Pureza nagô e nações africanas no tambor de mina do Maranhão," *Ciencias sociales y religión* 3, 3 (2001), 75–94; Mundicarmo Ferretti, *Desceu na guma: O caboclo do tambor de mina e um terreiro de São Luís – a casa de fainti-ashanti* (São Luís: Edufma, 2000); Mundicarmo Ferretti, "Non-African

syncretic or creolized beliefs are expressed. Yet it is clear that *terreiros* are places where Mina beliefs are dominant. Indeed, members are brought into *terreiros* through elaborate and secret initiations resembling those of vodun and candomblé houses throughout Brazil. In form, many rituals carried out in *terreiros* are obviously patterned after rituals found in societies on Africa's Mina coast. Moreover, many of the spirits appealed to in *terreiros* are of Mina origin.[4]

In the 1940s, anthropologist Octavio da Costa Eduardo, who conducted years of research in Maranhão, explained the dominance of the Mina belief system by comparing it to that of Upper Guinea. Upper Guinean cosmologies, he noted, were "less well-organized and more diffuse in structure" compared to those from Mina. That is, Mina beliefs and rituals were more "institutionalized" and, therefore, more resistant to change within Mina diasporas.[5] And, indeed, I have argued that spiritual authority in Upper Guinea was, like political authority, diffuse. This fact made Upper Guinean spiritism quite different from the belief systems of both Mina and West Central Africa.[6] Further, I have argued that the Upper Guinean spiritual system was incorporative – often accepting of the spirits and gifted people of outsiders. Over generations, the

---

Spiritual Entities in Afro-Brazilian Religion and Afro-Amerindian Syncretism," in *New Trends and Developments in African Religions*, ed. Peter Bernard Clarke (Westport, CT: Greenwood, 1998); Sergio F. Ferretti, *Querentã de zomadonu: Etnografia de casa das minas do Maranhão* (São Luís: EDUFMA, 1996); Sergio F. Ferretti, *Repensando o sincretismo* (São Paulo: Edusp, 1995); Sergio F. Ferretti, "Religions of Maranhão," unpublished paper (1985); Oneyda Alvarenga, *Tambor de mina e tambor de crioulo* (São Paulo: Biblioteca Público Municipal, 1948); Maria Amália Pereira Barretto, *Os voduns do Maranhão* (São Luís: FUNC, 1982); Olavo Correia Lima, *A casa de nagô: Tradição religiosa iorubana no Maranhão* (São Luís: UFMA); Euclides M. Ferreira, *O candomblé no Maranhão* (São Luís: Alcântara, 1984); Pierre Verger, "Le cult des voduns d'Abomey aurait-il été apporté à Saint Louis de Maranhon par la mere du roi Ghézo?," *Les Afro-Americains* (Dakar: IFAN, 1952), 157–60.

[4] Eduardo, *The Negro*, 104–5; Matthias Röhrig Assunção, "Popular Culture and Regional Society in Nineteenth-Century Maranhão, Brazil," *Bulletin of Latin American Research* 14, 3 (1995), 275; Nunes Pereira, *A casa das minas* (Petroplis: Vozes: 1979 [1947]), 24, 38; Pierre Verger, "Le culte des vodoun d'Abomey aurait-il été apporté à Saint-Louis de Maranhon par la mere du Roi Ghézo?" in *Les afro-américains* (Dakar: Mémoires de l'institut Français d'Afrique Noire, 1953); Ferretti, Maria Amália Pereira Barreto, *Os voduns do Maranhão* (São Luís: Fundação Cultural do Maranhão, 1977).

[5] Eduardo, *The Negro*, 104–5; Assunção, "Popular Culture," 275.

[6] On institutionalization of and continuation of West Central African practices in the Americas, see James H. Sweet, "The Evolution of Ritual in the African Diaspora: Central African *Kilundu* in Brazil, St. Domingue, and the United States," *Diasporic Africa: A Reader*, ed. Michael A. Gomez (New York: New York University Press, 2006) 64–80.

crioulo descendants of Upper Guineans may, then, have accepted myriad Mina rituals and gradually gravitated toward the more institutionalized spiritual system introduced by slaves from the region. Also important is the fact that slaves from Mina arrived in large numbers in Amazonia relatively late (in the post-1800 period). As in other parts of Brazil, Mina slaves who reached northern Brazil "re-Africanized" the population, introducing a coherent and unified ideology to *crioulos* suffering increased work as the slave trade was coming to an end and as planters were seeking to increase the labor burden on the slaves they held.

Whatever the case, it would be wrong to think that as blacks in Maranhão embraced Mina spiritual beliefs, all elements of Upper Guinean spiritism were forgotten. Within the broader Amazonian spiritual milieu one can still find traces of an Upper Guinean past. Most obviously, in some *terreiros* the *tambor de fulupa* (Floup) is performed. While drumming and dancing, participants honor, they say, the natural spirits brought by Floup ancestors from Upper Guinea.[7] In addition, the continued wearing of amulets (*mandingas*), the honoring of natural spirits found throughout the land, and the nature of many "Catholic" practices (especially with regard to communications with saints) in Maranhão can be read as "culturally encoded clues" or "practical memories" of an earlier period when Amazonia and Upper Guinea were firmly linked via an Atlantic slave-trading route. That is, present beliefs and practices – no matter how diffuse they have become with the passing of time – can be seen as memories captured in ritual form and passed down over generations through ritual practice.[8]

If only a few "survivals" of Upper Guinean spiritual beliefs persist in Maranhão today, it would be wrong to think that Upper Guinean spiritism was not more important in Maranhão in the eighteenth and early nineteenth centuries. Then, there were very few slaves from Mina in the

---

[7] Mundicarmo Ferretti, "Tambor de mina e umbanda: O culto aos caboclos no Maranhão," unpublished paper, 4; Mundicarmo Ferretti, "Tradition et changement dans les religions afro-brésiliennes dans le Maranhão," *Archives de sciences sociales des religions* 117 (2002), 105. The spirits are called *surrupiras* in Maranhão.

[8] On "culturally encoded clues" and "practical memories," Walter Hawthorne, *Planting Rice and Harvesting Slaves: Transformations along the Guinea-Bissau Coast, 1400–1900* (Portsmouth, NH: Heinemann, 2003), 6; Rosalind Shaw, *Memories of the Slave Trade: Ritual and the Historical Imagination in Sierra Leone* (Chicago: University of Chicago Press, 2002), 7–12. On honoring of spirits of the land, Eduardo, *The Negro*, 57–61. These spirits are called *encantados* and were, for Eduardo, "African-like." They are still recognized today; personal observations.

region and Upper Guineans were a majority in many colonial-controlled regions. Then, there were no *terreiros da mina*. Moreover, after 1759, Amazonia possessed few Christian churches and few Catholic priests. By embracing Upper Guinean core spiritual beliefs in Amazonia, Upper Guineans made *their* discourse about the relationship between the natural and supernatural realms meaningful in a new land.

Index

BOOKS IN THIS SERIES

www.ingramcontent.com/pod-product-compliance
Ingram Content Group UK Ltd.
Pitfield, Milton Keynes, MK11 3LW, UK
UKHW042154280225
455719UK00001B/348